Hawk's Nest

Hawk's Nest

A Novel

Hubert Skidmore

THE UNIVERSITY OF TENNESSEE PRESS / Knoxville

First Edition. Originally published in 1941 by Doubleday, Doran and Company, Inc.

THE APPALACHIAN ECHOES series is dedicated to reviving and contextualizing classic books about Appalachia for a new generation of readers. By making available a wide spectrum of works—from fiction to nonfiction, from folklife and letters to history, sociology, politics, religion, and biography—the series seeks to reveal the diversity that has always characterized Appalachian writing, a diversity that promises to confront and challenge long-held stereotypes about the region.

This book is printed on acid-free paper.

Library of Congress Cataloging-in-Publication Data

Skidmore, Hubert, 1909–1946.
Hawk's nest: a novel / Hubert Skidmore.— 1st ed.
        p. cm.—(Appalachian echoes)
ISBN 1-57233-280-8 (pbk.: alk. paper)

1. Industrial accidents—Fiction.
2. Construction workers—Fiction.
3. Appalachian Region—Fiction.
4. Depressions—Fiction.
5. Silicosis—Fiction.
6. Tunneling—Fiction.
I. Title.
II. Series.

PS3537.K38H39 2004
813'.52—dc22   2003026432

In memory of those who
died at Hawk's Nest

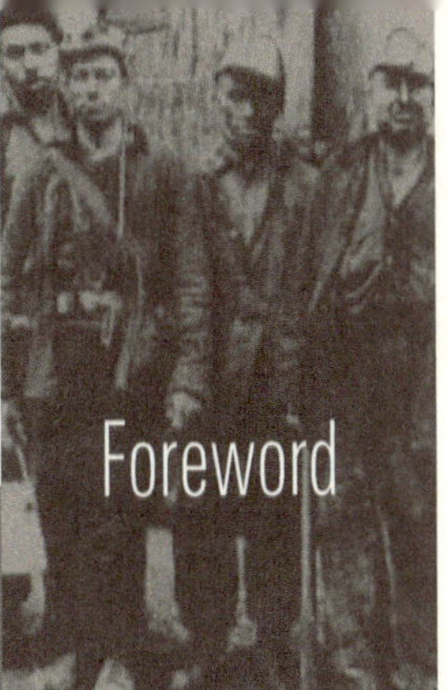

Hawk's Nest
A Novel of America's Disinherited

There's much more to the story of Hubert Skidmore's *Hawk's Nest,* first published in 1941 by Doubleday and Doran, than what the novel tells. By itself the novel recounts the tale of one of America's worst industrial disasters and the ensuing cover-up during a time when the rights of industry routinely overwhelmed the needs of labor. It is a kind of proletarian novel that stands alongside John Steinbeck's *Grapes of Wrath* (1940), Grace Lumpkin's *To Make My Bread* (1932), and Tom Kromer's *Waiting for Nothing* (1935). The time of the plot is 1930, the place Gauley Bridge, West Virginia, and a Charlottesville construction company has just been awarded the contract to dig a three-mile tunnel through Gauley Mountain to divert the New River in order to produce hydroelectric power. The call for labor goes out upon the land, full of hungry and frightened men. "Out of the south and out of the East they came, and out of Joplin, Missouri, and Picher, Oklahoma, searching their way toward the rocky irregular state. Depression-ridden and work-hungry, they set out, leaving their families behind. . . . 'Jesus Christ, Money in your pocket! A fellow said there was work in West Virginia . . .'"

Like Steinbeck's dispossessed Joad family in search of work and the promised land, Lumpkin's Appalachian immigrants, the McClure family, combating oppressive mill town hegemony, and Kromer's desperate and haunted narrator suffering the worst of want, Skidmore's *Hawk's Nest* tells a heartbreaking tale and, as a result, presents a more comprehensive depiction of the human price paid for the confluence of power, greed, fear, and debilitating socio-political attitudes during the Great Depression. In addition, Skidmore's novel—like Lumpkin's, with its backdrop of the Gastonia Mill Strike of 1929—creates a compelling psychological and emotional record of an actual event in history, pieced together by eyewitness stories and written accounts in the local and national press. The Hawk's Nest tunnel project began as a public power project for, and endorsed by, the state of West Virginia, but the force of the river's 162 foot fall would never produce power for the people of West Virginia; rather, it was designed and built to produce power for Union Carbide Corporation's huge ferro-alloy smelting plant along the Kanawha River. This sweetheart deal between the state and industry got underway with a 4.23-million-dollar contract awarded to the lowest bidder, Rinehart & Dennis Corporation, on March 13, 1930. However, at all times, Union Carbide maintained complete control over design and construction until the first power was produced in January 1937.

Of the five thousand men who eventually worked on the two-year tunnel project (with just as many turned away), some risked the press-gang methods of a one-way rail ticket and company store scrip, some endured baseball bat beatings at the hands of an exuberant roustabout employed by the local sheriff, some spent cold nights in an open field or under rocks for a chance to find a place in the foreman's line-up. The work consisted of ten-hour shifts, six days a week, for as much as 75 cents per hour and for as little as 20 cents an hour. The men, who were fortunate to be granted work, lived in twelve-by-fifteen-foot, thin-walled tarpaper shacks, equipped with one coal heater and double bunks for as many men who could fit. The shack rented for 50 cents per week, coal cost 25 to 50 cents per week, and electricity, if provided, 25 cents. Each man was charged the same rate no matter how many men were living in the same shack.[1] At times, as many as ten men would share the same shack—some the same bed—during alternating shifts. Working conditions, though less cramped, consisted of drilling, blasting, and hauling away the rock debris in tiny trains from a tunnel originally designed to be thirty-two feet in diameter, then widened to forty-six feet in diameter when rich sandstone deposits were uncovered. The excess debris, rich in silica, was used for an additional profit and mined at no additional cost and shipped to nearby Alloy, West Virginia, for processing.

Of course, the widening of the tunnel, unnecessary to the tunnel's original purpose, prolonged the work time inside the tunnel, as well as exposing the men to dangerous health risks due to airborne silica dioxide, an incipient cause of pneumonia, lung cancer, and tuberculosis, and the chief cause of acute silicosis, a disease verified for the first time by U.S. health officials as a result of the Hawk's Nest project. Official estimates placed the death toll of the Hawk's Nest debacle at 432 men, but epidemiologist Martin Cherniack, the author of *The Hawk's Nest Incident: America's Worst Industrial Disaster,* thinks the toll much higher, possibly 764 men or more.[2] What worsened the health conditions inside the tunnel was the use of dry drill bits and inadequate ventilation systems in violation of standard practice. The practice of wetting drill bits controlled airborne dust to some degree, but wet drill bits also made for slower drilling, impeding the progress of the tunnel, and thereby cut into contractor profits. Drilling began in March 1930 and was completed in December 1931, three months ahead of schedule.

In addition, racial attitudes of the time made the suffering even more intense for the 3,197 black workers, mainly from the South, who migrated to the job site, and who, of course, were predominantly assigned work inside the tunnel itself where the health effects of airborne silica would be the worst. Of the 1,488 men who worked inside the tunnel, 1,129 were African Americans, and they would represent more than three-quarters of the men who would die. (The actual figure is estimated to be 581, more than half of those who worked inside the tunnel.) At first, company doctors ignored the coughing and loss of breath, claiming the tunnel workers (especially "Negroes") exhibited unclean personal living habits, drinking and gambling addictions, and a lack of common sense. These vices, the doctors maintained, caused their sickness. After a time, when the number of sick and dying became epidemic, the doctors declared pneumonia or tuberculosis as the cause, or used the specious label of "tunnelitis," thereby absolving the company of blame. Area legends suggested that many of the dead went uncounted, especially those separated from their families, and were secretly buried or thrown into the river. Skidmore's eye and ear record this tragic chapter of history in the novel as well.

At the time, before Skidmore fully conceived his novel, the public Congressional investigation of 1936 focused the passion of labor activists and artists of the Left. Muriel Rukeyser's epic protest poem "Book of the Dead," for example, captures a surprising amount of detail about the disaster taken from those hearings. Josh White, whose pseudonym was Pinewood Tom, wrote a Woody Guthrie–like folk song called "Silicosis Is Killing Me"—"I said, 'Silicosis, you made a mighty bad break of me / Oh, Silicosis, you made a mighty bad break of me / You robbed me of my youth and health / All you brought poor me was misery.'" And in 1935, social worker-activist Bernard Allen, a.k.a. Philippa Allen, wrote a searing investigative report, "Two thousand dying on a job," for the leftist publication *New Masses,* which was founded in 1926 by political artists and writers like Michael Gold and John Sloan and featured political cartoons by Mischa Richter. True, much of the information that came out during the hearings had already been uncovered through newspaper and magazine accounts, and, certainly, the joint resolution establishing the investigative purpose of the House Committee on Labor of the 74th Congress, 2d session merely states what was then public knowledge:

> Whereas four hundred and seventy-six tunnel workers employed by the Rinehart and Dennis Company, contractors for the New Kanawha Power Company subsidiary of Union Carbide and Carbon Company, have from time to time died from silicosis contracted while employed in digging out a tunnel at Gauley Bridge, West Virginia; and Whereas one thousand five hundred workers are now suffering from silicosis contracted while employed in the construction of said tunnel at Gauley Bridge, West Virginia; and Whereas one hundred and sixty-nine of said workers were buried in a field at Summersville, West Virginia, with cornstalks as their gravestones and with no other means of identification.[3]

Returning from college in 1935, Skidmore became aware of the circumstances surrounding the disaster. Inspired by stories from eye-witness accounts and urged to fictionalize the event by his mother, he completed his novel in 1939. Doubleday then scheduled it for publication and distribution in 1941. However, coincident with Skidmore's efforts were state, national, and world events that would influence the fate of *Hawk's Nest*. On the brink of World War II, Union Carbide would be crucial to the production of war materiel—rayon, nylon, plastics, rubber, high strength alloys. As it turned out, Union Carbide was also instrumental in developing weapons-grade uranium for the Manhattan Project. In addition, the Smith Act of 1940, passed by Congress as the Alien Registration Act, made it illegal to belong to a group that advocated the violent overthrow of the government. This legislation later served as the basis for Congressional investigations and prosecutions of members of the Socialist and Communist parties in the late 1940s and early 1950s. This interpretation of the law was extended to the interests of business at a time when any labor movement was considered politically socialist. In 1941, Franklin Delano Roosevelt established the Office of Censorship and appointed Byron Price as director; he solicited the help of J. Edgar Hoover to monitor the press. In the early years of World War II, for example, Dalton Trumbo's 1939 antiwar novel, *Johnny Got His Gun*, was criticized as anti-American and suppressed. Many of these and other developments of the time contributed to an intolerant intellectual climate.

Furthermore, in 1938 and 1939, the WPA Writer's Project planned to publish the *West Virginia Guide*, a kind of pictorial/essay handbook to the history, culture, and economics of the state. After seeing the initial draft, Gov. Homer Adams "Rocky" Holt disapproved of the *Guide*'s contents, especially details about labor history, the abuse of the state's natural resources, and the disparity of wealth attributed to absentee landowners and corporations with out-of-state headquarters, and so he blocked its publication. At the same time, Texas Democrat Martin Dies, chairman of the House of Representatives' Committee on Un-American Activities, blazed a trail for Joe McCarthy to follow in the 1950s by conducting various witch hunts, accusing, among others, the Boy Scouts, Camp Fire Girls, the WPA, and Shirley Temple of subversion and radical leftist behavior. Governor Holt, who shared Dies's ideology, was paranoid about radical labor movements and hypersensitive to any representation of the state that was not good for business. Specifically, "[h]e insisted that the reports of the Congressional Committee that investigated the Hawk's Nest silicosis matter were unreliable. . . ."[4] The governor's astonishing vehemence paralleled the energy exhibited by Rinehart & Dennis Company and Union Carbide in whitewashing their responsibility in the affair. Holt would later serve as general counsel to Union Carbide and Carbon Corporation from 1947 to 1953. Due to this atmosphere, many West Virginians still believe Skidmore's novel—and Skidmore himself—posed a threat long after the lawsuits were settled out of court.

In her March 23, 1941, *New York Times* book review, Beatrice Sherman describes the narrative threads of Skidmore's novel:

Men who hadn't had a steady work for a year—or two or three—took fresh hope when they heard the news. Some of them went alone, promising to send money, as soon as they were paid, back to their wives and young'uns. Others packed up family, bedding and cooking pots and set out for the promised land where there were jobs. The author speaks with authority of the character and courage of the various types drawn to the big diggings, most of them with the single hope of pulling out of their destitute state and escaping starvation. The Reips came from their worn-out farm in Slaty Creek, W.Va., bringing their three sons, the eldest 18, and their little girl of 7. Peter Cermak and Anna were of Polish descent and came from Pennsylvania mining town where they could no longer stand the misery of their hungry families and where there was not the slightest chance of their getting married because Pete couldn't get a job. Lessie Lee Rucker, a youngster of 16, but already abandoned by a worthless husband, came cheerfully looking for a job as a waitress. From Cranberry Creek in the Blue Ridge more than fifty miles away came Lock and Daisy Mullens, just married and hoping that Lock could earn enough bonanza money to buy a promising farm for $500 in the home neighborhood. 'Long' Legg and Jim Martin and the colored boy, Owl Jones, came up by train the hard, hobo way from Texas, gathering others, hopefully looking for work as they passed on the news about the big tunnel.

After these "various types" converge on the job site, it is not too long before the harsh conditions and unjust treatment begin to surface—dust so thick men could not see more than a few feet, a loss of breath and energy, the inability to sleep, the fear of losing their jobs because of sickness. Hope suddenly turns to disappointment and despair, and like his other novels set in Appalachia, Skidmore dramatizes the heroic attempt to fight back against the destructive habits of industry and encroaching civilization and, in so doing, highlights the perseverance and stubborn pride he found in the mountain people he knew. Many of his novels, from his very first, *I Will Lift Up Mine Eyes* (1936), follow this same thematic pattern. *Hawk's Nest* unflinchingly relates a series of personal and family disasters due to the murderous conditions in the tunnel; yet, the beauty of the book rests on the simple hopes and dreams of these people who resist and suffer in humility. The need to right this injustice is plainly felt, but justice is never realized, which places this book firmly within the Appalachian consciousness. Nearing completion of the tunnel, the company methodically and hastily scatters its work force, burning the company shacks and belongings left behind, covering up the evidence of the disaster, and planning a nearby golf course to beautify the site.

Of the six novels Skidmore wrote, all were published by Doubleday Doran, a major publishing house; yet, only *Hawk's Nest* was withdrawn from the market immediately after its publication. Oddly, it was a novel that was not his last—one year later Doubleday Doran would publish and distribute *Hill Lawyer* (1942), a defiant story of a lawyer aiding mountain families in their fight to maintain their rights against out-of-state timber interests. Obviously, Doubleday Doran was not intending to sever ties with the author. Furthermore, Skidmore himself thought *Hawk's Nest* was his finest novel, one that received a favorable review in the *New York Times*, which concluded: "His book is not only an obvious [legal] brief for the unfortunate but a well told and honest story."[5] Skidmore "was heart-broken that it was not given a better reception." He thought his book had been condemned by a conspiracy. According to his twin brother, Hobert, in a letter dated 14 Oct. 1947, "he [Hubert] knew who or what was instrumental in having the book 'tossed down a rat hole' as we say."[6]

Interest in reviving the novel and the history that it tells has always been strong in the region. Martin Cherniack, who reinvestigated the Hawk's Nest disaster in the early 1980s, observed, "The building of the tunnel is only a generation or two removed from current memory. There are old men and women who remember it from their youth: the children of many of the best known protagonists are now in their fifties or sixties; and it was, after all, the landmark event in the history of an area that is deeply traditional and where consciousness of local history is wide spread. About fifteen years ago a historian of the area undertook a history of the tunnel project. He claims to have given up when death threats rose to double figures."[7] What further intrigued Cherniack were "crucial deletions" of routine documents from Union Carbide files concerning the tunnel project. "There was not a single document related to work on the tunnel, allegations of silicosis, or the hundreds of legal actions that were brought on behalf of the workers."[8] To Cherniack, this was an odd circumstance because of the enormous attention and exposure the incident received in the press at the time, which included the Congressional public hearings of 1936, the nine articles concerning the incident that appeared in the *New York Times* between 15 January and 23 February 1936, coverage in *Time, Newsweek,* and *Business Week,* not to mention the hundreds of the well-publicized lawsuits brought against Union Carbide and Rinehart & Dennis Corporation.

Moreover, in the early 1980s, the founding editor of the *West Virginia Hillbilly* and the publisher of *West Virginia Heritage,* Jim Comstock, tried to track down the rights to Skidmore's "lost" novel because the book was obtainable only through rare book dealers. Perhaps only a few hundred original copies are extant since the original production run was pulled after production and destroyed. According to historian Otis K. Rice, "criticisms and threats of lawsuits caused the publisher to withdraw all available copies."[9] Furthermore, Comstock found the Skidmore file at Doubleday empty of all documents pertinent to publication of the novel. Specifically,

Comstock believed that libel suits threatened by Rinehart & Dennis Corporation (Skidmore did not change the company's name in his novel, but spelled it Rhinehart & Dennis) forced the publisher to withdraw the book.

More recently, Hawk's Nest history provided some of the historical frame for Denise Giardina's 1998 novel, *Saints and Villains,* about the life of German theologian and humanitarian Dietrich Bonhoeffer. Giardina has Bonhoeffer travel to Gauley Bridge to witness the suffering there:

> "Anyway, they're drilling the tunnel now, been at it a year. Mostly black men working inside, but they got some white men from the hills around there too. Pulling people off the breadlines in Charlotte and Winston-Salem and Durham and putting them on trains bound for Hawks Nest. And keep looking for more, because word Doc's been getting, they're dying like flies up there."
>
> Dietrich had gone very still.
>
> "How are they dying?" he asked.
>
> "Don't know. Even Doc didn't know for sure, last we talked. All he knew was fellow name of Earl Harvey who rides the rails a lot has been up there and says so. This Earl has a reputation for being kind of crazy. Only saw him once myself, but I can vouch he's strange. Called Doc on somebody else's telephone, said there are skeletons walking at Hawks Nest. Dead men walking at Hawks Nest. And said they need a doctor. Then there was yelling in the background and somebody cut him off."[10]

From the facts and fiction about the Hawk's Nest disaster, there has been a strong suggestion of an attempted cover-up and an active willingness "to spin" the tragedy to fit the political outlook of both industry and labor. In the aftermath, an atmosphere of paranoia and distrust emerged. Indeed, the paternalistic laissez-faire attitudes of industry promoted the idea of "opportunity" in a place where there was none, and labor, of course, viewed industry as sacrificing the workers and the environment for the sake of profit. Certainly, these attitudes already fit the well-worn tracks of labor history of the West

Virginia coal mines and timber industry. Similarly, there is also a readiness "to spin" the circumstances surrounding Skidmore's death.

Skidmore perished in a house fire in Dauberville, Pennsylvania, on February 2, 1946. He was only thirty-six years old and had already written six published novels. The fire was investigated by state troopers and the U.S. Army, which gave the official explanation as a defective oil stove flue. He had been staying at a farm he had leased a few months before on the Dauberville-Belleman's Church Road, some ten miles north of Reading, Pennsylvania. He was on leave from the Newton D. Baker Rehabilitation Center at Martinsburg, West Virginia, where he was recovering from post-traumatic stress disorder or combat fatigue. He had been a first lieutenant in the 3103 battalion of the Signal Corps (intelligence) and served in the D-Day invasion of Normandy, then later as acting mayor in an occupation town in Germany. Returning from the war, Skidmore had become estranged from his wife, writer Maritta Wolff, author of *Whistle Stop* (1941) and *Night Shift* (1942), and who was living in an apartment in nearby Reading.

That evening he and a tenant at the farm, Paul Manwiller, had a few drinks at Trump's Hotel (now called Wagonsellers Kountry Inn) where they had been talking about their war experiences. About 9 o'clock, they left the hotel to walk home, and at about 9:30, Skidmore arrived at the stone foundation and wood-frame springhouse where he was staying, some fifty feet away from the main farmhouse, which was under renovation. Hours later, Manwiller was awakened by Charles Hoy of Mohrsville, who sped down the farm lane blowing the horn of his automobile alerting everyone to the burning springhouse engulfed in flames. Manwiller remembered seeing a light still on in Skidmore's room and calling out, but there was no answer. Skidmore's charred body was recovered from the wreckage the next morning. The investigation of the fire lasted only a few days, but there still remains a suspicion of foul play among those familiar with Skidmore's work. This belief is, perhaps, evidence of persistent paranoia about corporate conspiracy and cover-up, or, perhaps, something suggested by the ending of the novel itself—who can say?

Still, it is curious that the 4 February 1946 issue of *The Reading Times* reported: "Skidmore, whose latest novel was *Hawk's Nest*," when clearly it wasn't—*Hill Lawyer* was published in 1942, and it is also curious that the *Charleston Gazette* obituary would insist that of Skidmore's six novels, "[t]he best known, *Hawk's Nest*" was published in 1941"—a novel that was withdrawn and never distributed.

Flamboyant and outgoing, Hubert Skidmore never set out to be the bellwether for social or political causes, but he did set out to be a writer. He attended the University of Michigan and won the Avery Hopwood award for his first effort, *I Will Lift Up Mine Eyes* (1935), which would also begin his relationship with Doubleday Doran at the suggestion and encouragement of Sinclair Lewis, who was one of the judges for the award. Skidmore followed that work with a steady flow of novels, all set in the mountains of West Virginia: *Heaven Came So Near* (1939), *River Rising* (1939), *Hill Doctor* (1940), *Hawk's Nest* (1941), and *Hill Lawyer* (1942). Skidmore's writing is known for its accurate dialect and description of mountain folkways. For a time, Skidmore even taught folklore workshops. His themes came from the stories told to him by his mother, the former Daisy Mollohan (a "Daisy Mullens" appears in *Hawk's Nest*), who was the best-educated member of the family and who encouraged the advantages of education in her children—Hobert, Hubert, Cebert, Bill, and daughter Lula. Both Hobert and Hubert pursued writing careers after graduating from Clarksburg's Washington Irving High School (the same High School Appalachian writer Davis Grubb attended), and both had considerable success. Skidmore's stories would also reflect concerns inherent to the people who grew up and around Laurel Mountain where he was born and the area surrounding Webster Springs, heavily dependent on the timber and coal industry. His father, Cornelius Patrick "Neal" Skidmore, was a clerk and foreman for a glass company near Clarksburg, who moved the family to Elmira, New York, in 1927 to work for Corning Glass.

Hubert was born fifteen minutes after his twin brother Hobert on April 11, 1909.[11] Apparently, the women, acting as midwives, had set the chimney ablaze while boiling hot water. The fire began shortly after the first twin, Hobert, was born. Alarmed by the growing flames, Daisy herself carried the mattress out of the burning house to the shade of nearby tree, where minutes later she delivered Hubert as she watched the house burn. From that time on, family members noted that Hubert had an overdeveloped fear of fire and of being burned.

Tom Douglass

Notes

1. Martin Cherniack, *The Hawk's Nest Incident: America's Worst Industrial Disaster* (New Haven: Yale UP, 1986), 26.

2. Ibid, 104–5. "An estimated toll of more than seven hundred men, arrived at through a series of necessarily speculative but consistently conservative calculations, may well be too small. It is clear that many deaths occurring in Fayette County went unreported. It would be reasonable to suppose that less care might have been taken to record the deaths of migrants than those of local men. . . . There was, moreover, no clinical reason to limit the number of deaths from silicosis to those occurring before the end of 1937, since the disease might well have brought a slower death to workers for many years afterward."

3. U.S. Congress, House, Committee on Labor, 1936. An investigation relating to health conditions of workers employed in the construction and maintenance of public utilities: Hearings on H.J. Res. 449, 74th Congress, 2d session.

4. Jerry B. Thomas. "'The Nearly Perfect State': Governor Homer Adams Holt, the WPA Writers' Project and the Making of West Virginia: A Guide to the Mountain State," *West Virginia History* 52.7 (1996): 1–14.

5. Beatrice Sherman, "Tunnel Diggers," review of *Hawk's Nest* by Hubert Skidmore [368 pp. New York: Doubleday, Doran & Co., Inc. $2.50]. *New York Times Book Review* 23 Mar. 1941: 6–7.

6. Hobert Skidmore, qtd. in Shirley Young Campbell, "Lest We Forget: The Skidmore Twins Hubert and Hobert, Part III," *West Virginia Hillbilly* (19 Oct. 1989): 9.

7. Cherniack, *Hawk's Nest Incident*, 3.

8. Ibid.

9. Otis K. Rice, *West Virginia: A History* (Lexington: UP of Kentucky, 1985), 259.

10. Denise Giardina, *Saints and Villains* (New York: Norton, 1998), 58.

11. See Hobert Skidmore's *The Years Are Even: the Story of Identical Twin Brothers & Their Haunting Search for a Single Destiny* (New York: Random House, 1952).

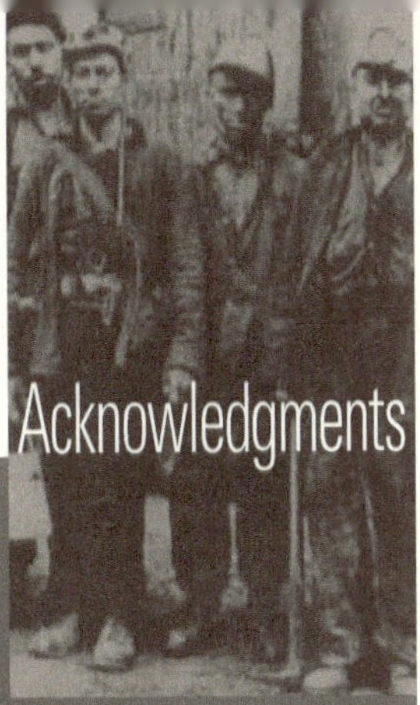

Acknowledgments

The press gratefully acknowledges Maritta Wolff Stegman for her interest in reviving Hubert Skidmore's lost novel. Let me also acknowledge Phyllis Moore for her unflagging support of my research; Gordon Simmons, formerly of Renaissance Books, for contributing an original edition of *Hawk's Nest* to the press; Sylvia Elzner of Bridgeport Public Library for her generous support; Patty Raikes of Fairmont, West Virginia, who compiled an invaluable biographical file; author Robert Skidmore, nephew of Hubert Skidmore; Pam Hehr of the Reading Public Library for her research expertise; James Presgraves of Bookworm & Silverfish for providing an original cover illustration of the first edition; Martin Cherniack for his provocative detective work; and Susen Douglass for her editorial assistance.

Tom Douglass

*A*s autumn gave way to winter, the nights chilling the hills beneath their bright covers, more and more men found their way into West Virginia. Out of the South and out of the East they came; and out of Joplin, Missouri, and Picher, Oklahoma, searching their way toward the rocky, irregular state. Depression-ridden and work-hungry, they set out, leaving their families behind with the great chat piles: crushed rock from which the ore had been removed.

"I'll send for you and the young'uns. First regular pay, I'll send for you and the young'uns."

Down from Michigan, from the quiet shops of Pontiac and Grand Rapids, Detroit and Saginaw. One young insurance salesman left Elmira, New York. Left his wife and two children with no money and no coal. They sat in the kitchen by the gas stove and the wife cried, watching the flame, afraid it would stop.

She only bought what they couldn't live without, knowing the A & P man on Lake Street extended their credit out of his own pocket.

"Ralph went to West Virginia, looking for work. We want to pay every cent we owe."

They came out of Ohio and Indiana and Illinois, listening along the road. There's work in Buffalo, in Rochester and Richmond. Stay away from the cities. The families are throwed out in the streets with their furniture. Lots of guys are heading for Texas, for Texas and Arizona and California They stand on a bridge with a gun, and if you ain't got a job and money in your pocket, they chase you the hell back.

"Jesus Christ, money in your pocket!"

A fellow said there was work in West Virginia.

"They're diggen a hole through a mountain in West Virginia. Even the niggers are maken forty cents."

Hawk's Nest

At the end of the black iron bridge which barely extended from stone ledge to stone ledge Lessie Lee Rucker stood shivering in the murky half rain that hung over the Kanawha Valley. The bright pink fuzz of her imitation angora sweater caught in streaks like wet hair and her sharp heels spiked the clay at the road's edge as she moved away from the abutment and then returned again.

Examining the road which followed the river up the deserted valley, Lessie turned and looked back over the bridge, her ears alert for the drone of a motor mounting its low arch. None came, and beyond the town of Montgomery shriveled somberly in the gray morning drizzle. As her eyes reached the flat walls of the hospital Lessie's hands rose to cup the tight clean bandage which fitted her head like a skullcap but for the few strands of blonde hair heaped into a pile at an opening on the top. Carefully she fingered the strands, trying to relieve their unbecoming soddenness.

Down the road a Ford rounded the bend beneath a huge overhanging rock and pointed its nose up the valley. Lessie stepped onto the pavement, almost indifferently, and raised her right arm. She did not wave but merely held it there, her fingers bent up the road toward Gauley Bridge.

The Ford idled down, but as Lessie stepped forward it turned sharply, rattled over the bridge and dropped down into Montgomery. She did not look after the car but remained where she stood, absently watching her right foot. As she exercised it, bending at the toes, water squashed and foamed out above the thin sole and Lessie's head began to bob in response to the movement. For a while she studied it, not thinking particularly, but fascinated by the mud-dirtied foam her shoe produced.

Presently she halted and her hand flew up again. A car muttered to a low halt just beyond her, throwing up a fine spray as it passed.

Thoughtfully Lessie stomped the red clay from her feet on the pavement, caught the door as it was thrown open and bent to step inside. "Howdy, mister," she said pleasantly, closing the door without banging it.

The plumpish, florid-faced man bent low over the wheel, looking sidewise at the bandage, his eyes candid and humorous. "Boy, sister," he exclaimed, touching the accelerator, "it looks like you spoke out of turn!"

Lessie smiled at him, her stubby fingers trying to fluff up the damp angora. "We had a car wreck," she explained genially. "A feller picked me up down by Cedar Grove yesterday—he was a driven devil, I'm tellen you!"

"What'd you do, smack into somebody?" He shook a pack of cigarettes until one jumped forward, half out of the tear. "Cigarette?"

"Thank you kindly," Lessie said, reaching inside her sweater. "I've got me some." She lighted a Sensation and settled back against the seat. "No sir, it wasn't that way a-tall," she explained. "He was comen up the valley, fit to kill, and I kept seein he was over on yon side of the road. I was goin to tell him, but when a feller picks you up you don't feel like headin in, do you? You know, it don't seem right to tell him what he ought to be doin, after he's picked you up that-a-way. Well, he was goin along, lickety-split for hell, and half the time he was on the wrong side of the road. And when we got to a turn he just sort of took a short cut. You couldn't of drove a cow between him and the hillside." She paused, memory clear in her face. "I was goin to get out, but there's this here job I heard about in Gauley Bridge, and I figured Id better get there as soon as I could. Well, sir, 'bout a mile yon side of London we come tearen round a bend, and there was a truck plunk in front of us! This feller—he was sellen somethin, I reckon—he tried to get back on his own side, but the car shot right off the road and clear out into a field!" She halted, a little breathless from the long recital, and then added, "Turned over three times. You never heard such a racket!"

"Fellows like that ought to be locked up," the plumpish man declared soberly. "He get hurt bad?"

"I reckon not," Lessie reasoned slowly. "When I woke up I was in the Coal Valley Hospital, in a clean white bed. They said the feller had gone back to Charleston. A nurse there, she lent me these clothes.

Mine was all gormed up. Reckon I must of been bleeden like a stuck hog. It was mighty nice of her, huh, wasn't it?"

The man nodded his head and was silent while he passed a chain of cars dragging along behind a decrepit truck.

"I figured I could get me this job," Lessie went on. "Way the girl told it to me, a company's putten a tunnel right smack through a hill up there, and men are comen in from every which direction, comen there to get the job. But I ain't never worked in a restaurant before."

"Yep," the man agreed, "the tunnel's goin' to bring a lot of work to Gauley Bridge. Ever time I come up here I hear they took on a couple hundred more men. Probably be the best thing that ever hit that town." He turned and looked at Lessie's round face, bland and white beneath the tightly wound cloths. "How old are you, kid?" he asked, his voice no longer darkened by her account of the accident.

"Sixteen, goin on seventeen."

"How long you been working?"

"This last place, 'bout a year," she replied enthusiastically. "And you never heard tell of better folks; just this man and his wife and their two kids. Five dollars a week they gave me, and my keep. First I just went to do their washings, and then they took me on regular. Lordie, they was nice to me. They was schoolteachers, both of 'em. You wouldn't believe it, but after I got the young'uns to bed of a night that man used to teach me things out of books. It never done much good, but I liked him for tryen. Honestly, you couldn't ask for nicer people."

"With two kids," the man ventured casually, "it sounds like a lot of work for five dollars."

"No it wasn't!" Lessie exclaimed earnestly. "No sir, it wasn't a-tall! After liven with my husband, it seemed like I had next to nothin to do."

"You been married?" he asked rather loudly, his eyes again running over Lessie's round face and slight figure.

"Sure," she replied, surprised at his lack of knowledge. "My name ain't Rucker. I'm a Lee. Lessie Lee. My folks live back on the Williams River. Ever hear of Williams River?"

The man nodded slightly. "Went clear back there hunting one fall. Where's your husband now?"

"He run off."

"Where'd he go?"

"I don't know, and I ain't worryen s'long as he don't come back. Mister, I'm tellen you, he wasn't worth a cryen dime! That man never done a lick of work from the day I met him, 'cept find washin's for me to do. Then I had to tote 'em back and forwards."

"Jesus Christ!" the man exclaimed and spat out the window.

"And I'll never forget it," Lessie went on. "One day I asked him for twenty-five cents—I wanted some dress goods. I was a burnen shame for folks to see on the road to Richwood—and damn if he didn't baste me in the jaw. Knocked a tooth out!" With a finger she pulled back the corner of her mouth, exposing a hole in a row of moderately clean teeth. "And it was my money too. I'd earnt ever cent of it over a washboard, down by the crick bank."

"Some men ain't worth a goddamn. Makes a fellow feel kind of ashamed he belongs to the same race."

"No," Lessie cried. "No sir! Men are al'right. Like I told you 'bout the one I worked for, wanten me to have some book learnin' and such. No, it ain't men, mister. It's them Ruckers. There ain't one of 'em worth a wet hole in the snow! Somebody ought to kill 'em all off, same as you would a snake. That's the way I come to look at it."

"Un-huh," the man grunted, depressed again. For a moment he fussed with the windshield wiper and then settled glumly back into the seat. "Hell of a day to be out looking for work," he said in sour consolation.

"'Tis kind of drizzlen," Lessie replied and suddenly sat erect, her eyes on the driver. "Mister, could I ask you somethin?"

He looked at her a moment, paused and said, "Shoot."

"Well, it's 'bout this feller that give me a ride yesterday. Like I said, they took me over to the Coal Valley Hospital, and I was layen there in bed. I heard a couple fellers talken outside the door, then this state trooper comes in and begins asken me a lot of questions. Scared me plumb out of my wits. I just shut up and never said aye, yes or no. I was scared sure he would put me in jail, and lordie, that'd a-been awful, with me 'bout to get a job and all. Well, he talked around a lot and I just kept my mouth shut tighter'n birch bark and after a while he makes ready to go. Then he tells me I have to go over to Fayetteville today and meet him in the county clerk's office, I think it was. Said I had to sign somethin so's I wouldn't sue this feller that picked me up—you know, sue him for rollen out into that field, like I told you."

"Fayetteville, for Christ's sake, in this rain!" the man exclaimed indignantly. "It's nearly sixteen miles the other side of Gauley."

"What I'm wanten you to tell me," Lessie continued, "is do you reckon that feller'll be worried too much if I don't get up there afore tomorrey? You see, I don't want somebody else to get this job afore I get there."

"The hell with him," the man said. "Why should you hike up there in the rain to sign something that you won't sue him just so's he'll feel better. Let him worry awhile, it won't kill him."

"Well, if you say so. But if a feller's nice enough to pick you up— you know, if a feller's that nice——"

"Go get your job," the man snorted, "and wait until this rain's over. Then if you want to hike to Fayetteville, go ahead."

"I thought it'd be al'right," Lessie said, "but I wasn't real sure. I knowed I wasn't goin to get no law on him, so I thought it'd be al'right."

The car slowed down, rattled over a spur-line track and approached the town of Gauley Bridge which clung to the narrow strip of flatland between the river and the sharply rising hill. Only the change of pavement marked where the state highway ceased and the village street began. Lessie, watching out the window, saw the houses draw together and then a store, a garage and another store. Back of the rain-splattered sidewalks men were clotted in doorways and beneath overhanging roofs, their clothes dark and somber through the mist.

"Lordie," she exclaimed abruptly, "all them men look like they was waiten for a funeral! Guess it must be the rain."

"There's the bus station," the plump man said, drawing into a flooded gutter. "I got to make a call in the drugstore."

Quickly, as though it had completely slipped her mind, Lessie began a futile effort to mold the loose hair on top of her head into some sort of presentable shape. Then she gave the sleeves and front of her sweater a quick ruffing and reached for the door handle. "Thank you very kindly," she said. "I don't reckon I ever would of got here if you hadn't come along."

"S'all right. I hope you get the job."

"I reckon I will now. The way the girl told me, they're needin somebody pretty bad, on 'count of that tunnel and all. Well, now, good-by, mister."

"So long."

When she had closed the door he leaned forward over the steering wheel and through the rain-streaked window watched the small figure, topped by a white-bound head, walk around a group of men, cut across the street and go directly into a door beneath a red cafe sign which wiggled and jerked electrically.

Leaving Memphis, puffing hard, the freight had headed north an hour before. Through the yards, through the scattered, half-lighted outskirts it went, gathering speed, and then, shrieking across Mississippi like a frightened animal, it bore its way into the night, the caboose lights whipped along like a tail it tried to pull in quickly, fearing harm.

Inward it sped, wanting Kentucky. The rapid tattoo increased, diminished and then clicked upward to a high, steellike stuttering; the smoke bent down across the flat-topped freight cars, cindery and blistering.

Knuckling at every joint, it screamed into a curve, pulled out again, rumbling a little, and plummeted forward.

Over its back two figures ran, cross-leaping, dark and almost obscured by the streaming smoke. Far forward the first dropped, squatting and crawling, found the ladder irons and lowered himself down the car's side. On the bottom rung he crouched, pulled together like a ball above the backward rush of broken stone and tie ends. The second followed, moving more slowly, bent partly sideways as he came down, his stick clumping against the red wall.

"No—Jesus, no! I'll get off!"

The stick fell twice only, flattening knuckles against the iron ladder rail, and the lower figure sprung backward, spread out against the wind, bounced on the road shoulder and rolled down the embankment, spewing gravel before it.

The freight could still be heard, a distant rumbling, when a tall, hulking figure came hurriedly up the track, paused, stepped over in the path and looked down the short incline. For a while the man stood, legs far apart, a small package caught at the end of an arm which nearly reached to his knee. His eyes moved along, examining the embankment which sloped down into the elder-stalked ditch. Finally his searching stopped and he went down the incline, his long legs planted stiffly in the crumbling dirt.

"Hey," he grunted, touching the sprawled figure with his toe. "Hey!"

There was no answer and he bent down, flopping Jim Martin over on his back. "Hey," he repeated, slapping Jim's face. Then he got up, wiping the sticky, dirt-thickened blood off on his trousers, and jammed the package into the front of his shirt. Squatting down, he caught an arm and a leg in either hand and swung Jim across his shoulders, jouncing himself to level the load, and methodically climbed back to the railroad bed.

A quarter of a mile further on, bearing his load easily, Long again left the track, found the creek-divided gulley and made his way down through the dense brush toward the shadow of a fire.

Four men squatted about in the little clearing looked up at Long but said nothing as he crossed to a level spot and placed Jim down on the ground.

"That sonuvabitch of a brakeman," Long explained. "He knocked him off. Must have been doin' fifty!"

A low moan escaped Jim's lips. The four men watched him quietly.

"We oughta lay for him with rocks," a lean man said. "We oughta lay for him and knock his goddamn brains out!"

Long looked down at Jim and then turned his broad, heavily browed face toward the fire. He said nothing, but as he drew the two small cans of beans and loaf of bread from inside his overalls one corner of his lower lip came out a little, twitching and jerking.

"He bad hurt, Mistah Legg?" a colored man asked, nodding toward Jim.

"Get some water, Owl," Long replied, dropping the beans down beside the fire. "We got to wash the dirt out of his face."

Sam Givens, the lean, half-toothed man, slid forward, an open jackknife in his hand, and began to cut the tops off the two cans. Hungrily the other two men watched him dump the beans into a smoked kettle.

"Rinse the cans out good," the quiet one offered. "It'll make more to sop the bread in."

The other squatted down, his chin fenced in his fingers, nodding firmly.

Owl, the colored man, came back with the syrup can filled with water, placed it down beside Jim and stood aside. Having rolled Jim over on his back, Long examined his face, his thick forefinger shaving away the dirt and coagulated blood. From below his right cheekbone, up across the corner of his eye, most of the skin and part of the hair had been torn from Jim's face.

Getting to his feet, Long reached inside his overalls, pulled out his shirttail and tore off a piece. Tilting the syrup can, he soaked the cloth and pulled it down over the wound.

"Jesus," Jim swore, muttering incoherently. "Oh, Jesus."

The face finished, Long ripped open the shattered tear in the right leg of Jim's pants, brushed the bruised knee a couple of times with the wet cloth and then took up one of his hands. For a moment he looked at it, laid it down and picked up the other. Both hands were badly torn.

"That dirty bastard," he muttered, "knockin' off a kid like that."

"It sure looks bad," Owl added. "Sure looks bad, Mistah Legg."

"Get me some more water."

By the time the beans were steaming above the slow fire Long had left Jim, his hands bandaged in the torn shirt, and stood before the fire.

"I heard somethin' in town," he said. "Man in the store there——"

"They ain't comin' after us," the worn-tooth man interrupted. "The law ain't comin', is it?" Gaunt, bony-faced, Sam Givens had left his home a week before, left the poor cotton rows which touched his back door, and fright came easily to him. For years he had lived on credit that did not stretch to planting time, on land that was not his own, on bad land and bad crops and bad markets, and he moved as an animal moves when its wind is gone and there is only furtive hiding and cleverness left.

"A nigger come into the store with a letter," Long went on. "I heard this feller readin' it to him. Guess it was from some of his folks, further north." He bent down and set the beans off the fire and they all drew up about the kettle, knives of shaved sticks poised in their hands. Owl opened the bread, dividing it.

"Seems like this feller that wrote the letter knowed about some work up there," Long stated, spooning some beans onto a lardpail lid and handing it to Owl. "Place in West Virginia somewheres."

The quiet man stopped eating, a knifeload of beans halfway to his mouth. "Work?" he asked incredulously. "You mean just one job?"

"Didn't sound that way."

"Mines," declared the cotton farmer. "Mines, I betcha. My wife had a brother that dug coal in West Virginia. Right after the war he got him a job. Married a girl from up there someplace. Sent my wife a picture."

"Ain't mines either, far's I could hear. They's a company puttin' in a power tunnel——"

"Oh, God Almighty," Givens exclaimed, "if they's a job there I'll crawl on my hands and knees! Four months I been lookin' for day's work—I ain't meant to be runnin' around the country. I get so's I can't write my old woman. I'm ashamed to tell her they ain't no work to be had." He paused, staring at the path Long had come down. "I'd work for next to nothin——"

"In the letter it said they needed more help," Long added, spreading beans over a slice of bread. "I been on the road four years, workin' here and there. A feller gets a feelin' 'bout where work is. You hear a lot of talk, bummin' round, but you get a feelin'. First year I run all over hell and gone, lookin' my eyes out for a job." His jaws showed bonily in the firelight as he paused to chew. "Went from Baltimore to Oklahoma to Kansas—and away the hell to the top of the state of Maine, pickin' taters, three cents a barrel. Ever time I heard they was work I went for it. After a while I slowed down." He took another bite, wiping his mouth with the back of his hand. "I got a feelin' they's work in West Virginia."

"Maybe," suggested the man who had not spoken, "maybe that nigger didn't mean it—the one that wrote that letter."

Long did not answer, but without raising his head he turned his eyes toward Owl, nodded, as though his own word was to be verified.

"No sir," Owl stated assuredly, "ain't no colored boy goin' send no letter less he means business."

The quiet man licked the blade of his knife and snapped it shut. "Where's West Virginia at?" he asked.

"Up north somewheres," Givens supplied anxiously. "Close to Pennsylvania, way I remember it. My girl had a schoolbook with all them states in it, all colored up, red, yaller and green. All four my young'uns was goin' to school the same time. Myrtle, the oldest'un, was clear up to number eight. Then the de-pression come along and they clear quit out. Never had no clothes or nothin'."

"I went acrost the corner of it once," Long supplied. "It's 'bout six-seven hundred miles to the northeast. A man could make it in two-three days if his luck was any good."

Beyond the shadow of light Jim Martin moved restlessly, the pain entering his numbed mind. Once he started to sit up, but when his hand touched the ground he gave a sharp, hurt cry and settled back; his head rolled to one side and his eyes fastened glassily upon the group about the fire.

"That po' boy is sufferin', Mistah Legg," Owl said. "Reckon I oughta give him some drinkin' water?"

Long nodded his head but spoke to the three men who stood before him.

"We'll head up across Tennessee and into Virginia. Someplace 'round Roanoke ought to be 'bout right. Then we'll cut over into West Virginia. If they's work there, we'll get it."

"Maybe we ought to start now," Givens said, buttoning an old army coat across his chest. "Again mornin' it'll put us where we can pick up a ride." Then fearful that he had spoken out of turn, he hastened on. "You heerd 'bout it first—you get the job if they's only one. But I'd kinda like to be there, case they was wantin' to take on another man. I'd send my woman a card, just kinda let her know if things was lookin' promisin'."

"Get some sleep," Long urged. "In the mornin' will be time enough."

"I'd kinda like to get started along," the man persisted hesitantly. "Be a shame to miss it——"

"You ain't goin' to pick up no freight through here tonight," Long said. "First place, it's too dark for you, and besides, there ain't none out of Memphis before daybreak."

The man looked at Jim's quiet figure, seeing his two bandaged hands held on his chest up near his chin.

"I was thinkin' I'd hitch up," he said. "I ain't had much experience ridin' freights."

"I feel 'bout the same way," the silent one added. "I ain't uset to 'em. Gets me scared all the time, thinkin' I'm on somethin' I ain't no business on; makes me feel sneakin'. If a feller picks you up on the road—well, you kinda feel like he's oblidgin' you."

"Okay," Long said, gesturing his hand. "See you in West Virginia maybe."

They moved away, their steps tentative and halting. Almost out of the circle of light they paused, whispered a moment and came back.

"I don't reckon, partner," Givens asked, "you'd mind tellin'—did you hear whereabouts they're buildin' that tunnel?"

"At a bridge, some kind of a bridge place," Long supplied readily. "The way this feller wrote it, you go to Charleston, that's the capital, then it's thirty-forty miles up the river from there. Kanawha, I think."

"Charleston," the man mumbled. "Charleston, West Virginia."

"Think you can remember that?"

"Sure, sure, Long."

Again they walked away, this time disappearing into the brush. For a while Long sat looking after them. Owl, who had given Jim a drink of water, pouring it slowly between his dry, stiff lips, came up and sat down beside him.

Through the brush they could hear voices, and presently Givens reappeared.

"We ain't feelin' just right," he said. "You don't reckon you'd like to come along with us?" he said.

"Nope," Long replied. "You get goin'. 'Bout four miles up the track you come to a highway. Take a turn right."

The man took a step, paused thoughtfully and called to Owl: "You want to come along, Jones?"

"No sir. I reckon I'll stay with Mistah Legg."

They both sat looking at the brush, moving imperceptibly where the man had disappeared. Presently they could hear footsteps climbing up the embankment.

Twisting about, Long stirred up the fire with his boot. "Ain't it a goddamned shame," he said, "the way men have to go 'round beggin' for work?"

Below a stump-clotted field and well above the dark, gurgling Cranberry Creek the Thorpe cabin squatted heavily against the rocky side of the hill. Though the sun, coming early to the cloudless sky above the Blue Ridges, had not yet found its way down into the valley, the hard-packed yard about the cabin had buzzed with activity for more than an hour. Soon after the last thin smoke of the breakfast fire had spiraled into the sky a tall lanky figure left the kitchen door, crossing the back yard in long, down-thrusting steps, and disappeared into the lean-to barn which haunched uncertainly against the hillside.

By the time Lock Mullens had harnessed the team and drawn the wagon around before the cabin a pile of bedclothes and a barrel of household goods had been stacked on the rickety, sloping porch. Beside the bulging, corner-tied dumpling of a crazy quilt stood an ancient valise, cracked and gray from its years above the rafters.

"The sun's up and full day's come," Lock said, seeing the last morning vapors recede, foglike, into the hollows, leaving the autumn hills damp and bright. "The sun's up and we'd best be headen along."

Halfway through the door Daisy Mullens paused, hugging a plump feather tick in her brown arms, and let her eyes come to rest on her husband. Furtively, hungrily she watched him, seeing the solid, downsloping shoulders, the arms, the back she had embraced for the first time the night before. Memory brought a bright flush to her cheeks and impulsively Daisy pressed her head against the bulging feather tick. It was the first time she had really dared look at her husband since he had crawled from bed, slipping noiselessly into his trousers, and stirred up a morning fire on the hearth. She had waited then, her eyes tight shut, until he had come and kissed her shoulder, saying, "You'd best get up now, honey. I'm goin' to the barn to feed the horses."

Beside her mother she had been busy over the stove by the time Lock returned, his hair wet and black and broadly streaked from the coarse comb. She was a married woman now, she knew, and the knowledge filled her with a warm, anxious realization, but the sound of Lock's voice behind her caused Daisy's breath to quicken as it never had and his plate rattled noisily when she set it on the table before him.

Hearing it, the saddlebag preacher, for whom they had waited over a month, laughed and banged Lock across the shoulder. "You must of had a big time," he roared, "she's still shaken like a leaf!"

Numb and burning with embarrassment, Daisy fled back to the stove, her ears large and fearful for the words Lock never spoke. "You all go right ahead," she had stammered. "I'll eat when the menfolks are done."

It had been a great relief when they left the room and she sagged down onto the bench beside the table, her heart thumping and her appetite completely gone. After a while she looked up to see Lock standing beside the woodpile, watching her through the kitchen door. She smiled timorously, got up, brushed imaginary crumbs from her fingers, straightened her skirt, walked into the bedroom and briskly began to fold and tie the bedclothes she had been making since that day, more than a year before, when tall, gangling Lock had first come across the hill to spend the night, thereby announcing his intentions of seeing her steadily.

"Landsakes alive, Daisy, get out of the way!" her mother cried, trying to wedge through the doorway. "We ain't got near all this stuff ready, and Lock's wanten to head over the ridge!"

Almost startled, Daisy hurried across the porch and down into the yard.

"Here, I'll take the ticken," Lock said, lifting it from her arms. "We'll put it here, under the seat, in case a rain comes on."

Daisy's father, in an elaborate pretense of observation, scrutinized the cloudless blue sky. "I don't hardly reckon it'll weather up," he predicted finally. "Seems to me you'll have a fine day to be headen out."

"Well, yes, I guess we will at that," Lock replied in stilted seriousness. "Leastways it ought to be fair till we reach Craigsville."

They were silent for a while, listening to Daisy and her mother clatter through the cabin, their voices loudly exclaiming over each small article narrowly left behind.

"Women make a sight of ruckus, don't they?" Daisy's father ventured. "Worser'n chickens when a hawk is circlen low."

Lock swung the valise into the wagon, carefully securing it against the plank side. "Well, yes sir, I reckon mebby they do."

"Man's got to get so he don't pay much attention to it," Sam Thorpe went on, casually picking up a bundle and handing it to Lock. "It'd set you plumb wild was you to pay any mind."

"I reckon they don't mean any harm by it," Lock countered. "No harm a-tall."

Sam bent over as if he were going to pick up a log and handed Lock the tightly wrapped quilt. "Oncet a man lets 'em know who's wearen the pants, they ain't nearly so much trouble. You just got to keep an eye on 'em. Women, as a general thing, can get around a man and he'll never know it."

"I 'low," Lock protected lightly, his back turned. "But Daisy's a good worker."

"Sure she is! Never no-mind, I had a time with her maw. Stubborn—Lord, it was like driven a balkin' mule! Don't guess I ever did get it all out of her," he ended, chuckling low. "More'n oncet I've stayed out there in the barn for a while when I'd just as leave a-been in the house."

Rounding the corner of the cabin, the Reverend Greengrove came to an abrupt, jolting halt, his small chin craned forward above the broad circle of his rigid white collar. "Whyn't you call me?" he asked loudly. "I'd a-been glad to help you load that stuff."

"Wasn't no chore," Lock thanked him. "We ain't taken nothin' but bedden and cooken things."

The preacher hooked his thumbs through his galluses and ambled across the yard. "It was a fine ceremony we had yesterday, I been thinken," he began, sucking at a ham sliver still lodged between his teeth. "Lots of folks, fine-looken couple—a good wedden is bettern a sermon, I allus say. Makes a man feel good, joinen together such a fine-looken couple for the holy bed of matrimony."

Noisily Lock thumped a box into the wagon. "We're thankful you come, Reverend," he said. "We been waiten some time for the wedden."

"You know," Sam interposed alertly, "Tom McCune's liquor ain't got the kick it uset to have. You don't spose he's runnen it off too fast, do you?"

"Kind of hard holden off, was it?" Greengrove went on, grinning, the parched skin drawing tighter across his bony skull.

Lock twisted about, angry and ashamed to look at Daisy's father. "You watch the team, Sam," he said presently. "I'm goin' round and get an extrey braken block."

The preacher looked after him, his mouth pursed like a dried apple. "He ain't feelen tetchy, is it?"

"Well, now," Sam drawled pointedly, "Lock's like most fellers. He figures preachers do a lot more talken than is called for."

Inside the cabin Mrs Thorpe dropped to her knees, half crawling beneath the bed. For a while she wiggled about, mumbling and tsching her tongue, and then one arm shot out from beneath the overhanging coverlet and placed a jar of green beans on the floor. Daisy, her arms loaded with a bunch of dried peppers, quartered apples shriveled on a string and a jar of beets from the year before, stood anxiously beside her mother's protruding hips.

"Now, Maw," she kept exclaiming, "I ain't taken another blessed thing! You'll need 'em afore winter's out; you'll need 'em bad!"

"Hesh up," her mother demanded from beneath the bed, "and take these yaller pears. Lock's a big eater, and you'd best have plenty. Lord Jesus, looket the dust under here! Daisy, I thought you told me you cleaned under the beds afore the wedden? For two coppers I'd—here, take another jar of these sour pickles. Your paw won't eat 'em. Says they put a edge on his teeth."

"Maw, that's more'n a-plenty," Daisy began and then paused, considering which of a few possible ways would be the most successful in halting her mother's unselfish giving. "I ain't tetchen another thing," she declared flatly, planting herself firmly at the foot of the bed. "Me and Lock's took the last thing from you and Paw we're aimen to!"

Slowly Mrs Thorpe's hips began to wiggle as she worked herself from beneath the bed. Her head rose from under the overhanging coverlet, her hair stringing down over her cheeks and a silvery cobweb extending from one eyebrow upward across her forehead, and she got to her knees, frowning ominously.

"Lookey here, my fine young lady," she charged, her finger marking off the words, "don't you start given me no back talk. You get out there and find a packen box as fast as your legs can carry you!"

"But, Maw," Daisy protested, "you ain't hardly got nothin left."

Mrs Thorpe swept the dust from her sinewy arms and clapped her hands as though she had been working in flour. "Get on out there and find a box, and don't you worry your purty head about me and Sam."

"But Maw—Lock and me—well, he'll be worken steady, and we don't want to take——"

"Go on," her mother shouted, swinging her arm threateningly. "They'll rob you in them stores there—fifteen cents I heered they was chargen for a handful of beans! It gets my mind sick, Daisy, thinken of you way off yonder with none of your kinfolks should trouble come on you."

"Lock," Daisy intervened, "Lock, he'll——"

"It's womenfolks I'm meanen. And nobody there but them outland folks. I've heered they're a shiftless lot, liven off their man's day's pay, buyen their grub in tin cans—law, think of it—tin cans!" For a moment she shook her head incredibly and then jerked her hand toward the door leading into the kitchen. "You heel it out there now and fetch a good-sized box. And bring that stone jar from the cellar house. The brown one. I'll fill it full of kraut, that's what I'll do!" In a wild sigh of exasperation she ducked her head and disappeared beneath the bed. "Tin cans—God have mercy on you!"

Daisy stood, her mouth shaping some protest, but without speaking she placed the jars down and hurried through the door.

As they squatted on the kitchen floor, carefully wrapping and packing each jar with pages from a worn old catalogue, the mother and daughter became suddenly, tensely quiet. Only minutes remained, Mrs Thorpe knew, before her last daughter would climb atop the wagon, turn her eyes toward the southwest and roll over the ridge into some world beyond. There would be no other footsteps about the kitchen while she worked, no singing from the cowyard, no quiet hum to accompany the rattle of supper dishes. Already, it seemed, she knew the long stillness of the days ahead, the lonely waiting for Sam to come in from the fields.

Feeling a lump clogging in her throat, Mrs Thorpe forced herself to speak, afraid she might whimper. "Use the corn first," she advised thickly. "Use corn first, always, cause it ain't near so lasty as beans."

"Lock, he likes corn too," Daisy managed. "He likes it fried, or just warmed up, or most anyways."

Her mother went on packing, her work-stiffened fingers awkwardly hugging the paper about each jar. "You got a fine man, Daisy," she said without looking up. "You make him a good woman."

"Yes, Mom," she promised, each word coming separately. "I'm to."

"There'll be times, girl, when it seems like there ain't no reason to a man, none in this world. But you just mind that Lock's yourn, for better or worse, as the preacher says, and keep your mouth shet. Many's the time I bit my tongue to keep from tellen your paw he didn't know one end from t'other, and I reckon we made out all right."

"Uh-huh," Daisy said, knowing her mother had not finished.

"And when he comes in of a evenin' don't go blabben to him 'bout what you got to worry and fuss with. A man has to do his own thinken, and he's got no time for your concerns."

"I won't," Daisy declared. "I'll take care of Lock like you allus took care of Paw. Just like you, I'll be."

Mrs Thorpe got to her feet, gathering the packed box into her arms. "Well," she admitted with some satisfaction, "you could do worse. I don't figure your paw's got any complaint comen. Leastways he'd better not let me hear it."

For a moment Daisy remained on the floor, her eyes fast upon mother's lean gray figure as she passed through the doorway and out into the bright, sunlit yard, bent a little forward with the load she carried. Then, getting to her feet, Daisy slowly crossed the kitchen and went into the bedroom. Before the cracked mirror she tied her blue bonnet about her head, bunching the bow neatly and allowing a few strands of sandy yellow hair to show. As she finished she went to the bed and gathered up the large flour sack that contained her new straw hat.

"I won't put it on till we get to Craigsville," she said, unconsciously repeating her mother's advice. "We won't be passen nobody but common folks afore we hit the state road."

In the kitchen she paused again, eying each corner and crevice of the room, the dark rafters, the puncheon floor, the place behind the wood box where they had once discovered a rattlesnake on a cold November morning. She saw the strings of pepper, hanging blood-dried behind the stove, the bread pan on the downthrown oven door, a square of corn bread, brown and yellow in its dark corner, the old zinc coffeepot on the stove, its mouth as brown as Enoch McCune's when he chewed tobacco.

"Come on, Daisy! Lock's a-waiten!" her father's voice called from the front yard.

Startled, she whirled about and hurried toward the door. Partway she halted ran back to the stove, slipped the bread pan into the oven and closed the door as she had done countless mornings before. Finally, giving the room a last, departing glance, she ran out the door, down the steps and across the hard, smooth yard.

"Take your time, Daisy," Lock said, checking the two planks which were to serve as a seat. "We'll get to Craigsville agin noon, anyways."

"Now as you come into Craigsville," Sam advised, "you'll see a kind of white house up against the bank. Two-story one, it is, with a porch front and back. Just call out and Mort will come runnen. Tell him he can bring the team back tomorrey or the next day."

Lock nodded his head and spoke the instructions he had repeated many times before. "Mort'll take me to this feller with the truck," he said. "The one that's taken us acrost to Gauley Bridge."

"Yep," Sam repeated. "Feller from over in Nicholas County, I heered he was. Mort says he'll do it for ten dollars. Seems mighty high, don't you think, Lock?"

"It's a right smart haul down to Gauley, I reckon. Better'n fifty miles, far's I can make out."

"Law, Sam, recollect the time you and me went to Gauley. Must be more'n twenty years now." Mrs Thorpe paused, looking up at Lock. "Two big rivers come together there, and after that they call it the Kanawhey. Must be a mile wide, that Kanawhey, wouldn't you say, Sam?"

"Well," he answered seriously, "somewheres around there, more or less. I'd think a couple of times afore I drove a horse into it, I'll tell you that."

"It's bigger'n anything I ever laid eyes on," Mrs Thorpe went on defensively. "Might be bigger by this time, for all I know."

They were silent, each one uselessly checking over the well-packed wagon.

The preacher, rubbing his face as the sun warmed it, leaned against a porch post and watched the procedure with bland, unthinking aloofness.

"Guess everything's all in," Mr Thorpe said perfunctorily.

"Looks that way," Lock agreed, taking a step forward and then awkwardly retreating to Daisy's side.

"You'd best hold your hat in your lap," Mrs Thorpe pointed out, wanting to postpone the final moment. It's apt to get something squashed agin it back there."

Mutely Daisy extended her arm, exhibiting the lightly filled flour sack.

"Reckon you'll be seeing some far and wondrous things there at Gauley Bridge," Sam said, breaking another silence. "That feller that come through here, norratin' it round bout them wanten men to work in that tunnel, he had some mighty strange tales to tell." He paused, looking across the filled wagon bed at his son-in-law. "When you get back, Lock, we'll be wanten to hear bout them things."

"Won't be long," Lock reaffirmed huskily. "Soon's I get me a little money saved up so's I can buy that piece of land there at the head of the holler—Daisy and me'll be comen back then, and most likely we'll have all manner of things to tell."

"Send us a letter sometime, if you get the chanct," Mrs Thorpe asked. "We'll take it acrost and get Samp Turner to read it for us."

"I will, Mom. Get Samp to write us a piece from you, if he's a-mind to."

Once again a silence settled over the yard. Lock turned about and looked at the sun, now clear of the misty ridges and moving up the sky.

"I reckon we'd best be goin," he said, taking Daisy's arm.

Not knowing what else to do, she let him help her up and over the axle and onto the seat. Wordlessly, while Lock took his place beside her, she sat looking, down at her parents as they backed slowly away toward the porch.

"Write us now, Daisy," the mother called. "Write us right off soon."

Daisy nodded her head vigorously and Lock, snapping the reins across the horses' backs, headed them up toward the ridge where the road bent down into the valley beyond.

No other word was spoken. The wheels clanged over the rocky, rutted clay and the harness chains rattled, but no word was exchanged between the two on the wagon seat and the older, slightly bent figures before the cabin. They only waved at each other and looked and looked and looked.

Topping the ridge, Lock pulled the team to a halt and they stood up, their arms gesturing above their heads. Down the hill, in the cabin yard behind them, Daisy saw her mother pull off her apron and wave it above her head quickly, almost desperately.

With a little cry she flung the flour sack outward, waving it all her might. It struck Lock against the shoulder, making a fine, crunching sound, like a step in a mow of hay.

"You'd best set down, honey," Lock said, starting the wagon over the ridge. "You'd best set down—you'll ruin your new hat."

Nearly fifty miles beyond White Sulphur Springs the Midland Trail found the gorge of the New River, running west and a little north, and slowly climbed to the tableland where the river had run long ages before. Above the road shallow gullies came down from the mountaintop, draining Fern and Mill, Opossum and Osborne creeks. Gently they began, spread like a soft fold near the mountaintop, laurel-filled and only soggy. Farther down, below the bright line of the highway, they dropped steeply, wearing into the gray truncated rocks, tumbling their waters down into the deeply trenched New River.

From the back seat of the salesman's car Pete Cermak tried to look into the valley below. Through the black spruce and blown oak he could glimpse the opposite side, a wall of rock that rose sheerly to its crown of dark pine. Here and there, against its cragged side, laurel grew and sometimes a birch, unreasonably rooted on a narrow ledge. Topping a knoll, he could see the river in the far valley ahead, glistening around the bleached stones, opaque and moss colored where it flowed beneath the overhanging cliffs.

"We gonna git to Hawk's Nest soon?" Pete asked the slender driver. His bony Polish face was drawn and tense as he slid forward on the seat, his pale stubby beard glistening in the eleven o'clock sun.

Beside him Anna Dubinsky straightened up, her eyes fixed on the face in the rearview mirror. She did not speak but her arms moved restlessly, as though she sought to restrain Pete without attracting the attention of the face framed in the small glass. Since they had left Carbondale, Pennsylvania, three nights before, walking across the black hill in the fog, Pete had talked of little else but the work he would find, and now, as they rolled over Gauley Mountain, Anna grew tense with apprehensive dread anxiety. If there was no work, she knew, Pete might send her back home.

Impulsively each hand cupped a sleeve of her sweat shirt and she watched the bald spot of the salesman's head, waiting for his answer.

"Hawk's Nest is just up here a little ways," he said, screwing about. "It's quite a sight if you've never seen. it. And," he went on, "right down in there someplace is Lover's Leap. Must be a couple of hundred feet high—straight down! They got a story around here about a couple of Indians jumping off of it. They come from different tribes—this fellow and girl—and the old chief wouldn't let his papoose marry this guy. They were enemies, I guess. Anyway, they used to meet there on top of that cliff, and one day they decided to get it over with. So they held hands and jumped. Hell of a jump it must of been too!"

"Dey die?" Pete asked naïvely.

"Gosh, you ought to see that cliff!" Jim Hathaway exclaimed. He paused to straighten up his coat which had been folded neatly over the back of the seat beside him. "Too bad I wasn't selling embalming fluid them days. I'd a-done a little business, maybe."

"Is it true?" Anna asked, feeling it was time to make some sort conversation. "Is the story true?"

"Aw, you never know. These West Virginians are a windy bunch. They'd rather lie than eat. But," he went on earnestly, "I don't put much credit in it. They got a cliff over in Ohio and they tell the same story about it. It's one of two things: they either made it up or a hell of a lot of Indians were jumping off of cliffs. I only seen one real Indian. He didn't look like he'd jump off a cliff for his own mother."

Anna turned to smile at Pete but, meeting Hathaway's eyes in the small mirror, she asked, "Do you go very far, selling embalming fluid?"

"Three thousand miles every month—all alone," the man replied importantly. "First I head out of Erie, covering Ohio and touching Indiana. Then I come back through Kentucky and Virginia and West Virginia. Out of Charleston I head up for Pennsylvania, making a few calls in Maryland." Again he caught his folded coat as it threatened to slide down on the seat. "We ain't been able to do much in Maryland. Seems like they don't die up there, or they go somewhere else to do it."

"We come from Carbondale," Anna ventured. "You go to Carbondale?"

"Yep," Hathaway replied, "but things are kinda quiet up there. I ain't placed a good order in that town since the mines shut down."

"No work no more," Pete injected somberly. "That's why we go. We get a job in West Virginia, in tunnel."

"We're getting there fast, brother," Hathaway said. "Hawk's Nest is right over that ridge. I'll stop and show it to you. The upper end of the tunnel is right there at the foot of Hawk's Nest."

"If you're busy . . ." Anna began tentatively.

"Plenty of time," Hathaway declared. "Make a call at Gauley Bridge and one at Summersville, and I'm through for the day." He reached over and took his hat down from a little hook above the corner of the door. "I kind of got an interest in that tunnel anyway," he went on. "Big job like that always helps business a little."

Anna and Pete settled back, worn empty with the man's talking, with his insistence on postponing the end of their journey which had begun so desperately three nights before.

By ten o'clock that night a heavy fog had settled into the Y-shaped valley which formed Carbondale. Smoke from the burning slag piles threaded dark filament across beneath the misty sky, and then low over the houses came the fog, dense and milky. The miners' shacks, like great clods of earth, sat lumpily, row after row, the night giving them a solid, permanent appearance their insubstantial structure did not warrant.

Here and there a window lamp reached out, squared by its frame, to cast a faint light on the broken, raggedy boardwalk which fringed either side of the dark road. Shadowy figures passed, hushed by the night and the fog and the cold threat of winter that came down from the black hills.

A door opened, emitting a burst of yellow light, and a child darted diagonally across the street, up two steps, over the porch and quickly into another door.

Anna and Pete, having left the bare Polish Recreation Hall, walked up the middle of the road, their voices low and their shoulders hunched a little forward.

"You stay, Pete. You stay," Anna kept repeating in an urgent voice. "You'll find work."

Pete continued to stalk along, his eyes on the road, his lean face drawn and set beneath the murky light of a street lamp.

"Once you start runnin' you'll never stop. There ain't no work no place, Pete. In Pittsburgh rich men are sellin' apples on the street. You stay, Pete."

"No."

In sudden anger Anna's voice rose. "You're thickheaded, and you won't listen to me! Like Joe Molesky. He thinks he can get work in California. California's fine! Now he's in jail; robbin' a gas station so he won't starve." She grew quiet again, and they walked on. "There ain't no work no place, Pete. You stay."

"West Virginia ain't California," he stated flatly.

"In a little while the mines will open," she went on, pleading. "Winter's comin'. The company will get orders. See, it's cold already." She folded her arms across her breast, shivering to verify her statement. "Least you got a house here in the winter."

"I don't ever go back," Pete declared angrily, the words rushing out with new release. "The old man's goin' crazy. In his eyes he's goin' crazy. The kids ain't got nothin' to eat, and the old man's goin' crazy. For supper we just got taters, and ever time I take a bite I feel it here." He slapped his hand against his chest. "I look at the kids and the old man, and I t'ink I go crazy too!"

"Maybe the mines will open," Anna repeated lamely. "Then there'll be work for everybody."

"One whole year I don't work," Pete protested, outraged, as though she had not spoken. "All the time I eat. Now I don't do it no more. All the time we want to get married. I don't got no money. I no can buy you dress, nottin."

"I don't want no dress, Pete," she said, stepping a little closer to him.

"Goddamn sonuvabitch!" Pete cried, kicking at the road. "I don't do it no more. I go to West Virginia. I work in tunnel."

"Maybe there ain't no work," Anna said. "Maybe that man just come here to talk."

"I go see."

He broadened his step and Anna hurried along after him, seeing the way his great shoulders lurched forward with each downthrown foot. They passed a quivering, bug-clotted street light, and Pete, a little ahead, started down the alleyway which led to the Cermak shack. Briefly Anna hesitated, then ran into the darkness and caught his arm, tugging him about.

"I'm goin' too," she declared. "I'm goin' with you."

Pete lowered his head, his eyes covering her tall, angular figure. "No, Annie. You no go."

"I'll get my clothes," she said, her voice suddenly alive and vibrant. "On the corner—twenty minutes. You wait!" She started swiftly back toward the street.

In a few long steps Pete had overtaken her. "Annie!" he cried. But seeing her eyes, he halted, his voice lowered and he spoke slowly, the words colored by what he was unable to say. "It's long ways, Annie. One—two hun'red miles. We got no place to sleep. No money."

"I know, Pete."

"You wear out your shoes. You got no more."

Impulsively she grabbed his arms, clenching them tightly in her strong hands. "Twenty minutes, Pete. I ain't got much to bring."

Mutely he stood watching her run down the street, her white sweat shirt a soft blob that melted into the fog. With one last backward look he plunged into the darkness of the board-fence alley.

By Saturday they reached the broad Shenandoah Valley, where the river flowed strangely north through the fertile heart of Virginia. Through Warrenton and Waterloo, Sperryville and New Market, riding trucks, cars, walking, over the first finger of the Blue Ridges they went, and into the valley beyond, where every road led to a cavern. Gorgeous. Unbelievable. Prehistoric. They looked at the billboards and moved on, finding their way across the valley to the shadow of the Shenandoahs, tan and richly autumnal beneath the high blue sky.

That night, without knowing it, they slept inside the West Virginia state line. The clear sun of an October morning awakened them, slanting down through the low-growing pines to turn a carpet of needles red and rust gold. They sat for a while squinting their sleep-filled eyes and rubbing the chill from along their arms and legs.

As he got to his feet Pete's eyes caught the glisten of water deep in the hollow below. "We take a bath!" he exclaimed, drawing Anna up. "Nice cold bath!"

Gathering up their two bundles and the last of a quart of milk left from their supper, they scrambled down the knoll, Pete holding the snapping branches aside for Anna, who followed.

"Nobody can see nottin," Pete exclaimed, slipping off his shirt and looking up the densely pined hillside where the motor of a transport coughed and choked as it topped the knoll and rolled on down the valley.

Anna found the small piece of soap inside her imitation-leather kit and followed Pete into the creek, feeling the cool water curving against her ankles.

"It's not deep," she said, disappointed. Experimentally she bent down and splashed a handful over her knee, allowing it to run down her leg.

"I know, I know," Pete cried, hurrying over the mossy rocks. "I got the idea!" Picking up the milk bottle, he waded back into the creek, lean and tall and brown. "You drink," he said, holding out the bottle.

After she had dipped a handful of water into her mouth, rubbing her teeth energetically with one finger, Anna accepted the bottle, carefully drinking half of what remained.

"No. All," Pete urged.

Anna shook her head and handed it back to him. In a long gulp he drained the bottle, squatted down and methodically washed it out. Filling it from the creek, he stepped toward Anna. "Now you get showers bath," he chuckled, spilling it down over her shoulders.

With a shrill little squeal Anna began soaping her firm, slender body while Pete emptied bottle after bottle of water over her. After she had rinsed the lather from the back of her neck Anna took the bottle from his hand and filled it herself.

"Don't make so much noise," she reprimanded lightly.

Ignoring her, Pete continued to splutter and slap the water over his body as though it contained ice. "Ah! Feels fine!" he crowed. "Feels fine all over!"

"Wait a minute. We'll wash your head." Tugging him by the arm, Anna found a large rock and climbed on top of it. More conservatively now, she poured water over his thick, sun-streaked blond hair, allowing him only enough to form a lather. Refilling the bottle, she poured it over his head, washing away most of the soap.

"Eyes, eyes, eyes!" Pete cried, jiggling up and down, trying to fling the lather from his forehead.

Anna slid down off the rock, bent in one movement to scoop up more water. Slipping, she tried to regain her balance, and the bottle landed against a large stone, breaking into sharp, irregular pieces.

"Here, bend down," she urged, grabbing Pete by the back of the neck. Gradually he got to his knees and stretched out in the shallow creek, his face buried in the water. Anna, kneeling beside him, splashed and washed the soap away.

"You try to make me blind!" Pete charged, his red-rimmed eyes blinking rapidly. "I no take you swimmin' no more!"

"You act like a baby," Anna reproached softly. "Soap can't hurt you. Here, let me see if your hair's clean."

As he bent down, while Anna examined his head, Pete reached over and playfully pinched her side.

Drawing her right arm back, Anna slapped him on the back end and was halfway to the creek bank, laughing and squealing, before Pete realized what had happened. For a moment he stood, one hand covering the red spot, staring after her with wide, amused eyes.

"No! no!" she cried as he had caught her up in his arms, tickling her just below the armpits. "No! You got to shave!"

Abruptly as he had grabbed her Pete released Anna and began to finger his whiskers thoughtfully. "That's right," he agreed seriously. "I shave. Maybe we get more rides, ain't?"

After he had honed the old long-bladed razor Pete sat in the creek cupping the cake of soap in one hand while he worked up a lather with the other. Having dressed, Anna came and sat on the rock before him, cleaned off the mirror of her cheap compact on the bottom of her skirt and held it out for him to see.

"Here, give me that razor," she commanded as Pete finished and started to get up. Pulling his head over in her lap, she carefully cut away the remaining shiny whiskers at the corners of his mouth and at the base of his nose. "Sure, I shave fine," she answered his statement. "When I uset to cut the kids' hair I always shaved their necks."

It was shortly before eleven o'clock when Jim Hathaway topped the ridge of Hawk's Nest hill and pulled off onto a broad strip beside the road. A small path, yellow and dry in the shale clay, led from the road through a clump of pines.

Pete and Anna climbed from the car and stood waiting while Hathaway picked up his uncreased coat from across the seat, locked and secured every door and snapped and pocketed his key case.

"How far to Gauley Bridge?" Pete asked restlessly. "How much more we got to go?"

"That's Gauley Mountain just ahead," the man replied. "We wind around it for a while and then drop right down into the town. Four or five miles ought to put us on the main drag." Turning, he led the way toward the broad scar of the path.

Pete started to speak but halted abruptly, noticing for the first time that one of Hathaway's legs was considerably shorter than the other. Surprised, he stared at the cumbersome four-inch sole beneath the sharply creased trouser leg and looked toward Anna, with wide, astonished eyes.

Anna nodded, caught Pete's arm, and together they followed the hollow sound of the man's lame foot along the path toward the brink of the hill where a rocky ledge extended, flat and narrow, from the very top of the great stone wall. Nearing the precipice, they moved cautiously, inching their way toward the front, quieted by the tremendous, gaping space that fell sharply away from the flat stone at their feet.

Close to the edge Pete halted, his eyes fastened on the river far below, and gradually eased himself back to his full height. Anna crept to his side, awed and not speaking, as their eyes followed the course of the dark green river which hurried down through the valley, sending up a low, muted drone as it pounded over its rocky bed. A short distance below Hawk's Nest the river, striking another wall of stone, had turned again, bending sharply to disappear at an angle in the course it had worn.

"If a man fell off there he'd have time to eat his lunch before he struck bottom," Hathaway chuckled, pleased that they were so profoundly impressed with what he had shown them. "Scare you, fellow?"

Pete looked at him for a moment, his face caught in a tenseness, "Deep like hell!" he declared. "Makes your head dizzy!"

"Come over here," Hathaway urged, stepping cautiously toward the far end of the ledge, "and I'll show you something." Where the stone fitted back into the hilltop he drew a clump of chokecherry aside and waited for Pete and Anna to look over his shoulder. "See that, down yonder?" He pointed, indicating a cluster of flimsy, temporary shacks scattered to either side of a small railway track which led, through scaffolding and loose-torn earth, toward a dark hole, like the open mouth of a mine, in the base of the mountain where the river turned in its course. "See that hole—right yonder—that's the upper end of the tunnel. The little things walking around are men."

Pete and Anna gaped in silence, and presently the man went on. "That's where the water's going in. They'll build a dam across the river there, and then the water will run in that hole. It comes out down near Gauley Bridge. Three miles, I think it was, a fellow said it was going to be. Three miles, straight through Gauley Mountain."

Anna stepped back, her face still and thoughtful. "Is that where the men all go to work?" she asked soberly. "Down there, by the river?"

"Nope," Hathaway replied. "See, they got this all figured out. Company men came in here and measured it all long before they got started. They got that tunnel laid out, this fellow said, within an inch of where it's going to be." He took a few steps up the incline and waited for them to follow. "One crew's starting here, and another is coming through from the other end. We'll see that opening just before we get into Gauley. My guess is, the lower end is where you'll find the foreman."

"I go see him now," Pete said.

As Jim Hathaway stood beside the car unsnapping his key case he puckered his mouth in conversation. "Wouldn't surprise me none," he advised gravely, "if you wouldn't be better off if you went right into Gauley. I'd be willing to bet they've opened up a hiring office down there now."

"Sure," Pete said gratefully. "Sure t'ing."

Carefully the salesman edged his car back onto the highway, and they rolled over Hawk's Nest hill and down into the ravine beyond. The road, winding its way about the brim of Gauley Mountain, dipped into the gullies, damp and shaded, and then bent across the next knoll, looking down, as it had for more than fifty miles, on the dark, rocky gorge that cradled the river.

Watching from the windows, Pete and Anna saw more and more people appear along the highway. Men, somber in their work clothes, walked the road's soft shoulders, sometimes alone, sometimes in groups of three or four. Now and then they passed a woman, bareheaded and with a grocery sack in her arms, pausing to hold her children until the car had passed. Once, in a ravine, Anna saw a woman squatted before a hut made of sheet tin and patched with wet, streaked cardboard. Most of the front side was open, and inside a dry-goods box, a chair without a back and a white iron bedstead rested on the hard-packed clay floor.

Anna, twisting about, watched the woman who sat heavily beside a small fire, idly punching the ashes with a stick she held in her hands. She hardly raised her head when the car passed, and as a clump of brush concealed her Anna saw the woman drop her head a little, one arm wiping up across her face, the movement seeming to have no meaning at all.

As the wagon crossed the ridge and clanged deeper and deeper into the shaded hollow Lock and Daisy Mullens did not speak. Beneath his broad-brimmed black hat Lock's face was quietly serious, his lips moving ever so slightly. Nearing the bottom of the valley, where the road ran along beside the creek, he took both check lines in his left hand and his other arm slipped about Daisy's waist, not drawing her to him but only held firmly, as if to halt her jouncing.

She looked at him wordlessly and allowed her body to accept the curve of his arm.

"We'll be comen back someday soon," Lock said consolingly. "Tain't like we're aimen to be gone forever."

"I know, Lock." Her voice was low, constrained, and showing none of the fearful loneliness she felt. "We'll be comen back someday."

"It won't take no time a-tall," Lock went on, more cheerful now that Daisy had spoken. "That feller said they was payen fifty cents a hour and a man could work twelve hours a day if he was a-minded to. I been figuren, Daisy. In a week's time, not counten Sundays, a man could bring in thirty-six dollars, from a Monday to a Saturday. Thirty-six dollars," he repeated, stressing his words incredulously. "Why, Daisy, if we was to go saven, wouldn't surprise me none if we was headen back in here long bout this time next year. That's a sweet piece of land, there at the head of Greenbrier. Room for corn and taters a-plenty! I been over every foot of it, and I know it like I know my name. Corn'll grow ten feet tall—Enoch McCort says he'll let me take it off his hands for five hundred dollars. That's all we'll need, Daisy, just five hundred dollars and a little more to go on till our first crop gets in."

"It'd be a purty place to live," she contributed halfheartedly. "We'll set the house a-facen east, so's the sun'll come in of a monen, the way it does at home. Mom allus said it was like haven pleasant company to open the door of a mornen and let the sun come in."

"Just whichever you want, honey," Lock said, tugging her toward him. "And—an—well, I wasn't goin to tell you, but I been thinken, Daisy, whilst we're liven to Gauley Bridge and I'm worken in the tunnel—well, if things turn out the way I got 'em planned—I was thinken we'd buy us a good cookstove. Might as well get it whilst we're here and then fetch it back when we come."

"Oh!" Daisy cried, straightening up. "I seen one in a catalogue. It had a warmen closet and a place beside the firebox where a body could keep water heaten all the day. It would be such a fine thing and last clear out of our time." Suddenly she was quiet, settling back in Lock's arm. "But I reckon that'd be too costly."

"Not if work's good and steady, like this feller said it was," he went on quickly. "We might as well get a good one whilst we're at it. We'll be eaten a sight of meals off'n that stove, I 'low, and so we might as well be gitten a good one."

"Land, won't Mom be surprised when we come riden back with a big shiny cookstove! I won't let 'em know till we get back, and when they see what I got in the wagon it'll just take the words plumb out of their mouths."

"That's the way I got it laid out, honey," Lock said, snapping the check lines importantly. "If I get good steady work, like the feller said, we'll just go right ahead and get us that cooken stove."

His arm slipped further around Daisy's waist, and they clung together, not speaking, as the horses plodded on, their heads rising and falling monotonously with their steps. As they left the woods, moving beside a dark fence that zigzagged the limits of a farm, Lock spoke again, the words low and filled with anticipation.

"We'll aim to get back in the fall," he said. "Agin the time snow falls we'll get the house up, and duren the cold months I'll finish it off. Thataway, when April comes again and the snow's gone, I'll be ready to do my planten. First year I'll get me in a sizey tater patch, and up near the woods there I'll sow to corn. It's good land, Daisy, and it lays well. If a man works it proper he can get him a fine liven, and there ain't no mistake about that."

"We'll get us a cow, first thing off," Daisy interposed. "I'm partial to a Jersey, if we can find——"

"Sure, we got to get a cow," Lock agreed firmly. "We'll have to have a cow for the young'uns." He stopped abruptly at the mention of children but hurried on. "It'd be a fine place to raise young'uns—they can run loose like a pack of hounds." He called to the horses, starting them up the next hill, and pulled his wife closer to his side. "Law, Daisy," he declared simply, "there ain't nothin' on earth a man cares for so much as a piece of land to call his own."

All that morning Lock and Daisy rode toward Craigsville, through shaded hollows beside the creeks, the road clay-damp and cool to hornets and bees, up the far hills, dry-rustling with sedge and goldenrod and brown-stemmed asters withering in the sun, and across barren knobs where the low-growing laurel and scrub pine drew back, revealing withered stones, blanched like bones, beneath the high autumn sky. Into the valley beyond they went, finding the creek again, and, then up the next hill, over a meadowy knoll and out onto the smooth surface of the state highway.

Now and then a car whirled by and the horses shied, drawing away. Lock and Daisy watched them, quiet-eyed, almost distant in their trepidation and mistrust, and Lock gathered the check lines tautly into his hands. Nearing the houses which stood to either side of the road, Daisy opened the flour sack and slipped her yellow straw hat out into her lap. She looked at it, straightening the cluster of roses about its brim, and, removing her bonnet, pinned the hat securely to the knot of blonde hair high on the back of her head.

From the corner of his eye Lock watched her, his face glowing a little as he saw her quick fingers stab the loose strands of hair up beneath the hat.

"Yesterday, Daisy," he said, not turning about, "You sure looked purty, standen there on the porch aside yore maw, them flowers in yore hand and that purty blue ribbon round yore waist."

"Law, I was scared out of my wits," she admitted with a little laugh. "I kept thinken, if I have to speak a word, I'll keel over right here on the porch, afore the preacher and everybody. I ain't never been so scared, less maybe it was the time I got baptized."

"I never felt good neither," Lock confessed. "And yore paw kept shoven me in the back, like I wasn't close enough to the preacher."

They both laughed, not loudly, and seeing the town loom up ahead, they became suddenly quiet and Lock's eyes began to scan the upper side of the road. "Yonder it is, I reckon," he said presently, "that one there, with the porch hine and fore."

"Lock," Daisy said breathily, "it's goin to seem quare, liven yonder at Gauley with so many folks around."

"We'll make-do somehow, Daisy, you and me," he stated encouragingly. "The pay's good, and come this time next year we'll be headen back home. . . ."

By two o'clock the worldly belongings of Lock Mullens and his young wife had been loaded into the clattering frame of Jerry Walker's truck, a boxlike bed affixed to what had once been a Model T Ford. The windshield was missing and from its two frames wires stretched tensely forward to hold the cracked front fenders up off the wheels. A box had replaced the seat five years before, and the rear wheels, lacking fenders, wobbled over and back, as though they followed the contraption against their own better judgment.

"That was Persinger," Jerry called across his shoulder. "Last town between here and Summersville. Ever been to Summersville?"

"No," Lock managed above the clatter, stiffening his bent arm so Daisy might hold on tighter.

"It's the county seat," the heavy figure called back. "Lots of folks live round there. Got a relief office too. You on relief?" Raising one foot to avoid the heat that streamed up through the floor board, Jerry laid it over the rusty motor hood.

Lock looked at his wife quizzically. "No," he called against the wind. "Never heard of it."

Jerry, a man nearing fifty, turned his face, gray brown with whiskers, back toward the loaded truck bed. "Never heered of relief?" he exclaimed. "Jesus Christ, half the country's on relief! Best damn thing the govermint done since the compression set in."

Lock made no reply, and the truck rounded a bend and moved on for half a mile before Jerry spoke again. "Guess you come from purty far back, huh?" he asked.

"Head o' Cranberry Crick," Lock said defiantly, not liking the man's tone.

"Between relief and the tunnel," Jerry reasoned, "they're comen down outter the hollers fastern hogs down a greased hole. You're the second bunch I hauled down this week. Monday I fetched some over from Camden. Reip, the feller said his name was. Any Reips back where you come from?"

"None I'm knowen of," Lock said tensely.

"Funny name, anyway," Jerry said, concluding the conversation.

Almost an hour later the truck rattled into Summersville, turned sharply at the courthouse corner, ran past a dozen or more stores, beyond the undertaker's and rolled into a filling station, crunching gray gravel beneath its thin old tires.

"Reckon a feller could have a little water?" Jerry called raucously to the overalled attendant who came forward. "This thing's hotter'n a bull in a pasture!"

"Help yourself." The short, scrawny attendant smiled, looking at the tall dark young man huddled beside his wife in the truckload of dusty nondescript household belongings.

"Kind of warm day to be moving, ain't it?" he offered pleasantly.

Lock and Daisy exchanged swift glances. "Why, yes sir, it is kind of," Lock said. "But they's a breeze stirren."

"Goin to work in the tunnel?"

Hesitating, amazed that a stranger should know so much about their intentions, Lock fumbled a moment before he answered: "I give a feller my name. I was figuren on it."

"I guess Gauley's filling up pretty fast," the young man reasoned. "They've been working six months now."

"They—they—that is," Lock stammered, "they still got work for a feller, ain't they?"

"Yeah, sure," the attendant replied, "if a man's willing to work like that." Abruptly, as though he had already said too much, he turned and disappeared inside the little red-and-white service station.

Jerry spun the dangling crank, leaped onto the box in time to catch the stuttering motor, and the truck rolled out off the gravel and continued down the highway. For a while Lock and Daisy sat looking behind them, noticing for the first time the little crowd of boys who had gathered on the sidewalk to stare at the mudsplashed dusty truck.

Presently Daisy, seeing the tense look on Lock's face, touched his arm and murmured, "Real purty little house that feller lived in, wasn't it?"

From Summersville on, the road seemed mostly downhill, following Little Elk Creek through the narrow valley as it hurried down to join the Gauley River. Lock was silent, watching the farms, seeing the yellowed fields, the corn and grain dark-waved with the wind that stirred across them. Once or twice he spoke to Daisy, but their words were few, and they traveled the miles together as though no one else rode the makeshift truck.

"Look down yonder," Jerry called, pointing toward a field that stretched from the highway down to a broad bend in the creek. "See them graves, yonder clost that black walnut! Them's girls killed by the Indians. Long bout suppertime—way the story goes—and they went out to do the milken. Indians was hid over in yon holler, ringen a cowbell to fool 'em. Scalped 'em afore they could get back to the house. Menfolks was off in the woods. Lots of them things around here. See there, that sign tells you bout it. State put it up."

At a glance Lock saw the blue iron sign, stiffly erect at the road's edge. "My grandpaw was a Indian fighter," he said, seating himself again. "And my grandmaw's sister was took by the Delawares. I reckon they was purty fierce them days."

"Makes it kind of inneresting, way the state puts up them signs," Jerry said congenially. "If a feller took the time, he could learn a lot, just driven along. Well, tain't more'n twelve-fifteen miles to Venetta. We'll be gitten there purty soon. Reckon that's where you're goin live, huh?"

Lock crawled forward a little. "I don't know," he admitted. "I figured I'd go see the company man first. The one that signed me up. He said they'd be houses a-plenty, houses the company was goin to let us use."

"God damn," Jerry swore over his shoulder, "them fellers go round promisen everything 'cept chicken on Sunday." He paused, spat forcefully toward the side of the road. "Take my word for it, feller. When we get to Venetta you hop out and see can you find yourself a place.

If they is one, move in! Then you go talk to the man bout a job. Way they're moven in now they'll be liven in coal mines afore winter comes on."

"Ain't there no houses?" Lock asked fearfully.

"Christ, yes, they's houses. But the company's moven 'em in here by the hundreds, niggers and all! Used to be a coal mine runnen there at Venetta. Them houses is in purty good shape, if you can git yourself one."

A few miles further along the black asphalt highway ended, and the jouncing ceased as the ancient truck rolled onto the smooth cement. Down the embankment, below the weed-grown railroad track, Lock saw the Gauley River, broad and flat and opaque. Here and there a man walked the tracks, and once, beyond a square white building, they passed a string of children rail-walking their way home from school. Against the steep hill beyond the river a clump of houses rested, somber and weather-blackened, atop the tall posts which supported their lower sides. A few, near the center of the group, were placed on a strip of level land, their gray hard-packed yards giving them a bald, barren look.

The truck lurched sideways, pulled across the highway and came to a halt straddling a small ditch which divided the highway from the railroad.

"That's Venetta," Jerry said, shoving his hat back on his forehead. "Gauley Bridge is a couple of miles down the road. By contract I'm s'posed to haul yore goods down there."

"You figure that's the best place . . ." Lock began, pointing across the river.

"'Less you want to live in one of them shacks they're builden up around Hawk's Nest. Course yore goin to have a couple miles walken to work, forward and back, but time winter comes the wind'll be blowen through them company shacks same as a rail fence!"

Stiffly Lock got to his feet, helping Daisy up, and they stood looking out over the river, seeing the mine high against the hill, the long straight line of the track which stretched down to the decayed tipple, the gray-black slag pile, the earth-colored houses, some with fallen and sagging porches, their doors and windows dark holes—a deserted, desolate place unreasonably brought to life again, unkept, unchanged.

"Yonder's a feller goin over in a boat," Jerry said, pointing down the steep incline. "Whyn't you get him to set you acrost? Me and the missus will stay over here ontil you get back."

"That feller you brung down before," Lock asked, climbing over the plank siding, "did he move over yonder?"

"Yep," Jerry answered. "Moved in that one down near the end of the row."

"Reckon if I went to see him he could accommodate me in finden a place?"

"Now, that's an idee," Jerry said enthusiastically, hopping down. "I'll go long with you. Me and that Reip feller had a nice talk. If he ain't home, more'n likely his missus can help us out." Almost before he had finished he cupped his hands and bellowed down the embankment: "Hey, feller! Any chanct of a man gitten put over to the other side?"

The man paused, small in the broad river, turned his boat and nosed it back toward the shore.

"You stay right there," Jerry called to Daisy. "We'll be back afore you can name it. If they's a place, we'll take yore stuff across and you can straighten up whilst yore man's down gitten a job." Pausing to spit, he lowered his voice and spoke to Lock. "I'll take you down to the company office. Just might be a chanct you can get on in the mornen."

Lock did not answer but walked along the railroad track sideways, pausing at the top of the path to wave brief reassurance to Daisy.

Moving forward to the front of the truck, Daisy watched the rowboat which jutted in little spurts across the river to the path below the double row of shacks propped against the farther shore. In the late afternoon sun her yellow hat shone brightly above her calico dress, and she stood, erect and rigid, amid the scrambled truckload, her eyes hard upon the figure in the back of the boat.

As the school children passed they stared at her, twittering at first and moving backward down the railroad tracks. When they had gone a few feet beyond, a small towheaded boy suddenly yelled, "Hillbilly! Hillbilly! Snake-eater! Snake-eater!" and the whole crowd, shrieking with him, turned and fled down the tracks.

Crossing over the bridge near the joining of Gauley and New rivers, which formed the Kanawha, Jim Hathaway let his car idle down and drew up to the curb beyond the bus station. It was almost eleven o'clock, and the single street was deserted but for a few people clotted around the Charleston bus, absently watching the driver strap luggage to the roof.

"Thank you very much," Anna said, following Pete to the sidewalk.

"Yes, t'ank you, t'ank you," Pete echoed, leaning over to see inside the driver's window.

"That's al'right," Jim replied cordially. "I like to have company. A fellow gets pretty lonely, driving three thousand miles every month."

Now that they were parting a formal stiffness arched their words. Pete kept nodding his head, backing away beside Anna. "Maybe we see you again sometime, huh?" he said. "It was very nice."

"Sure," the salesman said with a little gesture of his hand. "I get through here every now and then. Maybe I'll see you."

"Sure, sure t'ing," Pete smiled, following Anna a few steps up the street, where they halted to get their bearings.

On the side where they stood the bus station, garage and several stores lined the sidewalk, extending backward to the broad curve of the newly formed Kanawha. The opposite side held little, being only a small strip of land between the sidewalk and the railroad embankment which had been graded against the steep hill. Above the tracks and scattered about the hillside were several houses, well fenced and well kept.

"I guess everybody lives up against the hill," Anna ventured. "It's nice. The houses are clean."

"Sure," Pete agreed. "Not like Carbondale. Not smoke all the time." He raised his arm, indicating two cows eating their way across a field high against the hill. "Look."

"Must be nice living up on a hill like that," Anna said. "Maybe we can find a place up there."

"First t'ing," Pete said, taking her arm, "I got to find a job. I go now."

They walked along, past a dry-goods store, a narrow stairway leading up to a dentist's office and a beauty parlor, past the Ford sales agency and a garage, and came to a slow halt near the shelter roof of a filling station adjoining the bus stop. Anna, digging into her little leatherette bag, found a handkerchief with a knot tied solidly in the corner of it. Bringing it to her mouth, she caught the cloth in her teeth, pulled it loose and let the quarter roll out in her hand.

"I been keepin' it," she confessed. "For bread if we got hungry."

Pete stared at it and raised his head, smiling. "That's good," he said. "Now you got money, huh?"

"See that place," Anna said, pointing toward the half-curtained window of a cafe. "We're goin to get coffee."

"No. I got to find a job quick."

"Come on," Anna said. "You haven't had any breakfast. You only ate good one time yesterday."

Pete shook his head firmly. "You go, Annie. If I find a job I come back soon. You go get coffee."

Taking his arm, Anna attempted to guide him toward the cafe. "You can't look for work without even a cup of coffee," she declared flatly.

"No." Pete held back. "I get a job, then I like coffee."

"Come on, Pete. You know what you promised."

"No." He tried to free his arm.

Suddenly a horn shrieked behind them, and they jumped to get out of its way. A heavy truck, dusty and gray from the long journey, rolled over the drive and into the gas station. Its tall cratelike bed was crowded with Negroes, and across the rear a half dozen were seated, their legs dangling over the end. They did not talk much but sat looking from large curious eyes at the street of the town. As the attendant came out and took the gas hose down from its hook several of the men dropped over the sides of the truck to the ground, exercising their legs to remove the stiffness.

Pete and Anna watched them, listening intently.

"No gas, brother," the driver called, swinging down from the cab. "But she needs some oil." He bent over, unlatched the hood and raised it.

The attendant replaced the hose and got a spouted quart jar of oil and brought it around the truck.

"Looks like you come a long ways," he said friendlily. "Tennessee license, ain't it?"

"Yes sir," the driver answered. "We come straight through too. Never a stop."

Having emptied the bottle, the attendant let down the hood and snapped it into place. "They goin' to work at the tunnel?" he asked, nodding his head toward the rear of the truck.

"I reckon that's right, brother. I brought them black boys better'n five hundred miles." He paused, throwing out his arms and stretching his shoulders. "Where's the company office, you know?"

As the young man started to explain Pete caught Anna by the arm and pulled her a little further up the street. "I go now," he said anxiously. "You wait . . . there!" He pointed toward the green-faced cafe.

Anna nodded her head. "Here. I'll keep your bundle."

Pete thrust his small package of shirts and shaving articles into her hands, spun on his heel and ran up the street toward the road the salesman had pointed out to him. Anna watched him disappear, and then, picking up her own bag, went slowly into the restaurant.

She stopped inside the door, seeing the dark drab counter which ran down one side of the room, the half-dozen bare-topped tables placed about the floor and the little group of shabby wicker furniture near the front window, apparently a place for people to wait and rest. At the back she saw the splotched swinging kitchen door and a little farther to the right two doors marked Gents and Ladies.

Placing her package on a stool beside her, Anna seated herself at the counter, the quarter still held in her hand.

The kitchen door swung open and a young girl with an oval face marked by two splotches of rouge came along behind the counter picking up a heavy glass of water as she came. Halfway up she saw the truckload of Negroes and halted, the water in one hand and a soiled menu card in the other.

"Gosh," she exclaimed, "they get them dinges in here by the truckload. Another one come in yesterday. Seems like they already got enough to dig that whole mountain down. What're you goin to have?"

"Just a cup of coffee," Anna said, laying her quarter down on the counter.

Lessie Lee Rucker jabbed the menu card in between the sugar bowl and catsup bottle and went on looking at the Negroes for a moment. When the last one had climbed back onto the truck she gradually disappeared into the kitchen and returned with a thick cup of coffee. She stared at the coffee for a moment, bent down and brought a tiny container of cream out from beneath the counter.

Anna shoved the quarter forward and Lessie picked it up, went to the front end of the counter and rang up the nickel. As she placed Anna's change down on the counter near the cup she let her hand remain there, palm down, displaying five blood-red fingernails. "That's an awful purty color, ain't it?" she asked pleasantly.

"Yes, it is."

"I had 'em kind of pink yesterday, but I like this color better. It only costs ten cents. You can get it over at the drugstore."

Anna drank her coffee slowly, feeling it stream warmly down her throat. She did not answer immediately but sat looking at the patch bandage stuck to one side of Lessie's head.

It'd be an awful purty color for a dress too, wouldn't it?" Lessie went on. "If it was made up right it'd be real nice for Sunday." Seeing Anna's washed gray sweat shirt, she looked at it awhile and then continued. "'Less you don't like bright colors. Some folks just can't stand 'em. I oncet know'd a girl that never wore anything but black, with maybe a little white around the neck."

"How'd you hurt your head?" Anna asked, draining her cup. "It looks like it was pretty bad."

As though she had completely forgotten it, Lessie let her hand feel the bandage, touching it cautiously as if she expected it to either pain her or fall off.

"I was in a car wreck," she explained freely. "Driven up from Cedar Grove with a feller. Knocked the sense right out of me."

"Does it feel better now?"

"No, it don't hurt," Lessie explained. "You don't suppose I'm goin' to have a bald spot, do you?" she asked, her voice a little disturbed. "Lord, it'd sure look funny on a girl, wouldn't it?"

"Sure, it'll come in again," Anna said.

"I s'pose. You want some more coffee? You can have it if you want it. We always do that with the breakfast coffee. We ain't made the noon coffee yet."

Anna smiled, sliding her cup forward.

Lessie, returning from the kitchen, leaned back against the glass case that held the pies and watched Anna drink the second cup.

"You goin' to stay here?" she asked bluntly.

"I don't know," Anna replied. "Depends."

"You come by yourself?"

Anna shook her head.

"He's up looken for work, I reckon."

"He just went up to see," Anna replied, setting her cup down. "Maybe you can help me. If Pete gets a job, we'll be wanting someplace to live. You know where we can get a room cheap?"

Lessie thought for a moment, her eyes raised a little as she pondered the situation. "Sure!" she exclaimed, clapping her hands together. "Mrs Kinner, up where I live, has got one empty. There was a telephone man in here last week—a real nice feller from Charleston—but he left day afore yesterday. She'd be pleasured haven you. She's a widdy woman but just as nice as she can be."

"How much would it be?" Anna inquired. "We can't pay very much."

"I don't know for two," Lessie answered. "But she'd be very accommodaten, and they's a bathroom in the house. I pay four dollars for one."

"Do you think . . ." Anna began, halted and started again. "Do you imagine she'd let us have it and settle for it after the first pay?"

Lessie stared at her, candid and straightforward. "Ain't you got no money a-tall?" she asked.

Anna shook her head. "Not hardly any."

"Well, of course she would!" Lessie exclaimed, leaning down over the counter. "I'll tell her bout how you ain't got any money until your man gets a pay. Don't you worry bout it at all. Would you like some toast?"

"No, thank you. I'm not hungry."

Lessie was so close she could look into Anna's coffee cup. "What's your name?"

"Anna."

"Mine's Lessie. Lessie Lee Rucker. I'm a married woman myself."

"Is your husband in the tunnel?"

"Lordy, no!" Lessie exclaimed. "That man wouldn't pick up a shovel if he fell over it on the path! I reckon he's way off yonder somewheres, sitten on his butt, figuren out someway to eat without worken."

"Did he leave you?" Anna asked, her voice lowered by the intimacy.

"Well," Lessie replied robustly, "a feller to the courthouse over at Fayetteville said that's what it was. He 'lowed I could get my papers on the grounds of desertion. That's how he named it, but I ain't caren much, just as long as that snag-toothed hound don't come back no more. I got me this nice job here. By the time it's seven o'clock I ain't got a thing to worry about until the next mornen. That's the kind of liven I like, don't you?" She stopped, hearing the screen door squeak and close softly.

A small wiry woman, bent a little beneath the shoulders of her faded dress, stood hesitantly by the door and then edged herself onto a stool near the front of the counter. Her weathered face under the brim of her old sailor hat was quiet and timorous, and, having carefully piled her bundles onto her lap, she laced her stiff fingers together and laid her hands on top of the load.

"Howdy," Lessie said, placing a glass of water down before her.

"Howdy-do." The woman's voice was constrained and uncertain.

"Kind of warm to be traipsen, ain't it?"

"More'n common. The roads is so hard."

Lessie nodded her head knowingly. "It must have been right chilly afore the sun got up. Frost is comen on now."

"Was kind of sharp when we set out," the woman answered, her voice so low Anna could hardly hear her.

"You want to eat heavy?"

"No, thank ye. I thought I'd just have me a bite afore we headed back. My man's to see the doctor. He's got a bealen on his thumb."

"Lord, ain't them things painful!" Lessie exclaimed. "It's enough to drive a body out of his mind." She let her eyes run appraisingly over the back shelf. "Would you care for some pie?"

"Pie would set nice," the woman replied cordially.

Lessie slid back the door of the glass case. "They's cherry, apple and custard. And one piece of raisin, but that's kind of dry."

"The cherry sounds appetizen."

"It is," Lessie said, slicing off a sizable piece. "I et some last night for supper."

Placing the pie and fork and paper napkin before the woman, Lessie went into the kitchen and brought out a cup of coffee. "It's from the mornen," she explained, "but it's kept hot on the stove."

The woman smiled brokenly and raised the cup to her politely puckered lips.

"Anything else?" Lessie asked.

"No, thank ye. This'll be a great plenty."

While Lessie was busy filling the ledge by the faucet with washed glasses before the noon trade, Anna watched the small woman sitting stiffly erect at the counter. Finally, as she finished, she touched a forefinger to either side of her mouth, wiping away the moisture and crumbs. Belatedly seeing the napkin, she picked it up and touched it daintily to her lips. Laying it back on the counter, she pressed it flat with her heavily knuckled hand and got an old purse from beneath the bundles in her lap.

"That'll be ten cents," Lessie said, coming up.

"It was right satisfyen." Carefully she dug into her purse and produced a dime which she put on the counter with a slow quiet movement.

"Stop in the next time you're down," Lessie invited courteously.

"Thank ye," the woman said, gathering the bundles into her arms. "I misdoubt if we get down here again afore snow flies."

"Well, good-by."

"Good-by," she called from the door, nodding politely to Anna before she left.

The door closed softly, and the restaurant was silent.

"You know her?" Anna asked Lessie.

"No," she answered, going back to the glasses. "But she was awful nice, wasn't she?"

"Yes," Anna said, her brows caught together in thought. "I was sure you knew her, the way you talked."

"Huh-eh." Lessie explained. "But ever few days some of them back-country folks come in. They're awful poor, but there ain't no nicer people on earth."

"It was nice," Anna ventured, "the way you give her a cup of coffee."

"Land, you can't let on you're given 'em anything. I reckon she figured the pie was a nickel and the coffee was a nickel. If she knowed, she'd be real put out. Hill folks are awful touchy that way."

Anna got up, crossed to the wicker furniture and looked out the window, scanning the road for a sight of Pete.

As she started back there was a bump against the swinging kitchen door and a scrawny, thin-necked man, wrapped in a grease-smeared apron, appeared.

"You'd better set the tables up," he called to Lessie. "It's gitten on to'ards noon."

"I was fixen to make ready to," the girl answered, gathering both hands full of knives and forks from a box tray. "We sure are busy here at dinnertime, and supper too! We just sit around duren the day, but when mealtime comes we can't even stop to say howdy."

Anna made no reply, counting the tables and the number of stools along the counter.

"We could feed 'em fine," Lessie went on, rattling silver onto the first table, "but they all come at oncet, stompen in here hungry as wolves!"

"Lessie," Anna asked, walking toward her, "do you think he might take on someone else? I'd be willing to work just for my meals."

The girl paused, gaping at Anna in complete astonishment, and dumped both handfuls of silver on the table. "Lordie, I bet Mister Johns would be glad to do that!" she exclaimed. "I bet he'd do it in a minute."

"Who's Mister Johns?"

"Why, didn't you know? He's the man that owns the place. That was him," Lessie declared, pointing toward the kitchen door. "He was just in here a minute ago."

Anna took a few steps toward the kitchen door, came back and picked up her little bag. "I think I'd better go in there," she said, pointing toward the ladies' room, "and clean up first."

"No," Lessie said, urging her toward the kitchen. "Mister Johns don't care anything about that. He uset to cook in a loggen camp! Come on."

"Wait a minute, wait a minute." Anna tugged back. "I don't know what I'm going to say."

"My land," Lessie exclaimed. "I'll do the talken. You just come on."

Five minutes later, when the swinging doors closed on the kitchen, all the details had been completed. Anna was to work an hour at noon and from five until seven in the evening. In return she was to get her meals and two meals a day for Pete, plus an extra dollar at the end of the week.

"Gosh," Lessie cried happily, hurrying back to the unfinished table, "it's goin' to be nice haven someone to talk to. Mister Johns never says much, and I never had nothin to do but look out the winder, oncet the busy part was over."

"You show me where everything is," Anna said, glowing a little with her unexpected success. "Do you write the orders down on a pad or something?"

"No," Lessie explained loudly, dropping the silver again, "you just go back and tell Mister Johns. They ain't only two or three different things. And most of the time they eat what we got special. But if someone comes in and wants a short order, why, you go tell Mister Johns just the same."

As Lessie led Anna behind the counter Mr Johns stuck his small scrawny head in through the kitchen door. Furtively he watched Anna, studying the gray sweat shirt which gave her a somewhat husky, rough appearance.

"Lessie," he called, "you'd better give her one of them big aprons."

"Huh?" the girl said, straightening up.

"One of the big ones that come up around the neck," the man repeated. "Give her a big apron." Abruptly the door swung shut behind him.

"Oh. He wants me to give you a big apron."

Anna stood still, looking down at the clothes she had worn for three days. "I've got a dress," she explained guiltily. "But it's all wrinkled and mussed."

"We'll iron it this afternoon," Lessie explained brightly. "Them big aprons don't look much good on a girl." She paused, watching Anna industriously brushing the sleeves of her sweat shirt. "Your man's goin' to be terrible surprised when he comes back," she went on. "Walken in here and finden you worken and all."

"Yes," Anna said. "Yes, I guess he will."

"**Y**ou ever work in a tunnel before?"

"Nope. Never did."

"Mines?"

"No sir." Long shifted his weight, anxious to get through the lengthy application spread out on the clerk's desk.

"Where'd you work last?"

"Steady?"

"Yeah, steady. Where'd you work?"

"Oil fields," Long said, drawing his mouth together. "Corpus Christi. Two years ago."

"Married?"

"Nope."

"Dependents?"

"Guess not."

"How old are you?"

"Thirty-one."

"American?"

Seeing that the man, dressed in khaki shirt and knee boots, did not even look up, Long paused, caught the sides of his trousers in either hand and gave them a sharp tug. "Siberian," he said tersely.

The man's head shot up. He tossed his pen onto the rough table. "You being funny?"

Long made no answer. For a moment they stared at each other, and the clerk picked up his pen again.

"Where's your home?"

"I come from Nebraska. Kearney, Nebraska."

"Ever go to school?"

"Some. One year to high school."

The man flipped the application over, blotted it against the covered desk and picked up a small white card, swiftly scrawling Long's name, age and nationality in the proper places. Then, opening a large ledger, he ran his finger down the last page of entries.

"Take this card to the company doctor," he said, swiveling about. "You'll find him across the road, there where that car's parked, if he hasn't gone back to his office. He'll examine you. If he signs your card, report to the walking boss at Number One heading six o'clock this evening."

"Night shift?" Long queried.

"Night shift."

"What's the pay?"

Impatiently the man laid his pen down again, his movement an elaborate pretense. "Look," he said, raising a finger at Long, "you're not working yet. If they put you on, they'll tell you what you're paid."

Long took the card and stepped away from the head of the line. "Okay, brother."

Walking past the men lined against the rail, following it to the door, he went out and along the side of the building. As he went he could hear the man's voice rasping questions at Owl, who answered them in a fumbling, repetitious way.

"Owl Jones, cap'n. That's my name all right."

"Owl?"

'Yes, cap'n."

"Owl, for Christsakes! Don't you know your own name? You mean Al! You married?"

"Ain't rightly married, cap'n."

"You ever work in a mine or tunnel?"

"No sir. Never did."

As Owl came out of the door, his face shining from the ordeal, the small medical card white in his enormous hand, Long led the way across the road and once again they tied onto a line of men. Jim, who had been leaning against the unpainted building followed them but did not join the line.

"You get on?" he asked.

"Yeh, I guess so," Long said, nodding his head backward. "Goin' to see the sawbones."

Mutely Owl looked at his card and held it out toward Jim.

"He say I make a good muckah. What's that?"

Jim glanced at the card, seeing the word written across one corner. "A mucker's a mucker. I never heard of one."

"You probably clean out the crapper," Long chuckled.

Owl studied the card closely, his head moving with slow resolution. "No sir," he vowed. "Owl ain't goin' do nothin' like that."

The man ahead twisted about, pinching the tiny butt of a cigarette from between his lips. "A smart sonuvabitch, wasn't he?" he said, gesturing across the road.

Not answering, Long studied the thin, nervous face of the man. "They takin' many on?" he asked presently.

"Sure. Takin' on all they can get."

"Plenty of work?"

"Six days a week. Night shift don't have to work Sunday night. That bastard's puttin' me on the night shift."

"Won't make any difference once you get inside that hole," Long said. "You can't tell whether it's night or day."

"If there wasn't so many sonuvabitches comin' in here beggin' for work, a feller could get on day time."

Long ignored him, saying nothing.

"You'd think the governer'd keep them out," the man continued indignantly. "If he ain't goin' to do that, we ought to get first choice of the jobs."

"Yeah? How long's it been since you worked?"

The man fidgeted restlessly, puckering his mouth.

"I'll see you down the road," Jim said as the line crept forward a little. "Give the doc my regards." He raised one hand, now half covered with a dirty strip of bandage.

"Just the same," the man continued, "they ought to do somethin' 'bout all the wops and Polacks comin' in here, and the niggers——"

"Aw, shut up!"

"Well, it's the goddamn truth. They ruin a feller's chances of makin' a decent livin'. Man's out of work four or five years and a good thing like this comes along and——"

"For Christ's sake, shut up!" Long said, swinging his arm. "You sound like an old woman!"

Half an hour later the eight or ten men ahead had passed in and out of the doctor's temporary office. Long edged his way to the door, followed by Owl and the men who had passed before the employment clerk and received their medical cards. As the scrawny-necked man came back through the green curtain Long stepped inside.

"Take your shirt off." The doctor spoke without turning around. "Sit down on that chair." Long pulled off his jacket, dropped his overall straps and removed his shirt. The room was practically bare but for two chairs, placed close together, and a table upon which the doctor had scattered a few papers beside his black kit.

Long sat down on the chair the doctor indicated and waited for the man to finish reading the headlines of the *Charleston Gazette.* "Ever have any lung trouble?" he asked, edging away from the newspaper but still reading it. "Tuberculosis, consumption . . . ?"

"No, nothin'," Long said.

"Hernia? Got any ruptures?" Abandoning the paper, he lifted his stethoscope from about his neck and placed the ends in his ears.

"Naw, Doc. I guess I'm al'right."

The doctor bent over, pressing the mouth of the tube against Long's chest, moving it about. "You look sound," he said half aloud. "Cough."

Long obeyed, hawking from his throat.

"Again."

He moved the instrument, placing it over Long's right lung. "Again."

After he had tapped Long on the back he stepped away, his hand extended behind him. "Give me your card." Signing his initials across the bottom of the card, the doctor handed it to Long. "Give that to your foreman," he said. "That'll get you on the pay roll."

"All set?" Long asked, reaching for his shirt.

"Yep. That's all. Send the next man in." The doctor had already gone back to the newspaper, turning its pages desultorily.

Outside Long found Owl anxiously waiting, his ear near the door and his card partially crumpled in his fist. "What'd he do?" Owl asked quickly. "What'd he want?"

"Ah, he ain't goin' to hurt you," Long chided. "Go on in. He just wants to see how strong you are."

Shaking his head dubiously, Owl ducked through the green curtain, the card held before him like a defending weapon.

A few minutes later, as Long and Owl rejoined Jim at the edge of the road, the sun was dropping down behind Gauley Mountain, throwing its long shadow out over the river and making the overcast day seem even colder.

"How'd you come out?" Jim asked, coming toward them.

"Okay," Long said, smiling a little. "Looks like we run head on into a job."

"You too, Owl?"

"Yes sir, Mistah Jim."

"God damn!" Jim swore enthusiastically.

"Six o'clock we check in," Long went on. "Number One headin', working twelve hours."

"Whatta you get?" Jim asked anxiously. "The pay good?"

Long nodded his head toward the employment office. "That snotty bastard wouldn't tell me." For a prolonged moment he looked wondrously at his medical card. "Five long months without no sign of work, and then I finally got my hands on that thing!" With a broad, free gesture he flipped the card, smacking it soundly in empty defiance. "God damn, payday on Saturday!"

"Gosh," Jim said, "that's slick!"

"Don't worry," Long declared, "they're pushin' this thing ahead fast as they can. You'll get put on soon's you can hold onto a shovel."

"I hope so," Jim said lifelessly. "But they're comin' in fast. Must have been a dozen men go into the office while I was waiting for you." Reaching down, he loosened one of the bandages from the palm of his hand.

"Hey, smart guy," Long said, slapping his hand away, "you take it easy. Me and Owl's got a job. You wait till that heals up. We'll have something comin' Saturday, and that'll hold us till you're workin'."

"Maybe I can go fill out an application," Jim suggested. "He might put me on the waiting list."

"Ah, that pencil pusher!" Long declared disdainfully. "Take it slow. The way I see it, this company wants to get the job done and get the hell back to Virginia or wherever they come from. There'll be work for you when you're ready."

"Maybe," Jim said, not convinced.

"Sure," Long stated confidently. "I'll get in with the foreman. By the time you're ready he'll make you a straw boss."

Jim smiled, hearing the low chuckle in Long's voice. "Well, we still got a dollar and ninety cents," he said. "We'd better go and eat if you two are going to work all night."

"I ain't hungry," Long said, "and it must be after five anyhow. I'm going to walk up the road and find that Number One headin'. How 'bout you, Owl? Hungry?"

"Huh?" Owl asked dully. He had been watching half-a-dozen colored men who passed up the far side of the road and crossed over the bridge. "What's you say, Mistah Legg?"

"I said how's your gut, black boy?" Long laughed easily, filled with a new sense of security, feeling the anxiety leave him like a load he had carried. "You hungry?"

"You?" Owl asked experimentally.

"Naw. I'm goin' to work."

"That's where I'm goin' too," Owl declared.

As they started up the road Jim fell into step between them. "I'll bring somethin' up tonight," he said. "Maybe I can find a place to sleep around close by."

"Sure, sure!" Long cried expansively. "We'll go up there and build you a little old house! When we get that done me and Owl'll go in there and dig a hole with our bare hands! Boy, I'm tellin' you, it's sure goin' to feel nice when I get me that little envelope on Saturday. I ain't had no pocket money since Hoover got in the White House!" He stopped, searching the hills as if he expected his eyes to fall upon the thing he sought. "You reckon they got any good liquor round here anywhere?"

His face twisted humorously, Jim loudly sniffed the air. "Seems to me I smell some," he said. "Way the wind's blowing, it's comin' down from the hollow there."

"Damned if I don't smell it too!" Long declared happily. He inhaled noisily, his forehead drawn in speculation. "Far's I can tell, it ought to be just about right by Saturday."

Owl, who had fallen behind, examined the air and then trotted to catch up with them. "I don't smell nothin', Mistah Legg," he said. "I don't smell a thing!"

"You ain't tryin', Owl." Long laughed. "You got to get the wind comin' from the west."

"I got that wind, but I don't smell no likker."

'You'll smell it Saturday."

A dilapidated Ford, rolling down the mountain from Hawk's Nest, rattled over the railroad tracks and coughed to a halt beside them on the road. A hollow-cheeked man, his shirt bleached with sweat where galluses crossed his shoulders, sat behind the steering wheel. Beside him sat his wife, wearing a man's coat and holding a baby cloaked in a tattered piece of quilting. A rolled mattress stuck out of the car toward them, and back of it, across the seat, lay several rough bundles and the top of a two-burner oil stove. Perched above these, on the back of the seat, two small boys and a younger towheaded girl stared out like frightened animals. They were all barefooted but the girl, whose feet were wrapped in the remnants of a pair of sneakers.

"Howdy, feller!" the man called.

"Hi," Jim saluted, taking a step toward the car.

"I'm just gitten in. I don't reckon you fellers know where the office is for that company that's puttin' in a tunnel round here."

"Sure," Jim said. "Right down the road a piece. See that new shed built down yonder? The other side of the road? That's it."

"That 'un right yonder?" The man stuck a dark finger against the windshield, indicating the building.

"Yep," Long injected, "that's the one. Just go right in and tell 'em you want a job. If there's a line, just step up to the end of it."

The woman bent forward a little, holding the baby closer to her breast. "Are they still taken on men?" she asked apprehensively.

"Just left the place myself," Long said. "I'm headin' for the job now."'

Mutely Owl extended his hand, exhibiting his medical card in silent corroboration.

The woman made no sound, but her tired face seemed suddenly to sag and she lowered the baby to her lap.

"Thank you kindly," the man said, starting the rattling Ford again. "I'll go right——"

"Yes, thank you, thank you," the woman cried, straightening up. "We're much obliged."

Silently the three men watched the car roll down the highway, stiff and tottery on its old clincher tires. The children lifted up the rear curtain, which had been torn from the back of the seat, and stuck their heads out.

Long waved at them and, sticking his fingers between his lips, gave a long shrill whistle, rising at the end to a sharp, piercing crescendo.

The two boys and the girl did not bat an eye but only continued to stare blankly as the car went down the road, rolled off the highway and pulled up before the employment office.

"Scared as rabbits!" Long said, heading on up the road.

"They looked awful poor," Jim declared, falling into Long's great stride. "Poor as hell."

"Sure, but now they'll get a job!" Long said happily. "Everybody in the whole damn valley is goin' to get a job! We'll all be diggin' a hole right through that great big old bastard of a mountain up there!"

8

By the end of November, when the sky above the pronged valley remained gray for days at a time, work on the tunnel was well under way. Number One heading had gone into the base of the mountain, and Number Four, beginning at Hawk's Nest seven miles up the winding river, had started down to meet it. Midway in the route marked out for the tunnel, near the spot where Big Creek and Honey Branch flowed into the New River, another opening was made. Here in a low flat gulley between two spurs of Gauley Mountain, where the air vent would be on the finished turbine, men, working from the surveyors' chart, dug down to the level of the proposed tube.

At this mid-point openings Number Two and Three were cut. One crew, digging back down the valley from Number Two, estimated the spot where they would meet the men working upward from the entrance nearest Gauley Bridge. Another crew bored through the upper spur of the mountain, their drills pointed toward the men digging their way down from Hawk's Nest. The project became, during those weeks, almost like two separate tunnels, each boring through a spur of the mountain, each with a crew working from either side of that spur.

And so the plan of the tunnel was effected. Four crews bored their way across the top of the river's W, a total of nearly three miles through the two spurs, while the river wound its way for nearly seven, pounding down over its rock-chocked bed, dropping one hundred and sixty-eight feet, before it touched the lower end of the tunnel where its diverted waters would, one day, be returned again.

With all four headings opened, work moved forward. No day passed when more men, more families did not arrive by one of the three routes leading into the forked valley. Down the Gauley River they came, down the New River gorge or up the broad Kanawha from Charleston.

Rickety trucks, jalopies crammed with bedclothes and household furnishings, wagons, road-dusty and creaking over the hard highways, and some by bus, their belongings tied in paper, their work clothes bound together with rope. Negroes and sharecroppers up from the South, Polacks and Italians and Slovaks from Pennsylvania, from bituminous fields and bootleg mines, men from Ohio and Michigan and Indiana, off the farms and out of the factories, and some from Missouri and Arkansas, from the lead and zinc mines; men who came down from the Ozark Mountains, their tongues still strange with a language centuries old, their frames tall and lean and angular with the way they had lived.

Work-hungry, they plodded into the head of the great Kanawha Valley, wanting nothing more than a job, nothing more than a little money to send to their women and kids. The memory of bare, oil-cloth-covered kitchen tables made them silent. Some did not even ask what they would be earning.

I'm ready for work now.

They went to the green-shingled post office near the railroad underpass and sent penny post cards.

I was took on today. Satiday is when we get paid. Is the young' uns well?

Mister . . .

Yeah?

Uh . . . I'm wanten to send this . . .

Yeah?

I can't write so well. I kind of stove in my fingers.

What can I do for you?

Just tell her I'm al'right. That I got took on.

Oh.

Ast her is the least'un sick.

Anything else?

Come payday I'll send her money.

Where does it go?

Bessie McTeer, Picher, Okleyhomey.

There you are.

Thank ye kindly. Thank ye, sir. My fingers is kinder stiff.

The rooming houses were full and the shacks along the river were full. They searched Glen Ferris and Old Gauley, Venetta and Gamoca, and they climbed the side of the mountain, but the houses were all full. Along the Cotton Hill road they built shacks, and they built shacks in the hollows where the wind would not rip them apart, and then they kept looking because at night they knew the winter was not far away, and the children ate their breakfasts with the bedclothes bundled about them.

In Venetta, where the Cooper Coal Company had built their miners' shacks above the river, there was not an empty house. Shortly before the place had been deserted, black and empty and barren. Now every room was crowded, and from some of them two washings strung out from the same kitchen yard. In the daytime the women spread newspapers over the beds on the floor. It was impossible to get from the front to the back without stepping on them.

At the lower end of the settlement, where the shacks stopped and the road went down to the rottening tipple, Tom Reip had found a home for his family the day Jerry Walker had driven him down from the Slaty Fork country back of the Williams River.

Situated on the upper side of the road, the two-room house built of rough timber, with stripping nailed over the cracks, was a muddy, dark-streaked shelter, topped with tar paper and resting upon six-by-eights that had been sunk into the clay earth to support its lower side. Formerly the place had a front porch with a door leading into either room, but the roof had been ripped from it and now the floor extended like a ledge out over the yard. The rest of the front was weathered and dark but for the single window cut into the bedroom wall. One pane was missing, and a week before Maw Reip had covered it over with greased paper and flour-and-water paste. It gave the house a queer look, as though an eye was partly closed, squinting down at the road.

Dragging the old splint-bottomed rocker they had brought down from Slaty Forks onto the porch, Maw Reip sat down, placing a kettle on the floor beside her. From a flour sack she filled her lap with apples, small gnarled remnants of a harvest already past, and began to patiently peel and core them. Her fingers, stiffly bent about the paring knife, were thick at the joints and the inside of her thumb was toughened and calloused, but her hands moved rapidly, expertly, peeling, cutting, coring, saving all that she could of each defective apple.

With her head held forward a little Maw Reip's shoulders seemed more bent than they actually were, but even as she straightened up they still seemed to sag with some heavy load she carried. Her hair, which had been blonde and then sandy, was now turning gray, and the little color which remained gave it a soiled, unkempt appearance. Her face was older than it should have been, although her oldest son, Ely, had passed his eighteenth year. Beneath colorless brows her eyes seemed pale in age-darkened sockets, and from the corners of her nose deep lines ran down past her mouth, shadowed by lesser grooves moving out toward her gaunt cheeks. The cords of her neck were strong, straining to her heavy, bent shoulders, and in her forearm, as she manipulated the knife, the muscles could be seen moving beneath the brown weathered skin. Not a tall woman, Maw Reip was rugged, bony, knotted by years of hard field work which had toughened her skin, brought the bones closer to the surface and made the long scar which extended down across her forehead seem white and shallow.

In the back of Maw Reip's mind there was the memory of a cabin, solid and squat against the hill above Slaty Creek, its walls heavy against the wind and its floors solid for a person's foot to step upon. The great stone fireplace, nearly filling one whole wall, warmed both rooms, and the thick rafters overhead were dark and sturdy, as though they had grown beneath the upsloping roof.

Rocking on the sagging porch of the shack, Maw Reip remembered the solidity of the cabin where her four children had been born as she remembered the fields which spread about the hillside. In her mind she could recall how far one had to walk to reach the barn, the henhouse, the hogpen; how many corn rows could be planted across the upper field, how full the corncrib had to be to last out the winter.

She thought of the long years when the children were growing, first Ely and then Mark and then Virgil. For weeks at a time they would be all alone on the little knob, with no one going down the creek road to call to them. The boys had hoed a row each, and she and Tom had taken two apiece, heaping the dirt about the potato hills, cutting away the weeds and mounding it up. They had shucked corn in the same fashion, and the boys had ridden on top of the wagon when they brought the hay down from the field at the top of the ridge. And she recalled the spring, seven years before, when she had laid down her hoe and returned to the cabin although the sun had not yet crossed the sky.

By the time Tom and the boys came down for supper Viney May was asleep on the bed beside her, small and red with a hand no larger than her thumb. They had prepared their own supper that night, and Mark had offered to fry an egg for his sister, and they had all been very quiet because they were not sure of the thing which had happened.

As the sun came down the sky, glistening on the Gauley River and filling the valley with soft evening light, Maw stirred restlessly, pulling herself back, and refilled her lap with apples from the sack.

"Law," she thought aloud, "I hope they ain't no varmints got into the house. They'd gorm it up somethin terrible was they to get in afore we got back."

In her mind she retraced every step of their departure, renailing the cabin doors, making the windows solid so the house and furniture would be safe against their return.

"I reckon they'll get in the spring shed," she went on soberly. "They ain't no way to stop that, but I can ready it out. Just so's they don't get in the house and gorm it up . . ."

She stopped, seeing Daisy Mullens' slender figure coming down the road at an angle, crossing over from the side where the McClungs, Butchers and Stumps lived. In the soft light Daisy's hair was as yellow as butter, and her dress, freshly washed and ironed, swung a little stiffly above her dark, greased shoes.

"Howdy, Mis' Reip," Daisy called, halting where the yard met the road's edge.

"Come on up and rest yourself," Maw invited pleasantly. "I ain't seen you in some time. Tuesday it was, I reckon."

Daisy climbed the steps and started to seat herself on the edge of the porch.

"Don't you set there," Maw cried, running into the house. "It seems like a body can't keep these places clean in any ways a-tall." Dragging out a rugged old chair, she placed it beside her own. "You don't want to get yore clean dress all nastied."

"I been paperen the room," Daisy said. "The walls is so thin and bare I been tryen to cover 'em up."

"It's a sight of a job," Mrs Reip agreed, "but if a person's uset to being clean-like, you can't abide them dirty walls. Did yore man get took on steady?"

"Yes, Lock, he's worken full time now. Saturday is his first full pay."

"You'll be glad of that, I reckon," Maw Reip said, nodding thoughtfully. "I used up most every speck of paper in the house fixen up my walls," she apologized, "but yore more'n welcome to what I got left."

"Thank ye," Daisy said. "If you got any store paper, I'd be obligeed. I'm tryen to do it all in that brown store paper."

"I'll get it for you afore you go," Maw said. "Won't you have a bite of apple?" She held out a cored portion, cleanly peeled.

"You maken a pie?" Daisy asked, biting into the piece. "Apple pie would taste good. They're mostly gone."

"I thought I'd make a little butter out of these. I got 'em agin the hill back there, and of a winter the young'uns like apple butter on their bread, so I thought I'd put up another quart."

"That'll be nice."

"When winter gets here it'll come in handy. There's times I get to worryen bout moven down here. It ain't like liven back on the knoll, where a body's got a little somethin to depend on. Land, the cellar house uset to be full, and late like in the fall it allus done my heart good just to see them things lined up on the shelf. Seems like I allus knowed we'd make out someways, long as there was something left in the cellar house. It ain't goin to be like that down here, Daisy. Ever mouthful we get we're a-goin to have to pay for."

"I know," Daisy said, flattening a pleat in her skirt between her fingers. "I know, and everythin at the store is so dear."

Maw Reip did not answer at once but sat digging the point of her knife into a worm-rotted apple. "But I oughter be glad Tom was took on there at the tunnel," she admitted presently. "The crops never done a bit of good this year, somehow. Corn never growed shoulder high. We worked it; we worked it hard, but it seems like the ground's all wore out. When it come time for the second hoein a body could pick it up and it'd run through their fingers like sand, dryer'n a chip.

Lord, and there wasn't enough taters to cover the cellar-house floor, and them no bigger'n walnuts."

"It was dry on Cranberry Crick too," Daisy supplied. "Folks up there will just about make it through the winter and that's all."

Maw finished the apple, pared and dropped it into the kettle. "There was times afore we come down here when I'd wake up wringen wet in the night, wonderin and wonderin. Our boys is near man-growed now, and Viney, she's turned seven. It takes a sight to feed 'em." She hesitated, looked directly at Daisy. "Worst of it was, the year before was just as bad, and the one afore that. Tom, he never wanted to leave Slaty, but it seemed like there wasn't no other way to turn. The land quit given, same as if it was plum wore out."

"I reckon," Daisy said softly, feeling the tenseness creeping into Maw's voice.

"Three years runnen," Maw went on, "we could near fetch the crops down from the hill on our backs, me and Tom. We worked hard, and the boys helpen, but it never seemed to do no good. The taters wilted, and when you hoed there was a cloud of dust hangen over the cornfield until night come on. First two winters we made it through, someways. We et stuff from the cellar house—beans I'd put up afore Viney was borned. But this time we knowed there wasn't no way to piece out the winter. The boys knowed too, I guess. When Tom heered 'bout the tunnel wanten men—the boys, they named it, same as we knowed."

"There wasn't nothin else to do, I guess," Daisy managed.

Maw let her hands come to rest in her peeling-filled lap. "Nothin else on airth," she said, shaking her head. "But it ain't the way I'd have it, was I to have my druthers. This here valley is filled with a shiftless lot, far's I can tell, and it ain't no place to raise yore young'uns."

"The boys are near growed," Daisy ventured. "Ely is big, and Mark and Virgil is goin to school."

"Virgil, he's goin regular, and the teacher put him clear up in the Sixth Reader, but Mark—Mark ain't goin to school no more," Maw admitted thickly, as if the words were not her own.

"He's not?" Daisy asked in surprise, knowing how ambitiously Maw had planned their education.

There had been no school within ten miles of Slaty. Maw had taught them the little she knew and then, on the first Monday after their arrival in Venetta, she had crossed over the river with Mark and Virgil and Viney May, climbed up the riverbank to the railroad track and accompanied them to the schoolhouse. Looking neither to the right nor left, she strode into the square white building, passed up the aisle between the two rows of desks and came to a halt before the young woman standing at the blackboard.

"These are my young'uns," Maw declared, indicating Viney May and the two boys who stood awkwardly before the whole classroom. "I'm wanten them to have more book larnen."

The young woman dusted chalk from her fingers, allowing her eyes to run over the two tall boys standing beside their mother. The one with a great mop of black hair was a head taller than the second and larger than any child in her classroom.

"How much schooling have they had?" she asked, sliding onto the chair back of her desk.

"None, regular," Maw admitted hesitantly. "But I taught 'em their letters, and Virgil here's been nearly through the Blue Speller. Mark's a good scholar too." A little breathless with the speech, she paused, adding, "We just moved down yonder acrost the river."

"Well," the teacher faltered, "I'll be glad to have them. I don't know just what to do. I expect they'll have to take placement tests to see what grade they'll be in."

"I reckon Mark is big enough for the Seventh Reader," Maw stated helpfully, "and Virgil, he'll be in the Sixth. Viney May oughter go with the least'uns. She can't say her letters yet."

A low chuckle like a buzzing started in the back of the room, and presently the entire building was filled with raucous laughter. Virgil and Mark felt the back of their necks burning and they moved restlessly, hurt with the embarrassment their mother had caused them.

"Ridge-runners! Ridge-runners!" a shrill voice called from a back corner.

The teacher sprang to her feet. "John Keener, stand up!"

The laughter quieted, suppressed beneath lowered heads. At the rear of the room a chunky, rawboned youngster got to his feet.

After the teacher had stood John Keener against the blackboard, his back to the room, she again faced Maw. "If you'll just leave them with me," she said, "I'm sure we can find their rightful place."

Maw started to speak but, seeing how the color had spread across the cheeks of her two sons, she bowed and left the room. Rowing back across the river, which always filled her with fear, she remembered their scarlet faces, remembered the raucous laughter and the patient look in the teacher's eyes.

"I never meant nothin'," she thought aloud. "I never meant nothin' a-tall."

That evening when Virgil and Mark came home she was bent over the stove. For half an hour they sat on the edge of the porch looking out across the river, but she did not speak to them. Even after they came in to take off their good pants and she saw that Mark's eye was purplish blue from his cheek up through the brow she did not mention it. A sense of guilt swept through her frame, nameless and oppressive. Ely, returning home from work with his father, saw the black eye and began to laugh at his brother. Maw whirled from the stove, calling sharply, "Ely, you quit plaguen Mark! Stop it now, or I'll take a stick to you!"

Three days later she learned that Mark had been placed in the fifth grade, and after the first endless day, when he listened to the tittering of the small youngsters about him, he had not gone back to school. Maw pled with him, but Mark remained silent and disappeared up Sand Branch and onto Gauley Mountain. That night he argued with his father, hotly refusing to return to school, and Tom had whipped him. For a week he left the house in the mornings with Virgil and Viney May, coming back in the evening, silent and hostile. Finally Viney May could bear the secret no longer and blurted it out one evening at the table. Tom whipped him again for lying, and Mark rowed across the river and walked to Gauley Bridge. It was nearly midnight before Maw heard him cross the porch and slip into the bedroom where the boys slept. Tom was awake and heard him too, but neither one spoke, and the following morning no one mentioned the occurrence. After that, somehow, Mark understood that he would not be compelled to return to the Fifth Reader.

Daisy looked at Maw Reip but received no answer. "I seen Mark goin over the river with Virgil and Viney." She repeated her question. "I thought he was goin to school, the same as them."

"He rows 'em over of a mornen," Maw admitted, "but he ain't goin to school no more."

"Well, land, I never knowed that," Daisy said with slight energy, wanting to avoid the point. "I reckon he'll be wanten to get him some work now."

"He's naggen his paw mornen and night," Maw said. "He says he's turned sixteen and they's lots of fellers ain't no older'n him gitten took on there at the tunnel. Tom knows I'm agin it, count of Mark bein so young. But the boy's headstrong and seems like he can't get nothin else on his mind but earnen him some pocket money and goin to that there picture place down yonder to Gauley."

"You ever seen one of them?" Daisy asked quickly. "Mis' Stump was tellen me it was just like watchen real people."

"No, I ain't seen none," Maw replied, her voice stiff colored with what she had said.

"Lock's goin to take me Saturday. He says when he gets his first regular pay we'll go to the picture place. Just kind of a special treat," she ended somewhat apologetically.

"They must be somethin extrey," Maw agreed. "The boys is all for goin every night, if we was to let 'em. Tom, he named it bout us all goin sometime."

"Maybe we could all go together," Daisy offered cordially. "It'd be kind of nice, like goin to a party."

Maw nodded her head, running a hand through the peelings in her lap to make sure no apple had evaded her. "I'll name it to Tom," she said. "He might feel better was you and Lock to come along. He puts a sight of stock in your man, says it's just like knowen somebody from home."

"Lock's the same," Daisy declared. "I reckon he don't talk to the men down yonder very much. He says they got queer ways, and some of 'em is black. I'm seen 'em on the road, and they're enough to scare a-body to death. Blacker'n coal, some of 'em."

"I uset to hear my paw's brother talken about them colored folks. He seen 'em when he was to the war, but I never figured they'd be so black. I don't reckon they'd hurt you though, more'n anybody else, if you was minden yore own business."

"I guess not," Daisy said, getting to her feet and following Maw into the kitchen, which also served as a bedroom for Viney May and her parents. "But it allus scares me if I see one comen on the road. Lock, he says some of 'em are good workers, there at the tunnel. Says they're stronger'n bulls."

"I 'low."

Going to the wash box, Maw dumped the apples into a pan of water sitting on top of a dry-goods crate. "There ain't much to these apples," she said quietly, "but it gives me somethin to do. I worked all my days, and it just ain't in me to set on the porch and look at the sun."

"If Mark gets took on," Daisy offered, "you'll have your hands full. Three men worken in the family will keep you traipsen mornen and night. And, landsakes, they'll be maken a sight of money all together! It'll just come rollen in!"

"I ain't thinken bout that," Maw Reip said, crossing to a shelf and getting down a bunch of folded brown paper. "If it's good days now, they'll be bad ones to foller. When I get to thinken bout all of mine worken—all but Virgil—I allus get uneasy in my mind. It ain't never seemed right somehow. It's like they ain't growed up yet, and when I see 'em goin down the valley carryen their dinners in a bucket—I don't know, it just don't seem like they're my boys any more."

9

The nights were colder now, colder in Kentucky and in Pennsylvania's mine-gutted hills, colder in Missouri and Indiana and Illinois. A man walking down from Michigan's northern peninsula, walking the crooked road through sand and swamp pine, felt the night coming and knuckled his toes against it, thinking he'd walk south if there was no job. Two boys headed for a glass plant in Zanesville, Ohio, crept into the glowing shed of a pottery, and a red man with clay in his skin showed them where they might sleep.

"Winter's coming early. It'll take more coal," a man in Elmira, New York, said to his wife. "Everything happens at once, doesn't it?" She sat still, turning the worn collar on his white shirt, wetting the thread with colorless lips. That night he wrote a letter to his brother in Akron.

Me and Mabel are worried. It doesn't seem like the depression is going to let up, and nobody's buying any insurance. I'm out all day and most of the time in the evening. I only made $7.00 this week and I don't know what to do. The finance company took the car, but I don't mind walking. Gas for the car costs enough to buy milk for the kids. Today I walked all over the South Side and I didn't get a nibble. How are things in Akron? We're trying to rent the garage but haven't had any luck. We aren't going to buy coal until we have to, but we can't wait much longer. The kids say the floor is cold. I don't know what I'm going to use for money. Me and Mabel are worried, and I don't know what I'm going to do. I don't know where to turn.

The next morning he got a letter from Akron and tore his own up. After he tore it up he took it down to the empty furnace and burned it, afraid that his wife might see it.

By noon the days were warm, but the nights were cold, and to the north, along the Canadian border, the newspapers said, it had already snowed. Three inches of snow in Watertown. Forty-two days until Christmas. The postmaster at Santa Claus, Indiana, had already received his first letters. Michigan beat Ohio State 7–0 and Thanksgiving turkeys would be cheaper than any years since '29. In the back of the papers the *For Sale* and *Instructions—Male* columns almost crowded the *Help Wanted* department off the page. There was one for selling vacuum cleaners, the hearty Fuller Brush ad and two for selling insurance.

In Akron it was not much better.

Along the spine of the Blue Ridges it was cold. From the upper tip, where Elmira lay at the head of a broad valley that stretched southward over four states, it was cold. At night it crept down from the mountains, rotting the last grapes, pinching the tight-skinned apples, and then receded a little, but not as far as before.

Men left their homes, walking the streets, the roads to near-by towns, and finally they were gone for a day, two days, a week. Mister, I'd get to Alaska if there was work to be had when I got there. Thanks for the lift. Most people are scared to pick up a fellow. On account of the bums on the road.

In Gauley Bridge all four headings were now being operated at full speed. At six in the morning nearly a thousand men went into the holes beneath the mountain, working twelve hours, and another thousand came from the shacks and huts and shanties, from the homes where they roomed or the company's boardinghouses, at six in the evening. Two shifts, four headings, two thousand men driving a great hole through the base of Gauley Mountain, a hole thirty-two feet wide to divert water from the downsloping New River to a hydroelectric plant at Gauley junction. Three years before the State of West Virginia Power Commission had licensed the organization, a subsidiary of the Union Carbide and Carbon Company, to develop electric power for public consumption.

Surveyors had arrived, heading their lines across the two spurs of Gauley Mountain which ran down to the New River, showing the way the tunnel would go. People watched them, saying it would be a great thing for the valley, saying that in a time of depression it would bring a great deal of work. Plans were made, superstructure built, tracks laid to the openings, and the time had long since passed when men had left the coal company, left the dollar and eighty cents they could earn in a day's time; and gone to work for Rhinehart & Dennis, contractors from Charlottesville, Virginia, who had succeeded in getting the $16,000,000 contract.

With the population of the town more than tripled, with the number of available working men multiplied ten times over, the company had made arrangements to roughly house the imported families until the tunnel would be completed.

Searching for level ground to erect a group of shacks, they had gone over the valley from the bridge leading into Gauley as far up as the opening of Number One. Below the highway, near where the New River flowed into the wide Kanawha, a few shacks had been erected just above the stores that marked the location of Old Gauley before it was burned during the Civil War. But knowing the attitude of the townspeople against the imported migratory workers, especially the Negroes whom they had brought in by the carload, the company was forced to look farther.

As the road neared the entrance to the tunnel it turned, twisting through Cane Branch gulley, and wound its way up the mountain, crossing over the first spur. In that space, from Old Gauley north, the valley was exceptionally narrow, running sharply down to the rocky river bed. Across on the far side Cotton Hill rose steep and forbidding, offering no piece of land broad enough to support even a half-dozen shacks.

Following the highway up the mountain, hoping to keep as close to the tunnel entrance as possible so the men would be more available, they reached the summit, a broad, rounded knoll which bulged between Cane Branch and Big Creek. This was determined as the most likely spot. From the round ridge, running along the top of the mountain spur, men could walk down to the Number One heading, and from the other side, by following the course of Big Creek they could reach the middle gulley where Numbers Two and Three had been sunk.

Here, on the high knoll looking out over the branching of the Kanawha, they erected a double row of shacks, running along the ridge like a street unexpectedly come upon in the woods.

The shacks, hastily constructed and with no protection beneath the floors, were built of wide planks nailed to two-by-fours, with stripping over the cracks to keep the wind out. For the most part each shack consisted of two equal rooms, separated by a thin wall, each having a door at the front and back. A window was placed in either end of the building, a hole was cut in the roof for a flue and a door was made of planking so it might be closed against the cold.

In these houses most of the colored men were placed. A man and his wife and children were given one room, another man and his family the other. As the work proceeded during the early fall and more men were imported it was often necessary for families to double up, so that by the time winter had set in two families were sharing the same room.

Along the rear end of the ridge additional shacks were built for the unmarried men, similar in size and shape and hastily made from the same rough boards nailed to an insubstantial frame. In each of these shacks the company built bunks by standing a two-by-four from the floor to the ceiling and roughly fencing off the corner. The bunks were broad—wide enough to accommodate two men—and were built in double decks so that each corner held two beds and enough bed space for four men. The beds were box shaped, and since the men could not afford mattresses of any sort the bins were filled with straw. There was no other furniture in the room.

Hardly larger than ten feet by fourteen, the rooms were easily lighted by the single naked bulb which dangled from the unfinished ceiling. The men sat on the bunks which filled the four corners of the room, and at night, after they had gone to bed, the breathing of fourteen to sixteen men filled the room with a droning, weary sound. In the morning there was not enough floor space for them all to dress at once, but it was a shelter, and since they had arrived penniless after months of unemployment they crowded into the shacks, mumbling and discontent but afraid unless something should happen to bring an end to their sudden fortunate position.

Just beyond Hawk's Nest and near the foot of Lover's Leap another similar camp was built for colored families and for the men working on Number Four heading. On a flat piece of land at the foot of the towering wall of stone the houses were set up, facing the river, in the shelter of the mountain. In every way they resembled those on the knoll above Number One, and the square one-roomed places of the single men contained the same bunks, the same straw boxes and the single electric light strung from the ceiling.

Farther down the river, near where Number Four cut into the mountain and only a short way below the tall fearsome face of Hawk's Nest, the third camp was built. This one, limited to white people, extended from a large commissary down toward the entrance to the tunnel and consisted of similar shacks, erected rapidly on short pegs above the earth and topped with tar paper so the rain ran down toward the back and streaked the raw board walls, staining them brown and finally black.

The single men who did not live with families were housed in a large boardinghouse, erected by the company and standing like a long low shed beside the commissary where checks were cashed and food supplies purchased.

In this way, as the December skies darkened, as winter deepened and the tunnel moved farther and farther into the mountain, Gauley Bridge saw three new settlements spring up to house the hundreds of workers that crowded the streets at night, moving aimlessly from the bus-station cafe down to the motion-picture theater and back again. People driving out from Gauley on Sunday saw the three settlements, saw the shacks atop the knoll, crowded together along a clay path which turned wet and slippery as the first snow melted and ran down the hillside. From the precipice of Hawk's Nest they could look down upon the other two: the camp for Negroes at the foot of Lover's Leap and the larger one, just below Hawk's Nest, where the shacks strung along in a line between the tall commissary and the long shed where the unmarried men lived.

Beside these, in the gullies and in barns, beneath rock ledges and in outbuildings, they saw that other people had moved their few belongings into the temporary homes; backward, their eyes hungry and distant, their children thin—and always a little path leading toward one of the four entrances to the tunnel.

Each man was charged a dollar and a half a week for rent, there no distinction whether he was a married man with a full for himself and family or one of the hundreds of single men who were placed in the bunks.

But many arrived who had no money, and they hung about the outskirts of the town, finding whatever shelter they could until the time they could earn a little money and find it possible to pay the charges assessed them.

On a windy Thursday in December, as a cold rain came up the valley, chilling and gnawing at the hills, Roger Pugh and his wife arrived in Gauley Bridge. A tall and deep-shouldered Negro, stooped a little with dragging a sack through cotton rows, he had gone to Tennessee to visit relatives, hoping to find work of some sort until another season, another crop would feed them again.

In Tennessee he had heard of the tunnel, heard of men who had been working for months earning forty cents an hour, and that night he and his wife had headed north and east, asking at the Crossroads when they could not read the signs, hurrying as fast as they could for upper Kanawha Valley and a job that would last through the winter.

Reaching Gauley Bridge, Roger found the employment office, sat in the chair for the company doctor and hurried back up the road to tell his wife that he had been given work, that he must find Number Four heading before six in the morning.

At daybreak Roger passed down before the commissary, before the shacks sending up their spirals of breakfast smoke, and reported to the foreman. He worked all day, clearing out the muck and crushed stone, without eating, and his wife, waiting for him, searched the valley for a place in which they might live.

It was nearly four o'clock when, below the railroad tracks and three miles from the village, she found a long row of coke ovens, made her way to the low, igloolike ovens, clambering over the rusty, rotted track which had once carried the coke back to the now abandoned plant.

Carefully she examined each one, searching until she came upon an oven whose rounded top had not fallen through. Squatting down, she looked in the narrow door, seeing that a few bricks had crumbled from the back, leaving a torn hole that admitted a murky beam of light. Getting up, Nettie Pugh found a flat board and crawled through the oven door. Diligently she worked, scraping away the filth and dirt which had accumulated. A rat, squeaking shrilly, ran past her knee and left a little trail in the dirty snow as it sought another home.

By five-thirty she had cleaned the floor and, her eyes now used to the semidarkness, saw that, while they would never be able to straighten out, there would be enough room for herself and her husband to sleep until they could save the necessary money to move into a regular house.

Back at the tunnel mouth, she waited until Roger appeared, his eyes squinting and unaccustomed to the light, his shoulders covered with a fine layer of dust.

"I got us a place to lib'," she declared, falling in step beside him. "I found us a place we can sleep awhiles."

By the third day they had saved four precious dollars from Roger's pay. That evening he returned to the coke ovens to find his wife standing beside their little store of provisions.

"Dat man was here again," she said dumbly. "Look what he done!"

"What man?" Pugh asked.

"Dat company man what come yisterday. The one dat say we gots to go move to a company house."

"You tell him we ain't got no money?"

"I tole him," Nettie said. "He run me out of the place and den he blowed 'em all up!"

Following her finger, Roger looked at the row of deserted coke ovens scattered in a shambles over the narrow railroad track. In three different places dynamite had been set off. Only a pile of torn earth and red broken bricks remained where they had slept for the two nights past.

# 10

Slat McCune, a fat squat man with a slow, dented forehead overhanging his almost colorless eyes, had been brought to Hawk's Nest tunnel by the contractors. Soon after his arrival he was made, through the influence of Rhinehart & Dennis, a deputy sheriff of Fayette County.

A heavy man, with a tight, mean mouth, Slat McCune had a body like that of a sloppy woman. Beneath his shirt he seemed to have breasts lying in flat heavy folds, and his buttocks were obese beneath his tautly drawn trousers.

Supposedly Slat had been made a deputy sheriff to keep peace and order in the camp on the hill, but in hiring him the company had a much broader intention. Niggers, they said, were lazy and more given to drunkenness than mortal ambition, and an employer's only protection against spasmodic unco-operative labor was to take their own good in his hands and see to it that they earned a steady living. And who was going to watch that they did not haul out their razors during a crap game and slit one another's throats from ear to ear? Everybody knew that a nigger shot crap just as long as he could borrow a dime. Everybody knew that, and no employer wanted the responsibility of having his workers sent back home with a slit in their throats big enough to stick your head in.

Everybody knew that, and Rhinehart & Dennis got Slat McCune appointed deputy sheriff to watch over the camp on the hill. They called him their deputy, but the people living on the hill had another name for Slat. Beside the epithets, when they talked among themselves, they called him the shack rouster.

Owl's initial experience with the fat-rumped Georgian came the morning after he had completed his first twelve-hour shift.

Leaving the tunnel with Long that morning, he had found a walking boss and asked for his pay. The man handed him a slip of paper showing the hours he had worked and the amount due.

"Take that over to the commissary," he instructed. "They'll cash it for you. Then go up the hill to Number One camp and find yourself a room."

"My name's Legg. Can I have my time? I need the money." Long waited for a moment while the man ran a pencil point down the page of the notebook.

"You go on last night too?"

"Yep."

The walking boss marked another slip and handed it to Long.

"Three sixty," Long said tersely. "How come? That's only thirty cents an hour. I heard it was forty."

"You heard wrong." The man shut his time book and walked away.

Owl extended his hand, holding the small card before Long's face. "Dat's what I got," he said, not knowing at all.

"Jesus, you only got three bucks! Three bucks for twelve hours in that hole. Hey!" He took several steps after the boss, Owl's card in his hand. "Didn't you make a mistake here? Ain't he got more'n three bucks comin'?"

The walking boss halted, ramming his time book into his pocket. "Three bucks is what he's got comin', and that's what he gets. What the hell are you, his mother?"

"Twenty-five cents an hour," Long went on, ignoring the crack. "We heard forty."

"Say," the man asked bitingly, "what do you think he is—an engineer? If he don't want that, he don't have to come back. We got more men comin' in here now than we can use." He pointed toward the opening of the tunnel where a group of men were clotted near the entrance.

"See them men," he said. "They're waitin' to go on. If anybody don't show up on the day shift, they're waitin' there to take his place."

Long's eyes narrowed, anger tightening at his throat. He knew of the carloads of men the company was still bringing in, of the word they had spread to the east and the south of jobs that were waiting. "Say, fellow," he went on, his voice controlled and his words evenly spaced, "didn't you used to pay forty cents? I just want to know if a guy was lyin' to me."

The walking boss looked at him closely, trying to sense what might lie behind Long's words.

"I'm just askin'," Long continued. "I heard from a feller that you was payin' forty cents."

"We ain't now," the man said tentatively.

"You used to, eh?"

"Yeh, some of the men used to get forty."

Long drew his lips together. "That was before the company got more men in here than they could use, eh?"

The walking boss squared about and looked directly at Long. "Say, what the hell are you, one of them goddamn reds! What're you askin' all them questions for?"

"Aw, keep your shirt on! It ain't no skin off your nose."

Defensively, as though he had been duped, the man stepped angrily toward Long. "Listen, mister, if you don't want to work here I can fix that up in a minute!" He yanked the notebook from his hip pocket. "Time like this you ought to be damned glad to get a job."

Owl stepped forward, cautiously touching Long's arm. "Mistah Legg, us go get us some breakfast."

Long hesitated, looking at the two timecards he held in his hand.

"We got to find Mistah Jim," Owl went on uneasily. "That pore boy ain't had nothin' to eat noway."

A sound came from Long's throat, not a laugh but a short breathy gasp of contempt. "Hey, chief," he called bitterly after the walking boss, "where do you keep the commissary?"

Inside the long barnlike room, lined with rough temporary shelves and heated by a single potbellied stove which rested on a piece of sheet metal, Long looked about for the clerk. Finally, at the rear, beyond a pile of cheap tinny cooking utensils, he found the man sitting behind a high makeshift desk.

"Can I get these cashed?" he asked. "We just come off the job."

"Yep. Give 'em here." The clerk examined the two cards and pulled open his money drawer. "Which one is Jones?"

"Dat's me, cap'n," Owl said, stepping up. "Yes sir, dat's me."

Laying down bills in two separate piles, the clerk dumped some change on each of them. Owl picked his up, fingering it hungrily. The wonder of having money of his own started him mumbling, and he backed off a few steps, chattering incoherently and rubbing the two bills with his heavy fingers.

Long did not move but stood counting the money that had been placed before him. There was only three dollars and twenty-four cents. He counted it again and than a third time. "How much you got there, Owl?" he asked, twisting about.

"I ain't right sure," Owl replied, holding out one pink-palmed hand with the money spread over it. "I ain't right sure."

Long counted the change into his own hand and picked up the two bills, separating them carefully. "You only got two dollars and seventy cents," he said quietly. "You're short too."

"Dat's right," Owl declared in utter astonishment. "The boss man said three. I s'posed to get me three."

Long looked back at the clerk who sat on his high stool patiently, blandly awaiting their complaint. "We're short," he said. "He's due for three and I've got three sixty comin'."

"No you haven't. You got exactly what's due you. We have to charge ten per cent for cashing those."

"Ten per cent! For the love of jumpin' Jesus! Where do you get off with that stuff?"

"Those are my instructions. Ten per cent. That leaves three twenty-four for you, and he got his; two seventy."

Before Long could speak the front door slammed and a tall slender woman came into the store. Climbing down off his stool, the clerk crossed the room and found his way back of the counter. Long's eyes followed him steadily, outraged at the man's insolence, ready to demand a fuller explanation. But when the woman quietly began naming her wants he halted and spoke to Owl.

"Put your money back," he said tensely. "Lay it back down."

"Yes sir, yes sir," Owl said, slipping it off his palm onto the desk. Feeling the anger in Long's voice, he moved back a little, nervously watching the clerk.

For several minutes they waited while the woman gathered a little pile of supplies before her.

"And a half a pound of white pork," she said, her voice carefully modulated. "Lean white, if you got it."

After the clerk cut and weighed the sowbelly the woman asked what she owed and carefully counted out the change.

"I reckon that's all," she said stiffly. "I could use a pound or two of beans, but I only got four cents left."

The clerk ignored the statement, slipping her purchases into a brown sack.

The woman looked over her shoulder at Long briefly and turned back to the clerk. "You reckon you could in any ways let me have them beans till my man comes off this evenin?" she asked quickly.

"I told you before, Mrs Crump, we can't extend credit," he said flatly, crumbling the top of the sack together.

"I'll fetch my man's pay over soon's he gets in," she hurried on desperately. "We've a need for somethin' in the house. I could get them beans to soak and they'll be ready agin the time my man comes in." She slipped the four cents onto the counter. "I can give you this and fetch the rest over soon's my man comes home. I wouldn't ast, only we need it."

"Nope. Can't be done."

"We're tryin' to get ahead," Mrs Crump stated, her voice a little harsh and quiet with the courage behind it. "Payin' out ever day to get the checks cashed takes so much. If you could help us make it through till Saturday, we could sort of catch up, I reckon. I ain't askin' for much—just the beans———" She stopped abruptly. The clerk had already left her and gone around the end of the counter. She stood for a moment, her chin caught in close her throat, then picked up her package and left the store.

Long waited until the clerk had climbed back onto his high stool. "We got more'n that comin'," he said shoving the money toward him. "Let's have it."

The clerk picked up his pencil and bent over a tall ledger. "You got exactly what's coming to you," he said indifferently. "The company says I'm to charge ten per cent for cashing those checks. That's what I do."

Long felt his temper rising like a scorching flame along the sides of his neck. With one hand he thrust the money down beneath the clerk's face. Owl watched him, his feet shifting restlessly.

"Give us back our checks," Long demanded. "We'll take them someplace else. A bank don't charge no ten per cent for cashin' 'em."

Casually the clerk gathered up the money. "You can't get them cashed anywhere else," he said. "They're only to be redeemed by the company."

"What! That's the worst goddamned holdup I ever heard of! We work all night in that damn hole and then the bunch of bastards charge us ten per cent for cashin' the pay check they give us! What the hell kind of friggin' is that?"

"Those are my orders."

Long paused, trying to control the quiver which threatened to fill his voice. "You mean that piece of paper ain't no good anywhere else?"

"Only the company can redeem them," the man replied monotonously.

"And it costs us ten per cent ever time we cash one?"

"That's right," the clerk said authoritatively. "If you want to wait till the end of the week and get it all at once, we don't charge you. But if you cash them each day, it's ten per cent."

Long relaxed, placing his hands on the edge of the desk. "How about credit? How about findin' a place to live and get our grub here and pay you at the end of the week?"

"Nope. Sorry." He stuck his pencil into the corner of his mouth and bent down again. "No credit allowed. See that sign up there."

"Well, how the hell we goin' to live till Saturday?" Long demanded angrily.

"That's not my problem, mister."

"What the hell's the matter with that? We ain't goin' to buy no more'n we got comin' to us. You see us through to Saturday. Then we'll get squared up. Whatta you say?"

"Nothin' doing. We can't extend credit. If you want your checks cashed, it'll cost you ten per cent."

Long drew his hand down over his chin while he mulled over some stubborn thought. "That woman that was just in here?" he asked. "Her man work for the company?"

"Who? Mr Crump? Sure. Number Three. He's a chucker."

"And she was wantin' to buy grub?"

"Yes. She got it."

"How about them beans?"

"She didn't have enough money. She'll have it when her husband gets home this evening."

"And you mean you can't even give her credit until she comes in here with his time—just till he comes off this evenin?"

"Listen, you don't know these people," the clerk pointed out, his knowledge brightening his face. "If we started giving credit, they'd all want it. Think of the bookkeeping we'd have to go through. God, it'd be a full-time job!"

"And when she comes this evenin," Long continued, "it'll cost her ten per cent to get his pay slip cashed, eh?"

"That's right. Having the money on hand and everything causes a lot of trouble. The company can't afford to do it for nothing."

Long hesitated, looking about at Owl, who had crept back to his side, and then reached down and gathered up the money from the clerk's desk. Carefully he counted it out again, handed Owl his and put the rest in his pocket.

"You " the clerk said, pointing his pencil at Owl, "will find a room in Number One camp on the hill. See Slat McCune. He'll fix you up."

"Yes sir," Owl said, nodding his head. "See Mistah McCune."

"There's a boardinghouse," the clerk said, bending over his ledger again. "The men all eat there."

"Yes sir." Owl thanked him and started for the door.

"Say, bud," Long asked, turning to go, "do you do this for the company every day?"

"It's my job. I do it."

"Well, feller, I'm tellin' you—you must feel like the worst damned bastard in the country."

Outside Long and Owl parted. A bleak sun was breaking through the gray sky far above the mountain ridge, casting a barren light into the valley. The river seemed dark and cold, winding down between the rocks toward the Gauley, and the steam rising from the engine that hauled crushed stone to Alloy drifted upward like a luminous white cloud, shining a little in the weak light of the sun.

"Looks like we're takin' a beatin," Long said, his anger subsiding, "but there's nothin' we can do about it right now."

"No sir," Owl agreed ponderously. "It don't look dat way." He shook his head soberly, wanting Long to realize that he understood the gravity of the situation.

"You go on up on the hill and get yourself a bunk," Long said. "I'll go find Jim. Maybe he's looked up a place for us."

"Yes sir, Mistah Legg," Owl said, not budging.

"If you're tired as I am you'll jump in the first bed you see." Long moved down the road a little. "Get to sleep. I'll see you tonight."

"Um-huh, um-huh," Owl muttered, his dark forehead drawn in thought. "Dey's just one thing, Mistah Legg."

"Yeh, what is it?"

"I want you to give this to Mistah Jim," he said, holding out the two dollar bills he had received from the clerk. "He been buyin' me grub eber since we left Tennessee."

Long accepted the two dollars, separated them and handed one back to Owl. "You keep that," he said. "We can get along on what I have. I'll tell him you sent this one. After we get settled we'll figger out some way of livin' cheaper. That damn company ain't goin' to screw me if I can help it."

"Ain't goin' to screw me either," Owl added gravely.

"That's the spirit, black boy," Long chuckled and headed down the road.

Owl waited until he had gone several yards and then, keeping to the edge of the highway, he rounded the bend and started up toward the group of shacks scattered over a clearing at the top of the mountain. Nearing the ridge, he left the concrete highway and followed a path which led through the woods, up between two tall rock ledges and onto the rounded knoll where the flimsy shacks had been built.

Walking between them, seeing the washtubs hanging to their bare, porchless fronts, he found a man sitting in a doorway, his head lowered as he dragged away at his pipe.

"Good mawnin'," Owl said, trying to avoid the mudhole that lay between the sloppy path and the shack.

"Mawnin," the man answered. Behind him, Owl saw, two women and several children were crowded into the one half of the two-room shack. A little girl, with her wiry fingers of hair caught with torn strips of cloth, leaned against her father's back and stared at Owl.

"You know a man named McCune?" Owl asked. "I'm lookin' for a gentleman named McCune."

The man took his pipe from his mouth and looked up. "I know him, but I ain't seen him," he said begrudgingly. Turning, he called inside, "Marty, you see de rouster?"

A tall, bony-cheeked woman appeared beside the girl in the doorway. "Yeah, I see him," she said. "Bout ten minutes ago. He went on down yonder." She pointed along the side of the shack toward the far end of the settlement where the unmarried men were quartered.

"Thank ye," Owl said, moving off. "I'll go find him somewheres!"

"You know dat man?"

Owl stopped, facing the man who had spoken from the doorstep. "No, I neber laid my eyes on him. I was just took on last night."

"Den you stay way from him," the man advised gravely. "He's a mean man."

"He sure is that," the woman added. "Meanest white man I eber heered of."

"I gots to find him," Owl replied. "The man in the commissary say he show me where 'bouts I'm goin' sleep."

"When he tell you that," the man went on, "you stay out of his path. Dey ain't no good in dat man."

"Yes sir," Owl promised thankfully. "Me and him ain't goin' hab' no business. Mistah Legg, he's lookin' out for me."

The man nodded, clamping his pipe in his jaws. Owl studied him for a moment and slopped down the path, over a slight rise and onto the level portion which stretched backward toward the highest point of the mountain. There, before one of a dozen or more shacks, he found Slat McCune standing in a doorway. For a second he hesitated, seeing the guns strapped to McCune's thick, round thighs, and then he walked a little closer.

"You Mistah McCune, sir?" he asked, doffing his hat.

"Yeah. Whatta you want?"

"My name is Jones. Owl Jones. I worked the night shift, and the boss man say if I come up here, you goin' to show me where I'm goin' to lib'."

"Whatta you do?"

"I don't do nothin'," Owl stammered, frightened by the man's harsh, throaty voice. "I just come up——"

"No, you dumb bastard! Whatta you work at? Mucker? Chucker? Steel?"

"Yes sir, yes sir!" Owl blurted desperately. "I'm a mucker. That's what I am. A mucker."

"Get over in that one," Slat commanded. "Go in there and find an empty bunk and get into it. I'll see you later."

"Yes sir, cap'n," Owl said, hurriedly crossing the path toward the shack.

"And I'm tellin' you now," Slat called after him, "I don't stand for no back talk 'round here. When I tell you somethin', by God, I mean it!" His fat jaws wobbled when he ceased talking, and his mouth puckered together beneath his small nose.

"I'm goin'," Owl said. "I ain't lookin' for no trouble."

"Somebody will show you where the boardin'house is. You get your meals there."

"Mistah Legg, he tells me——"

"I said you'd eat at the boardin'house. Now get the hell in there and shut up!"

Mumbling to himself, Owl stepped over the clay-spattered doorway and into the almost square room which formed one portion of the shack. In each corner, supported by two-by-fours, he saw a double-decked bunk. Men lay in most of them, partially dressed and covered with dirty gray blankets and odds and ends of bedding they had managed to accumulate. There was no furniture in the room but the four tiers of bunks, and the floor, made of unfinished boards, was covered with a layer of heavily tracked clay. In most places it was dry and covered with a film of gray dust, but near the doorway, where Owl stood, it was darkly wet and slippery.

"What's you want?" a light coffee-colored man spoke from an upper bunk.

"I s'pose to stay here," Owl replied. "Mistah McCune say I s'pose to stay here."

"Where he at now?" the man asked quickly.

"Ober dere," Owl replied, pointing across the path. "Dat house ober dere."

"Come on in 'fore dat sonuvabitch come over here."

When he had gone inside the man in the upper bunk spoke to a fellow whose head was partially covered with a torn blanket. "We got any empties in here?" he asked.

The second man tossed the blanket back and rolled over.

"Up there," he said, pointing to a far corner. "The one on top. Dat feller got sick and he went home yisterday."

"Get up there," the first one instructed Owl. "Dat's your bunk." Without another word he laid back down, sighing deeply, as though he could scarcely get his breath.

Owl crossed the room and, standing on tiptoe, looked up at the unmade bed, without sheets and the blankets knotted in the center of a straw-filled mattress. Stepping on the corner of the lower bunk, he pulled himself up and fell wearily back on the knotty bed. Only then did he realize that he had not eaten any breakfast. For weeks he had followed Long, eating when he did and sleeping when he did, and now suddenly on his own, muscle-sore and almost unbearably tired, he had forgotten to get himself any food.

"Mistah Legg done forgit dat," he consoled himself. "He done forgit all 'bout it." Almost before the thought was finished he had rolled over on the coarse mattress and gone to sleep.

A week before Christmas Jim Martin went to work, helping carry steel to the drillers in Number One. His hands were healed but for one scab at the base of his right thumb, and his head, with the exception of a few black specks of cinders beneath the white scar tissue, showed no other trace of the night he had been knocked from the freight outside Memphis.

Following Long and Owl the first day, Jim edged along the track, his eyes fixed on the light bulbs which hung from the roof of the tunnel at intervals of twelve or fifteen feet. At first the walking had been easy, the tunnel seeming warm after the damp, cold snow which lay over the valley, but beyond a quarter of a mile the air became milk colored and thick and the light scarcely reached the floor of the shaft.

"You get used to it," Long said, hearing Jim stumble behind him. "Up near the heading it is worse. The first crew blasts just before they go off, and that makes it so thick you could cut it with a knife."

"Jesus," Jim swore, "I can't see as far as I could spit. Don't that stuff hurt your eyes?"

"Some—come on. You'll get used to it."

Jim paused, squinting through the heavy dust at the next light, seeing it like a soft blob, like a light in a fog that glistened a little near the globe but radiated scant light.

"One good thing," Long called across his shoulder, "you don't have to stay up near the drillers. It's worse there."

Jim did not answer but searched his way along, listening to the stumbling feet of the other men arriving for work, hearing here and yonder a cough.

"Can't they wet it down?" he asked, snuffling loudly.

"Christ, yes," Long exclaimed, "but they don't!"

"It's wet some where us muckers works," Owl said quietly, "but that don't keep the dust from the drills and blastin' from comin' back. The boss man, he ain't more'n ten feet away an———" Suddenly Owl grabbed Jim and pulled him aside, pressing him against the wall of the tunnel. A dinkey train, crawling into the tunnel with a chain of dump cars, had almost come upon them before its light penetrated the dense cloud of suspended dust.

"Holy hell!" Jim roared. "Can't that bastard see no better'n that!"

"He can't see no better'n you can," Long said, waiting for them to catch up. "When they get close enough you see 'em all right."

They said no more but walked steadily on, their feet placed solidly, their eyes straining into the half-light. Ahead they could hear voices, and then Long paused, guiding Jim around the dinkey which had puffed up on a side track.

"Your eyes gettin' any better?" he asked.

"Little," Jim replied. "After a while I'll get used to it."

"Sure," Long said. "You'll see as much as anybody else, and that ain't a helluva lot."

Passing the engine and on ahead where the first crew was placing steel bands about the walls of the tunnel, preparatory to erecting the wooden structures to hold the cement casing, they neared the upper end of the heading. Fumbling after the dark bulk of Long's figure, Jim stopped and looked about, wondering how far he could really see into the darkness. Behind, the string of lights stretched toward the opening, but it was impossible to see more than ten feet. Turning, he took a couple of steps and, missing his foothold, bumped into the blunt end of a steam shovel.

"Watch 'em, Mistah Jim!" Owl warned, grabbing for him. "I figured you seen that whirley shovel!"

"Goddamnit!" Jim swore between clenched teeth. With one foot he kicked the broad, rolling tread of the shovel's tanklike wheels.

"Hell," Long called apologetically, "I should have warned you, Jim. There's a light on them when they're workin, but the new crew ain't come on yet."

A short distance ahead, where twenty or thirty men clustered beneath the thin light of a single bulb, Owl came to a halt. Crushed rock and stone gave the floor of the tunnel a jagged, treacherous surface, and the water, covered with a film of dust, could hardly be seen as Owl moved toward the pile of shovels and picks.

"See you later, Owl," Long called. "Don't work too hard."

The crowd of men chuckled mirthlessly. "No sir," Owl vowed, "I ain't goin' to work too hard!"

Another thirty feet and Long came to a halt. A ledge about four feet high blocked the tunnel and, standing atop it, several men were dragging pneumatic drills into place.

Each crew worked all during its shift boring holes into the bench, and as they left the tunnel the biggest dynamite charge of the day was set off, blasting away the rock to the level of the tunnel floor. The stone shattered, cracking loose, and a fine cloud of dust charged the air, semi-microscopic and heavy, a cloud that the small ventilator with its insufficient fan hardly disturbed, a cloud that only became thicker when the next crew came on and set the drills into powerful, staccato action.

Finding his drill where the previous crew had left it, safe from the dynamite charges, Long dragged it onto the next bench, cut by the drifter drills ahead, and fell into line with the other men ready for the six o'clock working call.

"You stick close to me," he told Jim quietly. "When I call for steel you bring me a new point. Get yourself a stack of them and have 'em ready."

"Okay," Jim said uncertainly. "I'll catch on."

"Eyes hurt?" Long asked.

"I can see a little. But not very far."

"You never will, either," Long declared, "until we get through this damn rock. Here goes!" Turning, he kicked the snap, threw his weight onto the drill, holding it to one spot as it gnawed a rapid tattoo, sinking down through the stone and flushing up a fine cloud of dust that turned his work clothes white until presently, coming upon him, Jim saw that Long's overalls had taken on a ghostlike gray and over each eyelash lay a film of gray-white powder.

As work went on, the noise of twelve or fourteen drills was like the earsplitting squadron drone of airplanes. It sounded against the stone walls, thunderous and sharp, rolled over itself and searched the farther wall, but there was nothing to deaden it, nothing to soften it. As each drill pounded and jolted into the hard rock, biting and boring, it added to the incessant bombilation until the whole tunnel seemed to throb with deafening, relentless noise.

The metal sides of the dinkeys whined and tingled a thin echo to the pounding vibration.

Along the track where the muckers worked, following close behind the men who handled the sinker drills, boring from two to eighteen feet into the benches of stone which led the way up to the heading, the noise came back in constant, throbbing waves. Raising up, throwing broken stone into the dinkey cars, they felt it at the back of their heads like a pressure they might touch, and when they opened their mouths it made a difference in their ears.

In a futile effort to avoid the vibrating drone they caught their faces in half grimaces, their jaws set and their cheeks drawn back, like a person awaiting an explosion. When it became intolerable they would swallow hard, bending a little to avert the impact, and again set their jaws. But with fourteen drills going, with the clangor of the gasoline dinkeys, it was impossible to escape the noise.

Further up, toward the heading, it was worse.

On the first bench where Long worked, his weight thrown upon his drill so its point would sink deeper into the remaining ledge of stone, the drills about him jolted and hammered shrilly, but if a man looked at one the noise was so terrific only the jerky vibration told him if the drill was going or not. Working dry, because a man could sink a dry drill three times as fast as a wet one, the boring was a steely shriek that tore its way through the thunder of the tunnel. Ahead, toward the next bench and beyond that at the heading, where the drifters were boring into the forward wall, the noise was still worse.

Even Long, several yards behind, could tell the difference. When he was standing sideways across the tunnel the side toward the heading seemed infinitely more shrill.

And with the unending, deafening noise came the dust.

The narrow vent, intended to carry air into the heading, had long before been wrecked by falling rock and chip stone shot through the air by dynamite explosions. Never large enough to carry sufficient air to the inner tunnel and equipped with a fan too small to be effective, it was literally useless to the men who worked on the benches or the headings.

When new men arrived they remarked about it, pointing to the gaping holes, speaking of the torn canvas. But after a while they did not mention it any more.

"There ain't no air comin' in," they would say to the foreman. "That canvas thing is tore. . . . Look, see the hole in it!"

"Listen, you, there was a man workin' there before you come on the job. Now get back to work!"

"A man's got to have some air. He can't work unless he can breathe."

"If you can talk, you can breathe."

"But this dust is so thick you can taste it. And look in the water pail. A man can't drink that stuff. There's a crust on it as thick as cardboard."

"Shut your goddamned mouth and get to work."

"Why don't they fix that vent? Won't cost much of anything."

"Oh, you want to run the company, you wise bastard! Well, let me tell you something. There's a dozen men out at the mouth of the tunnel just waitin' to take your place. One more goddamned word out of you and out you go!"

Throughout the tunnel, from the drifter drills at the very head to the men who emptied the dump cars of crushed stone to be hauled and stored in a field at Alloy, a quickening was felt during these weeks. The unceasing thump and drive of the drills, the short rest periods, the dispatch with which a man was discharged if he refused to re-enter the tunnel soon after a charge of dynamite was set off, marked the speed-up which had already begun by the time Jim went to work. At first the foremen had waited half an hour after each blasting before the men were sent back to the tunnel, but as the weeks passed the time was lessened.

Just before ten o'clock, on his first shift, Jim was returning from the repair crew with a load of sharpened drills. He had found his way past the steam shovel and was headed into the section of the tunnel where the muckers were working, when he was halted by a shout that rang through the giant tube.

"All right!—get out!"

Jim waited, thinking someone was getting their walking papers.

"Way back! Get goin'—we'll set her off!"

Men brushed past him, dropping their shovels in a pile, and Jim tried to see their faces. Most of them were Negroes, but in the thick dust their faces seemed gray.

From near the head of the shaft he could hear a low, muted call. Straining, he thought he grasped the words, "Chucker—steel!"

Tightening his arm about the load of drills, he took a cautious step forward, paused and, finding the track, continued toward the heading.

Another man ran past him and then another. The second halted a few steps beyond, whirled about and ran back.

"Get out—quick!" he gave Jim's arm a tug, strewing the drills over the dinkey track.

"Huh—what——?"

Scrambling, Jim turned and raced down the length of the tunnel after Lock Mullens. They had not gone more than fifty feet when a deafening roar, like a sudden, jolting clap of thunder, broke behind them, angry and grumbling. Stone crushed and scraped against stone, clanging when it struck metal. Then the rumbling quieted, passing them like something they could feel and rolling out of the mouth of the cave to dissipate and vanish down the valley.

A great cloud of dust, like smoke fanned and blown, followed them down the tunnel, folding over itself like a blanket of fog which did not seem to lessen but only move about in the air, turbid and suspended.

"Jesus!" Jim gasped, flattening his hand against his forehead and shoving his cap back on his head.

"This your first shift?" the tall lanky man beside him asked. "You worked afore?"

"No," Jim admitted breathlessly. "I just come on."

"When you hear that call," Lock Mullens advised simply, "you'd best run for it!"

"Yeah. I didn't know." Jim squinted, looking at the man's face, wanting to remember it. The jawbones were rigid beneath bushy eyebrows; the nose was long and straight, and inside the nostrils the small hair had become coated and stiff with the powder of fine dust. "It's a good thing you seen me."

"Yep, I reckon it was," Lock went on easily.

Jim twisted about, looking back down the opening. Clouds of dust, thrown into the air by the dynamite charge, had not settled but seemed to wash through the air, crowding about the string of lights like some thick fluid flooded into the tunnel.

"How long do we wait?" he asked Lock.

"Longer the better. It's s'posed to be half an hour, but the boss, he don't usually give us that much of a wait. Soon's he can see his hand afore him, we'll have to head back."

No sooner had he finished than Jim heard, from among the crowd of men behind him, the call, "Let's get back! Come on, let's get back in!"

Without budging, the men stood looking at the dust which formed a gray wall above the dinkey track, their coughing the only answer.

"Did you hear me?" the foreman yelled. "Let's get back!"

A few feet moved, making a slow crunching sound.

"What the hell's the matter with you, you deaf?" the foreman swore, turning his angular figure about and facing the men. "I said we're goin' back in!"

There was no reply. The men waited, not stalling but glad for any few minutes that would give the dust a chance to partially settle.

"You, Robinson! Come on!"

A tall Negro took a few faltering steps. "Dat dust's purty thick, cap'n."

The foreman, Bill Hicks, started to speak but instead he walked over and gave Robinson a shove into the tunnel. "Don't talk back to me, you black bastard!"

Robinson stumbled awkwardly and came to a halt. No one else moved.

"You ought to wait for that dust to settle," a short stocky man said. "It'd choke a feller to death."

The foreman drew his lips together, aware of what he faced. "My orders are to get you back in there," he stated authoritatively, "and that's what I'm goin' to do!"

"We ain't had enough time," the stocky man continued. "Give her a chanct to settle down. Christ, we'll be fallen over one another."

Seeing the way the men moved, unconsciously edging toward the one who had spoken for them, the foreman had no alternative. "Hell, you're not scared of a little dust, are you?" he snorted angrily. "You get in there or I'll fire ever goddamned one of you! Now get goin'."

Gradually they began to edge along, the Negroes waiting for the others to set the course. They moved slowly, the foreman holding his ground as they filed past and into the tunnel.

"Come on, you!" he called to a young Negro who hung back. "Get the hell in here!"

"No sir, cap'n, I ain't goin' back in that place till that dust settles. It'll choke me sure."

Restlessly the other men paused, watching the two who remained behind. The foreman bellowed at them, but they did not move. Silently they waited, eying the foreman, eying the man who refused to return.

"Come on, you black sonuvabitch!" His word at stake, the foreman knew that a curt dismissal would not re-establish his authority with those who watched him, since he was aware that they knew to fire the entire shift on the spot would result in a serious loss of the company's time. If he made the threat good, it was more than probable that he would be put back on the crew himself.

The Negro took a step backward as the foreman approached. "Don't hit me, cap'n," he said, seeing Hicks knot his fist. "I ain't done nothin'. Don't you hit me!"

"Get back in there, you black sonuvabitch!"

"No sir." The fellow shook his head jerkily. "No sir."

With one lunge Hicks overtook him, driving his fist in a low, swinging arc at the Negro's jaw. The fellow staggered backward, his head knocking against the tunnel wall, and crumpled to the floor.

Hicks stood over him, clenching and unclenching his fist. When Robinson made no move he turned and called to the repair crew farther down the track. "Get this nigger out of here," he instructed. "Take him outside and get the walkin' boss to give him his time!"

As the men laid down their tools and came forward Hicks faced Jim and the others. "Now, get on up there! I ain't lookin' for no trouble, but I'm ready for it!"

They hesitated, angry-eyed and silent, then disappeared into the milky flood of dust that filled the tunnel ahead.

Day after day the quickening grew; the unceasing drills sinking farther and farther into the base of Gauley Mountain, each crew boring its way through rock and stone, hurrying toward the day when the headings would break through, forming the giant hole under the mountain, running from the foot of Hawk's Nest to Old Gauley, where gondolas of crushed silica rock were now being loaded for the proposed plant which would one day rise on the edge of the broad Kanawha, a metallurgical plant to consume the power which the great turbine would provide.

12

When Maw Reip awakened at five o'clock she was vaguely aware that it was snowing. There was no sound in the cold room but her husband's deep breathing, and in the silence beyond that she knew it was snowing, that the flakes were settling softly on the roof of the house, on the flat porch and over the yard.

Abruptly Maw sprang up, thinking of the three lunch pails she had to pack, and then halted on the edge of the bed, realizing that it was Christmas. Quietly she sat, feeling the sharp coldness that came through the thin walls, found her heavy shoes, pulled them on and noiselessly lighted the lamp.

The fire in the cookstove was roaring and groaning, and Maw had slipped into her dress and splashed water over her face at the wash box when Tom sat up in bed. His dark hair, graying about the temples, stood up like a brush heap, and above the flat neck of his heavy underwear his face was lean and bony. Unsteadily he sat watching his wife, his knotted fingers pulling down across his eyes.

"Don't make no noise a-tall," Maw whispered. "Ain't no use gitten the young'uns up till it's warm. It's the only earthly way we'll get 'em to eat afore they open their presents."

Tom threw his thin legs out over the edge of the bed, hunching his shoulders together, and got his trousers from the back of a chair. "Their eyes is goin to bust right outter their heads," he answered hoarsely, "when they see what you got 'em to the store. We ain't never had such store-bought things for Christmas."

Maw pressed her fingers to her lips and slipped the coffeepot onto the stove.

"I reckon you ain't gitten nothin." Tom grinned at her. "Don't seem like I seen anythin with yore name on it."

"I don't want to ketch anybody spenden money on me," Maw said quietly. "There ain't nothin I need in noways."

"I was goin to get you some purty dress goods," Tom went on tauntingly, "but I figured you already had you a dress." Maw looked at him, her lips drawn in a hushing way, but Tom continued. "And beads—'member when we was married and I said I'd get you some purty beads? Well, I was goin to get 'em, but I figured they was plum out of your mind by this time."

"Beads, at my age!" Maw hissed, trying to control her face. "Who ever heard tell of such a thing?"

"Wouldn't do no harm," Tom insinuated. "Might keep me from looken round for another woman. They was one down by the bridge the other day, and when I come by she kept rollen her big eyes like a heifer. She was real purty, too, and had some size to her!"

"Tom, hesh up. You'll wake everybody this side of the river!"

Meekly he settled down on one of the boxes, and only the gurgling coffeepot broke the silence of the room.

"I heered Ely putten a lot of stuff under his bed last night," he went on presently. "Sounded to me like somethin meant for a man."

"If you egged him on to spenden money on you——?"

"I just said if I had me a store suit I might step out a little," Tom said innocently. "Never named nothin direct."

"Quit talken sech foolishness."

"I just kinder got a little peep at them things. Lessen he's got it hid somewheres else, there ain't nothin in there for you, Nettie."

Maw paused, her dough-covered hands in mid-air, and looked at her husband. Not since the hot July, when stunting, searing heat came to the fields against the hill, had he called her by her first name. "What's come over you, Tom?" she asked loudly. "You're acten up worsen one of the boys!"

"Well, you're name's Nettie, ain't it?"

"If I hadn't slept beside you, I'd swear you'd been drinken somethin," she grinned.

"That's what makes me feel so good," Tom declared blandly. "Better'n any liquor I ever laid eyes on."

"Honest to the Lord," Maw exclaimed, squeezing the dough from her fingers, "you're gitten worse ever day you live."

"Ain't I allus told you that?"

"Tom, hesh up that kind of talk. The young'uns might be awake."

By six o'clock Ely and Virgil groped their way into the warm kitchen. Mark followed soon afterward, his eyes sleep-heavy and his lips forming slow contortions to remove some disagreeable taste from his mouth.

Tom, still filled with anxious, excitable good humor, plied Ely with questions concerning his mysterious gifts, and Maw, watching the potatoes that fried in a skillet beside the eggs, hurried across the kitchen, her voice growing vibrant with the hours that lay ahead.

"Get Viney up, somebody!" she called busily. "Virgil, you put the cups on the table—Tom! don't set there in the middle of everybody's road. Viney! Viney, honey—get up!"

Drowsily the girl sat up on her pallet, her tangled chestnut hair piling down over her face. For a moment she stared at the busy room, earnestly sniffing the pungent air.

"Well, sis," Ely called expansively, "ain't you goin to get up? It's Christmas!"

"O-o-o-oh!" she cried, as though she had been grievously deceived. "O-oh! C'ismas! C'ismas!" In two great leaps she crossed the room to the little tree Maw had placed in the corner against the curtain which protected the canned fruit.

Nearly four feet high, the tree was sparsely garlanded with popcorn, the strings dipping between the branches in soft crinkly loops. Here and there a shiny bulb shone red or blue, a bright statement of Ely's thoughtfulness. At the very peak and twisted a little to one side hung the red paper stocking Viney May had fashioned under the careful direction of her teacher. A red and white clump vaguely resembling Santa Claus protruded at the top, his face a little distorted where Viney's crayon had slipped.

Squatting before the tree, Viney stared at the packages piled about its base, little squeals of delight coming uncontrollably from her throat.

"Get up out of there now," Maw repeated a third time. "Get yore clothes on, honey."

"This'n mine, this'n mine," Viney cried, grabbing a square box from beneath the tree.

Dropping the egg turner, Maw ran across the room and grabbed the child. "No, no," she cried excitedly. "We ain't tetchin none of 'em till after we eat our breakfast."

"It's mine, it's mine!" Stoutly Viney tried to hang onto the box. "It's got my name——"

"Now you won't get none," Maw declared sharply, "less you run and put yore clothes on. Ely'll tie your shoes. Scamper!" With a little shove she sent the child toward the bedroom door. "Lord," she said, going back to the stove, her face flushed, "yore an worse'n heathens this morning. Ain't any of you ought to get a blessed thing for Christmas!"

"Maybe we ain't," Mark said. "I never heard I was goin to get anythin." He drew his lower lip low and stood behind the stove in an elaborate pretense of pouting.

"Oh, Mark!" Maw exclaimed. "You look so foolish!"

"You oughter see him when he goes in to talk to that girl there at the restaurant!" Ely laughed. "He gets red all over."

"I don't!"

"And he gets tongue-tied too," Ely went on tauntingly. "He goes in there and gets a bottle of sody, and then he can't do nothin but gawk at her."

"Like the devil," Mark protested proudly. "Me and Lessie went to the picture show last night."

Completely forgetting that his sister had gone into the bedroom, Ely gave a loud, shrill whistle and lunged for the door.

"Hey, sis! Put that down! Sis!"

As she was about to remove the paper from a package he snatched it from her hands. "I'll tan yore bottom!" he vowed, grabbing her in his arms. "Sneaken round where it ain't any of yore business!" Yelling and squawking, she tried to free herself as he carried her into the kitchen and placed her on a box beside the table.

"Hold her, Virgil, afore she gets into meanness."

Virgil, who had been sitting quietly at the table, made a gesture toward his sister but did not actually touch her. Instead his hand fell back, and from distant, somber eyes he continued to watch the others hurry about the room in tense, expectant activity.

"Set down now, afore it gets cold," Maw cried, carrying the coffeepot to the table. "Viney, get yore fingers outter that jelly. I'll baste you!"

Noisily they clambered about the long table covered with cracked oilcloth. On either side of the spoon dish Maw had placed a platter of fried ham and one of eggs, still bubbling in the hot grease. Biscuits steamed before Virgil's plate, and beside them stood the dish of fried potatoes, butter and two kinds of jelly and one of jam fitted in between. Before Tom the blue zinc coffeepot gurgled and sputtered to a quiet halt.

"Tom," Maw said, making her way to the table, "it'd be real nice if you returned thanks."

"At breakfast?" he asked incredulously.

"Breakfast, the same as any other time. We got a sight to be thankful for."

Tom looked helplessly about the table, and Ely sat the ham platter back down and lowered his head. The room was silent but for the low crackling of the kitchen stove and the squeak of the box as Viney twitched restlessly, peering over her shoulder toward the far corner.

"Our Father," Tom began, his voice low and constrained, "we thank Thee for this food Thou has placed before us. We thank Thee for our daily bread. We thank Thee that we are all well of body. In Thy name we ask it. Amen."

"Now," Maw said, rising up contentedly, "everybody retch in and help theirselves. They's plenty!"

One exclamation followed another, until the room seemed full and crowded with voices, with the clinking of forks and the rattle of coffee cups. Only Virgil remained quiet, speaking rarely, his eyes going furtively, guiltily toward the far corner.

As they had finished their second helpings Maw, seeing they could be held to the table no longer, shoved her chair back and started to get up. "Soon's I clear these things way," she said, "we open the packages."

"Come on, we'll do that later," Tom urged.

"Sure, Maw," Ely said, getting to his feet. "I want to see if I got anythin."

"Now, wait," Maw began, but Mark reached over and grabbed her skirt. "Set down, Nettie," he laughed, "we want to see what Santa brung us."

"Well, heavens, can't you———"

"Me first, me first!" Viney cried, running toward the corner. "Me first!"

"No, sis." Ely halted her. "You fetch the packages to Maw and she'll open 'em."

"All of 'em?"

"Sure. She'll say whose they are, and then she'll open 'em."

The girl paused, waiting for further instructions.

"Come and help me bring somethin," Mark said, catching Viney by the arm and dragging her into the bedroom.

Maw and Tom sat still, watching Viney and Mark and Ely trail into the bedroom and return with their arms full of packages. One by one they piled them beneath the tree, until the stack had nearly reached the lower branches.

"Land, it must be that Santy never went anyplace else," Maw cried. "Just look!"

"Reckon a feller ought to be able to get least one out of that lot," Tom reasoned loudly.

Across the table Maw saw Virgil, his face grave and almost hurt as he watched the others pile their gifts about the tree. She watched him, tempted to speak, but forced herself not to.

"Fetch me the first one, Viney May," she called brightly. "Anyone you come on!"

Ely and Mark seated themselves on the floor beside her, and Viney, her face glowing and bright, carried the first bundle over and laid it on her mother's lap.

"It's to Paw from Mark!" she declared, squinting at the writing on the brown paper. "Paw from Mark!"

Swiftly she unknotted the string, folded back the wrapping paper and displayed the gift. "A shirt!" she exclaimed. "A white Sunday shirt!"

Awkwardly Tom accepted it from Viney. "Doggone," he said thickly. "Doggone, lookit that!"

"Law, Mark, yore paw ain't had no white shirt in near twenty years." With a little nod she thanked him on behalf of her husband.

"Fetch another," Mark cried, but Viney had already crossed the small room and returned.

"That ain't as big as mine," Tom managed, chuckling a little.

"It's Viney May," Maw announced. "Viney May from Mark. Land, Mark, yore just given everybody things."

The girl stuck her hands out, trying to help Maw, and soon the wrapper disappeared. "Hair ribbon!" Maw exclaimed. "Yellow ribbon for yore hair, honey." She held the broad ribbon up, letting it stream down from her coarse hands. "And such a lot! Lands, there's enough to go around yore waist too! Ain't that the purtiest!"

Viney touched it experimentally and then jerked her hand back.

"Thank Mark, honey," her mother prompted.

The girl looked at her brother, giggled and fled back to the tree for another.

"Dig around a mite," Tom urged. "Yore gitten 'em all from one place."

From a far corner Viney dislodged a sizable package and, raring back a little, carried it to Maw's lap. Nothing was said for a moment, and Ely, feeling the silence, whistled shrilly. "Boy, what a whopper!"

"It's for Virgil," Maw explained quietly. "It's for Virgil from Tom and me."

Virgil stood up back of the table, watching the procedure, a stiff smile crinkling the corners of his mouth. Viney looked up at him enviously and tried to help with the unpacking.

"Gosh, what is it?" Ely and Mark got to their feet, crowding about Maw's chair.

"Here, son," she said, handing a heavy, folded blue bundle toward him.

Virgil accepted it, grinning self-consciously, and hastily unbuttoned the front and slipped the jacket on.

Again Ely's shrill whistle sounded. "Boy, oh boy!" he said, "a lumberjack!"

"That's a little beaut," Mark added, stiffly using the slang he had acquired.

"It'll be warm for school," Maw said, closely examining the shoulders for fit. "Purty color on you too."

Virgil moved his shoulders about, testing it, and edged back behind the table. "Gee, thanks," he said. "Thanks."

"Say," Tom declared loudly, "it's bout time Ely and Mark got somethin. Ain't there nothin in there for 'em a-tall?"

On and on the ritual went, with the wrapping paper piling higher and higher beside Maw's chair. Each piece she carefully folded and the twine was laid across her lap to be unknotted and rolled into a ball later.

Dress goods for Viney and one ready made, two suits of underwear for Tom and a heavy pair of arctics to wear as long as the snow remained on the ground. An eversharp pencil for Virgil from Mark, and a bright wool scarf from Maw alone. On the table beside her Maw placed the yard goods she had received from Mark, and finally, far under the tree, Viney discovered the large package with her name scribbled across it.

"This is for you, honey, from Santy Claus," Maw read, ripping the cord away. Unable to stand the anxiety over such a promising package, Viney began to teeter up and down, her hands flying uselessly, expectantly before her.

"There now, that's yourn."

Maw rested the box on her knees and Viney stared down at the doll laying flat in the tissue-filled box. For a long while she could not speak, seeing the golden yellow hair, the bright red dress and the tiny white shoes that fitted the doll's feet. "O-o-o-oh!" she squealed. "O-o-o-oh! Lookey!"

Tenderly she gathered it up, and in that moment the doll's eyes rolled backward as if it were awakening. Viney gasped loudly, tilting the doll backward a little. "Oh, Mommie! Mommie!" she squealed ecstatically. "Mommie! Lookey, lookey!"

"It talks too," Tom interposed softly. "Just you bend it down a little t'ward you." Viney looked at her father, back at the doll and again at her father.

"This-a-way," he said, reaching over and gently bending the doll forward. A tiny squeak filled the expectant silence, a word vaguely resembling Ma-ma.

Viney gave one loud scream and broke into tears, holding the doll before her like some wonder that had come unbearably close.

"Honey, what's the matter?" Maw said thickly, uselessly.

"Gosh," Ely exclaimed brusquely, "it's purty as a picture."

The girl twisted slowly about, looking at him through wet eyes, and began to nod her head in violent agreement.

"You hand me some now, Mark," Maw said gently. "Maybe Viney'd druther play with her doll."

For a while the room seemed stilled, but with the rustling of paper the tension passed and anxiety mounted again.

It's yourn, Virgil," Maw announced. "This 'un's for you from Ely."

"By gosh," Tom exclaimed loudly, "you're doin al'right, young feller. That's five for you!"

Hesitantly Virgil accepted it, removed the lid and held up two ties, silky and bright above the breakfast table.

"Now ain't them nice," Maw declared. "A blue one and a green one."

Virgil did not speak, only nodding toward Mark, his eyes remote and quiet.

"You'll be the best-looken feller in school," Maw went on brightly.

"That teacher'll be maken eyes at you," Mark laughed. "I allus did think she was worth gitten dressed up for."

Virgil grinned slowly and sat down again, embarrassed by the gifts, tortured by his inability to speak.

"Now hand me another one, quick!" Maw went on hastily. "It'll soon be time for me to get dinner on." She took the package and felt it inquiringly. "Um-mum, it's for me," she muttered half aloud. "Me from Tom there."

"Hey, how'd that happen?" Tom asked raucously. "I never put nothin there for you!"

Smiling warmly, Maw loosened the wrapping paper and raised the lid from the light cardboard box. "Well, bless my borned days!" she cried, holding up a dress. "Look at that! Store made!" Getting to her feet, she held the garment up against her body. "I allus had my heart set on a purple dress with white flowers like that," she said, her words quick and breathless. "Oh, it's such a purty color." She took a few steps, holding it before her. "Tom, you must have spent yoreself deaf, dumb and blind! It's a shame!" Her fingers ran along the collar of the dress, fingering the small circle of lace. "Oh . . . it'll last me to my dyen day."

"Gosh, Maw," Ely said, "that's purty."

"Say," Mark exclaimed broadly, "you get yoreself tyked out in that and I'll take you down to the moom pictures."

"It's purty, Maw," Virgil said. "It's purtier than anything I ever seen."

Maw paused in the center of the room, her moist eyes fixed on her husband. "You shouldn't a-done it, Tom," she charged. "There ain't no reason for a woman my age to have such a fine, purty dress."

Finally she sat down again, and the last of the packages were opened. A cap with turned-down, fur-lined ear flaps for Tom, a shirt for Ely and a drawing box for Viney May. With the final unwrapping everyone began to move about the room, examining and re-examining the presents neatly piled in separate groups. Virgil joined them, edging slowly about. As the excitement quieted down he got his cap from the back of the kitchen door. He did not speak as he went out, but closed the door softly.

Inside everyone listened, hearing his footsteps crunch along the side of the house and vanish.

"What's the matter?" Ely asked. "What's Virgil so still about?"

"He don't hardly talk," Tom added, going toward Maw who stood watching the door. "I never said nothin, did I?"

"No," Maw replied. "No, Virgil, he ain't hurt at nobody."

"What's the matter then?" Ely repeated. "Did I say somethin?"

"I should of thunk of it," Maw said guiltily. "Virgil, he never had no money to buy presents with. He wanted to get a tunnel job to airn somethin, and I wouldn't let him. He couldn't give nothin a-tall."

"Gosh," Mark exclaimed, "nobody cares. He's goin to school yet. He ain't s'pose to."

"I know," Maw answered. "I know, but I reckon it gives him a funny feelin."

13

Ralph Owens, an insurance salesman from Elmira, New York, arrived late in January. In his trade journal he had read of the $250,000 policy sold to Rhinehart & Dennis, who had contracted to build a power tunnel in West Virginia. It had been in an old magazine, and Owens had found it in the basement where he had come to spend a great deal of his time. He tore the article out and for three days he carried it in his pocket, reading, estimating, and one night he showed it to his wife.

"I looked on a map," he said. "West Virginia is almost four hundred miles."

"We'll be all right," his wife replied. "You go. Maybe they need a timekeeper."

"What about the rent? What if you and the kids are put out?"

"You go," his wife repeated quietly.

"It's so far," he cautioned, not looking up. "If the A & P man stops our credit——"

"We'll find some way. It sounds like you might get work down there."

He patched his shoes in the basement that night, and the next morning he hitched down across Pennsylvania. On the third day in Gauley Bridge he became weak with hunger and fatigue. Morosely he walked down the street, too scared to ask for a cigarette. He stayed away from people, walking endlessly up to the employment office and back again, thinking: I got to eat. I won't be strong enough to work if I don't eat. If I get a job I won't be strong enough.

By the end of the fourth day he had convinced himself that he looked too thin and weak for anyone to hire. He felt his jaws, and the bones seemed prominent and near the skin.

For an hour he stood in front of the cafe by the bus station and then walked to the end of the street near the bridge, trying to locate the back door. There wasn't any. The kitchen hung over the ice-edged river.

He went back to the entrance, passing close the window, hoping the place would be empty. Waiting across the street, he watched until the two men got up from the counter and left.

"I'll just ask for soup," he kept telling himself. "I'll scrub the place and just ask for soup." Almost before he realized it Ralph Owens was standing beside the cash register trying to answer the blonde girl who approached him.

"The manager," he repeated. "I'd like to speak to him."

"Huh?" Lessie said, watching the snow melt in his short whiskers.

"I want to speak to whoever's in charge," he said anxiously, fearing someone would come in.

"Oh. You mean Mister Johns."

"Is he in? I could come back."

"No. He went to the store. They's just me here."

Owens nodded awkwardly and backed toward the door. Midway he paused. "I'm looking for something to eat," he blurted. "I'd be glad to scrub the floors."

"Huh?"

"I'll scrub the floor," he said, gesturing his hand, "if you'll let me eat something. I'm hungry."

Lessie snapped her thumb against her teeth, her round face a mask of thought. "I wish Anna was here," she murmured.

"What?"

"Anna. If Anna was here she'd know." For a while Lessie studied Owens intently. "I'll tell you," she declared suddenly. "I'll run ast Mister Johns. You stay here, I'll be right back." She darted through the door, cut across the bus lot and headed for the grocery store.

Alone in the barnlike restaurant, Owens looked about, sniffing the air, eying the pies in the glass cases. Slowly he edged his way over and sat down at the counter. To the front, beyond the cash register, he saw that no one passed along the street. He listened, and there was no movement in the kitchen. Slowly his hand crept forward, past the catsup bottle and the spoon glass, and his fingers dug into the sugar bowl.

He was still holding the sweetening grains in his mouth when the door slammed and Lessie stood stomping the snow from her feet. "Sure, he said," she reported. "Sure. Only thing is, you can't have none of the beef. We'll need it all for supper."

The following day Ralph Owens was given a job carrying steel to the drillers in Number Two heading. He went to live in the company boardinghouse at the foot of Hawk's Nest. Sometimes when the dust made him cough he thought he would ask for a timekeeper's job. But he never did. Once before he had asked for a change of positions and his boss told him that if he was discontent he would have to leave. Every time he thought of the timekeeper's job he thought of that. On Saturdays, when he got his pay, he went to the drugstore in Gauley Bridge and bought himself a bottle of cough medicine.

And so, as the stragglers came into the valley, they gradually found work and settled down glad, in the winter of the depression, for whatever work they could get, accepting what was given them without question.

Those who had come earlier seemed like old residents. People meeting Tom Reip or one of his boys thought they had always been around Gauley. Only the real residents, who lived on the hill above the town, looked down on the busy street and recalled the days before the tunnel opened, when you could walk from one end of the town to the other and speak the names of everyone you passed.

"It's just like going to Charleston," the Reverend Mitchell's wife complained politely. "You hardly see anybody you know. And all sorts of people on the streets."

"Oh, yes indeed." Myrtle Kuhn quickly verified her statement. "I'd never think of going downstreet at night alone."

"You can tell the kind they are; not more than a handful has ever come near the church! Course so many of them are foreigners."

Miss Kuhn gathered up her sheet music from the piano where they had been practicing. "And the niggers—they shove you right off the street! I simply can't see why the company feels called on to bring so many of them in here. I'm certainly not against them, as I was telling Mother, but it does seem that something could be done about them. Mrs Pratt said she drove past one of the camps, and they live like pigs! You can imagine what goes on."

Mrs Mitchell twisted about on the stool, wiping her moist fingers with a handkerchief. "I told the reverend I was going to bring it up at the next meeting of the Delphians, but he seems to think it the affair of the town council. I know there're babies borned out there that ain't properly registered."

"As Mrs Pratt says, you can't expect anything but the scum when work's as free as it is here." Carefully she slipped her music back into a brown portfolio. "I don't think a day passes when we don't have a beggar at the door. It's gotten so we have to keep the shades drawn."

"It's a great burden," Mrs Mitchell echoed her husband's words. "A great problem. We'll be fortunate if we can keep our young people."

"And the way they take over the town!" Miss Kuhn declared in high exasperation. "Sometimes I think we ought to ask the state troopers be sent in here."

"Yes, yes," Mrs Mitchell agreed. "It's so outrageous. I suppose if they don't have a thing they feel they can come here and we'll take care of them."

Miss Kuhn snapped on her second galosh before she spoke. "And when the company goes we'll be left with them all on our hands. It's really too much to ask of the church." She paused, slipped her arms into a green cloth coat and latched the belt together. "Well, thank you so much for going over my music."

"Now, now, I do nothing but play the notes. And that's a privilege with your voice. The reverend declares your singing does so much to set the tone of his service."

Miss Kuhn laughed self-consciously, tucking her portfolio beneath her arm. "Oh, he's a wonderful man! I'm sure they'd never miss my poor efforts."

"Oh," Mrs Mitchell chided, "you mustn't say that."

At the door they parted, screaming a little at the cold air.

"Take care you don't get a cold," Mrs Mitchell called.

"Oh, I shall."

"Good-by."

"Good-by, and thank you for playing for me."

"It was a joy. And, Myrtle, don't forget Thursday night. The district conference expects a report from us."

"Oh yes. And I must bring the money. Mother has added another dollar, making it $14.85."

"How wonderful of her! I'm sure the Chinese children will be grateful. It must be so cold there. Well, good-by!"

"Good-by!"

Pulling her coat about her neck, Miss Kuhn bent a little against the wind and went down the parsonage steps, moving slowly so she would not slip, the notes of her song lilting through her mind with an ease she would never accomplish.

The snow had piled high over the state road, filling the ditches and spreading smoothly over the unused railroad track. Below the Gauley was frozen across but for a single strip down the center, dark blue and flowing like a vein that ran the river's course.

The coal company's shacks, above the tipple at Venetta, were roofed with the white blanket, and only here and there did the black coal-eroded soil show through. The houses standing against the hills seemed more drab than ever, and even the snow over the roofs and over their slate-colored yards did little to conceal their dingy dreariness.

Now, all through the days between late dawn and early dark, smoke trailed up from thin chimneys and a woman's wash froze to the line as soon as she had pinned it there.

Daisy Mullens had nearly finished hers, hanging it on a steaming line about the kitchen, when she heard a knock at the door and the plump figure of Mrs Stump hurried in out of the cold.

"Mercy," the large woman exclaimed, shaking the black shawl from about her head, "it's cold! And there's a wind blowin' over the river."

A chill burst of air swept through the room, turning milky white. "I thought it'd let up," Daisy said, drawing her arms from a suds-filled tub. "I waited so's I could put my wash out. It's been hung indoors until everythin's turnen yaller."

With a great sigh the woman sank into a chair beside the stove. Her hair was coarse and stringy, dropping from over her ears in strands to hang about her thick neck. Throughout Venetta it was known that on Saturday nights she drank at the kitchen table with her husband. They had no children, no particular home, but Mrs Stump possessed a warm, friendly manner, quick and bawdy of speech and as quick and generous with her sympathies.

"God!" she exclaimed breathily, looking at the lines of clothes stretched up and down the kitchen. "I ain't touched soap to a stitch in more'n a month. Hank's got on the same underwear he wore last week, but it's too hellish cold to wash these days."

"I was goin to wait over," Daisy said, "but it seems like this spell ain't goin to let up. A-body just sets around and sets around. I never had a blessed thing to do, so I figured I'd light into it and wash everythin up."

"Land, you and that Mis' Reip. I went into her house the other day, and it's clean as a pin. She must wear her knuckles to the bone."

Daisy bent back over the washboard, rubbing out the last of the clothes before she placed Lock's work shirt and trousers into the tub. "An' she's got three men worken," she said, "and Virgil and Viney May goin to school. I don't see how she finds the time."

"You wouldn't catch me workin' like that," Mrs Stump vowed, "and money comin' in faster'n you can count it. The Reips will be rich as grease if work don't give out."

"I reckon it takes a lot," Daisy said, "they's six of 'em all told. That's a lot of feet under the table of a mealtime."

From inside the waist of her dress Mrs Stump produced a small paper poke. "Have a piece of chocolate?" she offered.

"Thank ye kindly," Daisy said, wiping a soapy forearm across her face. "I won't stop for it just now."

The large woman got up and waddled to the table. "I'll lay it there," she said, placing a chocolate peppermint on the table. "Eat it when you want it." Going back to the stove, she seated herself and jammed her hand into the poke again. "You and Lock's gettin' along al'right, I guess."

"Just fine. He's worken regular, but don't seem like we can get as much ahead as we figured. But we ain't got no complaint comen."

"Me and Hank ain't so satisfied," Mrs Stump proclaimed. "We're plannin' to move on in the spring, if we can save a couple of dollars to rub together."

Hanging up the last of the clothes, Daisy tossed Lock's overalls into the tub. "Why, land, I never knowed that! " she said. "Where you plannen on goin?"

"Either down South or out to California. Like Hank says, we're just goin' to lay in the sun till our bellies get brown."

Daisy smiled as though she had never heard the story before. The first time she had been surprised and a little excited with the proposed adventure, but each time Mrs Stump had declared their intentions, their freedom and abandon, Daisy's excitement had lessened. "Oh, that'll be real pleasant," she managed, showing the layer of fine grit and dirt that remained when she drained the water from her hands. "Just seems like you can't get that dirt out no way you try."

"I quit tryin' long ago," Mrs Stump revealed. "Hank steps inside the kitchen and strips off and I get his other pants for him. In the mornin' he gets back in the old ones, and when he wears 'em out I just burn 'em up. There ain't no use tryin' to wash that dust out of 'em."

"It gets all over the place if I don't," Daisy said. "When Lock comes in I can sweep up a handful after him."

"I know. It's Jesus-awful."

While Daisy hung up the worn overalls and emptied the water at the kitchen door Mrs Stump sat placidly aside, smelling the damp kitchen and shuddering a little each time Daisy opened the back door and threw out a pail of water.

"Just lookey in the bottom of that tub!" Daisy said. "There must be a pint. Finer'n sand, it is. A-body'd think they was feelin flour almost, feelin it when it's wet that-a-way."

Mrs Stump nodded her head knowingly and changed the subject. "Is Mrs Reip's youngest boy still goin' to school? I heered they was some talk of his quittin' right after Christmas."

"Virgil," Daisy said. "Yes, he's still goin. He was put ahead to the Seventh Reader. From the way Mis' Reip talks, he may go right on through and then go away to that big school down there at Montgomery. That way he could be a teacher hisself."

Biting into another chocolate, Mrs Stump, in agreement to some inner thought, nodded her head stoutly. "I reckon the three that's worken must bring in fifty or sixty dollars a week. More'n likely they'll be gettin' them a car right off soon."

"I don't guess so," Daisy said, mopping up the floor. "They're goin saven so's they can get 'em a farm, same as me and Lock. They earn a-plenty, but they go saven."

"They'll be rich as John D. Rockefeller, with all them workin'," Mrs Stump said, getting up. "I always said money was made for spendin'. You might as well enjoy it whilst you're alive. When you're dead—the worms get you."

"Long t'ord spring," Daisy said, "Maw Reip's plannen on buyen a cow. I wisht me and Lock had us a cow. Maybe the milk would help him keep on his weight. He says I don't feed him enough, but I know that ain't it."

"He'll fatten up when spring comes. Don't you worry." She caught her shawl over her head and stepped toward the door. "Well, I guess I'll mosey along. I got some cookies I made. I want to take 'em over to Mrs Butcher. Lord, there's a family that could use a little more money. Seven kids, and he don't make more than twenty-two-three dollars. They can't hardly make ends meet."

"I was fixen to bake 'em some beans this evenin," Daisy revealed. "Pore Mis' Butcher allus seems so tired."

"That'd be neighborly," Mrs Stump answered. "Care for another chocolate before I go?"

"No, thank ye," Daisy said, indicating the table. "I still got this one."

That evening, when Lock had returned home shortly after the last light had faded over the snow-crusted river, he found their shack filled with the rich, pungent odor of baking beans.

"Sure smells good," he said, stomping the snow from his feet. "And I'm hungry as a bear."

Daisy took his heavy jacket, slipping it onto the peg behind the door, and placed his lunch pail on the box beside the wash pan.

"They ain't for you," she smiled. "I'm fixen 'em for the Butchers."

"Then you'd best keep 'em out of my sight," he warned. "On a cold day like this a man's insides is just yellen for beans baked in a pot."

Daisy reached up and kissed him on the cheek. "Wash yoreself," she whispered. "Supper's all done and waiten in the oven."

"Hey," Lock called, whirling about, "if yore goin to kiss a feller, kiss him proper!" Catching her in his arms, he pressed his lips squarely against her mouth.

With a little squeal Daisy drew away. "Goodness," she cried, screwing up her face, "you got that dust all over yore mouth!"

"It won't kill you," Lock laughed. "Leastways that's what the foreman said." Crossing to the wash box, he plunged his hands into the pan of water Daisy had prepared for him.

"I got a surprise," she said, lifting supper from the oven. "I got it at the post office today."

"Hear from yore folks?"

"No. Somethin else."

"What?"

"Guess?"

With a loud sputtering noise Lock doused the water over his face. He did not answer at once but worked his fingers into his ears, scrubbing the dirt from about his nostrils and eyes.

"The catylogue!" Daisy exclaimed as he halted to wipe his face. "The catylogue come today. And guess what."

"You're full of guesses," Lock grinned. "What?"

"They sent a letter. That company's got a store to Charleston. Right there in Charleston they got a store where you can see everythin that's in the catylogue!"

"Stoves too?" Lock asked.

"Stoves and everythin."

"Gosh, that's going to be real handy. You can pick out the one you want afore you get it."

After the supper dishes had been cleared away and the catalogue spread beneath the lamp Daisy and Lock bent over it, closely examining the pages.

"Here's the one I was thinken on," she said excitedly, "this here one with the warmen oven and the place for hot water. See this, right here. Well, that's a sort of box thing you put water in. It's right there by the fire, and that way a person's allus got hot water."

"It sounds dandy," Lock said. "Just what we was looken for." He drew back, wiping his hand across his eyes. "How much is it?"

"Fifty-nine dollars and fifty cents," Daisy said, looking up. "Lock, what's the matter? Does your eyes hurt?"

"It ain't nothin. That print's so fine."

"Lock, get your hands away and let me see."

Rubbing each eye with a finger, he blinked them for a moment and turned toward Daisy.

"They're awful red," she said thoughtfully, soberly. "Red round the edges."

"I got a cold in 'em maybe," Lock suggested. "It'll be gone tomorrey."

"I'll fix some warm salt water," Daisy said, springing up. "Maw allus said there was nothin so good for red eyes as weak salt water." She had crossed to the stove and was pouring water from the teakettle into a pan before she fully realized the dread which had gradually clouded her mind. "Lock," she said quietly, "Lock, is it that dust that makes yore eyes burn?"

"I don't know."

"Them other fellers—does their eyes burn?"

"Yeh, honey. Some of 'em, I reckon. Long Legg, a nigger named Pugh and two-three others named it."

Daisy got the salt box and put a teaspoonful in a glass. "That dust," she said softly, "it worries me near to death, Lock. It gets in everythin. You don't reckon it'd set a person blind, do you?"

"Good clean dirt never hurt nobody." He chuckled dryly. "Come read to me bout that stove, honey, whilst the water is heaten."

O n a Saturday morning early in February Lessie Lee hurried about the tables, setting them for noon dinner although it was not yet eleven o'clock. Her hair had been marcelled, and since it had not dried it gave her head, above her round face, the appearance of a half-peeled onion. As soon as she finished placing the knives and forks and spoons, the sugar, salt and pepper and catsup on the dark tables she fled back of the counter and snatched her patent-leather purse from behind the pie case. Digging into its tangle of cosmetics and paraphernalia, she found a chalky white pencil and set to restoring the white tips of her crimson fingernails. For a moment she examined them, wondering how a bottle labeled Rose Bronze could produce such a vivid shade of red.

"Lessie!" Mr Johns stuck his head through the partially opened kitchen door, his hands white and pink from the dishpan. "Lessie, you got them tables all set?"

"Landsakes, yes," she retorted nervously. "There ain't nothin' to worry about now."

"The sugar bowls filled?"

Lessie's breath came out in a long sigh of impatience. Abandoning her fingernails, she glared at the thin man caught in the swinging door. "I can take care of this place without batten an eye," she declared excitedly. "You dish it out and I'll give it to 'em."

"I don't want to lose no trade," the man said hesitantly. "I don't want 'em goin' downstreet cause they can't get waited on."

"They won't none of 'em leave," Lessie replied firmly. "Most of 'em is glad enough to set in here out of the cold, and the rest of 'em will have their grub before they hit the chair!"

Mr Johns did not retreat but stood looking at Lessie as if he suddenly expected her to break open with excitement. For three days she had been chattering and giggling and whispering with

Anna, their voices hushed and their eyes filled with some exhilaration he could not ponder.

The day before he had asked Lessie, hardly turning from the kitchen stove. "What's got into you girls?" he ventured casually. "You're whisperin' all the time."

"Nothin'," Lessie denied elaborately. "Nothin' in the blessed world."

He had wanted to pursue the subject, hungry to share their enormous secret. Outside of the daily trips he made to the grocery store he rarely spoke to an outsider, being morbidly reticent. On the two days before Lessie arrived to replace the girl who had quit Mr Johns had seriously considered closing the restaurant. Timidly he had gone out to take orders, fleeing back to the kitchen with them like a child seeking sanctuary. More than once a filled order sat on the kitchen table several minutes before he mustered enough courage to quit fussing about the stove and hurry it into the dining room. In the lumber camp he had cooked pots of food, dumping it out with a certain defiance. But one word spoken over the counter by a dissatisfied customer caused him to blunder speechlessly, the flesh crawling at the back of his neck. Lessie's arrival had been like a great release, and he looked with comfort at the kitchen walls, glad that they fenced him off from the embarrassed terror of the dining room. But when Anna had come to work, strong and firm and efficient, he had gloried in it, furtively watching her through a hole in the wall, enthusiastically smacking his fist against his hand when he saw her quiet an obstinate customer.

Sometimes when they were alone he stuck his head through the door, calling some unnecessary instruction, for it gave him a strange feeling of protected adventure. In the evenings, after he had taken off his apron and jerked into his coat, he would pause in the dining room to talk, but even then the unexpected approach of a customer filled him with uneasiness and he would slip quietly back into the kitchen.

Now, standing in the partially opened door, he eyed Lessie narrowly, trying to search her excitement under the pretense of his own anxiety. "You sure you're goin' to be al'right?" he began. "Lots of back-country folks come in on Saturdays."

"Honest to God!" Lessie exclaimed. "You'd think I never worked in a restaurant before!"

"Well, I just wanted to make sure. You seemed sort of anxious bout somethin'." He made it sound like a question.

"Just don't you worry none," Lessie said. "When they start comen I'll be ready for 'em."

The door closed slightly, and then his thin head came through again. "Saturday's a funny day for Annie to take off," he insinuated. "What she want Saturday off for?"

Lessie considered for a moment, searching for the best answer. "My Lord," she exclaimed presently, her outrage thin and feigned, "you work that poor girl to death! She makes out your menus and keeps the 'counts and waits on tables—she even fixed them new curtains for your winders! It's a wonder to me she don't take every Saturday off. You just come out here someday when it's dinnertime and listen to everybody yellin' cause the meat's cold and the taters are raw——"

"I just asked, that's all," he interrupted, allowing the door to fold shut behind him.

Fleeing to the front window, Lessie looked up the hill toward Mrs Kinner's boardinghouse, searching the white street for Anna and Pete. Part way up the hill, where a cross street met the sharp incline, she saw them, tall and hurrying, as they came down the center of the road where a path had been made. With a shrill little scream Lessie withdrew her face from the cold window and, yanking bobby pins from her hair, ran into the ladies' room, her fingers struggling frantically to release her hair from its caked unloveliness.

"Lessie," Anna called as she and Pete stomped the snow from their shoes. "Lessie!"

Pete unbuttoned his gray overcoat and folded its collar down. His face, above his white shirt and striped tie, was flushed with the cold and his eyes were blue and quick.

"Oh, my goodness," Lessie exclaimed, banging out of the ladies' room. "Oh, Annie, you look so purty! Take off your coat and let me see!"

Smiling, Anna slipped out of her new coat and carefully laid it over the back of a chair. In the center of the empty restaurant she pivoted about, her arms extended, while Lessie exclaimed over her new clothes. About the neck of the coffee-colored crepe dress heavy brown velvet flowers had been appliquéd, soft against Anna's neck. The cuff of each sleeve was a thick velvet band, and where the pleated skirt drew in at the waist a broad belt circled her body.

"Oh, Annie, it's beautiful!" Lessie cried. "It's the purtiest dress I ever laid eyes on." Whirling, she faced Pete. "Lordie, ain't she like someone in a moven picture?"

Pete nodded his head, a broad smile spreading over his face. "Better," he chuckled. "In the movies they got 'em skinny."

Lessie did not pause to listen. "Oh, Annie," she hurried on anxiously, "you scared?"

Anna shook her head, smiling at Pete.

"Brown's your color, honey," Lessie declared. "Brown and them nice gold earrings!"

"My grandmother sent them," Anna said. "She's always had them. From the old country. My mother wore them too."

"They're just lovely with that crepe dress!" Exhausted and breathless, Lessie dropped down on a stool by the counter. "Married in brown, you'll live in town."

"Sssh!" Anna cautioned, stepping to Pete's side. "Show Lessie your new suit," she urged. "Take your coat off."

"No," he said halfheartedly. "A suit ain't nothin'."

"Oh, come on, Pete," Lessie insisted, pushing his coat back over his shoulders. As she removed it she stood back, his coat over her arm, and looked at the couple standing before the rows of empty tables; Pete tall and lean and blond in his serge suit, and Anna, her hair caught up beneath her trim chocolate-brown felt hat, flushed and glowing where the cold had swept her cheeks. They stared at one another, grinning, as though their eyes had found a new delight.

"Stand together," Lessie urged pleadingly. "Right there—side by side."

"Aw," Pete said, gesturing with his hand. "One time today, that's enough."

Smiling indulgently, he moved to Anna's side, looking over the point of his shoulder to her. Anna caught his arm, pressing her cheek against him, and they both turned, like a pair facing an altar, and looked over Lessie's head at the pie case.

Lessie gaped at the tall, angular, handsome pair and a bent finger went up to wipe the moisture from her eyes. "Lordie, you make a beautiful couple," she blurted. "Just like somethin in a picture."

A soft squeak sounded at the back of the room, and they turned to see the kitchen door close, swinging softly.

"Hey!" Pete cried, jumping forward, "you drops my new coat!" He snatched the overcoat up from the floor, playfully slapping the dirt from its snow-dampened surface.

"I can't help it," Lessie sobbed quietly. "Everythin's so nice."

"You think Mr Johns knows?" Anna asked, slipping back into her coat. "He say anything?"

Lessie shook her marcelled hair violently. "I ain't let out a peep," she professed. "I never even told Mark. Ain't nobody goin' to know— just like you said."

"Us go," Pete said. "We git to Charleston too late, the place be closed up. We go, huh?"

Lessie slipped down from the stool by the counter and caught Anna in her arms. "I wish I could go too, honey," she said, half crying. "It's goin' to be such a purty weddin'."

Anna returned the embrace, holding Lessie erect. "We'll come back tomorrow," she said warmly. "We'll come back and tell you all about it."

"I wisht you was haven a picture took of it," Lessie said weakly. "I wish that."

Pete patted her on the shoulder, gently tugging Anna away. "We go now," he said a little thickly.

As they started the front door opened, sending a gust of cold air through the room, and a man, bent a little with the chill he had felt, stepped inside. His face was thin and red, and short bristles showed about his jaws where he had recently shaved. He stood by the door, pulling off his heavy cotton gloves and unbuttoning his overall jacket.

Anna watched him, vaguely aware that she had seen him before. Slowly, as she caught the imitation fur collar about her throat, she remembered him, confused only by the fact that he had shaved since the morning, a week before, when he had first come into the restaurant, faltering and timorous as he asked her to write a letter for him.

Since before Christmas the men who could not write had come into the restaurant, buying a sandwich or a piece of pie and apologetically asking Anna to write their letters. Sometimes, when she saw them waiting outside until the place was empty, she took them directly to a table in the rear corner and got out the nickel tablet and pencil. The men brought a stamped envelope and often a money-order blank for her to fill out. She did it carefully and slowly, telling them what their wives might like to know.

Pete had brought the first, a chucker on the same shift he worked, and after that others came, bringing a tablet the first time and a fresh, sharpened pencil. They left it behind, as a security, and Anna put their names on them and placed the tablets on the shelf together. By the end of the first month there were ten; ten letters to write, ten answers to read.

"Good mornin', m'am," the man said, taking a step forward.

"Good morning, Sam," Anna replied uncertainly.

"I got some money to send the missus," he continued stiffly, pulling a small fold of bills from his pocket. "I thought maybe you'd be so nice——" There he halted, aware that the three were silently watching him. He looked from Anna to Pete, seeing their new clothes, their freshly dressed appearance. "I never thunk," he said, backing away. "I never seen you was makin ready to go."

Anna looked at Pete quickly, questioningly. A week before she had written Mrs Sam Givens in Hawkins, Georgia; written her that the following week there would be more money. She knew, with four children, the little Sam could send from a mucker's pay could not be stretched through a full week.

Pete caught her glance, held it for a moment, stepped back and settled down on a stool, nodding his head. "We got the time," he said. "I talk to Lessie."

"Come on, Mr Givens," Anna called. "We'll write it fast."

"I don't want to hold you back," the man said. "I don't want to keep you."

"Come on." Anna headed for the table at the rear. "Your wife will be looking for it."

"Yes, that's the way I figured," the man replied, hurrying along after her. "Soon's I got my pay I come down. If it catches the evenin train, it'll get out today. The other way it'll lay over here till Monday."

Getting the coarse writing pad, Anna seated herself across the table from the man and quickly wrote "Dear Lily and children" on the first line.

"Anything special?" she asked, raising her head.

"I am senden you all eleven dollars," he said slowly and methodically, his eyes on Anna's pencil. "That's what I can do out of this week's pay. Last time I had to pay the doctor and the hospital and the electric for the shack where I live with a bunch of other fellers, and the boarden and my rent, but this time I can send you more. I can send you this eleven dollars. Work is steady, but they is a lot of fellers still comen in here. Maybe they's enough in this for them shoes for Myrtle. If they is, get 'em, and tell her her paw wants her to go back to school. If we get enough ahead to get her some dress goods, she oughter go. Tell her her writen is fallen off for a girl that's been clear to number eight. Tell her that."

Anna waited for him to go on, and when he did not she asked, "What else?"

"I reckon that's all, thank you." Uncertainly he looked toward Pete, who leaned against the counter talking with Lessie, his hat held loosely in his hand.

"What about you?" Anna asked. "She'll want to hear about you."

"There ain't nothin. I'm maken out al'right."

"Tell her some. She'll be worried," Anna urged, bending over her tablet again.

"I'm well off as could be expected," Sam Givens continued. "The cold is a sight fierce. You never see nothin like this in Georgia. Tell the young'uns the snow comes atop of your shoes of a mornin. I got a little cough, but I reckon it ain't a cold cause I don't cough up nothin. It's just a kind of ticklen in my lungs. Other fellers in the tunnel has got it, so I reckon it ain't nothin but just somethin you pick up in the tunnel. More'n likely it'll go away when good weather gets here agin. Is that misery in yore leg troublen you? I guess this will be all for this time. Write when you get a chanct and tell the young'uns snow's like cotton on the ground. Tell Myrtle to go back to school. If she gets some shoes and a dress, they ain't no reason they'll laugh at her no more. I'll send what I can next week."

"That all?" Anna asked.

"Thank you, yes."

"She'll like a letter tellin' bout you," Anna said, signing his name to it. "Where's your money-order blank?"

Sam laid it down on the table with the eleven dollars, and Anna quickly filled it in and addressed the envelope.

"Make the postmaster show you which end of the green slip to tear off," she cautioned. "Be sure you get the right one in the envelope when he makes it out."

"Yes, m'am, I will. Thank you, m'am." He got quickly to his feet, buttoned the collar to his overall jacket and started for the door. As he passed Pete he nodded his head a little, a brief salute for any hindrance he might have been.

"Annie," Lessie cried happily when Givens had closed the door, "Annie, Pete's goin' to get you flowers. Roses! Yaller roses in the winter!"

"Aw," Pete said crossly, "you don't tell that! You don't supposed to!"

Lessie's hand flew up and caught her lip. "Oh," she wailed pathetically, "I didn't know. You never said. I didn't——"

"We'd better go!" Anna interposed quickly. "It's late."

"Well—well," Lessie cried, running helplessly along behind them, "well—have a good time—I mean——"

Anna turned and smiled at her. "Do I look al'right?"

"You look wonderful. I wish everybody could know."

The kitchen door swung on its shrill hinge, and Mr Johns stuck his head through the opening. "If you don't want to come back tomorrey, it's al'right," he called. "Sundays is kind of dead."

"Sure, sure!" Lessie urged happily.

Anna and Pete paused in the doorway. "Thank you," she said. "Maybe we'll stay and go to a show tomorrow afternoon."

"There's that one with the clouds an' stars on the ceiling, like I told you," Lessie cried. "You go there. It's wonderful!"

"Me and Lessie can handle things till you get back," the man went on, directing his words at Pete. "You just have a good time and come back when you're ready."

"T'ank you, t'ank very much," Pete said, and they both went out the door, pressed together to avoid the snow and wind.

Mr Johns hurried forward and stood in the window beside Lessie, his apron looped behind a hand caught in his pocket. Silently they watched Anna and Pete go across the gas-station driveway, onto the sidewalk and around the corner of the Ford agency.

Uncontrollably Lessie began to whimper. Mr Johns looked at her and then back out the window, his eyes twitching and jerking.

"Gee," Lessie cried, "gee, don't they make a purty couple?"

"Uh-huh," he managed hoarsely.

"I wisht I could go with 'em," Lessie sobbed. "I never knowed anyone that was nicer——"

"They'll be comin' back," he said, his voice stiff and controlled. "What're you bawlin' for?"

"Because," Lessie wept, "just—because——" Throwing her hands over her tear-streaked face, she fled into the ladies' room.

Mr Johns looked after her sorrowfully and then went back into the kitchen, softly closing the door on the empty room.

15

During the winter's bitter, confining days Maw Reip moved aimlessly about the two-room shack, her arms and hands aching with their emptiness. In all her years in the heavy, squat cabin against the hill above Slaty Creek she never had known idleness, and now the undemanding hours drove her through the bare rooms of the coal-company shack with a relentlessness she could neither halt nor diminish. She went from one room to the other, cleaning, scraping, trying in every way she could to lessen the dread she had felt since the day they arrived in the valley with the children and furniture loaded in the clattering truck behind them. Never able to touch the thing she feared or even name it, Maw knew it as surely as she knew the cold which seeped through the cracks of the floor or the dust that lay in the bottoms of the tubs when she had hung Tom's and Ely's and Mark's overalls back of the stove to dry.

Ahead she sensed some violent, devastating time that would leave them at the mercy of things over which she had no control. More than once a cold, pounding fear had shot her bolt upright in bed, her arms already fumbling for her children in the darkness of the flimsy shack.

"Oh, Lord God," she would mutter, settling quietly down again. "Oh, Lord God."

Then, as she lay awake, listening to the five who filled the shack with their heavy breathing, her mind would bring up an old familiar memory which always associated itself with the fear and apprehension she felt.

Once, following the summer Ely was born, a wild, torturing storm had swept across the knoll, whistling about the walls of the cabin and rolling washtubs, like frightened animals, across the yard before it. Rain followed, wind-driven and fierce, and then, toward morning, it slackened and the day broke clear and yellow.

Beyond the woodpile, where Maw had boiled her soap and apple butter and wash, Tom had planted a young sycamore tree, saying that someday the children would play in its shade, saying they could sit beneath it during the long hours when the apple butter had to be stiffed.

The storm had passed and faint lemon-colored light was glistening wetly in the valley below by the time they went into the yard the following morning. Tom was in the barn and Maw, gathering up the dented tubs and buckets, rounded the woodpile and saw the young sycamore spread on the hard-packed earth, its roots bare and raw beneath the bone-white trunk.

Tom planted it again, but the sycamore never grew. Sometimes during the busy years which followed Maw remembered the tree, forever thinking how tall it would have grown, and then one night, soon after Virgil and Viney May had started to school in Venetta, she awoke with the horrible fear that the shack was being blown apart. After she had quieted down, staring into the darkness from her pillow, the image of the tree appeared, luminous and alive above her bed. From that time on the memory of its white mud-splattered branches came often, forming a pattern in her mind which she seemed to seek as she might some threatening danger that crept about those who slept.

Each time Maw could feel the sweat begin to drip from her armpits and she would listen sharply, as if she had already heard a noise in the dark house.

And so, as February came, freezing the river to the bottom and cracking it loose from its banks, Maw Reip felt her restlessness grow with each confining day. While the earth was covered and empty of giving, while her family had gone to school or to the tunnel, she wandered through the shack, counting and recounting the filled jars beneath the bed, trying to find in their number some additional assurance, some barrier against the dread she felt.

She would stand by the window, looking down the path, as if Tom or Ely or Mark might unexpectedly return from work. Unable to rest, she would go to the rag box back of Virgil's cot and fill her lap with scraps of cloth. Seated by the window, she would piece together the remnants, shaping them into the patchwork cover for a quilt. But her eyes turned again and again toward the path, and if she saw a dark figure coming up over the snow, her stiff, heavily knuckled fingers paused and she waited until she saw that it was not Tom and not Mark and not Ely.

Near the end of the month Maw sewed the last patched squares together and, spreading it over the bed, saw that it was large enough to form the upper side of a quilt. On Saturday, after Ely and Mark had handed over their seven dollars apiece and gone to Gauley Bridge to see the movie, taking Virgil with them, Maw broached the subject to Tom.

"I pieced out that coverlid," she said, carrying the supper dishes to the wash box. "You reckon they's enough extrey this week to get the cotton batten and the thread? I thought it'd be nice for the boys' bed. They only got two, and that old coat of yore maw's."

At the mention of his family's need all the expansive facetiousness of payday vanished from Tom's voice. "Sure, Nettie," he said. "You ought to get the fixens right off. Don't seem like this cold is plannen to let up."

"The rent comes out next week," Maw continued, "and it'll be coal from the next. Seems this is the likeliest time."

"You ought to get it then. The boys is worken hard. They got to get rest when they're abed."

"Virgil's needen shoes too, somethin fierce," Maw went on. "They'll have to be comen out soon."

"Maybe pay after next," Tom offered. "If this storm spells off, maybe we won't need so much coal." He paused thoughtfully and went on. "Nettie, how much is them wool comforts down there at the Bridge? If the boys is cold, they ought to get more covers."

"Law," Maw exclaimed, raising her hands above the soapy dishwater. "Law, them things are all out of reason. Six–seven dollars they're asken, and a body can see their hands right through 'em."

A low, sighing whistle escaped Tom's lips. "Maybe you could do better in Charleston," he offered. "Hank Stump told me him and his woman is goin down one day soon."

"Things are dear down there, from all I hear," Maw replied quietly. "Daisy Mullens told me she heard that preacher's wife from the Bridge bought a hat down there and paid eight dollars for it! Never had nothin on it but some black turkey feathers, neither!"

Tom chuckled to himself, his fingers shoving the crumbs into a little pile on the oilcloth-covered table. "I seen her the other day, driven past Number One openin. Looked like she smelt somethin turrible. Maybe she did too!"

Maw paused, snapping the suds from her hands, and gathered up a drycloth. "Tom," she asked, "is they any smell to that dust that comes outter the tunnel?"

"Not more'n common. A feller smells them gas engines, but he don't smell that dust, no more'n if it was sand."

Crossing back of him, Maw placed the six plates on the shelf above Tom's head. Playfully he watched her, jabbing his thumb into her ribs as she stretched upward.

"Stop that!" Maw demanded, slapping him over the head with the damp sugar sack she used for a towel. "Another inch and I'd a-broke them."

Tom ducked, and as she returned to the wash box he sat listening for some sound from the other room. "Where's Viney?" he asked presently.

"Gone acrost to play with the Butchers' young'uns, I reckon."

Biting his lip thoughtfully, Tom dug his hand into an overall pocket and drew out forty cents. Ploddingly he considered the money and, getting up, opened the door.

"Hey, Viney!" he bellowed down the road which led between the shacks. "Viney May!"

"Tom, close the door!" Maw demanded shrilly. "Landsakes!"

Across the road a streak of light showed through the partially opened door, and Viney's small dark head came through the crack.

"Come on home! We're a-goin to town. Heel it, now!"

"Oh, Tom, hesh up," Maw rebuked. "She'll be heartsick with yore foolen."

"Get on that purple dress with them white flowers! We're goin right into that drugstore and have us a sody. It's Saturday night, and we're going down there same as the boys!"

With an exasperated sigh Maw laid down her dishcloth and turned toward her husband. "We ain't got the money to spend," she pointed out bluntly. "And now you done called Viney. Tom, honest to the Lord——"

"Don't you worry yore head bout the money," Tom answered boisterously. "I'm treaten this time."

Maw eyed him sharply, her mind running back over the past weeks in rapid, close remembrance. "Where'd you get it?" she asked, puzzled. Then her drawn, thoughtful forehead relaxed. "Tom, you never got yoreself them gloves," she charged. "Yore a-worken bare-handed."

Viney slammed through the door in a gust of wind, whirled about and pushed it shut with her back. "Candy?" she asked breathlessly. "Can I get some candy?"

"You wipe yore nose," Maw instructed, going back to the sink. "I got these dishes to finish afore we set a foot out of this house."

Catching her about the waist, Tom lifted Maw from the floor and set her down facing the bedroom. "Now waltz yoreself in there and get yore purties on," he demanded. "Ain't no use goin down there after the streets is empty!"

Viney gave a shrill, hurried shriek and shot through the bedroom door before her mother.

"I'll do no sech thing," Maw declared flatly. "I ain't leavin this house till it's tidied up. There may be some——"

"Now you leave Sarey Stump be," Tom laughed, swinging his hand at the back of her dress. "Maybe she don't allus leave her house spick and span, but she's a good woman to her man." A little startled at the sound of what he had said but not realizing exactly what had occurred, Tom halted and considered it thoughtfully.

"Well," Maw conceded, brushing loose strands of hair back from her face, "well, al'right. It'll give me a chanct to get the cotton and thread." Quietly, almost demurely, she strode into the bedroom after the dress she had not worn since trying it on Christmas Day.

Half an hour later, when they had walked the frozen river and climbed up to the tire-rutted highway, a deep feeling of gladness and relief passed through Maw's bony frame. After the useless, confining days that tortured her provident soul she thought happily of peering into one brightly lighted store window after another. They could, she decided, even go in and price shoes for Virgil. He would be needing them soon, which was almost the same as buying them, and it would give her a chance to glance at the yard materials. Someday, before spring came and when they had saved a little more, she wanted to make Viney a dress and maybe an everyday one for herself.

On that same Saturday, as soon as he had drawn his pay, Ralph Owens, who had once averaged forty-five dollars a week selling insurance in Elmira, N.Y, cut up the path toward the highway and headed for the green-shingled post office at the upper end of Gauley Bridge. He walked a little stiffly, for his right hand, clenched inside his pocket, held all that remained of his week's pay after his board and room, hospital and doctor's fee, light charges and bed washing had been subtracted.

It was late and Owens hurried down the highway, walking rapidly through the slushy trenches traffic had worn into the heavy snow, finding his way over the company spur line, along past the Jungle, through Old Gauley and over the windy steel bridge.

On other days Owens passed men on the road, looking after them with a hungry, anxious loneliness, forever trying to break through the fear and helplessness that set him apart. But on Saturdays, which was payday, he spoke to those who worked beside him at the tunnel, and they answered him strangely, knowing that on Monday he would again be silent, a scrawny man who worked with frantic, killing desperation as a mucker in Number Two.

Leaving the bridge, Owens went through the underpass, darted across in front of a slush-splattered Ford and climbed the post-office stairs in quick, chopping steps.

"I'd like a money order, please," he said, shoving forward the slip he had prepared the night before.

A plump, pleasant woman who had relieved her husband so he might get a haircut began to fumble with the pens and order pads.

"I'm—I'm sort of in a hurry," Owens prompted timorously. "It's— I'd like to put it on the seven o'clock. You see, if it don't get to Charleston tonight, my wife won't get it Monday morning. She would be worried, and I don't want to do that." He stopped abruptly, seeing that the woman had paused to listen to him.

"There's thirty minutes yet," she explained. "We don't close the mails until ten of." Patiently, with a rolling movement of her plump hand, she wrote in the name and the amount. Owens watched, his body jerking in an involuntary effort to assist her.

With a soft, breathy sigh the large woman laid the pen down and blotted the long blue-green slip. "That'll be sixteen dollars—and—and——" She paused, examining a chart.

"Sixteen dollars and thirteen cents," Owens supplied promptly, shoving the money forward. "There's seventeen."

The woman went on peering at the posted rates, her head thrown back a little as if to improve her sight. "That's right!" she exclaimed presently. "Right to the penny!"

Going to the slat-top table which hung from the wall near the window, Owens laid the money order down and drew a letter from his inside pocket. His body relaxed a little and, drawing the folded pages from the envelope, he slowly reread the letter which he had written in parts since the previous Tuesday. He could almost recite it from memory, but his eyes ran down the lines, somehow erasing the loneliness, the fear and unending worry which filled his days.

"Dear Mabel," he read, "I suppose your letter will come tomorrow telling me you received the money. Usually I don't start my letters until Wednesday, after I get yours, but there isn't much to do around here tonight." Clearly recalling the following paragraph, Owens skipped to an indentation near the bottom of the first page. "Work is about the same. A man was killed in Number Three yesterday. Some rock fell on him, up near the heading. I guess the company is insured to cover such cases. Remember just before I came down here I showed you where they had taken out a $250,000 policy to cover accidents. From what I hear his people live in Virginia. The men all called him Norfolk. They have a way of doing that around the tunnel. They call me Cherry Valley. When they ask where Elmira is I always tell them at the upper end of Cherry Valley. One man, a Mr Legg—they call him Long—always says it must be quiet at the upper end of Cherry Valley. He says that because I sort of stay to myself and don't talk on the job. He's a very nice fellow though. I feel about the same, and I get the medicine regular, like you said." Again he skipped, avoiding a paragraph which recounted his physical condition.

"If you can, get Bonnie some overshoes out of this check. Montgomery Ward's ought to have some cheap, and I'd suggest that you pay the A & P man eight dollars. When he gives credit it comes out of his own pocket, and I'd hate for him to get in trouble with his company. Tell Dr Jones we'll pay him something as soon as we can. He's been good about waiting. Is his mother getting through the winter all right?

"Maybe, if things get better, we can get a rug to cover the bedroom floor before another winter comes. The linoleum must be cold on their feet. Tell Bonnie and Sarah if I was there I'd carry them to bed ever night and back down to the kitchen in the morning. I hope we can get some coal soon and heat the house all over. Living in the kitchen all the time like that must be hard on you, Mabel. Sometimes, when I think about those things, I think I'm not much of a husband." Again he stopped reading and turned to the seventh and last page.

"Don't you all worry about me," he read, a strange sense of unreal belief shimmering over the page. "Everything is fine with me, except that I miss you so much. I wish I was home. We'd all go to the movies if we could. Kiss Bonnie and Sarah for me and write a lot. I wish I could see them in their bed. I'll paint it again for them when I get home. Write me, Mabel, because I like hearing from you so much. It seems so long between Saturdays and Wednesdays."
Tearing the receipt stub from the money order, Ralph Owens carefully folded the long part and slipped it between the creased pages of the letter, patting it a little with his fingers so no blue-green edge would show. Then he licked the flap and sealed the envelope by pounding it gently with the heel of his hand. For a long moment he looked at the letter, holding it up with a feeling of pride and low, surging strength.

Everything he lived with during the entire week—the fear and loneliness and the cough—dropped away from him, and he stood there thinking that he had come through another week without getting the company down on him, that his boss did not think he was an agitator or troublemaker and that once again, during this bad winter, he had been able to send his wife and children nearly every cent he earned.

As had been his custom since his first payday, Ralph Owens left the long shed of the company boardinghouse soon after supper. and headed for Main Street, hoping he would find someone to talk with, someone, alone, who had left a wife and children behind them.

Beyond the bus station and the Ford garage, where the stairs led up to the dentist's office and beauty shop, a group of men stood in the doorway, idly watching those who walked from the underpass down to the brightly lighted Bijou Theater and back again. Nearing them, Owens slowed his steps, hoping someone would speak his name so he might stop and fall into easy, friendly conversation.

But as he passed the show window of the Ford garage a loud burst of laughter broke from the dark hallway, and almost before he knew it Owens had passed beyond and into the partially lighted section where the doctor's home and office sat against the sidewalk.

He slackened his pace and looked back, afraid to return now but hesitant to move on. Beneath the glaring lights of the moviehouse marquee he came to a slow, studied halt and stiffly began to examine the tier of colored pictures which illustrated the Western being shown. Furtively he watched the girl behind the ticket window, wanting to speak to her; maybe asking about the Hoot Gibson picture, maybe asking what was to be shown the following Saturday. As he stepped forward a man appeared through a door inside the ticket office and Owens turned sharply away, heading up the street as though he had suddenly recalled a forgotten errand.

The drugstore on the opposite side of the street was crowded and water puddled near the door where snow-clodded shoes had been stomped. Finding a place in the center of the room, Owens slowly removed his gloves, keeping well away from the counters where two young clerks trotted from one customer to the next.

At the back of the store four youngsters sprawled about a white marble-topped table, the comic section of a Baltimore paper spread between them. The Reverend Mitchell stood near the end of the soda fountain holding a glass and sucking a red fluid through his nicely puckered lips. Owens watched him, bending his head as the cherry-colored soda receded down the glass. As it neared the bottom his ears strained for the sucking sound, and when it came he relaxed and his eyes continued along the counter.

Midway he paused, caught by three figures who bent silently, politely over the polished slab of marble.

On the stool between Maw and Tom Reip, Viney May held her chin rigidly forward, considerably shortening the distance between her mouth and the dish of chocolate-covered ice cream that held her fixed attention. As she raised each spoonful her eyes grew larger and her mouth went forward with a bobbing movement, half opened and reaching for the ice cream. On one side of her Maw sat, stiffly erect, her head facing toward the Eskimo Pie and Cherry Smash signs which decorated the wall. But between the bites she brought carefully, almost daintily to her mouth Maw's eyes looked about, examining all the colored wonders of the store. Now and again she raised a slow, polite hand and wiped the corners of her mouth with a knuckled finger.

"Don't eat yourn so fast, honey," she spoke softly to Viney. "It'll make yore head thump."

Viney gave her a swift upward glance and expertly met another bite halfway from the dish.

Moving toward the front door, Ralph Owens closely examined the side of Tom's face.

"How do you do, Mr Reip?" he said, stepping up and touching Tom's shoulder. "I don't think I ever saw you downtown before." Tom twisted about on the stool, wiping his face with the back of his hand. "Howdy there, sir," he said cordially. "No, we don't get down much. My missus had some buyen to do."

Maw's eyes passed from Tom to the stranger and back again, but she said nothing. Her coarse hand gently rattled the package of cotton batting in her lap.

"I see," Owens sped on, warmed by Tom's friendly greeting. "I've got a little girl about that size. Her name's Bonnie. She's the oldest."

"Viney, here, she's our least'un. Only girl we got." Tom slid down off his stool and gestured toward Maw with one hand. "I'd like to have you make acquaintance with my wife. Nettie, this is Mr Owens. He works on the job with me."

Owens looked at her, seeing the colorless lips, the pale face and the deep, quiet wisdom in her patient eyes. Something made him take a step forward, and across his shoulders and down his arms he felt a vague warmth, soft and reassuring. "How do you do, Mrs Reip?" he stammered.

Maw's knuckled finger touched each corner of her mouth, and her head nodded politely. "I'm glad to be meetin you, Mister Owens," she acknowledged.

"Yes, Bonnie's just about her age," Owens repeated, placing his hand on Viney's head. He spoke directly to Maw, saying the words as if he had not said them before. "My youngest, Sarah, is only four."

Viney gave him a quick, roving glance and went back to her sundae.

"Yore folks come from round here?" Maw inquired politely. Behind the thin, blanched face she sensed the man's loneliness and fear, and she could not take her eyes from him. There were no words for what she felt, no way she could find to convey it, and presently she went on. "I mean, round these parts?"

"No, m'am. We come from New York State. My wife comes from Syracuse, but I've always lived in Elmira. It's sort of—well, over to the western part of the state."

"I've heered of New York State," Tom interposed. "Must be purty big from all a-body heers about it."

"It's a good state," Owens replied, looking from Maw to Tom and back again. "I don't guess I'd live anywhere else if I could get work there now. I just had a letter from my wife last Wednesday. She says there's not a thing doing in Elmira. And, mind you, that's a town that had plenty of factories."

"I reckon you miss yore woman and young'uns," Maw said, her lips softly shaping the words.

"Yes. Yes, I do," Owens replied, nodding rapidly. "I miss them all the time."

"A man hadn't ought to be away from his own. He's a need for them, same as they need him."

Owens put one foot up against Viney's stool and then took it down. "I think about them all the time," he admitted.

Tom watched closely but made no sound.

"Mebby," Maw said, "mebby you'll get home to them someday soon."

"I hope so." Peering carefully about the room, he stepped a few inches nearer to Maw. "I don't like it here much. There's something about the place. I don't know. It's just something."

"I reckon I know what you mean," Maw said. "It ain't nothin you can touch exactly."

"No. It's just something——" Halting, searching through his mind for the thing he could not name, Owens was suddenly, awkwardly aware that Maw's ice cream was melting in the dish. "Well—well, I'd better be going," he said hastily. "You go right ahead and eat——" Unable to finish, he hurried toward the front door, not pausing until he had gone outside and closed it behind him. As he started to cross the street toward the Kanawha Cafe, where he had eaten a piece of pie every payday night since Lessie had fed him on the third day after his arrival in Gauley Bridge, he saw Maw, twisted about on her stool, watching him with soft, knowing eyes.

Maw did not speak again until Tom had paid for the ice cream and Viney had followed them reluctantly out to the slushy sidewalk.

"That feller," she asked, drawing her chin down to avoid the cold, "does he work in the dusty part, there at the tunnel?"

"Yeh. He's a mucker," Tom explained. "He helps clean out after the blasten!" He waited for Maw to continue, and when she did not he asked, "Why?"

"He don't seem very stout," she answered. "He hadn't oughter be doin heavy work, seems like. Looks more like a schoolmaster."

"He is, kind of," Tom continued. "I've heered him come out with some whoppen big words. He's kind of quare too. Allus stays to hisself."

I 'low," Maw said, "I 'low he do."

They were silent as they went beneath the dark underpass and found the tire tracks that led back toward Venetta.

After they had finished their noon meal on Sunday, Long Legg and Jim Martin went back to their room and slept for three hours. The day was dark and windy, with a gale blowing from the east. Once, as he lay looking out over the dark water, Long saw a thin snow begin to pepper the air, blowing fine against the sweat-covered pane, and then the wind carried the storm across the hump of Gauley Mountain, leaving the valley bleak and forlorn.

Again the wind increased, whistling about the eaves and throbbing the loose window against the sill. Slipping off the bed, Long found an old pair of socks on the closet floor and, using his fingers as a prod, stuffed them into the draughty cracks at the bottom of the window.

He did not go back to bed but paced restlessly about the room, puzzled by the shortness of breath which had forced him to rest twice while climbing the hill after the noon meal. Crossing to the rickety dresser, he stood patting his stomach and watching his reflection in the blotched glass.

"I ate too much," he reasoned quietly. "I stuffed myself like a damned hog."

But his mind would not accept the answer, and as he stepped away from the mirror the unnamed dread continued to rise like something he could almost feel inside his chest. Experimentally he sniffed, trying to loosen any possible inflammation in his nose, and as that brought no results he began to cough, spitting into his handkerchief and carefully examining the saliva. There was no discoloration, no inflammation.

Jim Martin rolled over on his pillow, exercising his lips and drawing an arm across his forehead.

Long ceased coughing, and Jim rolled back, buried his face in a fold of the pillow, stretched a leg and slept again.

Quietly Long slipped into his shoes and got his coat from across the back of a chair. Drawing it on before the mirror, he tilted forward, opening his mouth and extending his tongue. He examined it minutely, not really expecting to see anything, and closed his mouth.

"It's probably the fumes from them damned dinkey engines," he thought, going toward the door. "They ain't no business usin' gasoline engines. When it's damp and the air's heavy them fumes hang in that hole all day. It ain't no wonder a guy gets out of wind——"

Leaving the thought unfinished, he slipped out into the hall and went down the stairs, still walking as softly as he had tiptoed about the room.

Smoke had already begun to slant away from the chimney of the small, steepled church, announcing the evening service, when Long slowly made his way back from Jessie Bail's, bearing a bottle of gin and a sack of lemons.

He halted in the hall to catch his breath and, wheezing audibly, threw the door open and stepped into the room. Sleepily Jim Martin rolled over, running hooked fingers through his matted hair.

Long set the gin on the dresser and ripped the paper sack half open, allowing the lemons to roll out.

"Didn't you sleep?" Jim asked foggily, squinting at the dresser.

Long crossed to the clothes closet and began searching along the top shelf. "Goddamn her, she took them glasses again!" he swore, tossing a rolled shirt from the shelf onto the floor.

"Huh?" Jim grunted.

"Glasses. She took 'em again." Long got two bottles of ginger ale from the floor beneath the window and placed them on the dresser. "I wish to hell she'd stay out of here."

"I'll get a couple." Jim got up and went out, his untied shoelaces lapping about his feet.

Presently Long heard him come back up the stairs and enter the bathroom down the hall, his feet dropping heavily on the linoleum-covered floor. Then there was a knock on the door and Mrs Higgenbottom came in, holding out two heavy tumblers.

"Don't you give Frank none of that stuff," she charged, edging her huge body up to the dresser, one hand held behind her back. "If he comes up here botherin' you, just let me know."

"Why don't you leave them glasses up here?" Long asked, halving a lemon with his pocketknife.

"They belong in the kitchen!" she stated sharply. "And you keep that lemon off my good dresser scarf. You'll cut it. And another thing, if I catch you cleanin' razor blades on my towels again, I'll fire you out of here. They're slit into shreds now. If I've told you that one time, I've told you a hundred. You and Jim don't pay any more attention to me than if I was nothin' a-tall."

Long ignored her, added gin to the lemon juice and filled the glass with ginger ale.

"You two are as bad as them telephone men," she went on, watching him carefully. "I work day and night, tryin' to keep this place partway decent, and what thanks do I get for it?"

"Here," Long said, stiffing the drink with the handle of a toothbrush and passing it to her, "give me the other glass."

"W-h-y, thank you," Mrs Higgenbottom beamed, drawing her left hand from behind her broad hips. "Just a drop on Sunday afternoons," she managed, backing for the door, "but don't you give Frank none if he comes up here. Mark my word!"

"You give him part of yours," Long smiled, squeezing another lemon. "He's your husband."

"I could have done a sight better," she snorted sharply, closing the door. "Indeed I could!"

An hour later, as Jim and Long finished their third drink and the gray sky began to sift darkness into the valley, Long's mind returned to the thing which had worried him for the past several days.

"Say, Jim," he asked casually, "you notice yourself bein' short of wind lately?"

"Yeh. A little. Was I snoring?"

"Naw. I just wondered." Long tilted his glass, and his Adam's apple ran up and down for a little while after he had finished the drink.

"I guess I don't get enough fresh air," Jim went on. "I just go from here to the tunnel and back—from one black hole to another!" He grinned, slightly pleased, and rolled his glass between the palms of his hands.

"Christ," Long declared, "that's it! I ain't smelled any good fresh air in a month. On the job we swallow dust for air, and this place is closed up tighter'n a rattrap. If you open a window you freeze to death."

Jim inhaled noisily. "This air's so stale it stinks."

"Yep, fellow, that's it," Long decided flatly. "We need us some fresh air." A little unsteadily he took Jim's glass and mixed another round.

"Yep, we ought to get some," Jim agreed.

"Now, that's a thing—I mean, that's a funny thing," Long went on, his words growing thick and lumpy. "I allus been outdoors a lot, and here I ain't had no fresh air for a month. That's why my wind is gettin' so bad."

"Shure. Shure. We ought to get out and get some air." Jim stared at himself in the scarred mirror, moving his head about as if he were trying to get squarely in front of his reflection.

"By God!" Long swore, slapping his knee loudly. "I got it! Let's walk up the hill and see Owl. I ain't seen that old booger in a coon's age! Whatta you say—we'll climb that hill and get us some air!"

"Shure," Jim managed, getting to his feet unevenly. "I'll bet you Owl misses us. He'll be wantin' to see us."

"Yeh," Long added gravely. "We hadn't ought to leave him by hisself like that. That ain't no way to treat a guy."

"He always liked you too," Jim went on. "You were just about everything to Owl."

"Yeh," Long commiserated guiltily. "Yeh, I guess that's right. I been actin' like a heel."

Jim got up and found his coat. "Come on, Long. Let's go up and see Owl. He'll be wantin' to see us pretty bad."

"Yeh, he sure will," Long reaffirmed, picking up his coat and following Jim out the door. He had taken a few steps down the hall when he whirled about, ran back into the room and wrapped the rest of the gin in the sport section of the *Charleston Telegraph*.

"Owl's got to have a drink," he kept muttering to himself; "Owl—he ought to have a drink."

Before they reached Number One camp, which spread across the ridge between Cane Branch and Big Creek, Long and Jim slackened their steps. The road, winding steeply up the hill above the lower opening of the tunnel, followed the ravines and crevices, bending out of sight and reappearing again along the further knoll. The wind caught up the snow beside the road, whipping it into little pools that settled softly over the slush of the tire tracks.

"This is a hell of a climb," Jim gasped presently. "Must be better than three miles up here."

"Yeh," Long managed. "Yeh, it is."

They moved on, not speaking until they reached the path which cut sharply up the hill toward the rows of drab shacks that crowned the ridge. Far below, near the river's edge, they could see the opening of Number One, a dim black scar in the side of the mountain. Crushed stone had spilled along the track from the tunnel to the point where the dump cars were emptied into the gondolas, turning the ground a dull skeleton gray.

They rested, peering down the steep embankment, staring at the opening torn like a giant bullet wound in the base of the mountain.

No word was spoken, and above the hushed murmur of the river their quick-coming breath sounded harsh and rasping.

From the corner of his eye Long saw that Jim's face had grown pale, blanched and white in the cold. The imbedded cinders above his left eye seemed unbelievably black in the gathering twilight.

"Wanta go on up?" he asked, trying to conceal his own breathlessness.

"Sure," Jim said, completely sobered now. "But let's wait a minute first. Let's rest."

"Yeh. Surest thing, Jim."

Finally they topped the ridge and found the broad path leading down between the rough tar-paper-covered shacks. Now the air was pumped in and out through their mouths, coming in successive, labored gasps.

"I'm pooped," Jim declared, kicking the snow from the top of a stump and flopping down.

Long said nothing but paced the rim of a slow circle, rubbing his hands over the thumping pound at the side of his neck.

"How about startin' south soon as we get a little money ahead?" Jim asked after he had rested. "Maybe we can find something in Texas."

"Ever been to Texas?" The words came out separately, quickly, his breath decreasing as they came.

"Nope."

"It's a big old trap," Long said, pacing. "You get in it, and it takes forever to get out."

"Louisiana, maybe."

"Huey Long's got it all tied up in a bag. If you can't vote you can't get a job."

Jim became silent, bent forward to ease his breathing. "I can't stay here much longer. This damn weather is getting me down. My wind's gone; I cough all the time."

Long stopped before him, his feet braced in the soft snow. "It's the gas fumes," he said. "They ought to use electric engines in that tunnel. A man breathes that stuff all day."

"Yeh," Jim added disconsolately. "It's thick as that damn dust. I'll bet our lungs are like the insides of a sand blower!"

Thoughtfully Long looked down over the hill. "Soon's it gets warm we'll ast for outside jobs. They'll be starting the facing soon. We'll try to get on as carpenter's helpers."

"In a pig's behind!" Jim snorted. "Way they're workin' us now, won't nobody come off that job until we hole through. Lock Mullens told me that McCune, the rouster, shags the niggers outta these shacks ever mornin' before six to be sure they'll get on the job."

"Hell," Long replied, "that's just a lot of talk. Come on, let's find Owl."

Jim got up, knocking the snow from the seat of his pants. "Want to take a little bet on it? That Mullens guy is too simple to lie."

They headed down the sloppy road that wound through between the shacks which housed the married workers. Here and there a weak light pressed an unsteady beam through the cracks about the flimsy doors, streaking the snow. Washtubs hung from the outside walls, and ashes paved a dirty path out to the road. Wind, fingering its way beneath the tar-paper roofs, had torn some in great gashes, and now they flapped and rattled with the gale which swept over the knoll.

"Once," Long went on presently, "when I was pickin' taters up in Maine a feller used to roust us out at four in the morning. Boy, I'm tellin' you, my back would be so sore when I got up I'd want to tie it to a plank, just to hold it straight."

"The way Mullens told it," Jim persisted, "this shack rouster don't come 'round just to wake 'em up. They got to get on the job, sick or well."

"Hell, that's just windy talk. He can't make 'em go to work unless they want to."

"Two bucks says Mullens is right," Jim offered, following in Long's footsteps. "He ain't the kind that talks to hear his ears roar. Next to Cherry Valley, they ain't nobody on the job that talks less than Mullens. He's a real old hillbilly."

"Two bucks?" Long called over his shoulder.

"Two bucks it is. Pay next Saturday."

"What's the matter?" Long asked, stepping aside until Jim overtook him. "You busted already?"

"Just about. Christ, by the time I pay the doctor and the hospital and the flower fund and the rest of the stuff I'm flat as a hot cake."

"You made nearly twenty-two, didn't you?"

"Yeh."

Long waited, and they had gone several steps before Jim continued. "I sent my sister five bucks. They got two kids. He lost his job. Now he's tryin' to sell magazine subscriptions. They was put out on the street just before Christmas."

"I seen it like that in the newsreel last night," Long said quietly. "Stuff all piled right on the curb, and this old lady sittin' in a chair and waitin' for something to happen. It was out in Chicago, I think." He halted, throwing his arm over Jim's shoulder. "You know, goddamnit, there was one part I had to laugh at. This dinge was goin' to be throwed out of his place—and you know what happened? Boy, you ought to have seen it! Everybody that lived in the house got out on the front steps and tied their wrists together. Formed a regular chain right across the door. Damned dispossess server come, and they wouldn't let him in. Just stood there, handcuffed together, lookin' a hole right through them two movers that had come along to toss the dinge's furniture out. Boy, it was somethin'."

Bending forward, Long saw that Jim's face was drawn and still. "What the hell you so long-faced about?" he prodded jovially. "I got enough to see us through the week." He drew twelve dollar bills from his pocket and held them out above the snow. "Jesus, lookit that! Big enough to choke a horse!"

"I'm not thinkin' about that. It was something else."

"What?"

Jim's lips drew together with tight determination, and his voice came deep and resonant. "I'm stickin' to that sonuvabitchin' tunnel, don't matter what!" he declared. "I got a job, and I'm——"

"Sure," Long added firmly. "We got work and the whole country's starvin' to death. Livin' in Hooverville and eatin' outta their hands. What have we got to worry about?"

Again Jim was silent, but when he spoke the loud protest was gone from his voice. "Maybe the company will fix them air vents," he said. "Maybe they'll do somethin' about the air."

"Damn right," Long went on assuredly. "If they fixed them and we got wet drills in there, like they're supposed to have—why, good God, it'd be a picnic!"

Jim moved away from Long's arm and looked up at the windswept sky, driven and gray beneath the early ghost of a moon.

"Spring ought to be comin' soon," he said. "Then it won't be so bad. The air won't be so heavy, and the fumes won't hang in the shaft. Once it's warm and I throw this cough off, I'll get my wind back."

"Hell, yes," Long declared. "It ain't nothin' to worry about. We all got the same thing."

Inside the square rough-boarded shack the air was dense with smoke and heavy with the smell of sweat and humectation. The double-decked bunks filled each of the four corners, crowding the small room which was scarcely heated by the midget potbellied stove set a little to one side of the center. With the exception of upturned dynamite boxes, brought from the tunnel, there was no other furniture in the room. Overhead a single naked bulb dangled from a rafter, casting a faint light over the twenty-two men congregated in the room.

On Sunday night, when no one worked at the tunnel, the shacks which stretched along the ridge in a ragged line from the boardinghouse to the insubstantial shelters where the married men lived were always crowded. But with a crap game in session shack Number Five was filled to overflowing, and the blanket which had been stretched over the single window confined the drifting clouds of smoke to the humid, stench-filled room.

On the four upper bunks that, like the lower ones, had been built wide enough to accommodate two men lumpy piles of torn, nondescript bedclothes marked the men who were attempting to sleep. Beneath them, on the lower cribs, several men sat watching the dice that rolled back and forth inside the squatting, kneeling ring of players.

All voices were hushed. Even the tense, fervent players spoke in deep, throaty whispers. A tall black man propped himself against the door, his feet stomping a little against the cold that seeped in over the doorsill.

Owl Jones threw a second seven, raked the change into a little pile beside the patch in the knee of his overalls and ploddingly counted out twenty-five cents again.

"Twenty-five cents, gem'men," he said, his voice hushed. "Twenty-five cents or any part of it!"

"You t'rowed three passes in a row," Stringbean, a slender coffee-colored man sighed. "'At's the end of you. You goin' to crap shure!" With an elaborate gesture he deposited fifteen cents beside Owl's quarter just as another dime fell.

From the upper level of the bunk in the back corner came a low, agonizing groan. Everyone hesitated, listening sharply. As the figure had settled down again the game went on.

"George is wheezin' like a horse with the heaves," a man spoke from the opposite bunk. "Reckon we best call that doc agin."

"We done call him four-five times," Stringbean answered concernedly. "Ain't no way to make him come."

"Dat man's sick inside," the fellow went on. "He ain't goin' be able to work tomorrey lessen he gets some medicine. Why don't that doc come?"

"Why don't a pig whistle?" a gaunt, bony man threw in from his perch on the rim of an upper bunk.

"Ain't right," Owl said soberly, gravely. "He's sick; he oughter be took care of."

The room was silent but for the heavy sporadic breathing of the men who attempted to sleep.

"That doc ain't carryin' his satchel up here in no storm," Popeye, the gaunt one, continued, sliding down to the floor. "We done ever thing we knows." He stopped, his head cocked toward the sleeping man. "Lan', lan'," he said blankly. "Listen at that man wheeze. Sound like a old wore-out parlor organ."

A chunky gray-haired man who sat on one of the dynamite boxes near the stove got to his feet, snapping together the metal buttons of his overall jacket.

"I'll go ask him," he offered, going for the door. "Maybe effen he don't come he's goin' gib' me some bottle medicine."

"Ain't goin' do no good," Stringbean prophesied. "Hain't been half an hour since they went after him for Burnie Colts. Burnie is dyin', sure as Scripture. If he ain't comin' up to see Burnie he ain't comin' to see George."

"I'm goin' ahead just the same," the man said, scrambling over the tangle of legs toward the door. "Ain't my time to sleep 'fore four o'clock. I gots nothin' to do."

Just as the tall black man moved to open the door a loud knock sounded against the boards. Grabbing their money, the men sprang up from the floor, stuffing it into their pockets. Owl fingered his clumsily, digging at a dime which clung to the bare floor. When he had retrieved his money he hastily stuffed the dice inside his left sock, wrinkling it deceptively. Someone pinned a funny paper about the light bulb, splotching the room with soft multicolors as the men pressed back against the bunks. No word was spoken, no sound made.

The knock was repeated, louder and more insistent, and the black man opened the door, stepping back.

It took Owl several minutes to recognize the two figures silhouetted against the growing darkness, and no one else moved from the drowsy postures they had assumed.

"Owl Jones live here?" Long called into the shadowy room. "I'm lookin' for——"

"Mistah Legg," Owl called, making his way across the room. "How come you up here? Howdy, Mistah Jim?" His head came through the doorway, craning as though he hoped to better his vision. "Ain't in no trouble, is you, Mistah Legg?" he whispered hoarsely. "Ain't nothin' the matter?"

"Naw," Long said, pressing forward. "Just come to pay you a Sunday visit. Come on, let us in. It's colder'n hell out here."

Owl closed the door behind them, and the dark man took his place again.

"What the devil's goin' on here?" Long asked, rubbing his hands briskly. "Baptist meetin'?"

Owl grinned, gesturing his hand toward Stringbean and then the light. "These gem'men is my friends," he stated softly. "Mistah Legg, he brought me clear from Looisanna."

The door opened slightly, and the stocky gray-haired man went out, his steps crunching briefly over the snow. Owl grabbed a dynamite box, drawing it forward in a low, inviting gesture as Stringbean's long arm went up to unwrap the funny paper from about the light.

Long looked around the crowded room, seeing the rough, disheveled bunks, the potbellied stove with a crack up one side. "If I didn't walk into a crap game, I'm a preacher's son!" He laughed, jerking his head toward the center of the room.

Jim opened up his coat and threw the snow from its shoulders. "What're you bein' so secret about?" he asked bluntly. "This place was black as pitch when we came down the road."

Relieved, the men moved back beneath the light. "That's on 'count of McCune. Effen he knows we got a little game he's goin' be down here quick as his feet'll carry him."

"That's prutty fast," Stringbean added. "That rouster moves like a ole cat catchin' a bitty robin bird."

"What the hells it to him?" Long asked. "He ain't no law-and-order, is he?"

"Yes sir, Mistah Legg," Owl replied earnestly. "The company fix that up right and proper. He carries a gun there and there." He demonstrated, slapping each hip. "And he's got him a big old club that long!"

"He's a deputy," Stringbean injected. "They brung him up here from No' Carolina, and he's law on this hill."

"That's right," Owl repeated. "The company fixed it for him to be a deputy. That's what he is al'right. He's a deputy."

"Well, good God!" Long exclaimed. "He wouldn't pinch you for shootin' crap, would he?"

"He don't zactly 'rest us," Owl began, struggling for clarity. "He tell us he's goin' take us to the sheriff but, Mistah Long, he don't zactly 'rest us." Owl paused, realizing that he had failed. "He take us to the sheriff effen we mean," he went on, pushing the words around in his mind. "Yes sir, he'd do that. But he don't 'rest us zactly for playin' with the dice."

Long stared at Jim questioningly and faced Owl again.

"If he won't pinch you," he asked, "what've you got the place shut up like a cigar box for?"

"'Cause Cap'n McCune goin' to come down here effen——" He stopped, mumbling incoherently, and gestured toward Stringbean.

"McCune comes bustin' in the do'," the lanky man provided, "an' grabs up all the money he can see. Effen we don't hide it fast enough, he's goin' take it ever time. He knocks de do' open an' slams his foot down on de money." He paused, breaking into a rumbling chuckle, one finger pointing to the bony man who had returned to the rim of the upper bunk. "Las' time he stomp his foot right on Popeye's hand. Busted two fingers wide open."

"Seventy-five cents," the man answered dismally. "That was my money. He ain't no right to take it."

"What do you mean?" Long asked, his anger rising. "Does the bastard come in and grab your money and keep it?"

"He sure does do that," Owl answered simply.

"Effen we opens our mouths," Stringbean added, "he takes us to the sheriff. The sheriff, he slaps the table with he's hand, and that costs ten dollars. It's a whole heap cheaper effen we just let McCune grab what he can get." He nodded his head toward the black man at the door. "Honey Boy watches the do'. We pays him fifteen cents. That's the best way."

Long pulled his heavy coat off and tossed it onto the foot of a bunk, jiggling the bottle of gin from hand to hand. "Come on," he said, holding out a hand for the dice. "I'm just itchin' for that bastard to come in here."

"You ain't goin' get us in no trouble, is you?" Stringbean asked fearfully.

"Who's got the dice?" Long repeated. "If there's any trouble, I'll handle it." Suddenly aware of the bottle in his hand, he whirled about and thrust it at Owl. "There," he said. "We brought you that. It tastes like hell, but you can feel it."

The room grew silent while Owl unwrapped the newspaper from about the bottle. "Thank you, Mistah Legg," he muttered. "Thank you. I ain't taste a drop——"

His words were drowned by George Teller's harsh, spasmodic coughing as he suddenly sat up in bed, thumping his chest in an effort to relieve his labored breathing. For a moment he coughed, his head bent down toward his outstretched legs and his eyes watering with the frantic effort. Finally he settled back, sucking his breath through loose lips, his arms falling limply at his sides.

Turning, seeing the inquiry in Long's eyes, Owl began to bob his head. "George has got the cough bad," he said soberly. "He been sick for a week."

"Why don't you get a doctor up here?" Jim asked, not trying to conceal his irritability. "You pay the company for one; why don't you use him?"

"We already gone after him fo'-five times, Mistah Jim," Owl returned apologetically. "Don't seem like he goin' to come up here."

"Well, go again," Long urged. "Keep goin' till you get him."

"Fellah just lef'," the dark man at the door said. "He's goin' to see can he get him."

Jim touched Owl's shoulder and pointed toward the upper bunk in the rear corner. "Give him a drink. He might feel better."

"Yes sir," Owl cried, stumbling about for a cup. "Yes sir. That's what we ought to do. Give George a drink. He ain't goin' feel de ticklin' so much effen he's got a drink." Getting the tin cup that hung from a nail in the rear wall, Owl uncorked the bottle and poured a stiff drink. Filling it with water and carefully replacing the board which served as a bucket lid, he carried it to the bunk.

Stringbean, reaching up with his long arm, helped the man to rise from his pillow, and Owl placed the cup to his lips. Jerkily the strong drink passed down George's throat and he settled back again, muttering indecipherably.

"He's goin' to feel better now," a stoop-shouldered man predicted from the back side of a lower bunk. "He's goin' to sleep."

Quietly the men waited, barely whispering, and the room was filled only with the incessant snoring of those who were to go to work at six o'clock the following morning and, consequently, had the first rights to the bunks that were alternately shared by the day shift and the night shift. At five o'clock they would be awakened, and the men who had worked the night shift would take their place in the fetid bunks.

"He's sleepin' like a chile," Stringbean said, tiptoeing back from the corner bunk. "Give me them bones, Owl. I feel the weather changin'."

Owl hesitated. "Mistah Legg," he urged, the words sluggish and difficult, "Mistah Legg, you hadn't ought to play with de colored boys."

"Why not?" Long demanded, dropping to his knees. "My money ain't Confederate. Come on."

"Dey'll ruin you," Owl warned lugubriously. "Same as taken it out of yo' pocket."

"Nuts! Give me them dice."

In unison the other men dropped to their knees, forming a rough ring about the palsied light that hung from the crossbeam.

"Roll for high man," Long called, drawing the bills from his pocket. "Come on, Jim, I'll stake you." He peeled two dollars from the twelve and thrust them into Jim's hand.

Owl fingered the dice, his lips working mutely, and handed them to Jim.

Following Jim and Long, the rest threw a single roll, and Stringbean, who had tossed an eleven for high, scooped them up with a broad, happy gesture.

"I'm shootin' ten cents," he called, rattling the dice about his body like a tambourine. "Ten cents to make me a dollar!"

At the door the watchman jiggled on cold feet, his neck craned forward like a ghoulish bird.

"Come on, ten!" Stringbean pled, unable to make his point after eight unsuccessful rolls. "Come on, Papa's waitin. Waitin' all night!"

Owl watched the dice, his eyes never leaving the floor. "A long illness is a sure death," he predicted dolefully. "A long illness is a sure death!"

After two more unsuccessful rolls Stringbean lost the dice and they passed about the ring clockwise. Blue smoke strung through the air, ribboned between the stovepipe and the blanket-covered window. On the rear bunk George slept quietly, his right arm thrown across his chest and his head tilted back as though his mouth reached upward to garner what air it could. Now and then a man awoke, drew the tattered blankets around him and again curled into a knot.

"It's your t'row, Mistah Jim," Owl said, passing him the dice when a seven had followed his five. "Treat 'em gentle."

As Jim bent forward, placing his twenty cents in the center of the ring, Owl's broad hand slipped back and began to rub the heel of Jim's heavy shoe. It was a slow superstition in his mind, but Owl knew it would help a white man's luck against the sovereignty of the colored. "Believe in 'em, Mistah Jim," he muttered endlessly. "You got to believe in 'em!"

"Okay, Owl."

Jim won the roll and then lost the dice, passing them on to Long. The game moved quietly, evenly, and the chocolate-colored man next to Long had just finished his roll when a brief, subdued knock came to the door. Everybody stopped, frozen, their ears cocked toward the door.

"Roll 'em," Long demanded. "I want to see that fat slob try to grab up this money!"

A second rapid knock followed and the players settled down again, their money held in their hands.

"That ain't him," Owl whispered thickly, nodding for the dark man to open the door.

A gust of wind squeezed through the opening and swept over the room as the stocky gray-haired man re-entered, his face fixed and heavy with the news he bore.

"The doctah comin?" Owl asked, partially getting to his feet. "He comin' to see George?"

In answer the man drew a small bottle containing a dozen shiny black pills from his pocket and held it out in his palm.

"Them black devils agin," someone said from an upper bunk. "Even if a man break his arm, they don't gib' him nothin' but them black devils."

Across his shoulder Long saw the bottle containing the familiar laxative. "What the hell's them for?" he asked. "Ain't the doc comin' to see about his cough?"

The man shook his head, unsnapping his overall jacket. Carefully making his way to the lower portion of the bunk he shared, he sat down and dropped his head forward in his hands.

"The wagon pass me on the hill," he said gravely. "When I come acrost the knoll they was takin' Burnie Colts away. A woman in de road say he been daid 'bout two hours."

Slowly, stiffly, the men got to their feet, staring wordlessly at the haunched figure crouched on the edge of the bunk.

"Burnie—he daid?" Owl managed.

"The undertaker done took him off'n the hill. The woman said he just got so he couldn't breathe no more."

"What was the matter with him?" Jim cried before he could conceal the wave of fright which spread along his spine. "What—what did the doctor say?"

"The doctah never got there," the stocky man answered numbly.

"They been sendin' for him since Tuesday," Stringbean injected. "Been wantin' him to come all de time."

"The undertaker said it was pnewmonia," the man continued, his head tilted up toward Jim. "That's what he told Burnie's woman. Said Burnie died of pnewmonia. Then he took him down the hill in he's wagon."

Long stuffed the money back in his pocket and took a step through the broken ring of men. "Why didn't the company doctor go to see him?" he asked, his voice cracking sharp in the room. "What'd they let him die like that for?"

"The doctah say he's busy."

"Busy, hell!" Long snapped. "What about that two bits they jerk out of our pay every week? He's not too busy to take that, is he?"

"I wouldn't know 'bout that, boss," the stocky man said dazedly. "I wouldn't know 'bout nothin' like that."

Again Popeye hopped down from his perch on an upper bunk. His feet hit the floor with a dull thud, and he slowly lifted his pointed finger toward the rear of the room.

"George is goin' die right up there," he predicted mournfully. "He's goin' die, and we goin' be right here with him!" His voice trailed off as he stared about the room, his eyes large and frightened.

"Don't you say that," Owl cautioned hurriedly. "Don't you say no sech devil thing!"

"That's what is goin' happen. George, he ain't gettin' his breath, just like Burnie. He's goin' choke up and die right up there where he's layin'."

Long grabbed his coat up from the bunk, jabbing his arms into the sleeves. "Come on, Jim," he said tensely. "We're goin' to get the company doctor up here if we have to drag him by the heels."

Owl followed them to the door, his arms gesturing vaguely after them. "Don't get yo'self in no trouble, Mistah Legg," he called through the door. "Don't you go do nothin' like that!"

"You stay here. We'll take care of this," Long yelled back, headed down the slushy road in great, downthrusting steps. "Come on, Jim."

They had crossed the ridge, found the road and followed its crooked, twisting way down to the foot of the hill before Jim overtook

Long. Falling in beside him as they passed through Old Gauley, knuckled a little forward against the wind, Jim brought two dollar bills from his pocket and handed them to Long.

"Better take this now," he said. "It's yours. I broke about even. And the bet's off, Long. The bet about the shack rouster is off."

Together, wheezing from the rapid, cold trip down the hill, they jogged over the bridge, past the bus station and down the partially cleared sidewalk.

Reaching the office of the company doctor, Long knocked twice, feeling the cold throb through his knuckled fist. A light snapped on overhead and the door opened partially, revealing the doctor in his shirt sleeves.

"They need you up on the hill," Long said. "There's a man pretty sick in Number Five."

"Al'right."

Long's hand flew up to hold the door as it threatened to close. "You goin' up?" he demanded. "The feller's in bad shape."

"I'll be up in the morning. I gave Colts all the medicine he needs," the doctor said irritably, watching Long's outstretched hand against the door. "I'll see him——"

"That's one trip you can save yourself," Long stated bitterly. "Colts is dead."

"He is?"

Long's upper lip drew out a little, his words sharply edged. "A man named Teller is sick in Number Five. He needs you right away. I came after you."

"That's not necessary," the doctor replied. "We handle those niggers——"

"Are you goin' up there?" Long demanded loudly.

The man looked toward the four shirt-sleeved men seated about his desk. "Deal me out," he called and turned back to Long. "What is your name?"

"Legg. I'm a driller in Number One."

"I've got your message, Legg," he said, "and I don't need you to tell me what to do. Now get your hand off that door!"

"You goin' on the hill?"

"I've got your message," the doctor said, nodding slightly. "Thank you very much. Good night."

When the door had closed Long stood kicking his toe against the step.

"That's all you can do," Jim said evenly. "We'll come back tomorrow if——?" Overhead the light snapped off.

"That sonuvabitch," Long swore, "that dirty, lyin' sonuvabitch!"

A s the worst of the winter passed and the snow began to recede into the hollows and clot beneath wind-swept ridges the great pronged valley at the upper end of the Kanawha waited hopefully for the coming of spring. The red clay, stiff and frost-crystaled in the morning, became mud at noon but congealed again into hard little ridges by nightfall.

Now that the cold wintry days were passing, more men came into the valley, walking slowly, with hunger at their sides and at their backs, deprived and driven by the winter when factories closed and the streets were dotted with soup kitchens and household furnishings. They came to the tunnel begging work, waiting at each opening as the shifts went on, silent and ashamed when they saw a man must lose his job before they could be hired.

During that month, as surplus labor began to drain into the valley again, the company declared another pay cut. The thirty-five cents was reduced to thirty, and the colored men were paid twenty-five. The cut was unannounced, coming quickly, and a man could accept it or leave. The night Tom Reip placed his pay on the kitchen table he counted it and Maw counted it, for it was the second cut in five months. Finally they saw it was true and they gathered the money up again, for their rebellion was impotent, their fear increased.

It's gettin warmer," Maw said halfheartedly. "Maybe we won't need so much coal. We can save on coal, and I'll get me a little garden out soon. We'll haft to work it out someways."

"We won't be able to lay none much by," Tom declared. "It'll take ever nickel I can make."

Maw washed the potatoes and set to peeling them, her face drawn with unconcealed worry. "If we can get along on what you make," she said finally. "Just if we don't have to dig into what we got put aside."

That night Ralph Owens could only buy a twelve-dollar money order at the post office, and it hurt him inside when he did it. Receiving his pay envelope, he had counted and recounted the bills, pulling each one between a tightly clenched thumb and finger, thinking the company had made a mistake. He considered going back to the foreman, but the torturing fear of getting the company down on him sickened his resolution. Hurrying to the bunkhouse, he settled miserably onto his cot and began to reapportion his pay.

Eventually, of the three dollars and sixty cents now deducted from his pay, he subtracted sixty from his allowance of a dollar eighty-four. Appending a brief, regretful note to his wife, he ran down the hill to catch the seven o'clock train.

That night, for the first time during the entire winter, Lessie Lee put his piece of apple pie back in the tin just before Mr Johns closed the cafe and went home at eleven-thirty.

"He must be sick," she decided, hurrying to meet Mark Reip, who waited outside. "He always comes in here on Saturday night, regular as clockwork."

"Maybe he went down to Jessie Bail's!" Mr Johns ventured with heavy facetiousness.

"Mister Owens?" Lessie screamed from before the mirror in the women's room. "Lord a-mercy, no! He ain't that kind of a feller."

"Still water runs deep," he answered from the empty, half-lighted room, enjoying the lively implications. "You can never tell."

"Why, there ain't any more chance of him goin' down to that place than there is of sin in heaven!"

To the hundreds of men who went into the tunnel on the day or night shift the five-cent cut made a lot of difference. For they were hungry and their people were hungry. Like Ralph Owens, they pulled in tighter, knowing that a difference of three dollars and sixty cents a week was the same as losing a full day's pay, knowing that they were losing it when ends could not be made to meet before.

Hance McTeer had left Picher, Oklahoma, saying to his wife: "I'll send for you the first regular pay I get. I'll send for you and the young'uns then." The postmaster of Gauley Bridge wrote a post card for him the day he got a job: "I was took on today. I'll send you money from my first pay." In the months which followed, when he sat across the table from Anna while she filled the pages of a tablet he had bought, Hance kept telling his wife he would send for her the first chance he got, and did the least one get over her cold?

The winter was a cold one in Joplin and Picher and Galena, with the wind blowing dustily across the great chat piles where zinc had been holed from the earth. Bessie McTeer saved and scraped and tried, wanting to get away from the sick hole of the Tri-State where miners had been dying for twenty years, but the children were sick and the tar-paper shack unbearably cold. Once they saved three dollars, living a week on soup beans and bread, but her second oldest girl caught a fever, and that and more money had to be spent.

When the second cut came, when the three-sixty was taken from his envelope, Hance McTeer knew he could not see his wife and kids again until he found his way back to the dead zinc mines and chat piles where the wind blew always, spreading the bone-colored dust and filtering it into the house.

He knew that now, and he told Anna to write it to his wife. I guess I'm meant to die out there in Picher, he said. Don't seem like we're ever goin' to get a chanct to get away.

It made a difference to Lock Mullens and Hank Stump, to Roger Pugh whose wife had tried to make a home in a coke oven and to Sam Givens from Georgia who put a lot of store in getting his children through the eighth grade. And it made a difference to Pete Cermak's family in Carbondale, Pennsylvania. Even Jessie Bail could see some change, but she had not expected much. "Tunnel workers and miners. They're all the same. Pick and shovel. They don't get enough to fill their gut. They ain't none of 'em spenders."

When Owl Jones got his pay envelope he waited outside the opening for Long to count it for him. After a full week's work there was only eight dollars and twenty-five cents, and it did not seem right. But it was, and he went back to the hill trying to total the rent and electricity, the doctor's quarter and one for the hospital. It never seemed enough to him, but Long had declared the amount was right after the cut and the deductions, and Owl accepted it wordlessly. But it hung on in his mind and he thought about it for a week, adding and subtracting as best he could. When he received the same amount the following week he realized that it must be correct despite his misgivings, and his mind no longer fretted with the problem.

Men walking to the tunnel talked, saying they ought to fight the cut, but seeing the new men stream into the valley, gaunt and empty-eyed, disowned and driven by their lean hunger for work, they became silent and stooped to pick up the drills and shovels. Within a week the feverish anger had passed, and they accepted the cut with a numb sense of horror, for there was nothing they could do, nothing they could fight with.

Even before the men had come to accept it the women had already made provisions against a leaner time, struggling to be provident on the scant little they had. Now two and three days would pass without meat on the table, and Daisy Mullens, like all the others, cooked beans and potatoes and cabbage again and again, trying to live through a week so there would be a little left over after the pay envelope was portioned out on Saturday.

Three weeks before the pay cut the Mullens' great black cooking stove, with the warming oven and water box, had arrived from Charleston by express, and Lock and Tom Reip and Hank Stump had hauled the two crates across the frozen river. It was nearly eleven o'clock that night before it stood, broad and black and shiny—almost filling one whole corner of the room.

"You could cook for an army on that," Mrs Stump had cried excitedly, tilting her plump body forward in the chair. "Look at that oven! Big enough to roast a ox!"

Smiling her answer, Daisy scurried about, helping Lock remove the paper and excelsior packing from the shiny rim and cast-iron legs.

"We 'lowed it was best to get a good one," Lock said, his pride glowing from his face like a reflected light. "When we get back to Greenbrier we'll allus have it. I promised Daisy when we was comin' down we'd get a stove first chance that come along."

"Land," Daisy cried, her arms overflowing with coarse brown paper. "Land, Mom's eyes will come right outter her head when she sees it in the wagon! She ain't never seen one with a place for hot water right inside it."

Maw Reip wandered slowly about the great stove, dragging her hand across the smooth fire caps, the bright nickeled warming oven and round knob which controlled the grate. "Laws, Daisy," she said quietly, "it'll last all through yore time. It's a thing you'll allus have."

Everyone edged about the room, admiring and exclaiming. Even Hank Stump, who always vowed that he would never buy anything that would tie him down, readily admitted that such a fine stove was a sound investment. "'Course me and Sarey," he ended somewhat definitely, "we just live wherever we hang our hats. But if we was to ever settle down, I'd get me a stove like that."

"You oughter grease it good," Maw advised sagely. "Take the skin from a piece of side meat and grease it good afore you start the fire. It'll keep the black from coming off, and it won't ever rust that-a-way."

"Is there any in the house?" Lock asked anxiously, wanting to get a fire started. "Is they any of that sow's belly left over, Daisy?"

"The last snitch went for supper," she replied, a little disappointed herself. "I got some store lard——"

"That ain't near so good," Maw declared, grabbing up her tattered shawl and heading for the door. "I'll slice off the rine from what I got and fetch it acrost."

Half an hour later the entire stove had been rubbed with the fatty side of the bacon rind and Lock started the fire, his ears cocked to catch every exclamation that filled the room. For a while the wood crackled and snapped, the flame moaning a little as it swept toward the flue.

"It draws good," he announced to the room. "And gives off a sight of heat now."

"I'll fill the water box right now," Daisy exclaimed, bringing the pail of water from the ledge. "It'll be warm to wash in when mornin comes."

Back of a rear cap tiny wisps of smoke twisted upward, bending across the top of the stove. Another larger one began just above the fire. Then, as the heat spread, the whole broad surface of the stove gradually clouded the room with smoke.

"Turn yore draft, Lock," Tom suggested politely. "I reckon you got it shet off too far."

Choking a little, Lock made the adjustment, but the smoke increased, rising in blue feathery streaks from the greasy surface.

"Maybe it's overheated," Mrs Stump offered. "Turn the damper a mite."

Excitedly, her arms shooting first one direction and then the other, Daisy struggled to help Lock halt the smoke that was rapidly filling the room.

"Let it alone," Maw called, waving a hand to clear the air before her face. "It ain't nothin. Nothin in the world but paint and that grease. It'll burn off in time——"

Twenty minutes later, when everyone had put on their coats and opened both doors, the stench diminished, and presently the room was emptied but for a few straggling ribbons of smoke that clung along the ceiling.

Satisfied, and feeling that they could properly leave now that the stove had returned to its right behavior, fulfilling all expectations, the neighbors got up and made for the door.

From the porch Maw Reip repeated the invitation she had made earlier in the evening. "Mis' Brake said I could have her quilten frames a week come Saturday," she began. "I'd take it kindly if you ladies would come and sew awhile on the Monday followin."

"I'll be there," Mrs Stump declared, oozing her large body down the steps sideways. "My stitches ain't even, but I'll be glad to help you."

"Stop by for me," Daisy called after her. "I'll wait and go long with you."

"Sounds like that is one night us men is goin to get a cold supper," Tom chuckled from the road. "Oncet the womenfolks start talken the fire can die right out and they won't pay no attention."

"Oh, hesh, Tom," Maw demanded briskly. "Supper's allus on the table, and you know it." She turned and called up the steps to Lock and Daisy. "Thank ye kindly for asken us in to see your stove. It's a sight for a body's eyes to see."

During these days the drills inside the tunnel bit and tore their way into the hard rock, ceaselessly boring the thirty-two-foot hole through the mountain. No trembling shook the earth as the repeated charges were set off, for the four headings were deep beneath the twin hills now, and a man leaving the job had a long way to walk before he reached the round tubular hole where the digging had first begun.

At the heading of Number One the drillers pushed constantly forward, driving the power drills into the solid wall of hard stone. After a sufficient number of holes had been bored they dragged the drills away, retreating, and the high ledge of stone was blown to a rough, jagged pile of rock. The muckers moved in, tearing out the broken stone until there remained only a low ledge which stood a few feet above the planned floor of the giant tube. Again the men came forward with their sinker drills, boring downward, preparing for the last blast to remove the stone platform which yet rose above the floor.

Back of this crew came other muckers, breaking the way for the steam shovel and the dinkey crews who helped to load the stone in chains of four to seven cars so that it might be hauled from the tunnel, placed in gondolas and shipped down the river.

The chuckers, who carried steel to the drillers, worked through between them, carrying fresh points through the dense, foglike dust when "Steel!" was called above the deafening, incessant pound of the drills. Track crews followed, laying and repairing the narrow-gauge line which had wormed its way along the tube.

Between these crews moved the walking bosses, who went from one end of the job to the other, watching, directing, ordering that men be shifted from one crew to another as the work progressed and returning to the superintendent to report and get his orders.

Farther back, near the entrance, the steel crew had already gone to work. With the walls of the giant tube shaped to size they began to put the steel reinforcements into place. Between these great bands that circled the hole at regular intervals the legging men placed the wooden structure, preparing for the day when the facing would be put into place.

At the mouth of the tunnel the dump crews emptied each string of dinkey cars into the gondolas that stood on the lower tracks. The small engines ran incessantly, disappearing into the dark hole and returning with another load of crushed stone. Ton after ton was removed, reloaded and shipped to Alloy, where a subsidiary of the Union Carbide and Carbon Company was erecting an electrometallurgical plant.

Engineers had known from the time they sunk their first test bores to determine the course of the proposed tunnel that veins of the silica stone ran as high as ninety-nine per cent pure, and as spring came on and the first green-yellow leaves broke bud-like from the branches the heading of Number One reached the valuable stretch of stone.

Early in the month engineers went through the tunnel where Number One and Number Two crews moved forward to meet each other, surveying and measuring. They came many times, carrying away test rocks and estimating their exact location under the hill.

"What're they fixin' to do?" Jim asked Long as they walked down the track from work. "They've had engineers in here all day. Do you suppose Number One and Number Two ain't goin' to hit?"

"I dunno," Long replied casually. "How could they miss? That's what they get smart engineers in here for."

"It'd be a funny thing though," Jim went on, "if the two didn't come together and they had to do it over."

"One time a feller told me a thing like that. He said the two crews was workin' each way, between New York and Hoboken. They seen too late that it wasn't goin' to come out even, so they went right ahead and built two tunnels side by side."

"I don't believe it," Jim returned. "Engineers wouldn't make a big mistake like that."

"That's what I told this feller. He just laughed though. Said his old man got an extrey year's work out of it. He was working in the sand. His old man, I mean."

"Just the same," Jim ended, laughing lightly, "it'd be a funny thing if they missed. It sure would make them engineers look silly, after coming in there so big, wearin' masks like they didn't want to smell the dirt we work in."

"Maybe they got them things on and can't see straight," Long chuckled, wiping the dust away from his eyebrows where it had settled in a thick, heavy coat.

Within the week the engineers' repeated trips into the tunnel took definite understandable shape for the men who went under the ground each morning and each evening.

Lock Mullens, who, because of his height and thickset shoulders, had been changed to a drifter drill, working at the very head of the tube, came to work one morning just as the night shift was going off. Muckers were still at work, clearing up after the last blast, when Lock made his way along the little track, past the "whirley shovels" and into the heading.

The three other men who ran drifter drills, boring into the vertical wall ahead, stood to one side taking instructions from a walking boss.

"Come here, Mullens," the man called; "you'll have to hear this too."

Through the dense cloud of dust which still hung in the air Lock could barely make out the boss's features. His face, normally reddened as though he stood forever before a blazing fire, seemed in the dim light to be scalded, as if the dust had suddenly turned to steam.

"Mornen," Lock said, nodding to the shadowy figures of the men who worked beside him.

"We're right about here now," the walking boss said, pushing his thumb along the parallel lines of a chart that indicated the shape of the tunnel. "Number Two's been cut down to there. Now," he said slowly, raising the map nearer the four attentive faces, "starting here we're going to broaden her to forty-six feet."

"Forty-six," Lock said. "That's fourteen feet more."

The walking boss eyed him sparely, trying to anticipate any question. "That's right, Mullens. Forty-six she's got to be. Today we'll slant her off a little at the sides. Tomorrow we'll cut in a little more. The crew back of you will shape it up." Turning, he laid out the proposed angles by pointing ahead and to the side with a slicing motion of his hand.

"Now, did you get that?"

"Yep," Lock said, trying to imprint the estimated angle indelibly in his mind.

"All right—get goin'. The muckers are comin' up."

Dragging their drills forward, the men raised them, placing the points against the forward wall and spreading their legs apart to lessen the jouncing vibration.

"What the hell do they want to make it wider for?" a man asked. "They can't get any extra water through here unless they enlarge the whole thing. Don't make sense to me."

"I'll bet they're wantin' to take out more of this damn dusty rock. They're haulin' it all down the river. Goin' to use it for somethin'."

"Give us more work," Lock declared. "I can use it since they give us that cut."

"Well, goddamn 'em, if they can give us a cut, why can't they give us wet drills if we are goin' to have more work!" With two fingers of his right hand he threw the lever, sending the drill into sharp staccato action. Lock's followed, and in a moment the narrow opening at the heading was throbbing violently with the ceaseless pneumatic tat-tat.

That day the widening of the tunnel began, and the work moved forward more slowly, but the number of cars hauling crushed stone out to the opening increased. The muckers and track crews, the steam-shovel operators and the chuckers saw the increased amount of removed stone passing from the tunnel, and as they worked word passed around, each man trying to determine why the tunnel, planned and cut at thirty-two feet, should unreasonably be broadened to forty-six feet.

"They're doin' it so's it'll hold more water," Roger Pugh ventured. "When it comes winter and de river is froze they'll be plenty of water stored up here to last."

"Aw hell!" another man replied from across the dinkey tracks, "they wouldn't do a thing like that. They'd make it all one size, don't matter what."

"They been figuring on makin' it wider here," a slender, dark-complexioned man interrupted. "They had it in the plans all the time. A feller that works in the office told me."

"Here comes the boss!"

For a while nothing could be heard but the thunderous drone of the drills and the high, piercing shriek of the steam shovel as it twisted about.

"Who's doin' the talkin' over here?" the foreman demanded, emerging from the fog.

"Ain't me, cap'n," a colored man replied obediently.

"Well, cut it out and get to work!" For a while he watched the men scoop up the broken stone, and moved on, disappearing into the milky dust toward the vague blob of light strung from the ceiling.

"Said the company figgered on makin' it bigger all the time, did he?"

"Yep," the tall one affirmed, bending to accept the weight of a loaded shovel. "That's what he said. They want more of that rock. It's got somethin' in it they want, I reckon. They're storing it in a lot down at Alloy."

"You reckon it's gold, maybe?" the second man asked briskly. "It kind of shines in places."

"Man alive!" Roger Pugh cried, "effen it's gold, I must have carried home a million dollars! When I take off my clothes there's a pile of money layin' right there on the flo'."

19

After the death of Burnie Colts and George Teller the men who slept in alternate shifts in the bunks crowded into shack Number Five became restless and afraid. For almost a week no one dared crawl into the upper bunk, and during the day, while the night shift slept, the bedclothes were dragged out of the door and spread across a row of dynamite boxes that had been carried up from the tunnel.

Finally the nearness of George's death became less real, and they spoke of it as something which might have occurred in another shanty, but no man living in Number Five ever forgot the quick businesslike fashion in which the body was removed and buried.

Coming in one evening, following the change of shifts, Stringbean had reached the shack before any of the others. The beds were still warm and disheveled where the night shift had slept. Seeing George's quiet figure, he tiptoed across the wide-cracked room and eased himself down on the bunk, waiting for the others to come in before he crossed the knoll to the long, loosely constructed building where the unmarried men were required to eat.

A strange quietness permeated the shack, and Stringbean looked about closely, expecting some sound. He saw nothing, but the feeling hung on, insistent and driving, like the loud moment of silence which precedes a familiar noise. Disturbed, Stringbean got up and moved about the room quietly, half expecting to find some stranger crouched in a corner, and then returned to the bunk.

Just as he was stretching out Stringbean's lanky body shot out of the binlike crib and his mouth hung open as he stared at Teller's bunk, suddenly aware of the knowledge he had already possessed. Sharply, fearfully he listened, knowing all the while that he had not heard Teller's harsh breathing since he had entered the room.

Step by step he crossed the floor, his lean body tilted forward as he strained to see in the upper bunk.

Teller lay, his mouth partially open, staring idiotically at the clapboard ceiling.

"George!" Stringbean called. "George!"

There was no answer and, rising upward on his toes, he saw that George was stone dead, his features frozen in a rigid mask.

By the time Owl, Honey Boy and the rest had reached the shack an ambulance had clanged up the hill, slipped along the ruts of the road that bisected the two rows of shacks and halted before Number Five. Owl, who had taken the path which formed a short cut, came through between the shanties and was nearly onto the olive-green hearse before he saw what it was.

Pausing at the corner beside a pile of ashes, he laboriously studied the *Howard C. Wayne, Undertaker* lettered in gold just beneath the darkly curtained window of the long automobile.

As he was deciphering it two men bore George's body through the shack door, tilting the wheeled stretcher a little to get it through the narrow door. Placing it in the ambulance, they gave it a slight shove, rolling it forward, and turned to face Stringbean and the rest who hung about the doorway staring incredulously.

"Where's his clothes?" the stubby, sandy-haired young man asked. "He got any?"

The men exchanged wordless glances and faced the brothers who drove the ambulance.

"He daid?" Owl asked.

"Yeh," Harold, the oldest of Wayne's sons, said. "Get his clothes if he's got any. We got to bury him in something."

"You takin' him away?" Honey Boy asked. "You goin' to bury him?"

"Sure." The stubby one pressed impatiently through the door of the shack, followed by the men. "Get his clothes," he repeated. "We can't bury a man in his underwear."

"He never had none," Owl said. "George, he just got his overalls and shirt."

"Give me them. Come on, we don't have all night."

Getting down on his knees, Owl dragged a cardboard carton from beneath the rear tier of bunks. One by one he laid out a pair of dust-covered overalls, a soiled denim shirt, pale and bleached from many washings, and a pair of coarse, cotton-ribbed socks from which the heels had been worn.

"You want these, sir?" he asked, holding them up.

"Christ's sake, no!" Catching the overalls by the shoulder strap and the shirt by a sleeve, Fred Wayne allowed them to drag along the floor as he turned to go.

The men watched him silently. Part way to the door the thickset young man wheeled about and walked back to the rear bunk. Kicking the canned-milk carton from his path, he reached up and dragged the shabby pillow from George's bed. Holding it by one corner of the slip, he snapped it in the air, slinging the pillow from inside its cover. He watched the floor, snapped the pillowcase a few times, dropped it and, reaching up, rolled the top part of the mattress down over the foot. Then, standing on the lower bunk, he examined the rough box which held the bed.

When he found nothing he hopped down and started out to the ambulance.

"Mister," Honey Boy asked, "ain't you goin' bury him in nothin' but he's work clothes?"

"That's all we got." Fred Wayne shrugged. "The company don't furnish anything else." He tossed the overalls and the shirt into the back of the ambulance and closed the door.

"Wait a minute, mistah." The short gray-haired man who had gone for the doctor the night of the crap game crossed to his bunk and pulled a package from beneath it. Returning to the doorway, he held it out to Harold Wayne. "Here," he said. "Put that on George. He ain't got no people here. They'd want him buried with a coat on."

As the ambulance clanged across the knoll, disappearing with the curve of the road, the men ventured out from the shack door, listening to the diminishing sound. They heard it rolling down into the gulley, out onto the highway and finally its loud, ringing clang as it sped down the hill toward Gauley Bridge.

"We oughter write his folks," Stringbean said. "George, he's got a woman and two boys down in No' Carolina. They'd like to know. We'll send 'em a post card."

"Mistah Legg," Owl put in anxiously, "Mistah Legg, he'll write it for us."

In the days which followed a heavy silence settled over the shack, and the men looked at one another without speaking. On Saturday they learned that another colored man had died in a shack at the foot of Hawk's Nest, and they sprang on the news almost hungrily, for it was the fear they had seen in each other's eyes for a week.

"If I had me enough money I'd go back home," Stringbean said that evening. "I'd head down the road and go home where I belong."

"I'm goin' home too," Honey Boy vowed. "It's a long time since I been to Geo'gia. I got a gal waitin' for me down there."

The talk increased, growing rapidly, spurred on by the fact that the days were warmer now and walking would be easier.

"Just soon's I get me a little money," Stringbean said. "Just so's I got enough they can't pick me off the road for beggin'. They put you in a gang if yo' ain't got money in yo' pocket."

Soberly they discussed it, knowing that by the end of the week, when room and board, light and coal and the other fees had been deducted from their pay envelopes, they possessed little else.

"I'll go down to the Jungle and live with Roger Pugh," Honey Boy said. "Me and Roger come from the same town, down below Memphis. But that ain't goin' to help none. The company take the rent from my pay just the same. Don't matter where a man lives, they charge him just the same."

Measure by measure they went over their earnings, discussing each expenditure. Now, following the cut which the company had imposed, it was impossible to earn much more than they actually needed to repay the company.

"If they never charged so much at the bo'rdinghouse," Owl said. "If they just never done that, we could get us a little travelin' money."

"Yes sir," Stringbean added. "Six dollars the cap'n takes. Six dollars ever week, and all we gets in the mawnin' is cawfee an Kayo syrup. An dat's half water."

"It ain't nuff fo' a man that's workin," Owl said soberly. "It don't stick to he's bones."

"I seen the cans in back," Honey Boy said. "They don't say coffee on 'em. They say cofferine. What the hell dat is, I never heard tell. Tastes like the bark off chicory."

"If they just give us a can of beans in the mawnin," Owl began. "I'd druther have me a can of beans."

Stringbean popped out of his chair, smacking his flat hands together. "We'll get us some beans!" he declared. "We buy us some grub and put it in here! Ain't no reason why we gots to pay that robber!"

Slowly Owl raised his head, a grin enlightening his face. "'At's a fine idea!" he declared. "We go to the sto' and buy us some grub. We can live on 'bout two dollars and save the rest."

"And we ain't buyin' it from the robbissary either!" Stringbean hurried on determinedly. "Us go to Gauley and fetch it from the Red Front."

Honey Boy dug down into his pocket and produced a wrinkled dollar and some change. "In a month we can save enough to get us home," he declared. "My gal be glad to see me comin' down the road. She ain't goin' let me cough all de time." Carefully he counted his money, half listening to the mumble of voices that filled the room. "I gots a dollah sixty-seven," he said presently. "We all put in the same——"

"Us make it one-fifty," Stringbean said. "We's six. Dat's nine dollahs. We can get us a mess o' eatin' for nine dollahs. If dat don't las, we can get some mo'."

Owl squatted down on his bunk, furtively feeling in the watch pocket of the pair of trousers he wore beneath his tattered overalls. As he worked his hand about, his face screwed from one side to another, and he drew out his money between a tightly clenched finger and thumb. Bending sideways across the bunk, he counted it slowly and patiently and slipped the remaining two dollars and twenty-three cents back into his pocket.

"Heah's mine," he said, passing Stringbean the bill and little pile of change.

Spreading it on his hand, the tall, slender man counted it and extended his flat palm toward Owl. "You short a nickel," he said. "That's a dollah forty-five."

Mutely Owl looked at him until, acknowledging the mistake, he returned to the bunk and went through the slow, painstaking motions of removing his carefully hoarded money again.

Sunday morning the six men did not go to the boardinghouse which Bob Camp ran at the far end of the uneven row of shacks. Sitting in the door and about the bunks, they ate their food from the supplies they had bought late the evening before. Owl boiled two eggs in a tomato can from the dump heap and the others followed suit, crunching soda crackers into their mouths with the eggs. Finishing, they shared a can of peaches, passing the can about for each to gobble his portion.

That evening they ate pink salmon, potatoes roasted on the back of the stove and two cans of baked beans, washing it down with coffee Owl had made in the water bucket. Each time they emptied a can it was carefully washed and the jagged edges pressed down so they would not tear a man's lips.

Owl, who stacked and restacked the precious hoard between the two rear bunks, went through the process once more, putting the canned meat in one place, the vegetables next to them and the pineapple and peaches by themselves. "If Popeye watches them in the day, like he promise," he muttered to himself, "I'll watch 'em at night. That way won't nobody come in here stealin' 'em."

"I watch 'em," Popeye reaffirmed. "You pays me a quarter ever Saturday, and I'll watch 'em like a hawk."

When the day crew came off Monday afternoon Owl waited outside until Stringbean and two of the others had joined him, slapping as much of the dust as possible from their clothes as they walked over the gray overcast ground.

"We better head on up," Owl said anxiously. "Popeye had done left fo' the night shift. We get the beans cookin'——"

They started up the path as rapidly as they could walk, tugging at brush and roots to help them over the steepest part of the incline. Finally reaching the rounded knoll that held the shacks, they cut through between Numbers Four and Five.

"We heat a can of corn an open de crackers and some tater chips," Owl began, reaching level ground. "By the time the others come up——" Rounding the ash heap at the corner of the shack, he came to an abrupt halt, hardly able to comprehend what he saw.

Standing beside a burning pile of packages, Slat McCune was busy slashing through the cans of food with an ax.

"What's you doin' cap'n?" Owl called, leaping forward, his eyes rapidly checking the corn and beans and tomatoes that oozed from the dented, hacked cans. "What's that yo'——" Without waiting for an answer he whirled about and ran into the shack.

Before any of the others could move Owl had reappeared in the door.

"You ain't no business doin' that, cap'n," Owl cried, his voice low and beseeching. "We paid our money——"

"Don't you cut that up!" Stringbean demanded, one hand raised to halt the ax McCune swung at the cans tossed in a heap in the road. "Don't you——"

"Get back there, you black bastard!" the paunchy man threatened. "Leave that stuff alone!"

"Mistah Slat," Owl begged. "We paid our money at the sto'——"

"You can't eat in the shacks," McCune declared, raising his ax again. "What the hell do you think the boardinghouse is for?"

"Please, cap'n," Owl said, reaching up and grabbing the ax handle. "We never knowed. We ain't goin' to do it no mo'. Just don't you burn up what we got an'——"

"Watch him, Owl!" Stringbean cried. "Get back!"

"Don't you do it, cap'n," Owl went on, throwing a folded arm above his head. "Dat's our grub, cap'n——"

The heavy brown mace swished through the air, cracking Owl across the arm and knocking him backward. McCune followed the blow with another, clubbing Owl over the shoulders.

"You sonuvabitch, don't you try to hit me!" he swore. "Get out of here before I bust your head wide open!"

Scrambling to his feet, Owl backed toward the door, kicking the steps with his heels to find his way. As he moved he continued to beg that the food be spared, the words coming repetitiously and with decreasing sound.

Grouped about the door, the men watched Slat McCune replace the mace and pick up the ax again. They did not speak, and McCune said nothing until he halved the last can of brown baked beans and kicked it, splattering, down the road.

"If I ever catch you eatin' in there again," he threatened, "it'll be worse! We got a boardin'house, and that's where you eat!"

Slinging the ax across his shoulder and giving the fire a last prodding kick, he turned and walked down the muddy road.

Silently the men watched him go, hardly aware of the odor of food that drifted up from the splattered road.

20

"It's getting warmer now," Lock said, marking off the corner of the garden plot with his shovel. "I'll be feelin better all the time."

Daisy did not answer but, taking the knotted length of string, she walked across the black, coal-dusted earth, showing how far the ground back of their house could be spaded.

"The days are longer now," he went on half aloud, "and a feller gets a chance to work out of doors. I'll be better in no time a-tall, Daisy." Placing his foot on the back of the shovel, he drove it into the ground, watching the soil break beneath the tangle of grass roots.

"It'll be nice acrost here for bunch beans," Daisy said, walking back beside the lengths of cord she had tied together. "Say bout five or six rows, and then one of beets and two or three of cabbage. Mis' Reip is fixen me a row of Early Round Dutch. She's got the seeds in a box back of the stove already."

Having broken the ground, Lock spaded across in a line beneath the string. "We'll get the beans in right away," he declared anxiously, "and the early sweet corn. We'll just plant the stuff we can bring in afore fall." He stopped, gasping a little, and leaned on his shovel. Daisy watched him narrowly, saying nothing but noting the heavy dilations at the side of his neck as Lock forced air into his lungs.

"Must be worser'n cutten rock," she said casually. "This yard's just been packed down and packed down."

"Yeh," Lock replied, forcing the flat shovel into the darkened soil again. "A man ought to have a regular spade."

"I'll step acrost and see if Maw Reip's usen her'n," Daisy offered. "She named it to me a'ready."

"Nope. Tom told me comen home he's fixen to turn up the rest of his patch." Lock grew silent, spading the earth and breaking the hard lumps with the side of the shovel. Before he had traveled halfway across the first row his breath began to burn in his throat and a small throbbing pain began on one side of his chest

Daisy edged toward him, her hand extended in apprehensive restraint, but said nothing. For more than a week Lock had talked of getting the garden plot broken, of turning and furrowing the ground for the first planting. Sometimes of an evening he would pull out the worn catalogue and search the pages, comparing and estimating each variety of seed so that their crop would be in before autumn had passed and it was time to take their cookstove and few belongings and head toward the fertile, rolling acres at the head of Greenbrier Hollow.

"We'll put in some pole beans," he would decide. "Plant 'em right in between the corn. When it comes time to head back they'll be dry in the shucks and we'll have 'em after winter comes on."

Another evening he would go over the same page, providentially preparing for days ahead. "I'd like to get me in a little patch of this Golden Bantam. It comes high, but if I got me a dozen rows in they'd be enough for seed corn when we get back to the holler. It'd be a thing, to see it growen there against the hill."

"Ah yes, Lock," Daisy would agree. "Nothin makes finer eaten than Golden Bantam."

"That's the way I figured we ought to work it out," Lock nodded soberly. "We'll have us a little eaten garden, and the rest we'll put in for seed when we get back home."

Daisy let the plate and drycloth settle into her lap. "Lock," she began, "they's somethin worken on my mind, and it frets me the blessed time."

His lean face bent toward her, his eyes moving in gentle asking.

"Can't we head back afore the end of October?" she urged. "We'll have us some laid by, and we could pay Enoch McCort the rest after we get settled. I'm fixen to do whatever you say, Lock, but you'd be a sight better off there at home."

Lock's eyes went back to the brightly colored seed pages, and he did not speak for some time. "It's a thing I hanker to do, honey," he said quietly, "but I reckon we'll stay on. Afore the snow flies we'll have us enough to own the place, and that-a-way it'll allus be ourn. I got it figured—with raisen the seed down here and layen a little by for winter—we'll be best off if we don't head home till late fall."

Daisy got up and continued to dry the dishes. As she passed from the wash box to the shelf her eyes turned again and again to the deep shadows the lamplight formed where Lock's cheeks had sunken into his gaunt face.

"I think I'll get some beans to plant with the corn," Lock went on presently. "We'll have that much more seed when we get back. Starten with a quarter's worth, I can have near enough to plant an acre next spring."

Now, as Lock struggled with the shovel, trying to break and loosen the hard-packed earth, Daisy moved toward him but could say nothing. Still ten feet away, she could hear his coarse, heavy breathing, and it filled her with terror.

"I'll go ast the Stumps," she offered. "Might be they got a spade."

Lock shook his head. "Hank don't plant none."

"I'll ast," Daisy said, running toward the back corner of the unpainted shack. "It just might be!"

Trotting back several minutes later, Daisy carried a heavy mattock in one hand. Ducking beneath the limp clothesline, she cut across the yard. "You dig with the mattock," she urged, "and I'll come along behint you and turn it over." Suddenly she stopped, seeing the throbbing feverishness that had drained the blood from Lock's lips.

Mutely he nodded his head and sat down upon the ground.

"Just you rest first, Lock," she cried, trying to conceal her fear. "They ain't no hurry."

Lock lifted his head as though to open the passage into his lungs. "I'm kind of wore out," he muttered.

"I'll fetch you a drink."

By the time Daisy ran back over the yard with a filled cup his harsh breathing had subsided, coming loud but regularly.

"They's plenty of time," Daisy urged carefully. "The Tuckers down yonder ain't near got their'n done."

Lock pressed his fingers against his lips with a steadying pressure before he spoke. "They're worken us harder," he said. "They're maken the hole wider. But the boss says we got to travel as fast as we done before."

The following morning, soon after Lock had gone down the path with Tom Reip and Hank Stump, Daisy piled the dishes in the wash box and hurried out the back door. Taking the shovel and mattock from against the boarded wall, she dragged them to the end of the row they had left unfinished the night before.

For more than an hour she worked, swinging the heavy mattock with all her might, sinking the blade into the earth and prying with the handle until the soil broke in clods. Finishing a row, she went over it again with the shovel, breaking the chunky dirt and crumbling it to a smooth surface.

The warm lemon sun had topped the hill and lowered its light into the valley when Maw Reip came over the road, walked through the Mullens' shack, calling for Daisy, and appeared on the back step.

"God's grace, Daisy!" she cried, seeing the mattock rise and fall with a heavy, solid thud. "What in kingdom come are you doin!" In one leap she hit the ground and was running across the yard, knocking the clothesline upward as she ran. "Put that mattock down!"

Daisy pried another clod loose and, leaning against the crudely fashioned handle, turned to Maw.

"Give me that!" Maw commanded, reaching for the mattock. "You ain't no business worken this-a-way!"

Stubbornly Daisy held on, one hand raking back the hair which strung down over her forehead.

"Leave me have it, I tell you," Maw repeated. "You'll hurt yoreself sure."

"No," Daisy protested. "It's too early. It won't do a bit of harm."

Maw gave the mattock a sudden jerk, yanking it from Daisy's hands. "I've had five in my time," she said, "and I know what I'm talken about! You get out of this garden as fast as yore feet'll carry you."

Daisy let her eyes run over the upturned soil, drying now as the sun spread over its dark rough surface. "I've got to dig it, Maw," she said. "Lock, he ain't fitten to, and he'll be heartsick if he don't get him a garden out."

"You tole him—bout the young'un?"

Daisy shook her head. "I'm waiten. It's a far time yet."

"Then get back to that house," Maw directed. "If you don't, I'll tell him sure as life! "

"Don't you dast," Daisy warned. "Lock, he's got everythin fig-gered out the way he's wanten it. He's a good planner, and I ain't goin to stand in his way. Just the other night he was tellen how he would work it and all. When it's warmer and he gets his flesh back———"

"Set down on the ground," Maw said. "If we get our heads together, we can settle this thing."

With a little sigh Daisy sat down, opening the collar of her dress and fanning her sweaty neck with an open hand.

"We finished off our'n last night," Maw began easily. "The boys flew in and helped Tom, and it's all turned now. We set the onions, and I got some lettuce in. It'll be nice eaten greens again."

"Lock started last night," Daisy admitted, "but he give plumb out. I thought I'd spade today, then we'd plant this evenin, after the sun's down. That way it'd be easier on him."

Maw nodded agreement, casting a surveying glance about the intended garden. "Lock seem to be gitten any better?" she asked, feign-ing casualness.

"None that I can see. He's so short-winded. How's Tom and Ely? Seems like I never lay eyes on the boys any more."

"They're a mite better, if anythin. And Mark, he don't complain a-tall, outside of the burnen in his eyes."

Anxiously Daisy twisted about, her words coming quick and urgent. "You think it's passen?" she asked. "You think it ain't nothin a-body can't get shet of?"

"You can't rightly tell. Times it seems like they're sound as stone, and then they get a little cold like Ely done, and they wheeze till a-body can hear it clear acrost the road."

"Maybe," Daisy broke in, "maybe it'll pass, now it's turnen warmer. It's just, maybe, somethin they catch from worken where its warm and then comen out."

"Mebby," Maw granted. "There ain't no real way of tellen. Turner Hatch, what's a foreman there, tole my man he's been worken in mines and sech for twenty years. Said the dust wouldn't hurt no more'n breathen in the fog."

Daisy settled back wordlessly, one finger tracing an endless pattern through the dirt. "Mercy," she said presently, "mercy, I hope so."

"Hope," Maw repeated softly. "Hope, I reckon that's about the most we got to go on." Then, as if their talk had been idle and without purpose, she clambered to her feet. "I'm goin after the spade," she called. "Don't you dig another stroke afore I get back."

Coming between the shacks, bearing the strong spade which she had brought down from the Knob the fall before, Maw set to work finishing the row Daisy had started. "I'll turn it over," she instructed, "and you come behind an break it up. Don't dig none. Just bust up the lumps."

Daisy tried to protest but, seeing Maw's firm, determined movements and receiving no answer to half-a-dozen appeals, she fell in line and began to hammer the clumps of earth with the edge of the shovel.

Over and back the two women worked, spading and breaking the soil for the seed Lock had already purchased. They talked little, calling now or again when a hawk ventured out of the woods or a robin hopped over the broken dirt, his head cocked sideways as he trailed them over the upturned soil.

Finally, as the sun reached the center of the sky, Maw sunk the spade into the ground with a sharp downward thrust and spoke to Daisy.

"You go in and rest awhile," she instructed. "It's comen noontime, and the young'uns will be wanten their meal."

"Land," Daisy said, looking down across the garden, "we done a lot, ain't we?"

"Enough for radishes and such. I'll come back soon as Viney and Virgil head over for school."

"Yore more'n kind," Daisy said. "It ain't a thing you've got a call to do."

"Why not, in the Lord's name?" Maw asked, stomping the mud from her high-topped shoes. "You quilted for me till yore eyes was maken spots on the wall."

"That wasn't nothin," Daisy protested. "We never got much done, Mis' Stump talken so much bout Flordia."

"She oughter have young'uns, like yore fixen to," Maw said. "It's a lonely road her and Hank is headen down. They talk all the time about Floredy, but when they get there it'll be somewheres else."

"I reckon," Daisy agreed. "I've seen her time and time agin. She talks big, but they's a empty look in her eyes."

"Well," Maw retorted, chuckling a little, "they's such a thing as overdoin it. Seems to me I been cooken and patchen for my young'uns since time out of mind. Patchen and cooken, spanken and huggen— that's bout all I ever got done."

"They're fine young'uns," Daisy declared warmly. "Specially that Virgil. He's as smart as he can be. Lock said he never seen anyone so quick to pick up a thing."

"He's done real good," Maw answered with reasonable pride. "The teacher has put him ahead three times. Reckon he'll get permoted agin when school's out at the end of the month."

"That'll be nice," Daisy said, placing the shovel against the wall of the shack. "He'll go on next year, I 'low."

"Yep," Maw said. "He's talken bout goin to a teacher's college, down yonder to Montgomery. Says he wants to work this summer, so's he can start gitten some money ahead."

"That would be nice," Daisy exclaimed. "Them places must take a sight of money."

"That'll be a far time yet," Maw said. "And I ain't sure I want him worken round that tunnel. It's a thing I ain't sure of in my mind yet."

During the changeable uncertain days of early spring, when men left the shacks and headed for the four openings with nothing heavier than an overall jacket to protect them from the winds that traveled up the river, many caught colds which seemed to hang on far past their expected time.

From the camps at the foot of Lover's Leap and Hawk's Nest, from atop the hill where Owl and the others lived and from the cluster of shacks between the railroad and the river, known as the Jungle, came repeated calls for the doctor. When he did arrive he passed from one tar-paper shack to another, examining them hastily and leaving behind a bottle of the black pills.

"If you men don't take care of yourselves," he would charge each time, "you're all going to die of the grippe. You work in that hot tunnel and then come out in the cold. What do you expect?"

"It ain't exactly like a cold, doctor," Mrs Crump insisted. "In the night he gets so he can't breathe to do no good."

"Naturally. His lungs are congested. Where do the Jacksons live?"

"Doctor," the woman persisted, "I ain't meanin' to get out of my place, but Paul's needin' somethin' else. I give them pills a'ready. They just sort of make him weaker."

"Wrap him up when he goes out. A changeable spring like this always means a fat graveyard."

Following his quick steps to the door, Mrs Crump slipped outside and closed it behind her. "Ain't there nothin' else you can do for him?" she begged. "He's a-sufferin' somethin' fierce. He gets chokin' spells——"

"Let him rest awhile. He'll be all right. Is that the Jacksons' place across there?"

Trotting down the wet clay path after him, Mrs Crump beat her hands together helplessly, trying to halt his departure.

"Paul can't miss no time," she declared frantically. "He's been off two days a'ready. The company will put us out if he misses any more."

"I can't help that."

"It's that chokin'. He don't cough like he's got a cold. The young'uns has had the grippe. But Paul, he——"

She stopped and walked back to the house, miserable and terrified at her own futile desperation.

During those days women went from one shack to another, asking for home cures, for broths and teas extracted from bark and herbs, that might cure a misery in the chest. They placed onion poultices over their husbands' chests at night and set a brew of red pepper, sugar and vinegar on the back of the stove to simmer, for word had gone around that it would relieve a congestion in the lungs. Once Nettie Pugh borrowed two dollars from her neighbors and walked to Gauley Bridge after Dr Robinson. She had made four trips after the company physician, but when he finally arrived he only examined Roger's eyes, listened to his chest, left a bottle of pills and departed.

"I gib' him dem a'ready. It don't do him no good."

"Give him some more."

That night Nettie had lain awake, listening to Roger's rough, labored breathing, lifting him up in bed when he seemed in danger of choking. The following morning she took the ninety cents left from his last pay, borrowed the rest and went for the old doctor who had served Gauley Bridge for years before any industry but mining had entered the ancient valley.

Robinson's examination was thorough, and Nettie, standing at the foot of the bed, watched him with wide, patient eyes.

"It's something they get in the tunnel," the old doctor stated, pouring out a bottle of reddish-yellow medicine. "I haven't been able to find out what it is yet. It may pass, but I don't think so. Meantime this will give him some relief."

As soon as Dr Robinson climbed back onto the highway, leaving the torn, patched shacks of the Jungle behind him, women fled across the cluttered yards and into the shanty Pugh and his wife shared with another couple.

"What he say?" they asked anxiously. "He gib' you somethin' fo' Rogah?"

Nettie held up the slender bottle, allowing the light to glisten through the shiny fluid. "It's to relieve him," she declared. "It's to stop the misery."

"Can you get mo' at the drugstore?" a lean, hard-boned woman asked. "We ain't no cash money to hire a regular doctah, an the company man just gib' me them black devils."

Proudly Nettie got a teaspoon from the cigar box on the table and frugally drained a dose from the bottle. The women watched her, grave-eyed and silent, and as Roger swallowed the medicine they looked toward him expectantly as if he might suddenly sit bolt upright in bed and toss the covers aside.

When his breathing eased he settled tiredly back on the pillow, and they fled from the house chattering and exclaiming over the miracle as profusely as if a permanent cure had been effected.

While the lung trouble increased, becoming more prevalent each week, drilling inside the tunnel was sent swiftly forward. Men waited outside the openings each time the shifts changed, and if a man did not show up they were taken on for a day. They grabbed at the chance, too stunned to speak, and went inside the great tube in hushed silence, wanting the others to know that they were not stealing another man's job, wanting to show the company that they were hard, willing workers.

If, as was sometimes the case, a man missed a full week's work, his ticket was taken from him and a new man was hired permanently. In that case the family was evicted from the company's house, where they had been compelled to live. Some left the valley, walking back over Route 60, and others dragged their few belongings into sheds or barns, waiting for the day their man would again be well and able to join the gang that waited outside the openings in the hopes of picking up a day's work.

In all the openings the digging was pushed forward at an ever-increasing speed. Each crew was fully manned, and as the tunnel was widened to forty-six feet, necessitating the removal of a greater amount of stone, the long, deep shaft became saturated with the dust which hung perpetually in the air. Sixteen drifter drills were now in use, churning up the fine powder as they bored farther and farther into the solid rock, and following the repeated blasts thick, impenetrable clouds rolled through the tunnel unendingly, finding no dissipating air.

Jim Martin, who began as a chucker carrying steel points to the drillers, was made a mucker during the second week in May. He worked on the bench immediately behind Long and the other men who handled the sinker drills, boring the twenty-four holes straight down. These were packed with dynamite, and following the blasting Jim and the others moved in, clearing away the stone and making a path for the shovel.

Here, at the innermost point of the digging, the tunnel was filled with "head" air, intensified from the dynamite smoke. This air, dry and dense with the constant flushing of dust from the drills, made the men sleepy and they would drowse incessantly, their heads dropping forward like a droopy, diseased chicken.

Hance McTeer, who had worked the zinc mines in Joplin, spoke to the foreman, suggesting that wet drills be used, but the man threatened to fire him, and after that little was said of the water hose which was strung along the floor. Wet drills were seldom used except on days when word was swept through the tunnel that the state mining inspectors were coming.

Weeks before, Lock had heard that a lookout was stationed near the opening to watch for the incoming inspectors. "It must be so," he told Tom Reip one evening as they walked the river path back up toward Venetta. "Ever time they tell us to hitch the hose on them fellers come through."

"The company knows al'right," Tom replied. "Turner Hatch— he's the foreman on the dump crew—he told me the company allus knows when they're due. I reckon they just keep the guard posted, so's they can work the dry drills right up until the time they see the inspectors comin."

Shortly after Jim had become a mucker word rushed through the tunnel that the water hose were to be attached to the drills.

Before the order had reached him Jim heard the call for water farther down the tunnel. At first he thought a motor might have ignited, but the alarm grew closer, louder, and his foreman stepped from the shadowy thickness. "Get some water on that!" he ordered. "Wet it down!"

Ahead he heard a voice calling to Long.

"Put the hose on them drills. Get 'em goin' now!"

The ceaseless tattoo stopped, coming like a loud, discernible silence. After a moment the drills began again, deadened and purling, lacking the high, shrill biting sound they had issued before.

A damp coolness passed through the tunnel and the air began to clear a little, although the difference was not much. Twenty minutes later four men came up the dinkey tracks, their faces covered to the eyes with protective masks.

"Here they come," Long called down to Jim. "Don't feed the monkeys!" he smirked facetiously. "Don't pinch the apes!"

The strong stench of exhaust fumes had lessened considerably, and the moist coolness pressed the finely particled dust back against the walls until it was possible to see as far as twelve or fourteen feet.

The inspectors passed on to the heading, examining the ceiling for loose rocks, watching and measuring the amount of work being done by each pair of drills.

After a few minutes they left, silent and wordless behind the masks that fitted tightly about their mouths and nostrils.

Work went on unbroken for nearly twenty minutes before Jim heard the call echoing along the tunnel again.

"Throw the hose off! Get the drills goin'."

Nearer it came, and his own foreman called, "Kick that hose back against the wall."

Ahead Lock and the others were given their orders.

"Throw that hose off! No more wet drilling!"

"Goddamn," Long called back. "It sure smelled good for a little while."

Presently, as the drill holes dried, the dust began to float upward again, filling the partially cleared air and dissolving the drillers' figures in the milky whiteness until they could be seen no more.

By ten-thirty that morning, as the sun spread across the sidewalk and began to filter in through the front windows, Lessie Lee and Anna had set the tables for the noon trade and scoured the long counter that ran the length of the cafe. While they polished the worn, blunt silverware two men came in, threw their coats over a chair and found places at the far end of the counter.

"Coffee," the shorter one said. "Black."

"Make mine the same." The second, a thin, wiry man, pulled a pencil and a tattered envelope from his pocket in preparation for the figures he intended to use.

"It's not very hot," Lessie said, coming through the swinging doors with a gray zinc pot in her hand. "We don't do much this time of day."

"Well," the thin one said, flipping his hat back on his head, "can't you heat it?"

Lessie looked at Anna and calmly answered the man. "Sure," she said, "but that's a lot for a nickel. Besides, Mr Johns is using the stove. He's fryen fish, and that takes a lot of room."

The man reached over and placed his palm around the coffeepot. Unperturbed, Lessie held it forward a little, waiting for his reaction. "Make mine a coke, sister," he said acidly, smiling at Anna.

The second one shrugged his shoulders and bent over his figures. "Okay. Give me one too."

By the time Lessie had opened the bottles and placed them on the counter with the container of straws the two men had drawn together. The lean one talked rapidly, his pencil sketching the figures which he emphasized by making little circles of dots about them.

"The way I make it, we can buy 'em for a dollar ninety. Now," he said, beating a little tattoo with the point of his pencil, "we ought to get somewhere between two-fifty and three for them. Say two seventy-five. That gives a profit of nearly a dollar each."

"How do you know the company ain't goin' to supply them?" the short man demanded. "If the dust is as bad as they say it is, why the hell don't the company supply masks?"

"George, I told you a hundred times! They just ain't goin' to do it!" He said the words slowly, separately, emphasizing each one with a thump of his pencil. "I talked to three-four foremen. They say the company ain't interested in supplying masks. Says it costs too much and the men don't need 'em. I'm tellin' you," he ended, reaching for his coke, "we could sell 'em like rafts at a shipwreck!"

George sat silently contemplating the figures traced on the envelope. "It sounds too easy," he said skeptically. "Two thousand men working up there in that dust, and none of 'em got masks."

"Jesus, it's a setup. You put in the three hundred bucks, and I'll get the stuff and I'll sell it. I'd come in here on payday and just haul the jack in!"

"What if the company won't let you sell 'em?" The thick-shouldered man rolled his coke bottle between his hands thoughtfully. "What if they say nothin' doin'?"

"It's a free country, ain't it?" the short man demanded shrilly. "I'll sell them right out of a car, there beside the road. They can't stop that."

"I'll have to think about it. There's something fishy somewhere. How about consignment?" George asked, leaning forward. "Let's get a couple hundred on consignment. If we can't sell them, we'll ship them back."

The wiry man did not speak but studied his figures in awkward silence. "I tried that al'ready," he admitted reluctantly. "We can't get 'em without cash."

"Oh," George accused sharply. "Tryin' to squeeze me out, were you?"

"Why, hell, no! I told you right at the first that you were in on it. I wouldn't cross you up that way."

George stood up, got his coat from across the chair and drew it over his heavy arms. "Seems to me, if the company thought them men ought to have masks, they'd get 'em. Ain't no company takin' a chance on being sued like that."

"What's the inspectors and engineers wearin' 'em for?" Slim asked, his anxiety growing. "You just ask anybody how it is inside that tunnel. Christ, it's so thick you can cut it with a knife."

"He ain't lyin', mister," Lessie broke in. "When them men come out of there they look like they been workin' in a flour mill!"

"Say, girlie," Slim said, tossing a dime on the counter, "you got big ears, ain't you?" With a dark, reproving look he followed the stubby man through the door.

Anna, who had been folding paper napkins into neat triangles and stuffing them into a green water glass, quit and called to Lessie. "What was the matter with him?" she asked. "He sounded sore."

"I don't know," Lessie said, confused by the man's attitude. "I just said when the men come out of the tunnel they look like they all work in a flour mill. Now what's the matter with that? Honest, some men——"

"What were they doing, selling something?"

"I guess. That little weaselly one wants to sell masks, so the men won't swallow that dust when they're worken."

Anna paused, her head tilted thoughtfully to one side as she walked across to the counter. "Masks?" she repeated. "Do they make masks for them to wear?"

"That little one that talked so feisty, he figured he would buy some and sell them to the men. Seemed like he needed three hundred dollars so he could order them. That's a sight of money, ain't it?"

Laying the unfinished napkins down on the counter, Anna ran out the door and across the sidewalk to the Ford coupe that had already started to pull away from the curb. Lessie moved to the front of the cafe, watching her through the window. For a while she could see Anna's head bobbing and nodding as she spoke through the partially opened door. Finally she drew her foot back from the running board and re-entered the restaurant.

"Didn't they have none?" Lessie asked. "What'd you want it for, Anna?"

Anna settled down on a stool beside the unfinished pile of napkins, her thumbnail making a little clicking sound as she snapped it against her upper teeth. Caught by her thoughtful seriousness, Lessie waited, knowing that in time she would be awarded the information.

"He says there's enough dust to kill the men," Anna answered, her voice distant and low. "He says they ought to have masks. They're workin' with dry drills, and they ought to have masks. He says they'll get potter's rot——"

"Potter's rot?" Lessie asked, her voice large and resonant in the empty room. "What's that? We never had nothin like that where I come from."

"It's something the men get when they work where it's dusty. The ones that make pottery, they get it, and miners sometimes."

"Oh," Lessie supplied, "you mean consumption!"

"They get that too. But this is something else." Absently she began to fold the napkins, the edge of her hand pressing each into a flat triangle. "I'm goin to get Pete one. He's had a cough all winter."

"I'll get one for Mark too!" Lessie cried anxiously. "He's got a birthday comen soon. I'll get him one for his birthday!" Suddenly she halted, her head twisting a little to one side. "Would it be al'right, Anna, to get him one for his birthday? What do they look like? I don't want to get him something that just looks like nothing a-tall."

"I don't know what they look like," Anna replied soberly. "Maybe like the ones they used in the war. They had some at the Army and Navy store in Carbondale. The kids bought them to play with———"

"Do you think it would be better to get Mark a tie?" Lessie went on, placing catsup and mustard jars along the counter. "A tie seems like a more choosey thing———"

Anna wheeled about on the stool and placed her folded arms on the counter. "Look, Lessie, I want you to think about something. Them men talking, it worries me———" Her voice was constrained, each word revealing the growing apprehension she felt. "Lessie—you noticed anything bout Mark's eyes lately?"

Lessie studied Anna closely, trying to sense what lay back of the question. "They're just the same. Brown with specks———"

"No, no. Have they been red around the edges? Do they burn—does he ever say?"

Lessie thought a moment and then plunked three catsup bottles down in a group. "Now that's a funny thing!" she exclaimed. "Just last Saturday, when I met him out there after work, he said his eyes was hurten. I swore he went to the movies, and he swore he never did. I never thought nothin about it, but I reckon he never, 'cause Mark, he don't lie———"

"Did you look at them?"

"Well—yes."

"Were they red around the rims, like he'd been crying?"

"Yes, sure! That's how they were. Just like when a kid's been bawlin. I never paid no 'tention. I figured Mark'd tell me if he was a mind to."

"And, Lessie," Anna went on quickly, "is Mark short of breath? Does he breathe hard, through his throat?"

"Bless my soul, he does that too! Anna, Anna, is there anythin the matter with him? What's maken it, Anna?"

For a while the long somber room was silent, and presently Anna went on, speaking almost to herself. "It's the same way with Sam Givens," she said. "He never had that wheeze when he first come here. Now, when I'm sittin and writin his letters, you can hear him breathe all over the place."

"And that Mister Owens—the one they call Cherry Valley. That man's got thinner'n a bean pole. A good wind would sweep him right off the place."

"That's what's causin it, sure as the world," Anna broke out suddenly. "It's that dust. I've got to get Pete a mask or he'll come down with t.b. I've seen it in Carbondale——"

"Lord, do you reckon Mark's catchen it?" Lessie asked fearfully. "You don't suppose he'll be spitten blood?"

She stopped, halted by the quiet slamming of the front door. Neither girl spoke, each one struggling to recognize the rather short man who limped slightly as he approached the counter, a friendly smile revealing his well-repaired teeth.

"Hello, there!" he called to Anna. "I don't suppose you thought I'd be coming through here again before spring?" Carefully he removed his coat and spread it across a chair, the sleeves neatly aligned.

"Why, Mister—er—er——" Anna floundered, going toward him.

"Hathaway," the man supplied. "Hathaway, the last man you do business with."

"I'm glad to see you again," Anna went on cordially. "Lessie, this is Mr Hathaway. He's the one that brought Pete and me into Gauley Bridge."

"Oh—how-ja-do?" Lessie smiled. "You sellin something too?"

"Yes," Anna interposed. "He sells—uh—embalming fluid. The stuff undertakers use."

As June gave way to the first hot days of summer the hundreds of workers who had been brought to Gauley Bridge began to move more freely. On their arrival during the late summer and autumn they had looked upon the pronged valley strangely, for the town had distrusted them, thinking them migratory and parasitic, and in turn they were isolated, having no standing in the community, no reason to expect any treatment other than that which the company fostered for them.

But, being workers whose roots began with each job they could find, they had turned during the winter toward one another. Men who had run from place to place, asking and begging for work, always alien and strangers in their own country, passed one another on the road and spoke, glad that they had been able to settle down for a while. Even Hance McTeer and Ralph Owens came to know what it meant to belong to the hundreds of men who had made Gauley Bridge their home. Separated from their families, they became a part of a new community, and passing on the street or in the post office, they spoke, aware that they were intruders who could never erase the animosity which was felt toward them.

In the Jungle and four camps where houses had been constructed of jerry stripping, in Venetta and Gamoca, in Gauley Bridge and Old Gauley the tunnel people knew their neighbors and went from one open door to another, visiting, talking.

As the growing days of spring had advanced Maw Reip, Daisy, Mrs Tucker and Mrs Stump had often gone against the hill together, a basket or paper sack in one hand and a sharp knife in the other. Through the morning hours they would move across the fields like grazing cattle, cutting the tender poke stalks, sheep's tongue, wild mustard and dandelion. When they had garnered enough of the tender stalks for a meal they headed back toward the dark miners' shacks, anxious to get the greens on the table for their men.

Walking side by side, they told of the homes they had known, of the cabin above Cranberry Creek where Daisy had been born, of towns where the Stumps had lived, of trailer camps and mining towns, and through it all they talked of a time when they would be settled again, solid and secure.

"Virgil, now," Maw related one morning. "He's allus talken bout us gitten a place. And Ely too. The boys is just like Tom, talken and plannen bout haven a place to call our own."

"That's nice," Mrs Tucker, a stringy, weary-voiced woman said. "My young'uns ain't got so much getup to them. They're all hankerin to get days' work, so they can go to the moven pictures. That's all I hear from one day's end till the next."

"Virgil wants to get took on," Maw admitted reluctantly. "He's named it over a hundred times. I was agin it, count of all the men gitten that cough, but Tom talked to the foreman and he said it never meant nothin."

"Lock's a mite better," Daisy offered. "He gets out of doors more, and that cough is lettin up. Just of a night, now and again, he gets a spell."

They stopped talking, each in turn holding up a strand of the rusty barbwire fence for the other to pass beneath.

"These greens oughter help," Mrs Tucker said. "We been liven out of cans the blessed winter. A man needs some fresh stuff. Leastways he gets puny if he don't get none."

"When me and Hank get to Floridey," Mrs Stump declared, "we're goin to have a fresh garden the year round. I seen in a magazine where a fellow can grow just 'bout everything he needs right outside his door. There ain't no winters there, and the sun shines ever blessed day."

Mrs Tucker dropped back, falling in step with Maw who brought up the rear of the little parade as it followed a diagonal cowpath down the hillside.

"You fixen to let Virgil go to the tunnel?" she asked. "Is he goin to get took on?"

"I ain't sure in my mind yet," Maw replied. "Tom, he 'lows it won't do him no harm, but I ain't sure in my mind yet."

Whatever reluctance Maw felt was diminished and erased by Virgil's insistence when the school term was over a few days later. Reaching home, he put his promotion card away and stored his books in a box beneath the bed. From that time on he talked ceaselessly of getting a job. Turner Hatch, the foreman with whom Tom had spoken, paved the way, and on Monday afternoon following the close of school Virgil returned with the news that he had secured a job and was to report for work the next morning.

"I just don't know what to say, Tom," Maw confessed that evening. "I wouldn't stand in his way a-tall, but I'm afeered was he to work all summer and get to maken steady money he wouldn't want to go back to school in the fall."

"He'll be goin back, I reckon," Tom reassured her. "He don't talk bout much else but gitten to that school in Montgomery."

"If he just worked a while," Maw went on, unwilling to give her final consent, "mebby he wouldn't catch the cough."

"The boy wants to make a little money of his own," Tom said, "and I s'pose he oughter. 'Member last Christmas how he shut up and left the house when he never got to give no presents. It hurts his feelin's for Ely and Mark allus to be given him a little. He figures he ought to earn a mite for hisself. A young feller allus feels like that."

"Well, if I was sure in my mind he'd go back to school in the fall——"

And so it was decided that Virgil could accept the job Turner Hatch had gotten for him, and Tuesday morning he went into Number One, carrying steel to the drillers on the first bench as Jim Martin had done when he had gone to work the previous December.

But Maw never fully agreed in the depth of her mind, for repeated talk spread through the clumps of workers' houses that more men were dying in the camps. Five had already died in Number One, the rumor said, and although the doctor had diagnosed them as pneumonia and consumption, Maw never forgot the dread and apprehension she felt that first morning when she saw Virgil leave the house with the others, his lunch wrapped in brown store paper and tucked under his arm.

With the coming of summer, when the work was speeded up despite the fact that the construction company was far ahead of their schedule, Maw, working about the yard or in the garden, sometimes heard the ambulance clanging up the road past the schoolhouse toward Summersville. She would stop, watching the olive-green car until it disappeared up the valley out of sight, her mind tortured by the blunt, oppressive foreboding.

Those who lived in the Jungle or the houses scattered against the hill above Gauley Bridge heard the impatient clangor more frequently, for the men, crippled as well as ill, were brought down from the camps and past their doors on their way to the hospital in Montgomery.

A day rarely passed when the undertaker's new ambulance did not go to one camp or the other, clattering its way between the opened-door shacks, and then came down the hill past the first opening of the tunnel, past the Jungle, past the Kanawha Cafe and drew up to the curb on the opposite side of the street. People paused on the sidewalk, waiting for the stretcher to be unloaded.

"Somebody get killed?"

"Nope. 'Nother nigger died."

"Pneumonia?"

"I suppose. Stand back a little."

"I heard one of them got caught in a stone crusher. Feller said it damn near chewed him up."

The two Wayne boys carried the sheet-covered stretcher across the sidewalk and into the temporary office.

"I heard about that," another said. "They got him down at the Coal Valley Hospital. This one died in bed."

"Pneumonia, eh? Probably out shootin' crap all night someplace."

The green-curtained door closed and the people passed on down the street, some remarking about the incident, some saying nothing.

During the third week in June Owl Jones became aware of the pain which broke in spasms across his chest and reduced his already impaired breathing to a laborious, struggling gasp. For days he tried to treat himself, climbing out of the bunk each morning to rub his chest with salve before going down to the tunnel, but he could bring no relief to the pain that doubled his neck forward in a sluggish, hacking cough.

Popeye had gone for the doctor the first day Owl missed work, and that evening Stringbean had gone again. Still the man did not come, and when Owl's choking spells grew worse on Saturday night he got up from bed at eight o'clock, pulled on his overalls and headed down the road. He walked slowly, not afraid but with the careful movement of one who is hurt and dares not antagonize the wound.

Reaching the village, Owl sought the Higgenbottom boarding-house and found his way around to the rear door. For a while he leaned against the wall, trying to control his breath, then, removing his cap, he knocked softly on the door.

A burst of yellow light shot out into the late gathering darkness and the plump woman stood back, holding the door wide.

"What do you want here?" she demanded irritably. "I've fed enough of you——"

"Mistah Legg home?" Owl asked, nodding his head a little.

"He's in bed. Go on away."

"I got to see him," Owl hurried on anxiously. "Please, ma'am, tell Mistah Legg Owl is here."

"Is there anything the matter?"

"No, m'am."

"Well, what do you want him for? He might be asleep."

"I'll be much obligeed, ma'am, if you see is Mistah Legg asleep."

Reluctantly she closed the door, and Owl could hear her slow steps disappearing down the hallway and then her voice calling, "Mr Legg! Someone to see you—round back!"

Receiving an answer, she returned to the kitchen but did not open the door again.

Presently Owl heard footsteps crossing the room and the door opened, revealing Long clad in his pants and partially buttoned shirt.

"Mistah Legg——"

"What's the matter, Owl?" Long asked, stepping out onto the little porch. "You in trouble?"

Owl fumbled for a moment, trying to co-ordinate his words.

"I been sick, Mistah Legg, and the doctah won't come."

"Did you send for him?"

"Fo'-five times."

"That sonuvabitch!"

"I come to see you, Mistah Legg. I thought maybe you'd go with me, so's the doctah would examine my ches'."

"What's the matter?" Mrs Higgenbottom called from where she humped over the kitchen table, a Sunday tabloid spread before her. "What's he want of you?"

"I'll be right down, Owl," Long said, ignoring her. "We'll go see that bastard right away."

"Yes sir, Mistah Legg. Yes sir." From the darkness Owl's voice came, grateful and warm.

An hour later Owl climbed the hill again, taking the steepest parts slowly, walked down the road before the shacks where the children still played in the lighted doorways and turned in at Number Five.

"What'd the ole sawbones tell you?" Honey Boy asked as Owl crossed the room and sagged down on his bunk.

"I'll bet he give you them black devils!" someone called from an upper bunk.

Stringbean sat up, his broad, grinning face toward Owl. "Bet he said you was bullin' round too much!" he chortled. "Bet he said you bettah stay away from the wemmin!"

Owl opened the bottle of medicine and placed it to his large pink-blotched lips.

"What's that?" Honey Boy asked. "What's that doctah say you got?"

Owl replaced the cork, pushing it in hard with the heel of his hand, and stuck it in his pocket.

Unused to the sight of liquid medicine, the men gathered around, curious and interested.

"What's the matter with you?" they continued to ask. "What did the doctah say you got?"

Owl raised his head tiredly. "He say I got tunnelitis. Dat's what he say."

"Tunnelitis?" Honey Boy said thoughtfully. "I never heard tell of no tunnelitis."

"Dat's what he say," Owl repeated. "Mistah Legg done took me down there, and the doctah say I got tunnelitis."

"We ain't got nothin' like that in Alabama," a tall ebony man vowed. "No sir! We ain't got nothin' like that!"

"Tunnelitis?" Stringbean exclaimed. "Boy, you got somethin' I never heard tell of!"

"Dat's what I got," Owl repeated again. "The company doctah tole me to open my shirt. Then he listened to my ches' and tole me to button up my shirt. He give me this medicine and he say I got tunnelitis. Yes sir, he say I got tunnelitis."

Early on the following Sunday morning Mark Reip left the house in Venetta to meet Lessie for a picnic. The sun had just climbed above the hill and was streaming down into the valley when he started for the Bridge. Daisy Mullens, who had gone early into her garden to gather leaf lettuce and green onions before the cool of the morning left the ground, saw Mark heading toward the path and called after him.

"How's Ely?" she inquired, shaking the loose dirt from the onion roots and dropping them into her caught-up apron. "He any better this mornen?"

"He don't seem so bad," Mark answered, his brown hair still shiny and wet from the wash pan. "Maw give him some of that stuff you told her about, from the drugstore. I reckon he'll go out in the mornen."

"Yore paw al'right?"

"Yeah, he's hoein in the garden."

"That's good," Daisy said, squatting down beside the long yellow-green rows of lettuce. "He oughter get all the sun he can."

"I'm goin to be out the whole day!" Mark declared, heading toward the path. "I'm goin way back on the hill." He made the statement loudly, his tone giving it a special emphasis.

"How's yore girl, Mark?" Daisy asked, pinching the leaves off near the ground. "Is she goin with you?"

"Sure! Sure she is."

As Mark went down the river path Lock ambled through the kitchen door, his shirt opened from the neck to the waist. In its gap the hair showed black against his white chest and his arms were thin and sinewy beneath rolled-up sleeves.

"You want me to help you?" he called.

Daisy shook her head. "Get a chair and set in the sun," she suggested. "Take yore shirt off and set in the sun."

Indolently Lock dragged a stool through the kitchen door, propped it against the dark wall of the house and sat down, tugging his shirt from inside his trousers.

"What if Mis' Stump was to come round here and see me?" he asked humorously. "I'm half naked!"

"It wouldn't scare her none," Daisy remarked dryly. "She's got a man of her own."

As though his entire body was filled with a heavy lethargy, Lock leaned back against the building, his head hung a little to one side and his chest pressed forward to meet the hot sun.

"That'll do you more good than medicine," Daisy said, starting toward the kitchen with her filled apron. "A-body can just feel the sun doin 'em good. Of a spring Maw used to make us young'uns set in the sun. She allus said we had to dry out after the winter."

Lock allowed his head to roll to one side, feeling the warmth against his neck. "I reckon yore paw got him out a good patch of taters," he mused drowsily. "This weather'll shoot 'em up like weeds."

His words came slowly, softly, for his entire body was filled with a lassitude he had not been able to throw off with the passing of spring. Following the days when Daisy and Maw Reip had spaded the small garden patch Lock had planted his seed corn, carefully estimating the hills and adding four or five corn beans to each one. Daisy had watched him, glad and anxious to see him working the soft ground, and then, unaccountably, his interest had slackened and he walked heavily along the rows.

"It seems like I ain't got no getup to me a-tall," he had explained repeatedly. "I'm wanten to do it in the worst way, but I just ain't got no getup any more."

Gradually Daisy had taken over the planting and hoeing. At first Lock protested, but his own body was lethargic and weighted, and if he did attempt to work over and back the small tract, his energy was soon exhausted and he sagged down on the kitchen step to catch his breath and rest his numb, tired shoulders.

Sometimes, when his old strength seemed to return and his voice boomed through the shack, Daisy thought she would tell Lock that during the coming January or February they might expect a child, but some unnamed dread always held her back. Seeing the loose way his trousers hung about his thin hips or the boniness of Lock's arms, she would be filled with fear and dreadful apprehension. Each time Daisy was glad she had not mentioned the child, for she knew after that Lock would never miss a day's work as long as he was able to stand on his feet.

Now, on Sunday morning, as the sun climbed the sky and crowded the bare doorway with its light, Daisy filled a pan with potatoes and brought a chair out into the yard to sit beside Lock while he dozed contentedly in the sun.

"You reckon, Lock," she offered, "I oughter rub yore chest with lard and turpentine? This sun would melt it right in."

Drowsily he shook his head. "This is fine."

Placing the pan of potatoes on her chair, Daisy reached over and drew the sides of his shirt back, uncovering more of his body.

"Good Lord, woman!" Lock cried protestingly, "you'll have me naked as a jay bird!"

"It wouldn't do you no harm," she replied, picking up the pan again. "The sun's the best thing a-body can get."

"It sure feels good," he agreed easily, rubbing a hand over his warm, hairy chest.

"If we was back home and you worken in the fields, you'd be brown as bark by this time," Daisy said. "Land, when you first come to see me Maw said you was just like a Indian, but she allus liked you though. Her and Paw both."

Lock tilted back, his head against the jerry stripping. "We'll be seein 'em afore winter comes agin," he said. "Way we got things planned, we'll be headen back round the end of November."

For several minutes they sat, quiet and wordless in the still morning sun. A young speckled robin flew between the shacks, squawking and protesting, and attempted to light on the clothesline. It flapped and wobbled uncertainly and dropped into the knee-high corn, rattling the leaves as it went.

"Lock," Daisy asked, "whyn't we just head back, one way or t'other, when November comes? We'll get by someways, and we'd be a deal better off back there." Lock did not answer, and Daisy waited, watching his still, immobile face that shone redly in the sun. "The hills will all be turned," she went on, "and it'll be dry and clear, with the nights comen sharp——"

There she halted, seeing Lock's head had fallen sleepily against his shoulder. Daisy let her hands settle down into the partially filled pan of potato peelings and her eyes became fixed in her head as she stared down between the shacks, beyond the road, toward the shiny surface of Gauley River as it flowed down to join the Kanawha at Gauley Bridge. No feeling seemed to cross her face, no emotion, but as she picked up another potato she sniffed loudly and pulled one hand across her eyes.

While June warmed to July, blanketing the hills with a dark green sameness from which the last splash of laurel and mountain pink had gone, the powdered, fine dust, billowing from the openings of the tunnel, spread over the grass and over the trees, leaving them bone gray and blanched beneath the sun that hung over the valley. When it rained the leaves were splotched but the coat of dust was never washed away, and by sundown the following day their mottled surface was again concealed beneath a new layer of dust.

A man walking through the grass left a little trail, as though he walked over a frost-covered land.

The water buckets were covered with a piecrust layer, and men tried to dip it off when they drank and blow it back from their lips when they finally brought the cup to their mouths, but it never really worked. They could feel it, fine as flour in their mouths. The hair in their nostrils and ears was covered with it, and it colored their eyebrows and lashes gray, making their eyes seem like damp pools in their bone-colored faces.

When they came from the tunnel the colored men were covered with the dust, and from a little distance they could not be distinguished from the white men. They stood together outside the openings, beating the dust from their clothes, thrashing it into little clouds that spread over the gray earth. Arriving home, they still made a little trail of it across the floors, for the dust was fine and seemed to come on forever, like the sifting of a house that had been mud filled at floodtime.

It was a thing they could never rid themselves of, and some of them carried their own drinking water in a milk bottle, and some of them put cotton in their ears, and they all worked with their mouths closed for they did not want to swallow the dust.

On humid, breathless days men would keel over from inhaling the torpid, ladened air inside the tunnel.

Once, when a shower hung dark and threatening above the stifled valley, extra help had to be called to carry men out of the tunnel. From four in the afternoon the air grew sluggish, moist and damp after the hot, sticky day. Yet no rain fell, and by the time the night shift went on the air was humid, clinging to the ground, since no breeze came over the river to stir it into motion.

Inside Number One the smoke from the engines was like a suspended blue-gray cloud that threaded its way through the ever-present milky dust. The men moved sluggishly, fetid and warm, their clothes clinging moistly to their bodies.

The gas engines, hauling crushed stone from the hole, left monoxide behind, the exhaust adding more fumes to the burnt gas which could not escape from the tunnel.

Just before nine o'clock a driller on the first bench, where Jim Martin worked during the day, straightened up, gasping for air. His head went back, his mouth forming mute, soundless contortions, and then he fell over. A chucker, carrying steel farther up toward the heading, found his body laying across a drill that whined and throbbed endlessly.

"Man down!" he yelled, peering into the wall of dust through which no figure could be seen. "Help! Man down!"

The foreman brought two muckers and they carried the man out of the tunnel, stretching him on the ground against the bank above the opening.

"Must a-been the gas," one suggested, seeing the man's pale, bloodless face.

"Yep," the foreman said sympathetically. "Go call the ambulance."

As he started to re-enter the tunnel he saw one man carrying another across his shoulder, staggering a little beneath the weight.

"Two more just went down," the mucker explained, lowering the man to the ground. "Better get some help in there!"

"It's them fumes," the foreman cried, running into the sparsely lighted tunnel. "The air's heavy and it hangs in the hole."

Before the ambulance had sped up the highway and turned off onto the torn, dust-whitened strip where trucks were loaded and unloaded four more men were added to those awaiting attention.

At eleven o'clock the rain had not yet fallen. The air, torpid and with no sign of a breeze, continued to lay like a weight over the ground. Inside the tunnel the fumes increased, and the dust, thrown up by the drills that tore their way into the solid rock, remained suspended like a fog brought to sudden, complete inanimation.

Muckers, working nearer the engines, became louder in their complaints, calling again and again for water to relieve the tight dryness in their throats, hoping that its coolness would diminish the throbbing pound at either side of their foreheads.

The walking boss ran through the tunnel, already aware that his men were dangerously in need of relief and knowing that no fresh air was entering the fume-filled tunnel.

"Walk some of 'em to the opening," he ordered the foreman. "Send 'em out two at a time. When they get some fresh air bring 'em back and send out two more."

"They're gettin' sick," Turner Hatch called after him. "I ought to take 'em all out."

"Jesus Christ, man!" the walking boss shouted, disappearing into the mist, "we can't shut the whole thing down!"

Before he had reached the heading, relaying his instructions from one foreman to the next, five more men keeled over where they stood.

As the men were sent out in relays the emergency lessened, until presently several minutes passed before the call, "Man down!" sounded through the dust. But off and on the cry came all during the night, and the following morning, when the walking boss made up his slip for the office, he marked off a total of twenty-eight men who had been carried from the hole during the night.

On an afternoon during the same hot, muggy week the news was first learned that the contractors had made provisions with Howard C. Wayne for the burial of men who died in the camps or were killed in the tunnel. Since late spring the deaths had increased, and with the ambulance going daily up to the tunnel and back, Anna and Lessie Lee began to hear the first rumors of the contract Rhinehart & Dennis had made with Wayne.

When Wayne, a florid, raucous man with broad yellowed teeth, had first opened his branch office in Gauley Bridge little was said since he was well known both at the Bridge and in Summersville, the county seat of the next county. Previously there had been no undertaker in Gauley Bridge, and with the incoming hundreds of workers it did not seem remarkable that some industrious man would open up a parlor.

Soon after Anna and Lessie had overheard the two men discussing their plans to sell protective masks to the workers at the tunnel they heard the first mention of the agreement which had been made with the undertaker. Anna did not tell Pete, for in an insidious way the rumor disturbed her and she did not want to state it as a fact until she was sure.

During those early weeks each time the ambulance returned from the tunnel she always ran across the street, waiting for the stretcher to be unloaded. Pressing through the crowd, she would examine, with a frightened quickening of her heartbeat, the face of the man being carried into the funeral parlor. Sickened at the sight of the bruised, torn figure on the canvas cot, she would find her way back to the cafe and drop onto a stool at the counter.

If the ambulance bore the prone figure of a man who had died in his home, the crowd would quickly dissolve and amble away. Knowing most of them, Anna often spoke, walking slowly back to the cafe.

"What was the matter with him?" she would ask.

"He had the same thing. Tunnelitis, they say."

"What's that?"

"Somethin' they get workin' up there."

Anna's face would become drawn and still. "Do they always die when they get it?"

"Don't ask me, lady. I never heard of it. Looked to me like he'd had cancer or somethin'. Wasn't nothin' but skin and bones."

"Tunnelitis," Anna repeated quietly.

"Yep, that's what the company doc calls it. 'Course, if you was to ask me, I'd say they was just workin' them men to death. Specially the niggers."

"Lots of them seem to be dying," Anna said. "They brought one down from the camp at Lover's Leap yesterday."

"Who's buryin' them? That's what I'd like to know. It must be costin' somebody a purty penny."

"The ambulance always goes up past Venetta," Anna pointed out. "Someone said that Mr Wayne had a graveyard over in Summersville. I don't know for sure though."

As the weeks moved on and sedge turned brown beneath the hot sun, as Honey and Cane branches dried up, it became well known along the street before the cafe that Howard C. Wayne, the undertaker from Summersville, had made an agreement with the company to dispose of the dead.

Anna told Pete, and the following afternoon, leaving Number One opening, accompanied by Long and Jim Martin, they fell to talking about it, for Jim, too, had heard the report.

"Sure t'ing," Pete declared, knocking the dust from his long-legged overalls. "He's goin' to bury 'em. The company fix it up."

"What the hell do you mean?" Long asked, beating his cap against his knee. After he had cleaned it he brushed the gray dust from the hair above his ears before he placed it back on his head.

"I heard the same thing," Jim said, starting up the path toward the shoulder of the highway. "A couple steel men told me. Said they heard it down at Jessie Bail's last night."

"Let me get this straight," Long said, falling in step beside Pete. "The company's got an agreement with this feller to lay away everybody that dies on the job? They already told him that?"

"Sure," Pete declared, "Annie tell me. That guy Wayne, he's goin' to bury all the dead men. Evertime he get good money, huh?"

"A fellow told me it was fifty dollars," Jim offered. "Fifty smackers for everyone he puts in the ground."

"Jesus," Long declared, "that's cheap enough."

"Sure t'ing," Pete replied. "The company say he'll get a lot of 'em so he say he'll do it cheap. That's what Annie tell me."

A shrill, sharp whistle broke from Long's lips, rising a little at the end. "Jesus!" he exclaimed.

"The company went out lookin' for someone to do the job, the way I heard it," Jim continued. "No one else would promise to bury them so cheap, so Wayne got the job."

"By God, that's an awful thing," Long declared. "Like tryin' to find someone that'll haul garbage cheap!"

"Step right up, fellows, step right up!" Jim cried mockingly. "Get your bids in. There's plenty of work here—plenty of work for the lowest bidder!"

"You don't make fun," Pete said solemnly.

"Hell, why not?" Jim retorted, finding his way along the edge of the highway. "Say, I should of got a bid in. I could put you guys in a box and stick you in the ground for ten bucks a throw—and still have money for beer on Saturday. *James Martin, Undertaker.* Say, that'd look pretty nice on a glass window."

They were all silent as two cars passed, rattling across the railroad tracks and dropping down toward the Jungle.

"I wonder," Long asked presently, "I wonder what the county 'lows for buryin' a pauper? Suppose a guy dies and he ain't got no money and no folks. What's the county pay for stickin' him in the ground?"

"A fellow told me thirty-five bucks," Jim said. "Some old geezer died in a shack down at the lower end of Gauley, and they paid thirty-five dollars for him."

"Christ," Long surmised, "that don't give this guy Wayne much extra, does it?"

"Maybe he's countin' on a lot of business," Jim said. "If the company can turn enough bodies over to him, he'll make plenty."

23

Maw Reip had gone to sit in the shade of a maple tree which stood at the far end of the garden, taking Ely with her. It was Sunday, and the stewing chicken was already simmering on the back of the kitchen stove, waiting for the dumplings which would be added when the sun reached the top of the sky. She settled back on one of the boxes Tom had carried home from the tunnel and began to string the bunch beans she had gathered from the three rows that ran across her garden.

Ely, stripped to the waist, lay sprawled on a tattered old blanket spread over the hammock he and Mark had made a week before. By lacing the staves of a barrel to two long parallel wires, the slightly concave sides turned upward, they had formed a crude hammock which stretched loosely from the maple to a post sunk in the ground a few feet away.

Maw worked silently, her knotted fingers unthreading the beans with quick, deft movements. Occasionally she tossed the beans about in her lap so the curled strings would sink to the bottom.

"Was you to stay home and rest another week," she said softly, "you'd stand a chance of throwen off that cough."

"I'm goin back tomorrey," Ely said, his lips barely moving. "I done lost four days' pay."

"There ain't no call to concern yoreself 'bout that," Maw reproved. "We got a mite put away, and Mark and Virgil and yore paw is worken steady."

For a while there was no sound over the yard but the low buzz of a bee making its way through the cucumber blossoms. Maw watched it, hearing above it the drone of a car across the river, and gathered up another handful of beans.

"I been thinken, Ely," she said. "We oughter get us a cow. If they was plenty of milk on the place to drink and good fresh butter, maybe it'd help——"

"You must have said that ten hundred times," Ely muttered indolently. "You been talken 'bout a cow since way last fall."

"I never wanted to cut into what we got laid aside," she confessed quietly, knowing the statement was old and worn of meaning. "Case we come on bad trouble, it wouldn't be all used up."

"Paw says you oughter get a cow," he added, wiping a hand across his sweat-moistened chest. "Why don't you get a cow?"

"I don't feel right about it in my mind," Maw said. "In part you boys helped earn that money. It'd worry me sick was we to use it and then a time was to come when one of you needed it bad."

"Get a cow," Ely said, dropping a leg over one side of the hammock. "You could always sell her if there was a need."

"I thought 'bout that, too, son," Maw said. "And maybe I could sell a little milk and butter to the Stumps and Daisy. I ought to near get enough to pay for her feed when the snow's on the ground."

"Get a cow, Maw," Ely repeated, blinking at the sun. "You been wanten one since the Lord knows when."

Maw looked at him, seeing the way his rib bones had neared the surface and the sunken hole between his neck and collarbone. "It would be nice if we had a cow," she mumbled. "That stuff you get in a can don't seem to have no real good in it. It don't seem to stick to yore bones." She paused, seeing that Ely was sinking drowsily into a nap. But in her mind she finished the statement, saying over and over, "Thin as hoe handles. They're all gittin thin as hoe handles. Even Tom, he's losen the flesh right off his bones."

Silently, as she turned the slender beans in her hands, Maw recounted the money hidden inside the mattress, estimating, figuring, knowing to the cent how much was concealed inside the heavy padding. Beside it she had placed another little sugar sack containing Virgil's scant savings, for in her mind she always kept them apart, thinking that he would be going away to school someday, thinking that he would be studying to be a teacher. The thing never quite seemed to be an actuality in her mind, but she would touch it, count it and set it aside, thinking that; thinking it forever but never really knowing how it was to happen.

Maw had finished the beans and thrown the strings into a clump of Jimpson weeds back of the outhouse when Mark came through the kitchen door and walked toward the shade of the maple.

His brown chestnut hair was damp, and above the open throat of his clean blue shirt his face was scrubbed and white. He had not been able to buy a suit yet, but his cheap cotton pants were neatly pressed, one leg being creased a little off center and showing a yellowish-brown trace where the iron had scorched. He moved across the yard with a soft, rolling step, his feet unaccustomed to the heelless sneakers that showed white and clean above the coal-darkened ground.

"You leaven a'ready?" Maw asked, gathering up the kettle of broken beans. "Tain't hardly noon yet."

"Yeh," Mark answered. "I'm goin now. I'll wait downstreet till they're ready." He walked slowly about, waiting for Maw to pass judgment.

"You got yore clean handkerchief?" she asked, eying him closely.

"Yep."

Maw settled the kettle of beans on her hip, speaking softly so she would not arouse Ely. "Ain't you wearen yore cap?"

"No, Maw. The fellers don't wear tem."

"Seems funny, goin out on Sunday bareheaded."

"They don't wear 'em," Mark repeated.

"Where's yore swimmen suit?"

Mark opened his shirt, showing the blue cotton suit that stretched over his chest.

"You'll burn up," Maw said.

Ely stirred and abruptly sat up, dragging a hand down over his thin face. Mark backed away, hoping nothing would be said.

"Lookit him," Ely cried derisively, "all sheiked out!"

"I don't like to see you goin off on a picnic without taken nothin," Maw said. "It don't seem right."

"Anna and Lessie is bringen everythin," Mark explained irritably, having said it many times before.

"Whatta you got on yore lip?" Ely asked, getting stiffly from the hammock and taking a few steps toward his brother. "Peach fuzz?"

"Shut up!"

"Gosh, if you kissed a girl with that, it'd tickle her to death!"

"Maw, make him shut up."

"Don't you go gitten out over yore head," Maw went on, ignoring the plea, "and get back here before dark."

"Get a picture of Lessie in her swimmen suit," Ely said condescendingly. "If she looks like much, I'll be down to see her."

"Ely!" Maw exclaimed. "Hesh that talk!"

"I'll bet she's flat-chested as all get-out."

"You shut up!"

"Mark, you go on over the river," Maw broke in. "Yore clean enough, I reckon."

With a sharp backward glance Mark followed his mother down into the dark cool doorway. Seeing that Ely was not following, he came to the point quickly. "Maw, I only got sixty-five cents left."

"That's a-plenty."

"No it ain't, Maw. Just let me have fifty cents. I'll give it back Saturday sure."

"Mark, we just ain't got it to spare," Maw began somewhat wearily, and then her voice rose accusingly. "You ain't spent two dollars since yesterday evenin, have you?"

"Maw, I just need fifty cents. I want to buy pop all around."

"Landsakes, we could live half a week on two dollars," she declared. "I don't see what you do with your money."

"Please, Maw. Pete's goin to bring bananas and oranges. That's how we got it fixed up."

"Sixty-five cents is enough for bottle pop," Maw said, pouring water over the beans. "A great plenty!"

"Aw, Maw . . ."

"Not another cent," Maw declared, shaking her head. "If she's goin to spend yore money like that, you hadn't ought to be seein her——"

"Please, Maw. I'll pay you back!"

"Here, runt."

Turning, Mark saw Ely's thin body framed in the doorway, his bare shoulders red where the sun had struck them. "Here. Don't buy any wooden nutmegs."

In a quick movement Mark accepted the money and headed for the doorway. Leaping out, he ran across the yard and down the road. For a moment Ely stood in the doorway watching him, then crossed the room and dropped tiredly on the bed.

"You'll spoil him, Ely!" Maw charged lightly. "He had a-plenty."

Ely smiled back at her and suddenly sat upright, his shoulder pitched forward as the low cough started in his chest and crowded its way out through his throat.

By the time Lessie and Anna had finished work at one-thirty Mark's clean blue shirt was damp with perspiration. Standing beneath the overhanging roof of the gas station, he jiggled from one restless position to another, his mind filled with worry. The pop he had bought an hour before was already sickly warm and one corner of the sack was soaked and torn.

Disconsolately he attempted to pick it up, thinking he would return it and get a new one. As he grasped the wrinkled sack the bottles rattled threateningly, clinking a little against the cement.

"Howdy!" Lessie cried, coming up unexpectedly behind him. "You think we was never comen?"

"Where's Pete?" Anna asked, shifting a large towel-covered basket to the other hand. "He was here a minute ago."

"He went to the drugstore," Mark managed, embarrassed by the bottles that slipped from the bottom of the torn sack. "He's comen right back."

"Land, I just can't wait to get in the river!" Lessie squealed her delight. "Lookey, Mark, I got a new suit!" Reaching inside the collar of her dress, she hooked the shoulder strap with her thumb, exposing a thin strip of red woolen material. "It's got green on the bottom."

"It's purty," Mark stammered awkwardly, squatting to retrieve the bottles.

"Well, come on, let's go," Lessie urged, gesturing with her hands. "We'll be sweaten like horses if we stand here!"

"Here comes Pete now," Anna said. "You all go ahead. We'll catch up."

"Sure, come on, Mark."

"Al'right." Slipping the spread fingers of either hand in from the sides, Mark attempted to gather up the bottles. They clinked and rattled, slipping from his grasp.

Anna reached down, gathered up Pete's sack of fruit and went out to the sidewalk to meet him, swinging the heavy basket toward him with a free, strong movement of her arm.

Lessie bounded along beside her, squealing and exclaiming over the food. "Chicken and coleslaw!" she cried. "Laws, we got a bushel! And there's enough sandwiches to fill a barrel."

"That's fine," Pete said. "Now we go and swim, huh?"

Alone, Mark fought with the bottles. Gathering the top of the paper sack together, he inverted and refilled it with bottles. As he sought to crowd the seventh one into the sack it ripped, and they all clattered to the cement, chipping at the edges. Hot, feeling his shirt cling and draw over his shoulders, he tried to retrieve the bottles in his folded arm before his awkwardness could be discovered.

"Mark! Come on!" Lessie cried from the far side of the gas station. "I'm dyen to get in the water!"

Helplessly he began to retrieve them again, standing the red and orange and purple bottles together and trying to grasp them in his hands. He caught a half dozen, but the rest bumped together and fell over, sounding loud and clumsy on the deserted street.

"What's the matter, Mark?" Lessie cried, running back. "You're a regular cow's tail!"

"Go ahead," Mark urged forlornly. "I'll catch up."

"What's holden you—" Standing above him, her feet wide apart, Lessie placed an outspread hand on each hip. "Well, for the Lord's sake!"

"Go on, Lessie," Mark pleaded, embarrassed. "I'll catch up!"

"Why didn't you say somethin!" Squatting down, she grabbed an Orange Crush and a bottle of grape. "Lord a'mighty, they're as warm as baby water!"

"Go on, Lessie," Mark begged. "I'm comen!"

Hearing the strained, beseeching voice, Lessie's attitude quickly changed.

"There's a whole world of time," she said. "You just wait, I'll fetch something." Running into the cafe, she returned with an empty cracker box and began helping Mark place the bottles inside. "I never knowed yore sack give out," she apologized. "I wasn't thinken of nothin but gitten in the river."

When they had finished Mark gathered the box up and they started through beneath the overhanging roof. Longingly Lessie looked at the cooler, thinking they should exchange the warm bottles for chilled ones, but she said nothing.

"Come on, let's catch up," Mark said, not looking at her. "Yonder they go."

They walked rapidly, feeling the hot pavement beneath their feet. Once, as a car passed and he stepped off the road, Mark bumped into Lessie, jouncing her with the corner of the box. He looked at her, smiling stiffly, apologetically.

"We'll put 'em in the river," Lessie said quickly. "When we get up there we'll just dump 'em right in the water."

"Sure," Mark said gratefully. "It'll keep 'em cool."

Nearing Pete and Anna, they slackened their pace. "You swim very good?" Lessie asked. "I can't."

"Not hardly a-tall," Mark admitted. "Slaty Creek wasn't very big. I never had no chanct to learn."

"Me neither," Lessie said. "I can dog paddle a little, that's all. But Anna, her and Pete is good swimmers. They learned in Pennsylvania."

"I'd like to learn," Mark said, shifting the cracker box to his other hip. "And to dive too."

"I'll bet you can learn easy," Lessie said. "I'll bet you anything."

After they had crossed the railroad trestle, smelling the hot pitch that oozed from the ties, and found their way along through the shade of Cotton Hill, Lessie and Mark followed the path that led from the railroad tracks down through a dump of willows and syca-mores to the little sandy stretch along the riverbank, where Pete and Anna stood looking out over the clear green water.

"Land," Lessie declared happily, shaking the front of her dress to stimulate a breeze, "it's cool as church down here!"

"Let's go in quick," Pete said. "We get cold."

"Sure," Anna said, glancing about. "We'll swim and then eat later. What do you say?"

"It'd take horses to keep me out of there," Lessie cried. Hurrying up the bank, she disappeared behind a shining laurel bush. Before he could turn away Mark saw her yanking her dress over her head, her arms waving above the dark green leaves.

"Come on," Pete said. "We go over there."

Beyond the flood-washed log where they had placed the food Pete and Mark stepped behind a large sycamore and began to pull off their clothes. Turning his back, Mark slipped out of his trousers, took off his shirt and sat down to remove his shoes.

"Come on, slowpokes!" Anna called. "We're ready."

Anna and Pete rushed into the water, kicking it into a white foam. As it reached their knees they plunged headlong, rose to the surface and swam a few strokes.

"Not very deep," Pete said, getting to his feet, disappointed. Standing waist-deep, he gestured for Mark and Lessie to follow them. "Just up to here," he said, holding his hands against his stomach. "You can swim fine."

Anna rolled and plunged in the water, splashing and churning it with her heels as she headed upstream, swimming on her back.

Hand in hand, Lessie and Mark waded into the stream. Beneath her bright yellow hair Lessie's scarlet suit shone brilliantly as they left the shade of the bank and waded into the water. Beside her Mark's thin suit hung limply from his narrow shoulders, and he kept tugging at the sides in an awkward attempt to conceal his reluctance and uncertainty.

"Don't be 'fraid," Pete called. "She's no deep. Come on, I show you how swim."

As the water crept up about her thighs Lessie began to walk on tiptoes, hesitant to let it touch her body. "Gee, it's kinda cold!" she squealed.

"No," Anna said, standing shoulder-deep in the pool. "Get wet all over. It's fine!"

Releasing their hold on each other, Lessie and Mark studied the water before them. As his muscles drew tensely toward his shoulders Mark ducked his head a little and threw himself forward, holding his nose.

Squealing shrilly, Lessie followed, scrambling immediately to her feet.

"Gee, that's fine," Mark called, throwing himself in the water again, slapping the surface with outthrown hands that sought furiously to keep him on the surface.

"Come out here," Pete called. "You swim fine!"

"Don't you do it," Lessie cautioned. "You stay here, Mark. That's too deep."

Mark looked back, laughing, and cautiously made his way out toward the main current of the stream.

"Come on," Pete urged. "You too, Lessie."

Like a contented seal Anna swam busily up and down the stream, traveling in a longer path, her strong firm arms knifing the water with slow assurance. Reaching a large boulder, she would turn, float downstream again and then swiftly make her way back.

Chugging and paddling, Mark reached Pete's side, his neck craned far out of the water and his feet touching the bottom every few strokes.

"Mark," Lessie cried, "come on back! I'm afraid."

"It's not deep," he said, standing up. "See!"

"No. But it's swift."

Ignoring her, Pete stretched out his arms. "Come on, I teach you," he offered. "Lay down. I hold you."

"Don't take him out any further. Anna, don't let Pete take him out."

"He won't," Anna called back. "Pete'll watch him."

"Now," Pete said as Mark came to rest across his arms. "I hold you. You swim."

Industriously Mark began to kick and paddle, his arms and legs thrashing the water to a white foam.

"No," Pete said. "You work too much. You drown me too!"

For a while he manipulated Mark up and down the stream, urging him to relax and work his arms and legs in a flowing, smooth rhythm.

Presently Mark began to tire, and Pete stood him on his feet, gasping for breath, and started up the river, half wading, half swimming toward Anna, who had climbed atop the boulder and was resting with her arms outthrown beneath the hot sun.

"Come and set down," Lessie invited, smacking the water beside her. Several feet from the shore she sat in knee-deep water, wiggling her toes luxuriously and, ducking her head beneath the water, timorously opened her eyes.

"You can see clear as day," she declared, rising up. "And it makes your legs look like they are wigglin."

Mark sat down beside her, panting heavily. "Pete's goin to show me some more," he said. "He's a good swimmer."

"You swim pretty good too," Lessie said. "But you better rest some."

They sat tilted back, the cool water flowing and curving about their bodies. Out in the stream Pete was clinging to the side of the boulder, trying to get Anna to join him. Playfully she kicked his hands free each time he grasped her, and presently Pete shoved himself away from the boulder, floating on his back out into the stream. He swam aimlessly about until, seeing another large white stone twenty or thirty yards across the main current of the stream, he turned and started to make his way toward it.

"Look!" Lessie cried, half getting up. "Pete's goin out in the river!"

"He's a good swimmer. Set down." Mark reached up, caught her hand and laughingly jerked her down.

"The water's swift out there," Lessie went on, "and it's deep as anything."

Anna, drowsing in the sun, made no move.

"He can make it, I bet you," Mark said. Moving one foot over, he allowed it to catch Lessie's, the toes knuckling down like the fingers of a hand. "I got you," he said. "You can't move!"

Lessie chuckled briefly, but her eyes did not leave the river. Approaching the current that moved rapidly through between the boulders, Pete was being carried downstream. His arms began to slacken their rhythmic movement, tugging harder as they rose from the water.

"I'm worried," Lessie said, getting up. "Look, Mark! Look!"

"He's al'right," Mark said uncertainly. "Pete swims as good as a fish."

Impulsively Lessie took a step forward, her eyes fast upon Pete. Suddenly she saw one arm thrash the water and then the other fumble. In a split second Pete's head seemed to rise a little, his arms slapping out over the water.

"Look, Mark! Pete's—— Look! Anna! ANNA!" In one breath her voice rose to a loud, terrified shriek, for Pete's head had disappeared beneath the water. "Anna! Oh God! Pete!"

Instinctively Anna jumped to her feet, her eyes moving rapidly over the surface of the water. For a moment she faltered, unable to locate Pete.

"There! Anna! Over there!"

Mark ran forward, wading deeper into the stream.

"Mark! Wait! Mark!"

Anna's body arched, bent through the bright sun and slid into the water, rising some yards farther out in the stream. Rapidly, evenly, her strong arms broke the surface and, sped on by the current, she swam swiftly toward the place where Pete's arms were thrashing frantically.

"Hurry, Anna! Hurry, hurry! Oh lordie——!"

Mark waded forward, backed up a few steps and started out again. Lessie hurried after him, half falling as she lunged to grab his blue swimming suit.

"No, Mark! You'll drown too! Don't! Don't!"

"Let go, Lessie. Let me go!"

As Pete went down the second time Anna reached the spot, treading slightly but allowing the current to carry her downstream as it would Pete. An arm rose above the surface and, humping her body, Anna disappeared beneath the water.

Paralyzed with fear, Mark and Lessie stood staring at the swift current.

There was a churning, thrashing of water and both bodies returned to the surface together. As they watched, Lessie saw Anna's head move backward, traveling with a jerky, fitful movement.

"Anna, come on," Lessie pled, foolishly extending an arm in an effort to reach her. "Come on—come on, Anna!"

Slowly, laboriously, Anna made her way backward, her left arm under Pete's shoulder and across his chest. As they escaped the main current of the river, several yards farther downstream, Lessie and Mark whirled about, splashed to the shore and raced through the underbrush.

By the time they reached an opening in the brush Anna had already got to her feet, supporting Pete with her shoulder, and they were slowly making their way to the shore.

Anxiously Mark stepped into the water, wading out to meet them.

With Mark's help Anna got Pete to the shore and lowered him to the ground. Dizzily he shook his head, pounding each side with the butt of his hand. His mouth hung open, and his breath, coming in harsh gasps from his throat, sounded like a repeated, exhausted plea for help.

"You—al'right?" Anna asked fearfully, urging him to bend his head forward.

Slowly Pete nodded, choking and coughing.

"My wind—I lose it all," he managed. "I choke."

"You went too far," Anna said. "It's swift."

"No. My wind. I couldn't breathe. I choke. It hurts here." He thumped his chest with his hand.

"What, Pete?" Anna asked, kneeling down beside him. "What hurts you, Pete?"

"It makes me choke bad," he gasped. "I almost drown—I get dust from tunnel——"

Anna started to speak but halted, and slowly her head turned aside and she looked up at Lessie, her eyes large and terror-filled as the import of Pete's words reached her mind.

"You just got tired, Pete," she cried. "You're just tired!"

"No," he said. "No. I got it. I can no swim no more."

24

August remained hot. No breeze moved over the river to stir the air, and it hung over the valley, sluggish to breathe, reflecting the dry, dancing heat. The path which wound through between the shacks in Number One camp was inch-deep with dust, and children, playing during the morning hours, left deep feetmarks with little ridges of dust separating the toes.

Early in the month the spring back of the camp dried up and water had to be carried from the valley below. On Monday mornings women jammed their washings into bushel baskets, crossed down over the highway, found the path, and, passing the opening of the tunnel, searched for a place along the riverbank where they could do their washing.

A few of them, not wanting to drag their children through the brush, washed near the opening, spreading their clothes over the willows. After they finished they bathed their children, drying them with bare hands beneath the hot sun, and washed their own dust-speckled ankles. While their clothes dried they gossiped, sitting in the flood-washed stones. Finally they got up and folded their clothes into the clean baskets. As they gathered up each piece they shook and snapped it to remove the thin layer of milky white dust which had settled over it.

Of a morning Owl Jones brought an old galvanized bucket down with him. Coming off the shift at six o'clock, he went to the river, brushed the film of dust aside with his hand and carried a pail of water back up the steep incline. Walking the highway, breathless and tired, he stood looking at the sharp incline of the short cut but trudged on up the pavement, taking the longer way home.

As he reached the shacks one evening Owl came upon a pile of household furnishings in the dry, trampled road. Approaching slowly, he saw Jeff Wall and his wife sitting on a packing crate just beyond the disheveled stack of belongings. Beside them their two children stood, strangely silent and immobile. The whole road was hushed, the people moving slowly, cautiously toward the Walls as though they anticipated some danger.

"You leavin', Jeff?" Owl asked, placing his bucket down on a backless chair.

For nearly two weeks Jeff Wall had been ill, confined to his home. The company doctor, thumping the man's chest, had diagnosed his case as tunnelitis. Since no credit was ever extended to them at the commissary where their daily pay tickets were cashed, the Walls had been short of food before Jeff had been in bed a week. After that the neighbors helped, giving two pounds of soup beans, a can of corn or whatever they could afford.

In the middle of the second week Slat McCune had walked through the open door and stood at the foot of the white, scarred iron bedstead.

"When you gettin' back on the job?" he demanded. "You been out nine workin' days now."

"Just soon's I can get up, cap'n," Jeff replied. "I'm wantin' to get back in the worst way."

"You get back in the mornin," Slat instructed. In the doorway he paused, his back to the silent, fearful room, and then ambled down the road to the place he kept near the boardinghouse, where the men were allowed to shoot crap and play poker for twenty-five cents a head.

The following morning Jeff Wall climbed from bed and attempted to make his way down the hill path. Just below the highway he faltered, wavering unsteadily, and eased himself down onto a stump. His breath was agonizing, coming in jerky, forced spurts, and a crippling pain tore its way across his chest.

The next day Jeff was worse than he had ever been. The shack was hushed and still, and the children, playing in the road, ran swiftly home when they saw Slat McCune wobbling his way down between the houses.

"He's comin'!" they cried fearfully. "He's comin' agin!"

Wordlessly Mrs Wall backed away from the door, taking her stand near the bed. Fixedly they watched the door, waiting for the broad, darkening figure to appear.

By the time Owl made his way slowly up the hill, carrying the pail of water, the Walls sat in the road, their few shabby possessions tossed into a pile at the end of the path which led out from the door of the shack.

"Whassa mattah, Jeff?" Owl asked, placing the water on the chair.

The man looked at him, his eyes mute and dull.

"De rouster was here," Mrs Wall supplied mournfully. "He t'rowed us off the place."

Jeff nodded his head, his lips working hard against each other but emitting no sound.

"He put you outta the house?" Owl asked.

Sure now that McCune was gone, other neighbors crept back, muttering helpless sympathy.

"He say we gots to get off the lan' b'fore night," Jeff said numbly. "If we don't get, he's gone to 'rest us fo' trespassin'." As he spoke Jeff shook his head, not sorrowfully but as if paralyzed by his inability to answer the question he repeatedly asked himself.

"When it get dark you come to my house," a woman offered. "We got a little bit of room."

"He say we can't do that," Mrs Wall said, fitting a tin skillet inside another and wrapping them in a corner-tied sheet. "He get yo' man fired if he catch us livin' with you."

"You gots to go someplace. You man's sick."

"He say we gots to go back where we come from," Mrs Wall repeated helplessly.

A short, broken sob came from Jeff's throat and his body shook convulsively. The children, seeing him, ran to their mother, squatting down in the road beside her.

"If we could on'y do that," Jeff cried to the ground. "If we could jus' get home, so's I could die with my own people."

The neighbors closed in silently, their eyes on Jeff's humped-over figure. One spoke, and then their suggestions came rapidly, one following the other, but their words held no reality. There was fear behind them and back of that the cold, relentless knowledge that other families had been sent from the hill, dragging their belongings with them.

"Stringbean," Owl said, "he's bad sick too. We're tryin' to send him home, but we ain't the cash money."

They all looked at him, knowing what he meant, and began to break away, hurrying across the dusty road and into the weathered, unpainted shacks.

"I gots thirty-five cents," a short stocky woman said, returning with her hand held out before her. "I can't gib' no more. That's all got."

"Here's sixty," another said. "That most makes a dollah."

One by one they offered their contributions, piling them on an upturned box beside Jeff's mute figure.

With his thumb and forefinger Owl dug into the watch pocket of the trousers he wore beneath his overalls and laid a dollar bill on the box.

Just as he bent to pick up his water a woman on the outer fringe of the crowd spoke in a low, forceful whisper. "Yonder comes the rouster!" she warned. "Yonder he comes!"

With a studied casualness the people moved back, lining up against the shack walls, talking in hushed tones and carefully avoiding the plump figure of Slat McCune as he came down the road kicking up a fine spray of dust that caught and hung about the tops of his shoes which were laced only halfway to the ankles.

"Get that stuff out of here before night," he ordered, hardly breaking his stride. "If it's not off the place, I'll burn it and haul you in for trespassin'."

Jeff Wall raised his head, saying nothing, and waited for the man to pass.

Slowly the neighbors moved in again, watching the road and spitting their oaths down toward the ground in tense, mounting resentment.

Arriving back at the shack, Owl discovered that Stringbean had grown weaker during the day. In the hot, fetid room he lay stretched on his bunk. Sweat streaked down his face, causing it to shine, and his eyes were yellowed inside their red rims.

"You want me to bring you some supper?" Owl asked, setting the water on the cracked, potbellied stove. "I can fetch it when I come back."

Wearily Stringbean rolled his head on the soiled pillow.

"Mebby," Owl suggested, "they will gib' me some soup in a bucket."

Again the man's head rolled on the pillow, his cavernous cheeks glistening. "The rouster was here," he muttered softly.

"What he want?" Owl asked. "What he say?"

"He say I gots to go to work," Stringbean managed. "I gots to be on the job tomorrey."

"You ain't goin' to work! You'd die sure." Thoughtfully Owl pinched his lips, silent beneath an obstinate problem. McCune arrived each morning, he knew, pounding on the door and driving the men out to the job. At the shacks like Number Five he flung the door open, snapped on the single light and beat his club against the corner of the bunks, calling for the men to roll out. Later he returned, before the night shift came in, making the same rounds, checking to see if any man stayed in bed.

"You gots to go away," Owl said, speaking almost to himself. "You stay here you goin' to die sure."

"I can't travel my way home. I ain't a nickel."

"You better start down the road. You'll be dead if you stay here."

"If I leave I'll die anyway," Stringbean said. "I'm too sick to get up."

An hour later Owl came back from the long bare room where the unmarried men ate carrying a fruit jar filled with kidney beans in a thick brownish-red broth. As he fed them to Stringbean, urging spoonful after spoonful into his mouth, he outlined the plan which had slowly worked its way through his mind.

"I'll take you out in de mornin', afore de rouster comes," he said. "I know a place agin the hill. I'll come up and fetch you back when I get off the job. McCune, he ain't goin' to know you ain't workin'."

Tiredly, almost indifferently, Stringbean accepted the plan. Just before daybreak the following morning Owl crept from his bed and quietly helped the thin man to his feet. Noiselessly they made their way through the door and along behind the row of clapboard houses.

At the far end of the row they hesitated, Stringbean leaning heavily on Owl's shoulder.

"We can go on now," Owl whispered, seeing that there was no movement in the road between the shacks. "Us head up for them brush right yonder."

Having crossed the clearing and concealed themselves in the undergrowth, they made their way slowly up the side of the little knoll and along its crown. At the far end a wall of jagged rocks rose upward, topped by a dense clump of hemlocks and cedars. At the base of the small cliff Owl led Stringbean through hazelnut and rhododendron bushes and halted beneath an overhanging ledge which extended eight or ten feet out from the cragged wall.

"You'll rest fine here," he said, lowering the man to the ground. With the toe of his shoe he kicked away the stones and sticks, forming a smooth bed of soft shale. "Just you sleep, and I'll come fetch you back this evenin'."

By a devious path he found his way back to the shack just as the others began to crawl from bed. Some mentioned Stringbean, saying his name quickly and with alarm, fearing he had died during the night.

"I don't know. I ain't seen him," Owl vowed in elaborate concealment. "I don't know a-tall——"

His words were stopped by a loud pounding on the door, and Slat McCune stepped into the foul-smelling, partially lighted room.

"All out," he demanded gruffly, his face still webbed with sleep. "Get rollin'!"

Without expecting an answer he passed from one bunk to the other, jabbing the crumpled, soiled bedding with his mace. Swearing loudly, he went out, and the men could hear him beating the doors of the other shacks as he made his way down the uneven row.

When his shift came off at six o'clock that evening Owl had got his water and was nearing the highway before he noticed that several men were gathering in a sprawling, attentive group beside a Ford coupé parked between the white guardrails and the hard surface of the road.

Approaching them, Owl stepped farther out into the road, hoping to pass as unobtrusively as possible. As he came abreast of the group he saw that two men near the center were in an angry, heated argument.

One, a thin, quick-moving fellow, stood on the running board of his car holding a pair of hoodlike contraptions in his hand.

"Get those damn things in that car and get out of here," the other man commanded, facing the smaller one belligerently. "Who gave you permission to sell them things around here?"

"I don't need permission," the wiry one protested shrilly. "This is a free country. I'm on the state road. This is a right-of-way——"

"I'm deputy sheriff, and I said to take them damn masks and get the hell out of here before I lock you up!"

"Why can't I sell them to the men?" the thin one demanded uncertainly. "They can use 'em. They only cost two-fifty!" He said the last quickly, looking to the men lined along the guardrail. "Two-fifty is a good price for a mask like this!"

"I wouldn't give you two-fifty for every nigger on the job!" He paused, shoving the slim one back against the car. "Now get in there and get goin' before I pinch you for peddlin' without a license!"

The wiry one held on, fumbling behind himself for the door handle. "Hey, give a fellow a break," he pleaded. "I bought all these things. I'll lose ever cent I got. Besides, the men need the protection."

The deputy placed his hand against the man's chest. "I'm through talkin'! Get in there and get goin' or I'll crack your skull open!"

Arriving at the shack, Owl set his water bucket down, found the path which ran along behind the buildings and, watching his chance, crossed the clearing when the road was quiet and empty in the late evening sun. Gaining the scrub growth, he found the base of the knoll, plodded up the small ridge and headed directly toward the dark clump of rhododendron, calling Stringbean's name as he went.

Ahead he saw the slender frame stretched on the ground, several feet away from the soft shale where he had left him.

"Stringbean!" Owl whispered hoarsely, dropping to the ground. "Wake up, Stringbean! Wake up!" Suddenly Owl's voice grew louder, and he bent low over the man's form.

Stringbean's heavy lips were parted slightly and his eyes had rolled backward and a little to one side. Impulsively Owl touched his face, spreading his palm over the forehead.

"Oh, dear Jesus," he gasped, jerking his hand back. "Oh, Lord Jesus!"

For a while he knelt beside the figure, muttering and mumbling incoherently. Then, in the darkening shadows, Owl slipped one arm beneath Stringbean's shoulders and one through behind his knees and lifted him unsteadily from the ground.

Crossing the ridge, he dropped down the knoll, feeling his way cautiously, came through the brush and, carrying Stringbean like a child in his arms, Owl reached the clearing and cut directly across it to the road which led through between the double row of shacks.

For a week Maw had slept fitfully. Both Tom and Ely were home sick, and no night passed when one or the other did not awaken her with his coughing. On Friday night she crept from bed several times, propping Ely up with a chair and pillows to relieve the choking congestion which threatened to halt his breath. Once, in the weak light, she saw Tom's eyes follow her across the room, and Maw stopped in the middle of the floor, frightened by the dumfounded terror she saw in them.

"You ailen, Tom?" she asked hoarsely. "Does yore breathen hurt you?"

Silently he shook his head, gesturing toward Ely with a limp hand.

"You'd best watch the boy close," he said. "He seems to be choken all the time."

Bending down over Ely, Maw raised his body a little, settling him back on the propped-up chair so that he rested in a half-sitting, half-reclining position.

Ely barely answered, the words coming from his throat on the burdensome breath he seemed to drive from his lungs.

When she had fixed the covers, tucking them tightly about his meager form, Maw slipped back across the room and lay down on the bed beside Tom. The shack became soundless, filled with darkness and the lumpy outlines of furniture. For half an hour she lay rigidly still, fearful of disturbing Tom's inconstant sleep. Her whole being was charged with a numb horror which took no form and which she could not name. Lying motionless, her ears alive to Ely's and Tom's harsh breathing, she felt the flesh along her thighs begin to jerk spasmodically as though it shrunk from some inward coldness. Whimpering a little, Maw clenched her jaws together, struggling to make no sound. Cold perspiration began to drip from her armpits and run in single drops down over her sides.

Caught in the dark, night-filled room, afraid and helpless with her fear, Maw pressed her tongue against her clenched teeth, struggling to hold back the cry which nearly broke from her throat. The old memory of the mud-splattered sycamore came back to plague her mind and she tried to shove it away, to free herself from its unnamed torture as she would seek to release herself from some tightening pressure that threatened to crush her skull.

Many times Maw clamped her jaws so hard her head shook, and then she would grow tensely still, holding herself rigid, afraid the thing which throbbed through her head would disturb Tom's unsteady sleep.

Presently Ely crouched over, gagging; his breath was coming in lumps. Maw was halfway across the room before she was fully aware that she had heard him, and then her blunt hands grabbed his body, holding him erect, his head tilted forward a little.

"Ely!" she cried. "Ely, cough up!"

He made no sign of an answer. Maw began to pummel his back with the heel of her hand, speaking his name over and over again.

As the choking ceased and his breath returned Ely sagged back against Maw's arms, limp and exhausted with the repeated spells that shook him.

"Is he al'right, Nettie?" Tom asked, attempting to sit up.

"I don't know, I don't know!" Her words came quickly as she tried to ease Ely back against the impromptu rest. Tucking the covers about him, Maw ran to the cooking stove and hurriedly stirred up a fire.

"I'd best fetch the doctor," Tom said. "He may take a turn for the worse."

"You stay abed. The night air will start you coughen agin. I'll call the boys." Placing a kettle of water over the blazing, open stove cap, Maw went into the other room and hastily roused Virgil and Mark.

"Get yore duds on," she whispered urgently. "Ely's worse. You'll have to fetch the doctor from the Bridge."

The two stared at their mother, seeing the thin hair stringing down over her worn face, and sprang from bed. Grabbing up their clothes, they rushed into the kitchen and dressed before the stove.

The fire roared up the flue, diminishing the cold autumnal air that came in off the river.

"Ely been coughen bad?" Virgil asked.

"I reckon he's took a turn," Maw said, her lips tight across her teeth. "Fetch the doctor with you. Run now! Tell him there's no time."

Dragging their clothes on, Virgil and Mark gaped at the bed in the corner where their brother had slept since the day he left the tunnel at noon, wheezing and weakened, and found his way back to Venetta.

"Don't leave till you get him, Mark," Tom called from the large double bed. "If the company doctor don't answer out, go straight after Robinson. Don't waste no time."

As Maw picked up the teakettle to fill the wash pan with hot water a low, suffocating moan came from the corner of the room, followed by a deep, rumbling cough which never seemed to escape Ely's throat. The pan rattled on the stove as she fled across the room.

Virgil and Mark stared after her, frightened, and then ran through the kitchen door, over the road between the dark houses and down the riverbank to the stump where the rowboat was tied.

By the time Dr Robinson had parked his car on the highway and followed Virgil and Mark across the railroad track the lights were all lit in the somber shack which stood on high stiltlike supports on the upper side of the road that passed through Venetta. Rowing back across the river, they scampered up the path, circled about the Stumps's place and, urging the doctor on, ran toward home.

Even before they reached the kitchen door they could hear Maw's weeping, her grief coming in broken, agonized cries. Inside the door they stopped, seeing Viney, still dressed in her nightgown, standing in the middle of the room sobbing hysterically as she watched Maw's shoulders jerk and throb as she wept into her hands. On the bed Tom lay, looking at the ceiling, his gaunt cheeks wet where the tears ran down toward the ends of his black mustache.

Before the sun broke through the cloud of smoke and coal stench which hung over the valley the main room of the Reip home had been cleaned and scoured. Ely had been dressed and moved into the bed where Mark and Virgil slept, and Maw, walking numbly across the dark, damp floor, placed the breakfast things on the oil-cloth-covered table.

No one ate much. Obediently Mark and Virgil tried, cutting into eggs with the side of their forks, their faces lowered to avoid meeting Maw's wet, inflamed eyes. Viney May whimpered incessantly, unable to control her grief. Once she broke completely, a long, wailing cry coming from her throat as she ran across the room and threw herself down on the bed beside her father.

"Let her cry it out, Tom," Maw said lumpily. "Let her get it over with if she can."

Virgil and Mark went back to their untouched plates, suppressing the nausea the sight of warm fried eggs brought to their throats.

When Maw had washed all the other dishes she crossed to the table and looked down at the boys' plates.

"You better eat somethin," she said hollowly.

Dutifully Virgil picked up his coffee cup, barely touching the cold, milk-skimmed fluid to his lips.

"I ain't hungry, Maw," Mark explained. "You set down and rest. I'll clear off the table."

Maw gathered up the fried eggs, put them both on one plate and covered them with a bowl. Placing them on a shelf, she noiselessly washed the rest of the dishes. Each movement was separate and individual, none flowing together, and each held for a long while as though it brought some sad consolation.

Finally she took a damp cloth and cleaned the cracked oilcloth, scrubbing diligently at the stubborn spots. Mark and Virgil moved back, their. eyes helpfully following each movement of her hands.

"You and Mark had best go out," Maw spoke to Virgil. "Take Viney and go out for a while. I want to speak to yore paw."

Thankful for some direction which came from outside themselves, the two got up, helped their sister from the bed and went out the back door, closing it softly behind them.

For several minutes Maw said nothing. Getting a wash pan, she filled it with warm water, gathered up a strip of sugar sacking and a cake of soap and seated herself at the table. Methodically she dipped the cloth in the water, rubbed it over the soap and set to washing her face, lathering it plentifully about her neck and along the hairline.

Tom watched her, drawing the covers up about his shoulders, leveling off the side where Viney May had rumpled them.

"I reckon I'd best go right off and find a buryen place for him, fore the neighbors start comen in," Maw began presently. "There's one down yonder agin the hill above the town."

"Get a good one, Nettie. One where the sun shines good."

Maw nodded her head, absently letting the washcloth come to rest in her lap. "He was allus so good to the others," she murmured softly. "Given them spenden money and things, when he thought I never knowed."

"He was allus like that, wasn't he, Nettie? Member when he was a little tyke and they'd been playen there agin the hill? It was allus Ely that looked after 'em, maken elder whistles and bean-shooters——"

Abruptly he stopped, seeing that Maw's head had fallen forward onto her folded arms. At first her crying was only a low whimper, tight and suppressed, and then her shoulders began to jerk convul-sively and her wailing came like a great lump from her throat.

"Nettie . . . Nettie," Tom called from the bed. "Nettie, the young'uns will hear you."

Gradually, her body shaking with the effort, Maw halted her cry-ing, twisting about so she faced the wall.

"Likely Hank Stump and Lock will dig the grave." Tom hurried on carefully. "I'll send for 'em soon as they get home from work."

Before she answered Maw got up and placed the pan of water back inside the wash box. "It'd be real nice of 'em," she said, "but it hadn't ought to be dug afore tomorrey. It ain't fitten that a grave should stay open through the night."

"I was thinken that," Tom said. "Might be they could do it the first thing in the mornen."

"I'll see that man at the Bridge," Maw replied. "Mebby they got someone there to do the diggen."

Tom ran a bony hand across the covers, his eyes following it thoughtfully. "What time you reckon we ought to have the sarvices, Nettie?"

"Long t'ords noon sometime. Seems like that's the best time."

"I favor a time like that too, when the sun's well up."

Maw unfastened the hooks and eyes which held the front of her gingham dress and slipped it over her head. "I thought we'd have the sarvices here, afore we went on the hill. There'll just be a few of us to go up," she went on tentatively. "The main part will be here."

"I'm goin up," Tom protested firmly. "I'll get an early start———"

"You'd best not, Tom. You'd give out."

Blankly he watched Maw as she wiped her heavy shoes with a damp cloth, and then he spoke again, his words coming even and sure. "I'll go up to Ely's grave effen it's the last thing I do," he affirmed. "Me and Mark can get a soon start. We'll be there agin the time the rest comes up."

"It's too far, Tom. You'd wear yoreself plumb out. You heered what the doctor said."

"Nettie, I'm goin!" he declared. "Me and Mark can start afore the sun's up. We'll be waiten when you get there."

Maw crossed to the piece of mirror nailed to the wall back of the wash box. "All right, Tom," she conceded. "We'll see how yore feelin by mornen." Taking the heavy-toothed comb from the tin rack, she set to combing her hair, drawing it tightly over her skull and looping it into a small thin knot at the back. When she finished Maw got a little flour from the sack which sat on a paper-covered box in the back corner. Never having used powder, she applied it bluntly, patting it on her face and neck in little splotches and rubbing it over her coarse, wrinkled skin.

"Tom," she said, coming back to the bed. "Tom, they's been somethin worryen me ever since mornen."

"What, Nettie?"

Standing at the foot of the bed, she caught the iron stead with each hand, pondering her words before she spoke.

"It's bout—well, bout the funeral, Tom. It's somethin I don't know."

"What is it, now?"

Maw's face drew a little to one side, her eyes red-rimmed above the flour which showed gray over her ashen skin.

"I was wonderin if we oughter have the undertaker for Ely. We never had none back on Slaty, but"—she paused, the words growing heavy in her mouth—"but—I don't know just what it is, Tom, but I got to thinken if it'll help Ely any, mebby we oughter———" Suddenly she began to cry, her head falling into her open hands.

"I'm just wanten to do whatever on earth we can for Ely. I just want to be sure we're doin everything we can—Ely's the oldest an——"

Tom's lower lip drew in beneath his mustache as he pulled his hand across his eyes.

"Nettie, don't cry no more," he asked. "It tears the heart out of me. I can't get up out of here and help do nothin——"

Maw twisted partially away, catching her mouth with her hand and holding it a moment before she spoke.

"I been wanten to ask bout it sence fore daylight, and I never knowed what to say," she commenced again, struggling to control her voice. "I've heered a peck of things bout what they do, and it worries me sick. But if it's the best thing for Ely, I figure we ought to try someways to do it."

"It must be the best thing," Tom added hopefully. "Everybody down round here allus has the undertaker. We never had none back home, but that don't mean it ain't the best thing."

Maw straightened up, blinking her eyes in a hard way. "I heered they cost a sight fierce," she said.

"We can make out someways. You just go in and talk to him. We can make out someways."

Maw looked at him, her face eased by his reassurance, and started toward the bedroom. "I'll go down right now," she said. "Folks will be comen in soon."

Inside the bedroom she found her dark blue calico dress and the purple flowered one Tom had given her for Christmas. Holding the blue one in the fold of her arm, she carefully examined the other, feeling the material and allowing her eyes to run along the seams as if to check their strength.

Pulling the blue dress on over her head, Maw tucked the thin ends of hair beneath the knot at the back, got her dark coat and slipped her arms into the worn sleeves. Quietly, then, she tiptoed to the head of the bed and, getting down on her knees, searched along the end of the ticking for the opening she had made months before. As she broke the thread Maw held her hand against the mattress as though she was afraid of disturbing Ely. Slipping her hand inside, she withdrew the old leather purse, brushed away the few feathers that clung to it, got to her feet and tiptoed from the room.

"I'd best be ready if they want somethin down," she whispered to Tom, holding up the pocketbook.

Tom nodded, strangely silenced by her low tone, and watched her cross the room and go out the back door.

When Mark had set her across the river, leaving Viney May and Virgil standing sad-eyed and desolate at the corner of the house, Maw climbed up the riverbank and onto the state highway. She walked slowly, her feet rising and falling with a monotonous heaviness and her old sailor hat bobbing slightly to the tense rhythm of her body. A car passed and she stepped off the highway, scarcely looking at it. After it had gone she continued along the graveled shoulder, not remembering to return to the smooth surface.

Nearing the overpass, where the houses drew together forming the town, Maw paused, breaking the monotony of her steps for the first time, and drew a knuckled finger across beneath her eyes. Clutching the old purse close to her, she passed in front of the post office, through the shadow of the overhead railroad, and crossed to the far side of the street.

In the bright autumn sun her heavy coat seemed unwarranted, and people stared after her, seeing the black hat, the dark coat and coarse shoes, but when she had gone on they only looked at each other, saying nothing.

Reaching the dry-goods and notions store, Maw opened the screen door and stepped inside. A young girl standing behind the counter glanced at Maw's somber, dark clothes and came through a narrow passage between the showcase and the counter.

"May I help you?" she asked, unable to keep her eyes from Maw's drawn, vigil-worn face.

"I want some dye," Maw said. "I'm fixen to dye me a dress."

"What color would you like?"

"Black, if you got some."

The girl led her to a rack against the wall, pointing out the two brands filed in small slits in the frame.

"What kind of material is it?" she asked, explaining that the dip dye could not be washed.

"It's kind of a silk," Maw said. "It's my good dress."

"Rayon?"

"I 'low."

"What color is it? Some colors will show through, you know."

"Purple-like," Maw replied. "Almost as dark as elderberries."

After the girl had given her the box, carefully instructing her to follow the instructions printed on the container, Maw took a dollar from the old purse, accepted her change and went through the screen door, unaware that the girl had hurried to the window, watching her cross the street toward the point where an olive-green ambulance was drawn up to the curb.

Reaching the front of Howard C. Wayne's temporary office, Maw hesitated, tugging at the collar of her coat to be sure that the blue dress did not show. Then, straightening her shoulders and sniffing to clear her nose, she opened the door and stepped inside.

The room was dark and cool behind the heavy curtains. Maw blinked slowly, feeling the coolness about her eyes, and spoke to the stocky, florid man who approached her.

"I come to see bout buryen my boy," she said. "I come to see bout buryen Ely."

Lessie Lee left the courthouse in Fayetteville, slanted down across the lawn past a dying geranium bed, hopped onto the sidewalk and started back toward Gauley Bridge. As she reached the edge of the town she stopped, a little beyond the last gas station, and removed the pink-feathered Empress Eugenie hat which tilted precariously over her forehead. Tucking her black patent-leather pocketbook under one arm, she held the hat in her left hand so the other would be free.

For several minutes she watched for a car to leave the white cement of the village street and head down the dark asphalt highway where she waited. Idly she stood, warm in the autumn morning, smelling the goldenrod and withering asters that colored the fields to either side of the road. Once she saw a rabbit venture out to the edge of the road and she yelled at it, waving her pink hat. Startled, the animal shot its ears erect, throbbing with its own intensity. Reaching down, Lessie gathered up a handful of gravel, flinging it at the rabbit. "You want to get killed?" she asked reprovingly as it scuttled back through the field. "You want to get runned over?"

A green Buick left Fayetteville, its motor mounting to a high drone as it passed the town limits. Lessie's right hand circled upward and outward, indicating Gauley Bridge. The two women in the front seat eyed her curiously but showed no sign of recognizing her request.

Lessie watched the car out of sight, muttering indictment, and resumed her stance.

A few minutes later a Ford coupe rolled to a halt just beyond her, and Lessie overtook it before the tall, slender young man had opened the door.

"Goin' down toward Gauley?" she asked, slipping onto the seat.

"Yep," he replied, easing into second. "I'm going back to Charleston. Want to come along?" He laughed a little, looking at her across his shoulder.

"I'd sure like to, now," she said friendlily. "You live down there?"

"Yep."

Lessie laid her purse and hat on her lap and settled herself comfortably. "Nice day, ain't it?"

"Good enough, I guess," he replied, trying to pass over the cordiality. "What're you all dressed up for?"

"I been to the courthouse," Lessie explained. "I got my papers this morning. Boy, I'm telling you, that judge sure was nice."

"Papers?" he asked, scrutinizing her face. "What kind of papers? You were born here, weren't you?"

"Divorce papers," Lessie declared proudly. "And like the judge said, I'm well off to be shet of him."

He looked at her closely, allowing his eyes to run to the floor board where one black patent-leather shoe rested on the other. Thoughtfully he watched the highway for a short while, eased down in the seat and allowed his thigh to rest a little closer to Lessie.

"So you're a free woman, huh?" he said warmly. "Free and footloose again."

"I'm shet of him ferever, that's all I know," she replied. "And I'm telling you, that's a God's blessing!"

"I'll bet you miss him, don't you? I mean sometimes?"

"Heck, no!"

"At night, I mean," he went on, his eyes closing partially, knowingly. "You must get lonesome after having a man around——"

"I don't miss him no more'n I'd miss measles. Like the judge said, he never done a bloomen thing for me."

"Not a thing?" he chuckled, allowing his right knee to drop over against her leg. "You should have divorced him then!"

Feeling the slight pressure, Lessie looked down at his knee, a frown wrinkling her forehead.

"If I had a girl like you around I'd know what to do," he continued, laughing warmly. "I wouldn't let you get lonesome."

Feeling his knee rub against hers, Lessie reached over and gave it a firm push. "Hey, get back over there!" she commanded.

"Aw, come on, let's be friends."

"Yeh," Lessie said, drawing away, "I'll be friends all right, but that ain't what you're after. Now behave or let me out, for certain!"

He withdrew, straightening up in the seat, and Lessie grabbed the opportunity. "Boy, lookey at that shumack yonder," she exclaimed. "Just like a fire on the hill, ain't it?"

"Yes. Un-huh, it is," he said restively.

"Long 'bout this time of the year, back where I come from," Lessie continued quickly, "it just seemed like the whole world was burnen up in glory. And I'm tellen you, when you looked up at the sky you could see ferever! You ever been back on the Williams River? It's lonesome back there, but it sure is purty in the spring and fall."

He watched her, pensive and silent, and settled back on the seat, drawing his neck up from his collar. "You're a funny one," he said. "And you're not dumb either."

"The heck I'm not," Lessie said. "One time where I worked the man and his woman was schoolteachers, and he done his best to make me learn out of books. He done everything he could, and it never helped a bit. Finally I seen him given up hope, and it made me feel awful. Honest, I'd a-done it just to make him feel good, but I couldn't in noways a-tall. Just went in one ear and out the other."

"Well," he laughed, "I wouldn't worry about it. You'll get along." Speeding up to pass the green Buick, while Lessie stared through the window at the two women, he waited until he was back on the right-hand side of the road. "What are you doing now?" he asked.

"I work in the Kanawha Cafe, there at Gauley," she answered. "There's me and another girl. Anna. She come all the way from Carbondale, Pennsylvania."

"Then you probably know something about the men working in the tunnel," he said. "I'm handling a case for one of them, or rather for his family."

"Surest thing!" Lessie cried. "My boy friend works there, and Pete—that's Anna's husband—he's been worken since way last fall. Oh, I know a lot of them!"

"Did you know any who have died?"

Lessie picked up her hat, stroking the pink feather gently. "Yes, I knowed some. Mark's brother was layed away just last week. He worked there and died. They buried him in the graveyard up on the hill. I never felt so awful in all my life. His maw just stood there beside the grave with tears runnen down her cheeks in a regular stream, holden his paw up with one arm. I felt like I just wanted to lay down and die."

For a while the slender young man watched the road soberly and then twisted about on the seat. "What is your name?" he asked.

"Lessie. Lessie Lee."

"And who's Mark?"

"That's my boy friend. We ain't engaged yet or nothin, but we sort of know, I guess you'd say."

"Why did his brother die?"

"Same as all of 'em. They said it was pneumoney or that tunnel stuff they get."

"Lessie, my name's James Wright. I'm a lawyer from Charleston. You tell Mark that maybe, in a little while, the people who are getting sick and dying in that tunnel are going to get something for it. We're trying to set up a precedent case now, and if we can, then it'll be easier for the rest. God knows, they've got something coming to them!"

"Really?" Lessie cried, sitting bolt upright. "Is there really some chance of it?"

"I hope so. The company's certainly to blame, but they've got everything around here pretty much their own way. It depends upon how much they want to spend to defeat us."

"Gee, Mister Wright," Lessie said, her voice clear and earnest, "I hope you can do somethin. I know a lot of them men, and it's a cryen shame what's happened to them. I can't look some of them in the face. Honest, I can't. It's just like somethin that's been caught and is starven to death. Once, back home, I come on a hound caught in a steel trap. It must of been there a week or more. Its pore sides was just like a washboard, and its eyes looked big as a dollar, and when you touched it it just shook and shook——"

"If I win this case for Seth Pritchard," Wright broke in, his voice colored by Lessie's intensity, "or if anybody can prove the company is responsible, then they'll all have some money coming to them."

"Lordie, that would be nice," Lessie said, quieting down. "They're all so pore. They ain't got nothin, or next to nothin either—— Hey, wait a minute! We're passin the cafe. Yonder it is, back there!"

James Wright swerved the coupe into the curb just below the drug-store and pulled on the brake.

"I wish we could talk some more," he said. "Maybe next time I'm up I'll stop in the restaurant."

"Sure. Now you do that," Lessie urged, gathering her hat and purse into her hand and reaching for the door handle with the other. "I'd like to know 'bout what you're doin. If the company's goin to pay anythin you could tell Anna, and I'd let Mark know, so's he could tell his folks." Outside, on the curb, she bent over, looking through the window. "Gee, mister, I sure hope you can do somethin," she said. "They're needin it so bad."

"I'll try, Lessie."

As she passed around behind the car Wright opened his door and slid from the driver's seat.

"Lessie," he said, halting her as she started across the road, "Lessie—I didn't know back there—I mean, when you got in the car——" His hand touched his coat front and then gestured toward her. "I'd like to say I'm sorry and—well——"

"Oh, that!" Lessie declared friendlily. "That wasn't nothin! You never knowed. Soon's I told you bout me nobody could have been nicer. Well, good-by."

"Good-by, Lessie. I'll see you again."

A truck rolled by and Lessie darted across the street, past the store fronts and onto the broad strip of cement which led to the cafe. At the screen door she looked back. James Wright raised his hand a little, smiling, and as Lessie walked into the cool, shadowy room he pulled away from the curb and headed down the valley for Charleston.

Inside the cafe Lessie sensed a silence which seemed to hang unnaturally over the counter and tables. On the verge of calling to Anna, anxious to reveal her good news, she hesitated and walked slowly past the single customer eating a plate of fried ham and hash-brown potatoes at the counter. Pensively Lessie stared at the food, knowing there was something odd in the way the knives and forks had been scattered about the man's plate and that the sugar, salt and pepper had not been placed before him.

"Howdy," Jim Hathaway said, twisting about on the stool. "You're the girl that worked here, ain't you?"

"Sure," Lessie said readily. "I remember you. You sell that stuff to the undertaker, don't you?"

"That's right. Providing, of course, I can get him to buy it. I drive all the way over through here, and all he takes is a dribble-drabble. Where's the other girl?"

"Who, Anna?"

"Yes. I think that was her name."

"Ain't she here?" Lessie asked anxiously.

At the back the swinging door opened slightly and Mr Johns stuck his head out.

"Lessie," he called, "hurry on back here. I need you!" His voice was filled with impatient concern, as if he could no longer endure some unseen, impending danger.

"Where's Anna?" Lessie asked, tossing her hat and purse on the counter. What's happened?"

"Come on in the kitchen!" The door swung shut behind him, and, tying her apron as she went, Lessie followed, pushing it open with her knee.

"What's the matter, Mr Johns? Where's Anna? She sick?"

"What kept you so long?" he demanded, wiping his hands nervously on the front of his apron. "I've been here all alone. It's nearly noon."

"Tell me," Lessie demanded shrilly, "where's Anna? What's wrong?"

Mr Johns waved his hand above his head in a frantic effort to lower Lessie's voice and ran to the swinging door, peering through the little glass to see if the solitary customer had been disturbed.

Lessie sprang after him, grabbing his arm and whirling him about. "Tell me," she commanded. "Where's Anna? What's she gone for?"

"It was Pete," Mr Johns declared. "They brought him down about two hours ago. He give out, up at the tunnel. They took him to the hospital."

"Pete?" Lessie gasped. "Was he hurt?"

"Just don't yell, Lessie. I'm tryen to tell you," the thin man pleaded anxiously. "He was overcome by the gas or somethin in the tunnel. They carried him out and called the ambulance. Anna, she's gone to the hospital. Rode to Montgomery on the bakery truck."

"Oh, Lord God," Lessie cried woefully. "Oh, I hope it ain't bad!"

"She said she'd call and let us know," Mr Johns explained hastily, fearful that Lessie would go and leave him. "Said she'd call sure."

"Oh, pore Anna. She's been worried sick. Was he bad?" she asked, whirling about. "Did they say?"

"I don't know. I been waiten for the call. It ain't come yet."

Impatiently Lessie passed through the swinging door and hurried to the front of the cafe. Standing on the doorstep, she looked up and down the bright, sunny street, half expecting to see some sign of all that had transpired during her absence.

"Lessie," Mr Johns called. "Lessie, don't go off!"

Back in the kitchen, she only partially listened to him, knowing his terror of waiting on customers alone yet trying to find some way in which she could be of use to Anna.

"What do you think we ought to do, Lessie? Maybe we ought to send him some grub over someway. You could call and see. Why don't you, Lessie? See if he's al'right. I can close the place up. We don't have to stay here. If you'll go with me, we'll go see——"

"Wait a minute, Mr Johns. Landsakes, I can't hear my ears roar!"

From the front of the cafe came a metallic pecking sound, and Lessie ran out to accept the forty cents from Jim Hathaway. As she passed his change across the counter the telephone rang shrilly.

"Answer it, Lessie!" Mr Johns called, coming through the kitchen door. "It's Anna!"

Reaching the telephone, Lessie grabbed down the receiver.

"Yes—yes, Anna. Yes. Yes. How's Pete, Anna? Oh. Oh, that's awful!" She stopped, her face drawn in painful muteness. Mr Johns wrapped his arm in his apron and crept forward, listening attentively. "But—but he'll be al'right—huh? Yes, Anna. Yes, we will. I'll tell him. We're al'right. Don't you think about us at all. I'll come if you want me, Anna. What?" Again she paused to listen.

"Ask her if we can send some grub over," Mr Johns interjected quickly. "We'll send whatever Pete wants."

Lessie shook one hand at him, violently demanding silence.

"Yes, Anna. I will. Whatever you say, Anna, but I could come down easy as not. Yes, yes. Good-by, Anna. Tell Pete I'll come see him—yes—yes. Good-by."

"Is he bad?" Mr Johns asked. "Tell me, Lessie!"

Lessie crossed and sat down at the counter, her hand held against her cheek as if she had been struck.

"Tell me, Lessie," Mr Johns pleaded.

"Not turrible bad," Lessie said quietly. "He's got that trouble in his chest. Anna said he can't leave the hospital for some time. Says the doctors think he'll get over it if he'll rest up good." Suddenly she wheeled about on the stool and faced Mr Johns. "She was cryen, Mr Johns," she began, whimpering brokenly. "Anna was cryen like a baby!"

"Oh—oh, my goodness!" he said sadly, backing away. At the door he paused, looking at Lessie as though she could relieve his dreadful apprehension, and then vanished into the sanctuary of the kitchen.

om Reip, limping down from the graveyard on the shoulders of his two remaining sons, had returned to bed, exhausted by the strenuous effort. For days he lay staring blankly at the ceiling, barely speaking when Maw or the others brought his soft food to the bed. Virgil and Mark moved about the house in estranged silence, grieved by Ely's death and the great emptiness his going had created. Once Virgil, seeking to explain why he could not eat his supper, suddenly ran out of the kitchen door into the darkness. He hid by the maple where the hammock hung, trying to swallow his crying, his right fist smacking his left hand harder and harder. For almost an hour he cried, remembering Maw's tired, bewildered face and oppressed with a feeling that he had hurt her, that his words, meant in careful explanation, had struck her like heavy inconsideration. By the sink Maw cried too, believing that her insistence had driven Virgil from the house.

On payday evening, two weeks before school reopened, Maw and Virgil seated themselves about the table near Tom, where he liked to have them, as Maw methodically counted over the money. Viney was out playing Go-sheepie in the road, and Mark had gone to Gauley to meet Lessie, since it was Saturday and a Western was playing at the Bijou.

When she had counted and recounted the pay, returning Virgil's seventy-five cents for spending, allotting for the groceries and rent, the undertaker's payment and three dollars for the doctor, Maw took the two dollars and forty cents which remained and slipped it inside the old leather purse. Presently she withdrew one of the dollars and handed it across the table to Virgil.

"Go put that with the little bit you got left," she said. "You'll need it for books and sech when school opens. You ain't got but two more pays comen."

Virgil looked at the bill, moving his head about in a wordless effort to speak, and slid it back across the table.

"You keep it, Maw," he managed finally.

"Put it with yore other, boy," she repeated. "You'll have a need for it. There'll be books and shoes——"

"Maw," Virgil blurted, twisting about to straddle the bench. "Maw, I figure maybe I won't go back this term. I'll stay out and go back next February."

"You'll do no sech a thing! You got yore mind set on gitten some eddication—yore goin back this term, and that's all there is to it!"

"No, Maw, I ain't."

"Son," Tom spoke from the bed, "do what yore maw tells you. Put yore money away like she says."

Virgil looked at his father, and then his eyes came back to watch his finger dig at a crack in the bench.

"I been thinken it over," he explained carefully. "I got along good last year, and I can finish off the eighth grade in one term. If I go back in February I'll be sent on to high school just the same when promotion time comes next spring. That way I can work until—— Well, gosh, we ain't hardly got enough now."

Maw gathered up the money, folding the bills with firm, sure movements. "You worked in that tunnel as long as yore goin to," she declared. "You got to stop afore it breaks you down."

"I won't be worken inside," Virgil said. "I spoke to Turner Hatch al'ready. I'm goin to be took on as a carpenter's helper. It's a good job, outdoors."

"When'd he tell you that, son?" Tom asked, roused a little.

"Last Tuesday. I asked him, and he said he'd see. Today he said I'd be changed over the end of next week."

"That's a fine job," Tom said. "Carpenter work is good work."

"Just the same," Maw broke in, "Virgil's goin back to school. He's got a head start, and he ain't stoppen now. We'll make out someways."

"Maw," Virgil explained persistently, crossing to the back door, "It ain't like I was plannen to give up. It's just until February, till we get a little ahead. We had to use most everything—it cost so much."

"Now, mark my word, son," Maw warned, "yore goin back to school no matter what."

"No, Maw, I'm not." Stepping outside, he closed the door softly.

"Virgil, you come back here! Come here, I said!" Running to the door, Maw continued to call down the path after him. "Virgil! Virgil! Come on back here!"

"Let him go, Nettie," Tom said quietly. "You'll only get him upsot."

Angrily Maw whirled back toward the bed. "You hadn't oughter let him talk to me that-a-way," she charged. "You know right well that boy ain't no right worken in that dirty hole! He oughter be in school!"

"I never said nothin like that," Tom declared.

"You did, you just the same as did!" Maw went on, the corners of her mouth quivering. Drawn, tense, shattered by the long grief which followed Ely's death, she moved easily to tears, striking out against them each time they threatened. "More'n likely you want him to keep on there. Well, I ain't goin to have it! We lost one a'ready down yonder, and I can't stand any more. I can't stand it, I tell you, I just can't. A-body can only go so far an——" She threw herself into a chair, dropping her head forward into her cupped hands.

"Nettie, Nettie," Tom whispered hoarsely. "Nettie, you hadn't oughter——" There he ceased talking too. Immobile he lay, looking from dry, frightened eyes at the ceiling, while Maw's sobbing crowded about the catalogue-papered walls of the room.

By the time school opened Virgil had been transferred to the construction gang, setting up the scaffolding for the powerhouse to be built along the riverbank just below Number One opening. Maw fought against the idea, but with money endlessly scarce and with Tom still confined to his bed, she gradually withdrew until, when the opening day of school had passed, she no longer mentioned it. And then a week later she asked Virgil if it might not be possible to have Mark transferred to the same crew, since the outdoors would be away from the dust and safer.

"You ain't hardly got none of that dust on yore clothes," she would say each time. "Just a mite. Effen Mark was to be changed over, more'n likely he'd get to feelen better too."

As October wore on, burning the hills bright gold and red, word spread that Number One and Two openings would be holing through sometime around Christmas. The upper shaft, where Number Four came down from Hawk's Nest to meet Three, would go through soon afterward, forming the long hole through the base of Gauley Mountain.

During the last hot autumnal days, with the sun high and clear above the valley, Tom Reip sat on the front porch, his chest partially exposed to garner what warmth he could. Down the road, on the opposite side, Lock Mullens rested, his long legs stretched over the weathered boards of the roofless porch. The day came, near the end of October, when they walked the road between the houses together. At first they both settled down on a stump at the far end of the row of shacks, waiting for the harsh, spasmodic breathing to pass, but the day came when they could make the entire trip without resting, and then Lock ventured across the river and into Gauley Bridge.

The doctor examined him, saying that he was well but for a little congestion which still blocked his right lung.

"It makes a heavy sound when he thumps it," Lock explained. "But he figures it won't do no harm lessen I catch a cold or somethin to clog it up."

Nearly a week later Tom made the same trip, and the following evening when Mark came off his shift he found his father waiting outside. Together they walked the path back, talking, pausing at the foot of each incline. The next morning Tom went to the timekeeper's office and asked to be put back to work.

"We're all full up right now, Tom," the man explained. "I'll take you on first chance I get."

Tom thanked him and made his slow way back to the foreman's office, asking to be given work cleaning up about the mouths of the openings. Again he was refused.

"We're layin' men off right now. The work's getting ahead. We won't be needing so many."

Returning home, Tom barely spoke to Maw. Seating himself disconsolately on the back steps, he remained there for more than an hour, looking out over the yard toward the place where the last of Maw's garden ripened and withered in the autumn sun.

The next morning he left the shack before Mark and Virgil. Reaching the job, they saw him standing with the group which always waited at the change of shifts outside the tunnel in the hopes of securing a day's work.

At ten o'clock Tom started back home, his eyes dull and deep in his head. At the bridge which passed over into Gauley he saw several men loafing against the thin gray railing. He barely spoke to them, standing a little apart, listening to their talk, and after a while he headed up the path for home.

"Why don't you go out and set in the sun, Tom?" Maw asked, seeing his restlessness.

"Aw, I'm al'right," he retorted shortly.

"It'd do you good, Tom. Open up yore shirt."

"Nettie, can't you let a man alone!"

"Now, Tom, I didn't mean nothin!"

"Well—well," he began angrily, not knowing why he was mad, "well, just leave me alone!"

The next morning he arose early, leaving the house before daybreak. Maw heard him pulling on his clothes in the dark room and spoke. His answer was a low mutter, and then the door closed behind him.

"I'll let your boy know if there's anything for you," the foreman said. "No use you making a trip all the way down here."

Tom moved a little to one side, digging the ground with his toe. "I allus worked steady till I took sick," he said. "I figured you'd keep my place."

"Hell, man, we can't stop work on your account. I'll let you know if anything turns up. Move along now."

Nearing the bridge on his way home, seeing the men who gathered in a clot near its end, Tom turned aside, waited for a while beside the road and then, barely nodding, hurried across the bridge and into Gauley, the back of his neck burning with some unnamed shame as he passed the men.

By eleven o'clock he had found the office of the Cooper Coal Company. Resting outside to regain his breath, he screwed up his courage to ask for work. It was a difficult thing for him since in all the years he had lived on Slaty Forks he had been his own boss and unaccustomed to asking for anything.

Inside the office he found a man in his shirt sleeves sitting behind a battered oak desk.

"Mornen, sir," Tom began, removing his hat.

The man nodded, raising his face expectantly.

"Is this the hiren office?" Tom asked stiffly.

"Yes, it is. What can I do for you?"

"Well, I was kind of looken for some day's work."

The man pulled open a drawer and spread a long application form on the desk before him. "What's your name?" he asked, picking up a pen.

"Tom. Tom Reip."

"Where'd you live?" he continued, filling in the blank.

"Up the river there. Venetta, they call it."

The man hesitated, the end of the pen gesturing before his face. "Where did you work last?" he inquired, not writing any more.

"Up to the tunnel," Tom supplied readily. "I worked there nearly a year."

"Inside?"

"Yes sir. I worked clost to the big shovel."

Making a sucking noise through the corner of his mouth, the man laid the pen down and gathered the application form up in both hands. "If you've been working at the tunnel we can't use you," he said, tearing the paper into strips.

"Well—well, I can dig coal," Tom began quickly. "I'm a steady worker—if you'd give me a chanct——"

"Those are my orders," the man said, tossing the scraps into a wastepaper basket. "We aren't hiring anybody who's worked inside that tunnel. Good day."

"Mister—I need it bad——"

"Sorry, fellow." Returning to his work, the man lowered his head, studying the paper with exaggerated diligence.

Mutely Tom began to tear at his hat as he slipped wordlessly out of the room.

The noon whistle was blowing by the time he crossed back over the bridge. Halfway up the path which led to Venetta Tom halted, sat down on a large stone and waited. For a long while the valley between Gauley Bridge and the mining shacks was silent but for an occasional car which passed on the road beyond the river. Finally, as the sun crossed the center of the sky, school children gathered about the white building above the road, their voices loud and shrill.

Through the branches of a cluster of yellow sassafras trees Tom watched them, looking for Viney May. Furtively he waited, not wanting to reach home while she was there and yet not knowing why. At last the school bell sounded and the loud cries diminished as the youngsters crowded in through the door. Getting up, Tom found his way home.

Reaching the kitchen, he settled down on the doorstep, not speaking to Maw.

"Come on in an eat, Tom. I'll heat the coffee."

"No. I ain't wanten nothin."

"Come on, Tom."

Hearing her scrape the pot across the stove, he got up, washed his hands and sat down heavily on the bench back of the table.

"Mebby you'll get took on soon," Maw said, filling the white cup beside his plate. "There ain't no call to fret."

"No I won't!" he flared angrily. "They ain't never goin to give me no work. Nor nobody else, neither!"

"Tom, you hadn't oughter say that."

"It's the God's truth," he declared loudly. "I been to the coal company. They won't even take my name."

"Mebby they ain't hiren right now," Maw placated. "They's time a-plenty. Mark and Virgil is worken steady."

"Damnit, woman, that ain't me!"

"Tom, hesh swearen!"

"When I told him I worked at the tunnel he just tore the paper up and throwed it away," Tom went on, his anger rising. "Had my name writ down and everthin! Then I told him and he tore the paper up right before my eyes."

"Tore it up cause you worked at the tunnel?" Maw asked incredulously. "Whatever did he do that for?"

"I don't know, I don't know," Tom declared, his fist pounding the table. "I don't know nothin! I been looken; I been looken ever day for work. But they don't want me no more. Ain't nobody wants me. I'm just like a old horse with the heaves. Somebody ought to take me out an shoot me!"

"Tom, hesh that talk!"

"It's the God's truth, Nettie! I don't know what to do. They let me work, then when they was through with me they throwed me out. And I don't know what to do—I don't know, I don't know a-tall!"

On the first Thursday in November when Owl Jones left the tunnel he did not climb the hill toward Number One camp but, reaching the highway, followed it through the cove of Cane Branch, up the slight rise and over the railroad track and then dropped down the embankment to the cluster of shacks which formed the Jungle.

Wearily Owl trudged his slow way, his tired steps made more reluctant by the news he carried. Standing where the graveled shoulder of the road met the front yards of the tar-papered houses, Owl stared for a long while at one sway-backed shack whose patched roof had been blistered and welted by the hot summer sun.

Slowly he made his way toward the bare frame door which centered the one-room place. Knocking lightly, he stepped back, leaning against a telephone pole that rose clean and tall from the shambled yard.

"Dat you, Rogah?" a soft voice called from inside.

Owl could not answer. Although in weeks past he had entered the door many times unannounced, now he hesitated, shuffling his feet in fearful anticipation.

"Come on in, Rogah."

Owl knocked again, knuckling the doorframe a little louder.

"Rogah, I got supper cookin'. Quit foolin' and come in."

"It ain't Rogah, Mis' Pugh. It's me—Owl."

A kettle rattled on the stove, and a woman's steps sounded across the warped floor. Cissie Pugh stood sweating and bright where the patch of evening sun reached through the door.

"I never knowed it was you," she explained, holding a gravy-covered spoon out before her. "Rogah's allus foolin'———" She halted, tilting her head out the door, and looked up the road toward the tunnel. "Where's he at? You seen him, Owl?"

Owl stepped back toward the telephone pole, crunching the brim of his hat in one hand. "I come to tell you," he began thickly. "This af'ernoon, up at de tunn——"

"Ain't nothin' wrong, is they, Owl?" In her anxiety Mrs Pugh stepped down into the yard, approaching Owl. "Ain't nothin' happened to Rogah?"

"Us go inside, Cissie," Owl said, urging her back.

"The rock never falled on him, did it, Owl?" she cried, the words coming loud and emptily. "Tell me, man, did the rock fall on him?"

Guiding her into the room before him, Owl stood with his eyes lowered, glancing about the floor in a furtive effort to find words to bear his message.

"They was some trouble," he began. "Rogah was workin' up ahead, on de bench——"

"Where's Rogah at?" Cissie demanded frantically. "What happened? Where did they take him? If he's sufferin', he'll be callin' fo' me——" Breaking past Owl, she made for the door, the spoon rattling on the floor behind her.

"Come on back, Cissie! Come on back!" Owl called, extending his hand toward her. "You can't go down there——"

She whirled about, her hands shaking and her lips working apprehensively. "Man, you drivin' me crazy!" she cried. "Tell me what happened? Where they got Rogah?"

"De wagon come and got him," Owl muttered. "'Bout two hours ago. They took him down——"

"To de hospital?" she interrupted loudly. "To de Coal Valley?"

Woefully Owl shook his head. "De undertakah got him, Cissie. The cap'n said I was to come tell you."

For a moment the woman said nothing, her mouth opening and closing emptily. Then she gave one loud scream, beating her arms together, and stumbled toward the door.

"I seen 'em carryin' him out," Owl went on, not knowing what to say. "I come soon as I got off—— Come back! Cissie, come back!"

Reaching the yard, faltering a little, Mrs Pugh leaned against the telephone pole, shoved herself away from it and started up the path which topped the road's shoulder. By the time she got to the pavement her steps had increased, and as she headed toward Gauley Bridge she broke into a trot, her sobs trailing through the air after her.

Frightened, Owl climbed up to the road, looking about for help. Supper smoke trailed upward from the shacks, and no children played in the yards. Before he could move again Mrs Pugh had broken into a dead run and, nearing the bridge which led into Gauley, her crying was obscured by the successive cars that passed on the road.

Owl took a few steps after her, paused and, with his hand covering his face, turned about and made his way back toward the railroad crossing.

Leaving the bridge, Mrs Pugh found the sidewalk, ran in front of the gas station, past the Kanawha Cafe and, dodging a truck, cut across the street toward the undertaking parlor.

Fleetingly she noticed that the familiar olive-green ambulance was not drawn up to the curb before the curtained windows and, driven by some unnamed dread, she threw the door open and ran into the dark, shaded room.

Potted palms sat in each corner, and a small desk, with two somber books on it, occupied the center of the floor. In a glance Mrs Pugh saw the green-curtained door which led into the rear and, sniffing loudly to halt her crying, she threw the curtains aside and stepped into the back room.

"What do you want in here?" a short stocky man demanded, rising from an instrument-littered desk. "What do you mean busting in like this?"

"I—I——" Cissie stammered, unable to control her voice. "Rogah—you got Rogah here?"

"Go back out in the other room," Howard C. Wayne commanded. "Go on out there, you——"

Ignoring his words, Mrs Pugh dodged his outstretched hand and ran to the metal table where the nude figure of a colored man lay, the arms placed rigidly at his side.

With her mouth caught powerfully in her hand to strangle the scream which welled in her throat Mrs Pugh bent over, staring into the dead man's face. It was not Roger, and she straightened up, looking, like a terrified animal, about the room.

"Get out of here, I told you!" the red-faced man demanded, swearing to emphasize his words. Catching her by the shoulder, he shoved her toward the green-curtained door. "You've got no business back here! Get outside before I throw you in the street!"

Stumbling to a halt, Mrs Pugh dodged his outthrust arm and, circling the long table, ran toward the other figure of a man which lay stretched on a large box near the back of the room. Before the stocky man could reach her she saw that it was not Roger and turned to face him.

"Where's my man?" she cried hysterically. "What's you done with him?"

"Get outside and I'll talk to you!"

Blindly she found her way through the curtained door. Wiping her wet cheeks with the palm of her hand, she tried to swallow her grief so she might force the words from her throat.

"Rogah—Rogah Pugh," she sobbed lumpily. "Where you got him? I wants to see Rogah——"

"Sit down there! You niggers ought to learn to control yourselves!" Wayne went back through the curtains, returning with a sizable stack of cards.

"Now, what's the name?"

"He's name's Rogah, sir," she whimpered. "He—he——" Her body shook, pulsating her breath in short, broken spurts. "He died 'bout fo' o'clock."

"What opening did he work in?"

"Nu—nu—Number One."

Wetting his thumb, Wayne leafed through the cards, restacked them and repeated his search more slowly.

"Pugh, did you say?"

"Y-yes sir."

"Get ahold of yourself. I can't understand a damn thing you're saying. He was buried about an hour ago."

Cissie sprang up from her chair, the clustered fingers of her hand digging at her lips. Her eyes, large and dumfounded, became fixed in her head. "You done buried him?" she asked hollowly.

"Yep. About an hour ago. The wagon isn't back yet."

Cissie's hand moved on up her face, pushing its way past her eyes and into her thick kinky hair. "Our Jesus have mercy," she moaned. "Our Jesus have mercy!"

Wayne knocked the cards into an even pile on the corner of the desk and casually laid them down beside the two books.

Cissie took a few steps toward him, fear and dread and dumb horror freezing her distorted face into rigid lines.

"You bury him in de clothes he work in?" she asked numbly. "You ain't changed he's clothes?"

"How'd we know he had any more?" the man asked. "A lot of them we get in here don't have anything but what they've got on. You'd better start back home now." He opened the front door and stood aside for her to pass.

"Why you didn't wait till I come? Rogah's got clean clothes——" Uncontrollably she broke into loud grief; her head dropped forward from her shoulders, her hands beating against her forehead. "Oh, Jesus—— Oh, Jesus——" Her weeping rose and fell, the words breaking through it in fitful, incoherent spurts. "Bury my man like a dog—you ain't no right—no right on Jesus' earth——"

"Here, you'll have to stop that," Wayne said, his broad teeth biting off the words. "I put him away like I did all the others. He's got a coffin and a grave of his own. Nobody told me he was married. He couldn't stay here overnight——"

"Where you take him?" Mrs Pugh asked, getting to her feet, her hand working at the lump which clogged her throat. "Where is de graveyard?"

"It's over at Summersville. Go home and get ahold of yourself. I'll let you know where he's buried early next week."

"Where 'bouts is Summersville?" she asked, her face grown strangely quiet. "Which way I got to go?"

"It's up the Gauley, about twenty-eight miles." Crossing the room quickly, he again swung the door open, standing a little to one side. "I'll let you know the first of the week. The company won't put you out before then. You can ride over on the wagon with the boys. They'll show you which grave it is."

Wiping her face with her forearm, Mrs Pugh stepped out onto the sidewalk, crossed to the far side, near the curb, and headed up to the fork of the street, following the branch which passed beneath the railroad overpass and beyond the post office.

For fifteen minutes she made her way along the side of the road, crying bitterly. Once she stopped, removed her apron and, wadding it in one hand, used it as a handkerchief to mop up her twisted, moist face. Across from Venetta and near the white schoolhouse she halted, turning sideways, and waited for a car to pass.

A man in overalls looked at her but did not lessen his speed. She had gone another fifty yards when a car came up the road, followed by a truck. As they neared her the truck moved out to pass the tan Chevvy and neither noticed her upraised thumb.

Hearing the clang of an ambulance bell ahead, Mrs Pugh looked toward Summersville. The green car swerved around a bend, straightened out and raced down toward her.

Standing beside the road, she watched it pass, a beaten, dull hopelessness filling her eyes as it sped by, clanging furiously, and hurried on toward Gauley Bridge.

She had walked nearly a mile further on before a truck, mounting the slow incline she had just left, chugged to a halt at her signal.

"Climb in back if you want to!" a man called, bending across the lap of the boy who sat on the seat beside him.

"Yes sir," Cissie replied, catching ahold of the tall, wobbly rigging and pulling herself up in the truck bed where she squatted on a pile of tattered blankets used for packing.

The sun had already gone down, leaving the rolling hills gray-cool and bleak as the darkening shadows of twilight came out of the hollows and ravines. A mile and a half beyond Summersville Mrs Pugh went into a roadside stand, where two transport trucks were parked, and asked for final directions. The road, she was told, that led to Howard Wayne's burial field, which he had rented from his blind mother, was two hundred yards back down the highway.

Returning, Cissie found the red clay tire-marked lane that passed through a ravine between two shabby fences. To one side, atop a knoll, a tall square-framed white house stood, distant and bare. Although a rolling field extended from the house down to the highway, the house itself was enclosed in a tight picket fence which seemed to hem it like the rigid boundary of a single country grave.

Leaving the road, Mrs Pugh trotted down the lane, stumbling a little when the tire tracks dipped into a ditch which had been formed during the rainy weather. A quarter of a mile from the highway she saw that the automobile tracks ended, crisscrossing the road many times, and up the side of a thorn-thicketed knoll a well-used path had been worn.

Darkness was coming rapidly and, fearful of arriving after night had fallen and being unable to identify Roger's grave, Cissie began to run up the path as fast as she could take the incline.

Once atop the knoll, which still showed marks of pastureland, she paused. In broken, uneven rows little mounds of earth were crowded together, one after the other. Standing there in the gathering dark, Cissie looked at them hurriedly and, seeing three freshly earthed ones near the far end of the last row, she ran across between the graves and dropped to her knees. The heavy, pungent odor of broken earth still rose from the ground, and occasionally the red clay crumbled, rolling down the slight mounds in little cascading rivulets.

She examined the first grave, looking at both ends and along the side for a sign of identification. There was none and, muttering prayerfully, she crawled to the next, about five feet away.

"Rogah, Rogah," she called softly, her outstretched hand feeling over the newly piled earth. "Rogah, were you—— Oh, Lord Jesus——"

Passing on to the third, she searched for a posted stick or end board which might bear his name. Twisting about, she stared at the three fresh graves, muttering incoherently, her eyes running from one to the other.

"Lord Jesus," she wept, dropping to her hands and knees again, "Lord Jesus, where he at?" Across and back she crawled, looking through tear-blurred eyes for some indication of her husband's grave, but there was no sign to distinguish one mound of earth from another.

Finally, when her grief had broken, rising loud and mournful from the dark-shadowed knoll, Cissie fell in the ditch formed by the lower end of the graves, and as she cried her hands kept digging and clawing at the loose earth, breaking and fighting the clods.

"Oh, Lord Jesus," she pleaded, "let me see him once mo'—let me see him once mo'——"

29

Rain had come to the valley, slow and mist filled. The sun, a pale lemon glow in a dark vapory sky, held little warmth, and when Maw hung out her washing it was still wet at evening and she brought it into the house and strung it over chairs and on a line stretched back of the stove. It filled the house with a steaming dampness, and Virgil, who had worked all day in the rain and come home with a threatening cold, sat by the cooking stove shivering and shaking.

That night Maw rubbed his chest with melted lard and lamp oil, covered it with a flannel cloth and made him sleep between blankets. But the congestion continued to gather, and from four o'clock on Maw stayed up, alternately rubbing his chest with the greasy oil and wrapping him in warm bedclothes.

"You'd best stay home, today," she told Virgil as Mark climbed from bed and got into his clothes. "It's still wet-like, and you hadn't oughter be out."

Just before noon Tom walked down to the drugstore, making his slow, breathless way back with a stubby green bottle of nose drops, thankful that there was something he could do.

For two hours the afternoon sun broke through the thick, rain-filled sky, and Virgil and Tom sat on the damp front porch, soothed by its thin warmth. Every few minutes Maw left her ironing board and came out with the bottle, tilting Virgil's head back so the fluid ran down his nostrils.

At four o'clock the noisy pack broke from the schoolhouse across the river, and Virgil, looking off down the road, saw Mrs Stump coming toward them, making her way cautiously around the mud puddles, her vision partially blocked by the load she carried in her arms.

"Where's she goin with all that stuff?" Virgil asked, a little apprehensive each time she neared a sizable puddle.

"Headen for Flordey, mebby," Tom chuckled dryly, "like Hank an her's allus plannen."

Again they became silent, watching the heavy woman's progress with the slow, distant patience of the sick.

"Nettie, you got company," Tom called, seeing Mrs Stump pass the last shack and start for their steps. "Mis' Stump's headen this way."

"Land, whatever for?" Maw asked, exasperation creeping wearily into her voice. "I ain't near done ironen, and no time to talk!"

Reaching the foot of the steps, Mrs Stump turned sideways, looking around the armload of pans and packages. "Howdy," she said. "Maw home?"

"Nettie," Tom called. "Nettie, Mis' Stump's out here."

Maw's iron clanged on the top of the stove, a chair scraped over the floor, and presently she stepped through the doorway. "Landsakes alive," she exclaimed, "where you goin loaded down that-a-way!"

Lumpily Mrs Stump started up the steps. "Me and Hank's headen out tomorrey," she explained. "I thought mebby you have some use for this truck."

Tom's tilted chair hit the floor as he got to his feet. "You goin off?" he yelped. "You leaven the valley?"

Mrs Stump did not answer until Maw had taken the two tin skillets, the stewing kettles, rolling pin, cheap yellow sugar canister and several worn paper sacks from her arms and placed them on the porch.

"Yep," she said, sighing her relief, "we got to talken last night. Don't seem like we're ever goin to get anywheres in this Jesus-awful hole!"

Virgil got up, taking a few slow steps toward her. "You—you goin to Florida?" he asked.

"Yep," she declared, accepting the chair Maw dragged onto the porch, "that's where we aim to hang our hats! Like Hank says, being here's like a pig in a mudhole. The more you try, the deeper you get in."

"Clar to Flordey," Maw exclaimed. "Landsakes, whoever heard tell of sech a thing! How on airth are you goin to make it?"

"We're just headen down the road, straight through Virginia and North Carolina. It's comen on cold now, and we figure we'll follow the birds south."

"Yore—yore walken all the way to Flordey?" Maw asked, her words loud and incredulous. "All the way?"

"Folks will pick us up, give us a ride," Mrs Stump returned, a little too defiantly. "Hank, he fetched a map from the gas station yesterday. We'll keep bearen east till we hit U.S. 1. Fore the month's up we ought to be in Flordey, eaten oranges right off a tree."

"I never heard tell of sech a thing," Maw said, flabbergasted. "Never in all my borned days! You told Daisy and Lock yet?"

"That I did," Mrs Stump nodded, glowing with the elation their daring brought. "I give her my dishes and stuff. I sold a mess of truck to the Dago in Gauley, but there's one bed ticken left if you got any use for it."

"Is Lock abed yet?" Tom asked soberly.

"Yep," Mrs Stump replied, hurrying on. "Hank says fore winter's out ever man in this valley will be sick or dyen! Somethin gets in their chests, he says, and they get to coughen——" Abruptly she broke off, aware that Tom had turned aside. "Tomorrow mornen we're headen down the road," she went on quickly. "Never a worry in the world. Oh, Hank's got a little hid in the insole of his shoe. Ain't no danger of us starven to death! He'll get a job picken oranges down there. I'll have me a basket too. We'll just walk along under them shady trees, fillen 'em up easy as you please. There's good fishen in Flordey too," she added, speaking directly to Tom. "Mebby we'll get a fishen boat, and I'll open up a little place for the men to eat."

"Send us a picture of them places," Maw asked. "I never seen oranges grown on a bush."

"Send one of the fish too," Virgil added. "Mr Johns has got one tied to his cash register. It'd be nice having one to look at ever day."

"Sure," Mrs Stump promised happily. "I'll send you all kinds of picture cards. Hank says if we like it there we'll buy us a house. If it suits you the same, more'n likely Hank could get you a job too, and you could live out your days there in Flordey."

No one answered, and the porch was silent as they waited hungrily for the large woman to continue. The sun, reaching a mounting thunderhead, shadowed and disappeared.

Mrs Stump, a little embarrassed by their still, asking eyes, got to her feet, blustering and noisy.

"Well, if you feel like gettin out this evenin," she invited, "stop over. There's a little stuff left you might want. Me and Hank ain't taken nothin but what we can tote on our backs."

"Thank ye kindly," Maw said, stooping to pick up the pans and paper sacks from the porch. "It was nice of you to fetch thesens."

"It ain't much. Just a handful of beans and some onions and macroni. There's one can of chili. Hank's got an awful tooth for hot stuff," she said, indicating the bright yellow can of chili con carne. "I thought maybe the young'uns might like it."

"We're ever so much obligeed," Maw said as Mrs Stump started down the steps sideways. "We'll be over round the edge of dark."

Tom, sitting apart, looked after the large woman, his dun, tired eyes tracing her path about the puddles as she headed down the road. Maw and Virgil stood motionless, watching her out of sight, and then, the bright-colored chili can still held absently in his hand, Virgil walked slowly into the house and laid down on the bed.

Soon after midnight Maw awakened, hearing Virgil's tearing cough. Quickly she heated the lard and oil, spreading it over his chest and back.

"You chillen, son?" she whispered, bending close. "You still cold along yore back?"

"A little," Virgil answered. "My head is clogged up."

For an hour Maw worked with him, trying to clear the congestion in his head and chest. At last he slept again, and she crept back to bed, slipping in between the covers so as not to disturb Tom.

"Is he bad?" Tom asked unexpectedly. "You reckon Mark oughter go fetch the doctor?"

"If he gets any worse, we'll send for him," Maw whispered. "You go on back to sleep. I'll listen."

Just as early day seeped into the still room Maw heard Virgil stir, a low wheeze sounding above the squeak of the bed. By the time she had reached him Virgil was sitting up, his shoulders bent forward as he fought to gain his breath. Throwing one hand across his stomach, Maw tilted him forward, thumping his back lightly, horribly aware in the shadowy room that the attack was identical with dozens that had racked Ely's thin body.

For several minutes she worked furiously, and when nothing else succeeded she dragged Virgil's body from the bed. Already his face seemed swollen, his neck and jaws unnaturally distended by the suffocating effort to breathe.

"Mark! Mark!" she cried. "Get up, Mark! Quick!"

"What's the matter, Nettie?" Tom yelled from the other room. "Nettie, is he bad?"

By the time Mark had bounded from his cot Tom's lean, gaunt figure stood in the doorway.

"Take his other arm, son," Maw called desperately. "We got to keep him standen up."

"Cough, boy, cough," Tom urged, extending and withdrawing his weak arms in a futile effort to be helpful. "Swaller the air down——"

"Hand me a cover," Maw called to Tom, swinging her arm toward the bed. "Fetch me that quilt. The house is cold."

As Maw wrapped the quilt about Virgil his head bobbed twice, limply, and with a slow, gradual intake of breath he straightened up, his eyes red and filled with water and his lips white far back toward his strangely flushed cheeks.

"You'd best get back to bed, Tom," Maw called. "It's passen off."

In the kitchen Tom sat down on the edge of the double bed, carefully pulling his trousers up over his bony legs. Tugging them beneath his body, he raised his weight with one stiff arm and eased them up over his hips, slipped his feet into his shoes and picked up his shirt. By the time Maw and Mark had led Virgil back to his bed Tom had a fire blazing in the kitchen stove.

Maw pulled her gray gingham dress on over her head, her thin hair hanging in two small braids down to her shoulders, and carried Viney May from the cot in the corner of the kitchen to the double bed where she and Tom slept. Then, remaking the cot, she went to the bedroom, picked Virgil up in her arms and carried him into the kitchen.

"He'd best sleep in here," she told Tom, "so's I can be closer to him if he gets another one of them choken spells."

The rain ceased and pale light sifted into the washed valley. Maw and Tom and Mark all stood about the kitchen, silent and anxious, each rising quickly to perform the simplest chore as though some hunger had been born in them during the night. Quietly they watched Virgil, hoping no one would mention that his choking spell had been like the ones Ely suffered during the last days when he, too, slept in a corner of the kitchen.

"I'll go fetch the doctor," Tom offered stiffly. "I'll go down when Mark heads for work. I figure he oughter come and look at him, anyways. More'n likely he just got a cold from worken in the rain." He looked at Maw, wanting confirmation for what he had said. She made him no answer, bending silently over the stove, her back to the room.

As Tom and Mark rounded the house, starting for the path, they saw Hank Stump and his wife climbing up toward the highway on the opposite side of the river. They stopped in their tracks, waving.

"They're headen out, Maw," Mark called, running back to the kitchen door. "Hank and Mis' Stump has done crossed the river!"

"I seen 'em," Maw answered, trying to control her grief-distorted face. "Yes, I seen 'em a'ready."

Without another word Mark rejoined Tom at the head of the path.

"She comen to wave 'em good-by?" Tom asked, glancing toward the kitchen door.

"Nope, I reckon not."

"You tell her?"

"Un-huh."

They had gone several yards down the path, winding along above the muddy river, before Tom spoke again. "Mark, was yore maw cryen?"

Mark only nodded his head. They both knew that the thing they feared had been named to them at last.

Dr Robinson spent an hour examining Virgil's chest, throat and back, making sure that his slight temperature did not indicate impending pneumonia. Maw watched his every move, saying little until he finished and she had followed him out into the back yard.

"How long did he work at the tunnel?" Robinson asked, shifting his black satchel from one hand to the other.

"Goin on five months," Maw replied. "But he's been worken outside some time now; he's been worken outdoors." She stopped, looking fearfully into the doctor's eyes. "He can't have the trouble," she declared, her words frightened and horrible to hear. "He only worked in the dust three months and a little more. He can't have the trouble——"

"I'm afraid he has, Mrs Reip. If he only worked inside that long, I'd be inclined to say no, but I've examined too many of these cases. I'm afraid he's got what the company calls tunnelitis."

"No," Maw cried, her voice rising sharply. "Virgil, he ain't got it!"

The doctor nodded his head. "They're all the same. He was younger; it showed up suddenly. He might have gone on for some time without our knowing it, but this cold showed it up. I've examined a lot of men, or I would not be so certain. I'll come back tomorrow and check again. Meanwhile keep giving him the medicine. At least it'll relieve the pain when he starts to choke. That's about all we doctors are able to do."

Maw started to speak, but as a cry broke in her throat she threw her hands over her face and ran to the far corner of the house. Leaning against the wall, she wept in a low, agonized way, her voice smothered by her hands so her sobs could not be heard.

In the next two days the long rain blew over, leaving the hills bare and dark before the coming of winter. At night the cold crept beneath the shacks, raw and penetrating, but by eleven o'clock the sun would break through, dissolving the caul from the frozen mud puddles and reducing the clay road to a bed of slush beneath the thin layer of coal dust. Now, during the bright hours, Virgil sat on the front porch beside his father, saying little and reading again and again from the history he had stored away with his schoolbooks the previous spring.

Once Anna and Lessie brought him some frayed movie magazines, two copies of *True Detective* and Jack London's *Love of Life*. In the morning Maw helped him out onto the porch, stacking the magazines on an upturned dynamite box beside him. Within a week Virgil had read them all, sometimes aloud to Tom, sometimes quickly and silently to himself.

One morning after he had leafed through the magazines, being sure that there was nothing he had not read, Virgil picked up the London book and fingered his way through the torn, soft-edged pages. Having read only one book which was not a school text, he looked at the first story indifferently, scanning the opening paragraphs to see what the characters were saying. In a moment he had turned the first page, reading avidly, and when Maw came out to help him in to his noon meal he went reluctantly, carrying the book in the hand he held across her shoulder.

"You hadn't ought to read so much, son," she cautioned, helping him back to the porch a few minutes later. "It'll ruin yore eyes."

Virgil hardly answered. Tilting his chair back, he hungrily opened the book, reading one story after another. By the end of the second day he had finished the last and turned back to the gnawing account of a man's horrible encounter with death. Over and over he read the tale, terrified each time the wolf approached, struggling with the man's faltering steps, and when at last he had lain down to die within sight of help Virgil would sit for a long while staring out over the river, bewitched by the man's struggle for life, awed and terrified by the slow, inevitable approach of death.

He read the story to Tom in a low, muted tone because his breath was weak, and the next morning Tom asked for it again. After Virgil finished Tom told him of a man he had known who was found beside his horse, frozen in a snowdrift. The man had died first, sheltering himself along the animal's back for warmth, and then the horse had died with its legs sticking out as rigid as fence posts.

"It'd be a funny way to die," Virgil said, leafing through the book. "Does a feller get warm just before he freezes to death?"

"I guess that's right. My pap freezed his foot oncet. He said the feelen went right out of it, same as it never had none. Never hurt him a-tall, he said, till he got back to the house and started to thawen it out in the well bucket."

"Must be funny, dyen that way," Virgil repeated. "This feller in the book says it don't hurt to die," he ended, staring at the slow movement of the river below. "Says living is the only time a feller gets pain. Starven would be a funny way to go."

"There's worse ways of dyen," Tom said. "Burnen, now that's a way I'd hate to go. Seen a horse burn in a barn oncet. Worst thing I ever seen. It screamed like a woman."

"That's about the worst of all, I reckon," Virgil agreed. "'Less it was bein scalded to death and dyen slow."

Tom settled down, pushing his hat forward to shelter his eyes. "When the Yankees was comen through that time an yore grandpap went off to war he seen a sight of dyen, to hear him tell it. Said it was funny, but when some of them fellers got shot they died so sudden they never even layed down their guns. Just died how they was, sitten or standen. But I reckon they wasn't none of 'em that wouldn't a-died in bed if they was to have the chance. Pap allus said he come home so's he could die in his bed, and he done that very thing, peaceful as you'd like."

Virgil made no answer. Shielding his eyes with one hand, he began the story again, reading slowly, extracting all meaning from each familiar word.

30

As snow rode into the valley on winter winds, death followed death like the steps of a walking man. With Number One and Two ready to hole through, and the other spur not far behind, the drills whirred and whined ceaselessly in the great shafts beneath the foot of Gauley Mountain. New men quickly replaced the ones who were fired when the emaciated bodies could no longer man the drills, and any mucker who staggered was sent home for a day, for two days, and then, if he was not able to return to the hole, another took his place, for all crews were kept at capacity, all work went on unremittently.

Seeing the men lined along the highway and gathered in silent, distant-eyed clots about the openings, every man hung on as long as he could, knowing that the winter was at hand. Resolutely they drove themselves back to work, saying nothing now of the dust, expecting no relief from the torn and unrepaired air vents; wanting only to keep their jobs so there might be a little food on the table, so a child did not have to go to school with an empty belly.

As the wet cold crept into the valley men coughed more, drawing slight phlegm from their lungs as repeated hacking spells tore through their bodies. No day passed when the ambulance did not nose its way to one of the openings and return to the Coal Valley or the undertaker's green-curtained parlor on Main Street.

On a Saturday night Lessie, preparing to keep a date with Mark, went into the women's room and retraced lipstick about the upper rim of her mouth. As she pulled her mouth together, imprinting part of it on her full lower lip, she heard the ambulance clang down the street and come to a low, whining halt a little farther on.

"Somebody must a-died," she called to Anna, leaning through the partially opened door. "Sounds like they're stoppen at Wayne's."

Anna left the *Charleston Gazette* spread on the end of the counter and ran toward the door. "I'll see," she called back, stepping into the windy street. "Might have been a cave-in!"

Quickly Lessie finished her make-up and, closing the door, fluffed her hair about the brim of the flat hat perched on her blonde head.

"She come back yet?" she asked Mr Johns, who stood at the front window, his arms wrapped in a white apron. "What happened? Who was it?"

"I ain't heard yet. Big crowd gatherin' over there."

"It's always worse on Saturday nights," Lessie pointed out. "I wish Anna would come back; yonder's Mark."

"Anna ought to stop always runnen over there," Mr Johns said concernedly. "It keeps her upset all the time, and worried." Raising on tiptoes, he tried to locate Anna among the crowd before the funeral parlor. 'She'd be a lot better off if she tried to forget it. Pete's not worken——!"

"Hesh!" Lessie cautioned sharply. "Here she comes. Don't let her hear you sayen a word 'bout Pete not worken. She's half out of her mind now."

Anna scarcely spoke when she came in, naming the man who had died at Hawk's Nest camp and settling down at the end of the counter, depressed, her hands absently leafing through the newspaper. As Lessie, going out to meet Mark, closed the door behind her the low mumble of the crowd diminished and inside only the big clock above the pie case advertising a Fayetteville jeweler broke the heavy, disconsolate silence.

"Don't seem like anybody else is comen in," Mr Johns ventured, fidgeting beneath the stillness. "You might as well go on home, Anna. Pete'll be wanten to see you."

While Anna got her coat and hat Mr Johns went to the front and pulled the strings which hung from the globe lights, darkening the long room. "He seem to be feelen any better?" he asked, nodding his head toward the hill. Anna shook her head morosely and, sensing that he had inquired too far, Mr Johns hastily added, "I always liked Pete. He's quiet and minds his own business."

"Some," Anna replied belatedly. "He walks in the yard a little when it's warm. But he lost three pounds last week."

"Three more?" His voice rose with surprise. "Maybe, Anna, you ain't feeden him enough. I saved some bean soup. Why don't you take——"

"It's not that, Mr Johns," she broke in. "It's hangin' round the house day after day, just doin' nothin'. Pete ain't the kind that can do that. He talks all the time about goin' back to work, and he's not strong enough to even climb the hill."

"Maybe," Mr Johns suggested timorously, seeing the tenseness gather in Anna's face, "maybe the company will be payen him somethin, like that feller told Lessie. They was talken 'bout it acrost the street when I went for sugar."

"Pete says he don't want that. He justs wants his health back so he can do a regular day's work. He's independent as a hog on ice." Nervously she began beating her felt hat against her knee. "He thinks we've still got money in the bank. I had to tell him that. If he knew we were livin' on what I make he'd—well, there's no tellin' what he would do. Leave, I guess."

"Leave you, Anna? Go off by hisself?"

"I'd wake up some morning and he'd be gone, that's all." The words came from her tight throat, thin and sharp. "He wouldn't live on my money. But I'd follow him, like I did when we left Carbondale."

"Good Lord," Mr Johns groaned, sinking onto a stool. Feeling Anna's mounting hysteria, he attempted to speak several times, and finally the words came. "Pete's just sick, Anna. He'll get well. When the tunnel holes through the mines might open up———"

"No, he won't," she snapped bitterly. "He's like all the rest; they don't get better, they get worse!" She waved her hat toward the far corner where the stack of coarse tablets lay on a ledge just beyond the men's room. "Look at them! They all thought the same thing. Hance McTeer wanted to bring his family here from Oklahoma. He wrote her about it in every letter. Now he's caught, and he'll die like the rest of them!"

Angrily tossing her hat and coat over the counter, Anna walked to the ledge and sorted through the tablets. Mr Johns gestured, trying to halt her, frightened by the shrill, desperate tone of her voice.

"See them?" she called, holding up three partially used tablets. "One. Two. Three. All dead and buried without ever gettin' home again! They wanted to—they wanted to like hell!" She tossed two back onto the pile and stood holding the third one up before her. "See that?" she said, flicking the pages. "We ought to give it to some kid goin' to school. It's almost new. That's Lindsey Means. We wrote two whole tablets to his dad, and he sent three dollars ever week. His dad lives in South Carolina." She stopped, examining the upper edge of the cover. "Ridgeway, South Carolina. He's a Baptist preacher down there, and he's only got one arm. Do you suppose, Mr Johns, I ought to send him this tablet? He might want it."

"Anna, you hadn't ought to talk like that," Mr Johns said persuasively. "What would Pete think if he heard you?"

"He don't hear me!" she retorted sharply. "But it's drivin' me crazy, always lyin' and kiddin' along. I can't do it much longer. Evertime that goddamn ambulance goes clanging past here I shake all over! I want to run out and yell and yell and yell!" She threw the last tablet back on the shelf, crossed to the counter and snatched up her coat and hat.

Mr Johns watched her closely, moving back a little, afraid to speak but wanting to stem the bitter hysteria which mounted in her voice. "Get ahold of yourself, Anna," he ventured softly. "Things'll work out."

"I'm holdin' on!" she cried defiantly. "I'm holdin' on all the time! I'll hold on forever and ever, if Pete just don't die. But when I see him walkin' round like a rat in a shoe box—— Oh God, it's awful!"

Nervously Mr Johns edged toward her, reaching out and withdrawing. Whirling abruptly, he ran into the kitchen, dug a bottle of dark whisky from the flour barrel and poured a good-sized drink into a glass. Filling it with water, he came back through the swinging door.

"Here, you'd better drink this. It'll help, maybe."

Anna stared at him, her face screwed up to control her weeping. "What is it?" she asked, daubing her eyes with a crumpled handkerchief.

"Just whisky. I always keep a little on hand."

"I know," she said tiredly, accepting the glass. "I seen you before."

"You did?" he asked, startled.

"Through the door," Anna said, drinking slowly. "Lessie tole me when I first came here."

Mr Johns's face dropped and his hands brushed flatly against the sides of his apron. "Well," he said meekly, "it's lonesome back there by yourself; a man gets down in the mouth——"

Anna looked up, smiling feebly. "You're awful nice," she said, finishing the drink. "I didn't mean to say those things, but I couldn't help it. Everything inside me seems so heavy anymore, and I can't laugh natural, like I used to." Her shoulders rose in a deep sigh, and she got to her feet. "I'm dead tired. I'm going home to bed."

"Yes indeedy, that's the best thing for you!" Mr Johns declared, walking to the door beside her. "And tell Pete I'm fryen chicken for noon tomorrow. We'll fix him enough to fill a wheelbarrow."

Anna nodded, moving about a clump of people who still hung along the curb talking of the death at Hawk's Nest camp, crossed the street and wearily climbed the hill toward the boardinghouse where Pete waited.

Mr Johns watched her out of sight, put out all the lights but the one above the cash register and, going to the kitchen, poured himself a drink from the bottle which still sat on the shelf above the sink. Distraught and upset by Anna's wretchedness, he gulped the drink before he picked up the pan of potatoes he had been peeling when Wayne's ambulance first screamed down the road.

A few minutes later there was a knock at the front door and Mr Johns sat bolt upright, listening sharply. Again the knock came and, grabbing the bottle of whisky, Mr Johns recorked it and jabbed it into the flour barrel, covering it with one sweep of his hand.

Peering through the glass slit in the swinging door, he saw the thin figure of a man outlined against the lighted street. Recognizing Ralph Owens and knowing his light had been seen, Mr Johns went down the long counter, slipped the night lock back and opened the door slightly.

"We're closed up," he said. "The girls are gone."

Ralph Owens' face seemed like a skeleton beneath the dark brim of his hat. "Could you put a sandwich in a bag?" he asked. "I want to take it along with me."

"Cheese, ham, bologna or egg?"

"I'll take one cheese. Could you put some mustard on it, please?"

"Why don't you come in?" Mr Johns invited. "I don't guess there's any use waiten out there."

Inside the lighted kitchen Owens stood staring at the pans of unused food, the roasted ham and block of cheese that rested on a zinc-topped table. While Mr Johns spread mustard and butter over the sliced bread Owens pulled a dime from his trouser pocket and held it in his hand.

"I ain't seen you in some time," Mr Johns said, knifing the cheese. "The girls used to watch out for you ever Saturday night.

"They were always nice to me," Owens said. "I wanted to come in, but after they cut my pay, I——" He flipped the dime over and over in his hand. "I never did very well here. They let me go today."

"Fire you?" Mr Johns asked.

"Yes. It wasn't the boss's fault. I couldn't do the work any more." He tilted his head, coughing into a cupped hand. "I'm going home. I don't know what else to do."

"They fired some at Number Four," Mr Johns said. "You work there?"

"No. Number Two. Eighteen were put off there, just on that opening. We got to be off the grounds by morning."

"Where you headed? You got a place to go?"

"I'm going home. I'll be home before Christmas. I live in Elmira, New York. I got a wife and two girls in Elmira. They don't know I'm coming home though. She doesn't even know I'm sick."

"She don't?"

"No. I never told her. I don't know what she's going to say." He paused, holding out the dime. "She took the girls to live with her folks. They've always been good to us, but they don't have anything either. We lost our furniture, mostly."

Mr Johns stirred up the fire and placed the coffeepot over an open lid, ignoring the proffered money. "How you goin? Bus?"

Pointing his thumb, Owens gestured it over his shoulder, grinning sickly.

"Long ways, ain't it?"

"Pretty far. I used to sell insurance in Elmira," he went on proudly. "I sold insurance for seven years."

"You did?"

"Sure. In 1927 1 made better than three thousand dollars. We lost it all in the depression. One of my kids is in school already." He threw out the information in a spurting, disjointed way, listening to his own words. "Now I'm going home sick, and I can't earn nothing. I worked hard in the tunnel. Stayed on nearly a year. I'd never done pick-and-shovel work before."

"How long have you had the cough?"

"Since early last spring. I tried to keep it down, around the job, so the boss wouldn't find out. I saw they were laying the worst ones off. I never wanted to get the boss down on me. I stayed to myself and never said anything. But I've been losing weight right along. I weighed a hundred and forty-two when I left home. My wife weighed more; she's a little taller than I am."

"You're pretty puny right now," Mr Johns commented.

Ralph Owens touched the legs of the overalls that hung loosely from his thin hips. "At night it feels like I'm all bones. But I can't sleep anyway." Seeing Mr Johns set two coffee cups on the table, he took off his hat, watching closely but saying nothing. His eyes, small and sharp, glistened with feverish intensity and his hands darted jerkily, the movements ending abruptly.

"I got so I could handle a shovel pretty good," he went on loudly, the words hollow and distant. His drawn lips were cracked and broken, and in the weak light of the kitchen his jaws seemed bluish purple beneath the stubble beard.

"I don't know what I'm going to do now," he sped on, the babble flowing freely. "I used to sell insurance in Elmira, New York. I went all the way through high school. I've got two girls; one's seven and one's five. I'm going to paint their bed when I get home. I'm pretty handy with things like that. I fixed up the basement for them to play in, but we don't live there any more. My wife's gone to live with her folks. They live on the South Side, on Maple Street; a green house near the corner of Clark. I don't think I got the boss down on me. I tried not to. I used to bite my sleeve when I had to cough. Sometimes I would make a noise with my shovel too. They just fired me because I'm so thin. But I always tried. I did everything I could."

Mr Johns filled a plate with food and set it on the table, his eyes never leaving Owens. Then he brought the coffee, filled a cup and put the pot back on the stove.

"Set down and eat," he said, his voice stilted and uncertain. "I'll make you another sandwich. You'll be hungry on the road."

"When I came down here," Owens said, slipping furtively onto the chair and picking up a piece of ham in his fingers, "people thought I was a bum. They wouldn't pick me up. They didn't know I'd been all the way through high school. I'll go to Hornell and look for work, and Bath and Corning. They're all good towns. Corning's got a glass factory. I won't cough; I'll put the covers over my head." He barely ceased talking, chewing the ham in great bites that forced the bones of his face nearer the surface.

"You saw me, didn't you? Every Saturday night I went straight to the post office. I sent the money home. I saved the receipts. I got them here, here in my shirt pocket. I pinned them in." Long after he had finished the statement he sat up and thumped his open hand against the left side of his chest. "I always tried. I watched and never coughed where the boss could hear me. But they fired me, that's what they did. They fired me. I'm going home now. I'm going home and tell Mabel."

On that Saturday when a tense, accumulating fear spread over streets of Gauley Bridge, when Anna climbed the hill crying and Ralph Owens walked back over Route 60 chattering and mumbling incoherently, people continued to pass up and down before the drugstore until late at night, listening, talking, gathering in clumps as though they were afraid to return home. The layoffs at the tunnel became an angry protest to be heard all along the street, broken only by mention of Wayne's ambulance, the number of deaths and the trial still being heard in Fayetteville which might bring compensation for the losses they had suffered.

Turner Hatch, who had been a foreman in Number One, left the bright lights of the Bijou's marquee and made his way back to the gas station again, searching for someone he could not name or even imagine, a person who could erase the fear and dread that had grown rapidly inside him since his curt dismissal from the job that afternoon.

In front of the Ford agency he stopped, studying the figure of a young man who slowly made his way down the wet sidewalk. "Ain't you that Martin boy?" he asked. "The one that worked with Legg, up near the heading?"

Jim nodded, hardly breaking his pace. "Yep, that's me."

"I ain't seen you in some time. Been out long?"

"Over two weeks." Jim's lips, grown thin and colorless, bit off the words, his jaws working dry motions beneath his pallid skin.

"How's Long? He still on the job?"

"Yep. You're workin' steady, I guess."

"No," Hatch replied. "No, I'm off the job now."

"Quit?"

"No, I got the cough. I worked in mines twenty years, tunnels too. But I got the cough. I was fired today."

"Jesus Christ," Jim swore. "You was always sayin' that the dust wouldn't hurt a fellow!" His eyes ran over Hatch's lean frame. "You ain't much more than skin and bones now."

"That dust ain't like nothin' I ever worked in before," Hatch explained uneasily. "The super told me it wouldn't hurt a man———"

"Yeh, and what's the super going to do for you now?" Jim asked acidly, moving toward the drugstore.

Hatch tried to stop him, wanting to talk. As Jim reached the curb he called, "I heard that colored fellow died yesterday," his voice unnaturally loud.

"Which one?" Jim asked. "Who?"

"Jones. Owl Jones. He came on the day you did."

"Owl?" Jim whirled, taking a step back. "Owl dead?"

"Yep. Died on the hill. Wayne hauled him over to that field in Summersville, I heard."

"Why didn't somebody tell Long?" Jim demanded. "He'd want to know. We all come here together."

On Sunday, which began with a heavy fog and degenerated into a drizzling, overcast day, Jim and Long left Gauley Bridge and walked up toward the square white schoolhouse. Soon after they had passed Venetta, seeing the dark, drab shacks propped against the riverbank, they caught a ride and reached Summersville at noon.

The lane which led through between the shabby fences was a swamp of red clay and stone. Clinging to the upper side, holding to brush and rusty wire fence, they came to the broadened place where the undertaker's sons turned the ambulance across the lane, backing it against the foot of the knoll.

"Jesus God, it's worse than a mudhole down here," Long swore, helping Jim make his way up the slippery incline. "It looks like the ass end of nowhere."

Atop the knoll they saw the rows of graves which stretched across the rounded hill toward the ravine beyond. Near them the earth on the recent graves still remained fresh and darkly red. Farther along, where the first ones had been dug, the mounds had already sunken, leaving shallow cavities in the ground. Here and there a stick marked the end of a row, and in one place a rough board had been driven into the ground for a headstone.

Barely speaking, Long and Jim looked out over the torn, sod-less ground.

"Holy God, what a place to bury them," Long said beneath his breath.

Pushing through a clump of thorn and white gum trees, Jim worked his way to the freshest, most recently turned earth.

"Pete heard through Anna that they were buryin' more than one in a box," he said. "Damn if it don't look that way!"

Long did not answer. His face, grimly still, was drawn into a rigid, whitened mask.

"Wonder where Owl is?" he asked finally.

"There's no telling. Might be any of these."

Finding a narrow passage between two rows of graves, Long started toward Jim, counting off his steps.

"Seven graves in a place eleven yards wide," he remarked emptily. "That's crowdin' 'em in close."

"That's just one to a grave," Jim pointed out. "Look, do you suppose this is Owl? It looks a couple days old."

"Might be. You can't tell."

Bending down, Jim tried to examine the color of the torn earth. "Those two must of been made yesterday," he decided. "But it's hard to tell in this damp weather."

"Them was made this mornen."

Turning, Jim and Long saw two boys and a dog standing back of them, at the edge of the thorn thicket.

"When were these made?" Jim asked, indicating the two at his feet.

"Yisterday. Them was made yisterday." The boy edged forward, one knee showing through his torn overalls. "Mister, it's a sight the way they put them niggers in there."

"How deep are they, bud?" Long asked.

"Ain't deep at all," the second boy declared knowingly. "Just—just down a little bit."

"Pap said it ruint our drinken water," the first one said soberly. "We live down yonder in the holler. He ought not to a-buried them like that. It ruint the drinken water."

"Which ones were made day before yesterday?" Jim asked. "Where would they be?"

Gravely the two boys looked at each other and then back at Jim. "We never come up Friday. We ain't no way of knowen."

Jim looked at the graves again and started back toward Long. "I guess there's nothing we can do," he said, his voice low and sorrowful. "We can't find him the way they're stuck in here."

"Pap says there's some white men buried in there too," the boy went on importantly. "Said the church is gitten after old Wayne. They're goin' to make him move 'em acrost yonder—against the slope yonder."

"You seen any of them buried?" Long asked.

"Sure. They chase us off, but I see 'em afore."

"Is there more than one in a grave?"

"I don't know, mister. They just fetch the boxes up here and stick 'em in the ground. Pap said he heered some had two in 'em."

"Okay, bud." Taking Jim's arm, Long helped him back down the muddy incline. "Keep your nose clean."

The boys followed them to the lane, their low-built collie waddling along behind.

"Say, mister, you know any fellers worken in that tunnel?"

"Sure. Lots of 'em."

"Pap says they're all dyen. Says they got somethin' worser'n cancer."

"You'd better go on home," Long called. "Go on, a rain's comin'!"

The boys stared at him, confusion and bewilderment darkening their faces.

"Pap says they're all choken to death!" one yelled, taking a step up the lane after Jim and Long. "Says they fall over dead in the road!" He paused, waiting for an answer, and when none came he called again. "He says they're dyen like flies, an there ain't nothin' that can stop it. Is that right, mister?"

Long did not answer. Offering his shoulder as a support for Jim, they made their way back toward the state highway, carefully avoiding what mud puddles they could in the treacherous, uncertain road.

"The way this feller named it to me," Lock Mullens explained, "you sign up with one of them lawyers, and if he wins out in court you stand to get a pile of money."

Going down the path after Lock, skirmishing anything which might cause him to stumble, Tom had gone several yards before he spoke again. "Mark said he seen a feller stop a colored man on the street. The nigger signed a piece of paper, and the feller give him a dollar and took his pencil back and told him he'd try to get him ten thousand dollars!"

"Mebby Mark didn't hear straight," Lock said skeptically. "He must a-said a thousand."

"No siree! Mark said he was standen close enough to tetch him. This feller is in here signen 'em up for some lawyers down to Charleston."

"I figure we ought to sign up first chanct we get," Lock continued seriously. "That way we'll get our money in case the company ain't got enough to go around."

It was not yet eight o'clock, and the sun, part way up, was only a soft blob in the rain-filled December sky. Leaves, caught in the brush along the path, hung wetly, adding their stench to the heavy decay which arose from the ground.

"Seems like we ought to stand a good chanct." Tom's voice was full and clear with bright wanting. "Nettie, she misdoubts it, but it stands to reason a feller ought to get somethin if he ain't ever goin to be able to do a day's work agin."

"There's one thing, Tom," Lock said, stopping to catch his breath. "The way the company looks at it, it ain't their fault. They say if a feller gets pneumoney or consumption that's his own lookout. Like Mort Tucker said, they tell how them niggers come out of there wringen with sweat an set in a chill gamblen all night. They say that's how they got the cough."

"That ain't where I got it," Tom protested loudly, "an it ain't where Ely got it neither. Nor Virgil, far's that goes!"

"I'm just tellen you, Tom. They 'low if a man loses a arm he's got somethin comen. But, 'corden to law, they ain't responsible if he gets him a cold an chokes to death."

Tom squared off in the path, his sunken eyes snapping fiercely. "Law or no law," he swore, "me and my boys worked in that hole, an now we're all dyen! What's goin to happen to Maw an Viney? Seems like there ought to be a law bout that! We worked hard and took care of ourselfs. What we kotched never come from no cold, you can bet yore hind-end! We're sick, and we got it in the tunnel, that's what! I'll get right up in court and name it too!"

Pacifically Lock laid his hand on Tom's shoulder. "I know that well as you do, Tom. Many's the night Daisy has helped me turn over when I was choken. An I'm near out of my mind, worryen bout her and the baby. Her heart's set on goin home and haven it there. I've been hangen on and hangen on, hopen to see my way clear. If the company don't pay us somethin, I don't know what will happen to us."

As autumn passed and Lock began to miss work Daisy made no mention of it, cold in her heart with the knowledge that he had already foregone the hope of returning. Finally she could stand the tightening apprehension no longer and she named it, calling the words bluntly and loudly across the supper table.

"It's way past time for us to head out," she charged. "Snow'll be flyen soon———" She halted sharply, seeing Lock's upturned face, his eyes dark and tortured.

"We can't make it this year, Daisy."

"You mean we ain't goin? We ain't goin a-tall!"

"Not now, Daisy. Mebby in the spring."

"Lock, you promised. You promised when we was married."

"I never knowed," he explained, his words wrapped in hurt and sick apology. "I never knowed it would turn out this-a-way."

"But you give my folks yore word!"

"There ain't no doctors back there, honey. You'll be wanten one, and I've a need for one. We'd best stay here, no matter what."

Crying, she left the house, coming back an hour later to find Lock still sitting at the table, his food untouched and his head caught in his hands, low over his knees.

Nothing more was said for over a week, and then, unable to stem the dread and terror which grew like a lump inside her breast, Daisy tore open the wound again. Lock worked part of that week, and all during the interminable, frightened days she paced the kitchen, feeling the heaviness of the child she carried, gathering to herself all the pity and hurt that hung about her.

By the time Lock came up the path from work she sat by the stove, her clothes partially packed and her face bloodless and quivering when she attempted to speak.

"What's the matter, honey?" Lock asked, seeing the worn valise, the unset table. "Yore time ain't near come, is it?" He dropped his dinner pail and ran across the kitchen, bending down to touch her face. "Yore pain ain't come——"

Daisy raised her head, struggling to hold back the tears which had already left her eyes dull and bloodshot. "I'm goin home," she managed thickly. "I'm set in my mind; I'm headen back home."

"Yore what, honey?" he asked incredulously.

"I'm goin home. I'm goin to have my baby back—— Oh, Lock, I'm scared! I'm scared to death!" Throwing her arms about his neck, she clung to him desperately, crying out her fear and terror. "Yore sick, and the baby's comen! I don't know what to do. We're all goin to die here! There ain't no chanct for us to last!"

"Honey," Lock said, drawing Daisy to her feet, his arms bent to accept her weight. "Honey, don't take on that-a-way. We got to last through someways. We got to."

For several minutes they stood in the center of the kitchen floor, the old valise at their feet, while Daisy sobbed and clung to him, the terror and pity gushing from her throat in loud unrestraint.

"Go ahead, honey," he consoled. "You got a thing to cry for."

"If—if anythin was to happen to you," she said, her words throbbing, "I don't know what on earth I'd do. When I hear that ambulance clangen up the valley it scares me to death!"

"Just don't listen to it, Daisy," he said gently. "You hadn't ought to let it upsot you, on count of the baby."

"I try, but it gets so it sounds like it's comen right straight to the house. I keep runnen to the door, scared it's goin to stop above the riverbank over yonder. If it ever done that, if it ever did, I reckon I'd just drop dead."

By the time word first came that lawyers were signing up the men Daisy no longer mentioned their return, walking through the house on heavy feet, lying awake at night so she could help Lock turn over when congested phlegm impaired his damaged breathing.

Going down the path, Lock was several steps ahead of Tom before he was aware of the distance between them. "Like I was sayen," he called, waiting for Tom, "the company looks at it different. Mort told me ever time a man dies they put it in the courthouse 'bout him haven pneumoney. All them fellers Wayne's buryen has been put down for pneumoney or somethin like that. The way I understand it, the law says they don't have to pay anythin if a man dies like that."

"I told you it was somethin else, Lock," Tom vowed. "They're just putten it onto that."

"I know it clear as day," Lock complied. "But when it gets to court that's the way they're goin to name it, sure's water is wet!"

"Well, it ain't right! A man works hisself to death——"

"What is it then?" Lock asked. "These lawyers have to pin it down to somethin so's the company can't worm out of it. That's the only way we stand to get compensayted."

Tom looked at him, angry with the question but knowing there was truth in what Lock said. "I don't know," he replied sharply. "But I'm goin down and sign up afore it's too late."

Again the younger man led the way, his steps broken and uncertain. Behind him Tom followed, bent a little at the shoulders, sucking his breath through his teeth with a windy, whistling sound.

They had neared the opening where the path cut through a field toward the state highway before Lock spoke again.

"How's Virgil feelen?" he asked. "He gitten any better?"

"Not a bit," Tom answered dejected. "He's losen flesh all the time, fastern it went off me. Last week he went twicet to see Doc Robinson. Now he can't barely walk by hisself."

"The doc do him any good?"

"Can't see none. It worries Nettie sick ever time. Virgil, he just comes home and mopes around, keepen to hisself. He allus done that, but sence he got to coughen and readen that book he just sets in a deep study the blessed time."

"If he gets company money he can head back for school," Lock said cheerfully. "Daisy says yore missus puts a sight of stock in that."

"We allus counted on it," Tom said, his head lowered and his voice windy. "Virgil was the puny one but the brightest of the lot. He read to me out of a book he'd never laid eyes on before, big as anybody."

"He goin to sign up too?" Lock asked.

"I'm doin it for him. He's too sickly to get off the place much."

Tom caught a dead branch, broke it into many small pieces and threw it aside before he answered. "Nettie's afeered Virgil can't hold out," he admitted softly. "His coughen fits is worser'n Ely's was. I've seen her afore, cryen back of the house. Nother time she'll just set in a chair, looken straight into nothin, and if you speak to her seems like she don't hardly know you."

Lock nodded understandingly but said nothing as he followed the sloppy path through the low field toward the end of the iron bridge.

Along the highway which led from Hawk's Nest down past the tunnel men were lined in little groups beside the pavement, their heads drawn together. The drone of cars interrupted their talk, and periodically they paused, waiting for the sound to pass. Some propped their gaunt bodies up with whittled canes and others, leaning against fences and telephone poles, kept holding their overall coats close about their necks. Few smoked, for it irritated their throats, and as the hum of a car faded their low, strangled coughs arose above the murmur of the Gauley and New rivers flowing together.

The largest group congregated at the end of the bridge, seating themselves on the cement abutment or tilting back against the railing that fenced the pedestrian walk to either side of the smooth-floored bridge.

Lock and Tom studied the straggling line and started toward the bridge, searching expectantly for a well-clothed figure, for a man who might be collecting names on the contractual forms he carried.

"Mornen," Lock said, nearing the abutment.

The men nodded, and one whose cheeks were red where the bones neared the flesh spoke. "You're Mullens, ain't you?"

"Yep. This is Tom Reip. He worked Number One."

"Never recognized you," the man stated. "You used to be a good-sized feller."

"We heered a lawyer was here from Charleston," Tom said cordially. "You seen one round anywheres?"

"One just went up the road," a short wiry man said, pointing toward the Jungle. "There's another one down at the filling station. They're getting thick as lice on a dog's back."

Lock and Tom edged into the group, finding places with stiff casualness, wanting to be taken into the talk. "You figure them fellers are goin to be able to get us anythin?" Tom asked, seating himself.

"Nobody's goin to help us," the tall red-cheeked man declared loudly. "They just want to get shet of us."

"Most of the lawyers are in cahoots with the company," another interrupted. "They're just signing us up so they can stall as long as they want to. Soon as the tunnel's through they'll chase us out, same as if we never done a lick of work for them."

"Now, they wouldn't do that," Lock began. "We can stay————"

"They're doin it a'ready," the man snapped back. "They're layen the sorriest ones off left and right, tryen to get shet of them!"

"That's the truth," a colored-man spoke from the edge of the crowd. "Layed off twenty mo' last night. Soon's they hole thro' they'll fire 'em by the hun'red. Guess they don't want to look at us any more."

"They done put some out in Number Three camp," a man beside him declared. "Put 'em on the road and tole 'em to ball the jack. Yes sir, that's what they done."

"Way I heered it," Tom returned, "they're fixen to lay it into the company bout so many bein sick and dyen. Ain't that a fact?"

"That Wright feller is tryen, over there in Fayetteville, I guess," the red-cheeked man replied. "But we ain't goin to get nothin from nobody."

"Them other lawyers————" Lock interrupted.

"Even if they got something, we'll never know it," the man barked angrily. "They got big pockets, an if the company fills them, they'll shet up bout wanten to help us. I seen 'em signen up the niggers. One feller asked for fifteen dollars to get home on. Said the lawyer could have all the rest he collected. Damn lawyer just give him a dollar and took his pencil back. Hell will freeze over 'fore that man hears from the lawyer again!"

"Ain't there nothin we can do?" Lock asked simply. "Nothin a-tall?"

"You can jump in the river," the man snapped bitterly. "Throw your kids in too, if you got any!"

Lock looked at Tom, and his eyes moved on about the group, slowly and steadily, seeing their slumped shoulders, the great pockets that cupped their sunken eyes.

"I ain't goin to do that," he said. "I can still work—someday."

"Just you go somewhere and try to get a job. Soon's they know you worked in the tunnel they quit talken to you. What're you goin to do then? Nothin, that's what. Just sit round on your back end, watching your kids go hungry, knowen that somethin is killen you inside."

Uneasily Lock got to his feet. "I'm goin over the bridge, Tom. You comen?"

Awkwardly Tom made his way through the outstretched legs. As he started after Lock the thin wiry man called after him. "If you sign up," he warned, "be sure you get your dollar!"

Lock gestured his hand in stiff, unaccustomed camaraderie and made for the street which led through Gauley Bridge. Ahead they saw other clots of men, caught along the street and in front of the stores like deadwood on a creek bank.

During these days, as the four openings drew together forming one long tunnel, completing the job, Maw Reip seldom left the hard-packed yard which surrounded the house. Before her constant vigil with Ely had ended on the hill above the town she realized that Tom could not be left alone. By the time he was able to walk the road before the shack with Lock, Virgil had gone to bed, regaining his strength slowly. When it seemed he might get well the coughing spells had become more frequent, more suffocating as they tore their way from his throat, and she stayed near the house, watching him unremittently. On sunny days she carried him onto the porch, leaving her work many times to go to the door, fearful that his throat would become clogged before she could reach him.

"You al'right, son?" she would ask each time.

"Sure, Maw. I'm fine."

"You feel a chill? It's damp along the ground this mornen."

"No. I'm warm as anything."

On the morning Lock and Tom walked to town Virgil laid his book aside and motioned Maw nearer.

"Maw, I been thinken a lot," he said. "It's funny how all them fellers worken at the tunnel are dyen."

"Go on back to yore readen, Virgil. You hadn't ought to think bout them things."

"I been over and over it in my head, Maw. There must be some reason 'sides the cough. If it was pneumoney, seems like women folks would get it, and the little ones."

"It does, for a fact, son," Maw agreed, trying to close the talk. "Would you like another glass of milk?"

Virgil shook his head, staring thoughtfully down the yard. "Sitten here, hearen the ambulance ever day," he went on quietly, "I get to thinken. Now I got the trouble and Paw's got it, and Mark, he coughs some too. But you and Viney, you ain't never had it. That's a funny thing, don't you think, Maw?"

"Son," Maw said, easing back toward the doorway, "you go on with yore readen. You ain't no business thinken things like that. Just set yore mind on gitten well."

"Maw, I don't think I'm goin to get well."

"Virgil, don't talk that way!"

"I don't care, Maw. If there was just somebody to take care of you and Paw. If a feller's got to die, one time's as good as another."

"Virgil," Maw pleaded, trying to control her quavering voice. "Virgil, hesh that!"

"I ain't aimen to upset you, Maw," he said apologetically, listening to see if her weeping had broken through. "But I got somethin set in my mind. I won't ever be able to work again, and Paw won't neither. A time will come when you an———"

"Hesh now, Virgil, hesh! I can't bear to hear you talk that way."

"I been thinken, Maw, till my head's bout to split," he continued determinedly, "tryen to find a way so's you'd have a little place of yore own when we're all gone."

"Virgil, for the Lord's sake, hesh up! Yore just sick and low in yore mind———"

"Don't cry, Maw. I got to tell you what I been thinken." He ceased for a moment, looking at her twisted, blood-drained face. "I want to tell you whilst there ain't nobody else home."

"Son," Maw broke in, "like you say, we're on hard days right now, but don't you go thinken like that. We'll get along someways. I can take in washens. We'll get along, son."

"I heered Paw and Lock talken bout them lawyers and how the company figures there ain't no call for them to pay the men. I been thinken bout that, Maw, and now you got to promise me somethin."

Maw wet her lips, swallowing hard, and nodded her head a little. "If it's anythin in reason, son. Anythin a-tall."

He settled back in his chair, his voice lowered and steady. "The way I see it, the fellers that worked in the dust is the ones that're dyen. Ain't none of the construction gang died but that nigger that fell off and kilt hisself. Ain't nobody on the outside died; only the ones in the dust." Behind him he could hear Maw pressing her back to the rough wall. "You listenin, Maw?"

"I'm listenin, Virgil."

"The way I got it set in my head," he continued, "it must be the dust that kills everybody."

"That's what Tom allus said!" she replied, her relief coming out with the words. "He allus layed it to the dust."

"If that's why it happened, and was they to prove it in court, then the company would have to pay for all the men that died."

"I reckon."

"It stands to reason they knowed what kind of dust it was," he explained, his voice carefully modulated, as though he listened through his words for Maw's reactions. "They saved the rock and hauled it down to Alloy, so they could use it for somethin."

"I heered," she agreed. "Lock said he seen it, all piled up in a field."

"The way I got it layed out," Virgil said, "if a person was to show that the dust was what kilt the men, the company would have to pay you somethin. Somethin for Ely an somethin——"

"Virgil, you hadn't ought to name it that-a-way," Maw reproached quickly. "It ain't a fitten way to talk. Tom's walken round now, and yore a mite better. By spring——"

"Promise me now, Maw," he went on relentlessly, "promise me you'll do what I'm goin to ask you."

"If it's in reason, son."

"I been talken to the doctor. He thinks it's a right thing to do."

"What is it, son?" Maw asked apprehensively. "Name it to me."

"Maw, when I die I want you to have them cut me open and see if it ain't the dust that's killen us."

"Virgil, in the name of God!" Maw cried.

"It's the only thing to do," he hurried on. "That way we can tell if it's the dust."

"Virgil, don't talk to yore maw like that! Hesh up now! Hesh!"

"I want you to, Maw. I fixed it with the doctor a'ready."

"You ain't no right to say that," Maw began, whimpering. "You ain't no right——"

"Promise me, Maw!"

"No, I won't! I won't, before God, I won't!"

"You got to, Maw. It's the only thing in the world I want."

"Son—son," she cried, "yore sick and low in yore mind. Yore frettin yoreself to death——"

"Promise now, Maw."

"No, no! Stop asken me——"

"Mebby if they find out," he explained, driving the words from his throat, "mebby then they'll know how to cure Paw and Mark. It ain't just for the money, Maw. It's the only chanct."

Her shoulders began to shake convulsively, and her grief broke through her hands as she started for the door.

"Doctor Robinson thinks the company is coveren up somethin," Virgil went on loudly. "He thinks they know, but they ain't plannen to let it slip out! They're fixen to run all the men off soon's the work is over, so's nobody will ever know. That's why you got to promise, Maw! It's my only chanct to help——"

There he stopped, hearing Maw run through the kitchen and out into the back yard, her voice breaking into a high, piercing cry as she fled across the corner of the garden toward the old hammock.

32

For two weeks Virgil lay on the cot in a corner of the kitchen, propped up to get his breath. Maw rarely left his side, working about the kitchen during the day and lying awake in the double bed against the wall at night. Her own face, tortured by grief and unanswerable worry, had grown thin, the flesh hanging in little folds at the corners of her mouth and where her jawbones traced their way up toward her ears.

During the second week Maw hardly slept at all. More than once she sprang from her bed at night, paralyzed with a cold fear that Virgil had died during her brief sleep. The fear of sleeping, of missing any warning harshness of breath which preceded a choking spell, caused her to freeze with horror, and Maw fought off sleep as she fought off the inevitable fact that Virgil's days were following the pattern of those which had ended Ely's life.

Sometimes during the day she read to Virgil from her ancient, worn Bible, but it was hard for her to keep her place and often she read the same passage two or three times, unaware that she repeated it. Frantic with worry, the memory of standing beside Ely's grave forever returning, and with a hollow emptiness ringing back of her ears, concentration was impossible for her. Many times Maw found herself standing in the middle of the room, not knowing how she got there, as though her distracted mind had left her body and she was only aware of it at some later, indeterminable time. It added to her worry, and she would try to remember what had happened, frightened by the blind intermediate period and made more desperate when she could not remember.

Virgil talked little, scarcely moving his thin legs and arms under the blankets. He would follow Maw around the room with his eyes, and when she placed her arm beneath his neck, lifting him to accept the spoonful of medicine, he would ease back down on the pillow, his eyes never leaving her worn, stoical face.

"Remember, Maw," he would say, "you promised."

"Hesh, son. Rest yoreself."

"You'll do it, won't you, Maw? Doctor Robinson's got everything fixed and ready."

"Rest now, Virgil. Rest."

"Say you promise, Maw."

Mutely she would nod, turning away.

"Name it, Maw. Name yore promise."

"I'll do what you ask, son. I'll do it."

He would become silent then, still on the cot, his arms thin in the flannel nightgown and his eyes following her about the kitchen.

At six o'clock in the morning on the last Tuesday of the month Mark, who had been up since three o'clock, ran down to the river, searching for the rowboat with the yellow light of a carbide lamp. Hurriedly he rowed across the river and raced down the highway after Dr Robinson. Racing back over the dark water as fast as Mark could pull the oars, they saw that all of the lights were on in the house and, from the single window in the Mullens shack, that Lock and Daisy were up and their lamps going.

As the boat scraped bottom, reaching shore, the doctor sprang out, bobbing his flashlight, and raced up the embankment.

Looping the tie rope about the trunk of a willow, Mark fled up the incline after him, his steps faltering and uncertain. Reaching the road which passed between the dark houses, he began to stumble, and with one hand stretched out before him he got to the empty, decrepit house where the Stumps had lived. With a sharp pain ripping over his chest he sagged onto the rotten porch and stretched across the damp, musk-smelling boards, the blood pounding and thumping behind his ears. As he lay, his arms outstretched, he could hear Maw's shrill, hysterical wailing as it came from the lighted windows and sounded through the dark, dawn-threatened night.

Dr Robinson placed his bag down on a chair, opening it. Maw raised her swollen eyes, staring at his fleet, expert movements. For a second she was quiet, whimpering like a child, then she sprang to her feet, her fists beating the sides of her head as one piercing scream followed another from her throat.

"Nettie—— Oh God, Nettie——" Tom cried, reaching for her. "Nettie—don't don't, don't——"

At the foot of the double bed Viney May stomped up and down, screaming and fighting to break free of Daisy Mullens' hold. Beside her Lock stood, extending and withdrawing his arms each time the child threatened to strike his wife.

Wiping his hypodermic needle with a piece of cotton, the doctor crossed the room and grabbed Maw's arm, holding it rigidly. "It's all right, Mrs Reip," he repeated softly, rapidly. "It's all right, Mrs Reip. It's all right."

Maw's weeping diminished, her lips shaking and her voice trailing in a low whine as she watched the doctor's hand. Quickly he injected the needle, withdrew it and pressed the cotton to the wound.

Suddenly, before he could halt her, Maw knocked him aside, ran across the room and threw herself on the floor beside the cot.

"Oh, Virgil! Virgil, boy!" she cried, clawing at the pillow. "Speak to yore maw, Virgil! Speak—speak—— Oh, Lord Jesus!"

"Try to get her to bed," the doctor spoke to Tom. "Try to get her to lie down."

As Tom crossed to Maw, his arms reaching for her, the doctor turned to Daisy and Lock.

"You'd better take the girl out," he advised softly. "Quiet her down if you can."

Nodding and urging Viney before them, Daisy started for the back door.

"Leave her with a neighbor and hurry back," Dr Robinson asked. "Somebody had better stay with Mrs Reip. She'll need somebody when she awakens."

Daisy and Lock exchanged mute, questioning glances.

"We ain't got no neighbors," Lock said. "I'll keep the girl. Daisy can come back."

"Where is everybody?" the doctor asked. "Are you the only families over here now?"

"They all died or left," Lock explained. "There's just the Reips and us now. That's all."

Robinson looked at them and back to Tom and Maw.

"Do what you can," he said, going toward the cot. "Mrs Reip is badly upset."

Nodding silently, Lock and Daisy went out the door, urging Viney along between them. Wordlessly they passed down behind the dark houses, each with an arm about the child. Cutting over the slushy road, they saw Mark emerge from the shadows of the old Stump place, his face ghostly white in the first faint streaks of dawn.

For a week following Virgil's burial Tom Reip did not leave the house. From the morning they came back down the hill, weak and without life, he did not allow Maw from his sight. Seeing her sit with a pan of unpeeled potatoes in her lap, her paring knife halted and still in her hand, Tom moved cautiously, trying to arouse her from the stupor which enveloped her. More often than not he failed, causing Maw to go from him in bitter weeping or to stare at him from remote, passionless eyes, her mouth working dryly as though there was no spittle to wet her pale lips.

Mark did what he could, attempting to draw Maw's mind from its relentless torture, and no day passed when Daisy Mullens did not come through the kitchen door, anxiously ready to share Maw's work, fearfully trying to lessen her burden.

Shortly before Christmas, seeing that Maw still walked aimlessly from one room to the other, mumbling to herself and making odd, unco-ordinated motions with her hands, Tom brought Daisy to the house and, leaving by the back way, headed through the thin, moist snow for Gauley Bridge and Dr Robinson's office.

At the bridge he passed the men with a slight nod, anxious to see the doctor and get back home as soon as possible.

"Hear you lost another'n," a tall red-haired man called.

Tom nodded, walking on.

"You down to sign him up? If the company pays us anythin, you oughter be rich!"

"Ain't no use dependen on it, Tom!" another called. "They ain't fixen to do nothin bout us!"

Leaving the bridge, Tom passed the gas station and was nearing the Ford agency when Lessie banged out of the cafe door and ran toward him.

"I wanted to ask bout Maw," she cried, overtaking him. "How's she feelen this mornen?"

"She ain't no better, Lessie. Don't seem like she takes any interest in anythin."

Lessie's face clouded, her mouth moving in the shadow of the worry and concern she felt. "Mark was tellen me," she said. "I'm comen up to see her tonight. Maybe I can bring her some sewin or somethin to do."

"We tried that," Tom replied. "Mis' Mullens fetched her some fancywork. Don't seem like she can get any heart for it."

"She still goin to the graveyard ever day, Mister Reip?"

"Ever day. Mis' Mullens says she just stands there with the tears runnen down her face." Swallowing, Tom looked at his shoes, squashing the toes a little. "I done everthin I know," he said sorrowfully. "If Maw goes, I don't know what will become of us. Just seems like I'm whupped, and I don't know which way to turn."

"Maybe," Lessie ventured helpfully, "maybe you ought to take Maw and Viney May and head back for Slaty Crick. Me and Mark—we'd send whatever we can."

"Thank ye kindly," Tom said. "I been over that in my mind a'ready. Nettie, she won't hear of it. Says she ain't goin off an leave the boys on the hill yonder by theirselves."

"No," Lessie said apologetically. "No, I reckon she wouldn't."

"It's more'n a man can stand," Tom went on lifelessly. "I lost two of my boys and broke down myself. If Maw goes, there ain't no use me holden out any longer."

"Don't talk that way, Mister Reip. You still got Mark and Viney. In time Maw will get over it. Gauley Bridge ain't a bad place to live in. When it gets warm agin you'll get work somewheres——"

Tom shook his head, his eyes, beneath his bushy brows, still and dull. "Ain't no use thinken that," he said wearily. "Ain't nobody wants me any more. I'd be just as well off dead."

Lessie shifted from one foot to the other, looking helplessly back toward the cafe. "Come on," she said, "I'll go see the doctor with you. Seems like he ought to find somethin to give Maw. We'll have a good talk with him." Without thinking, she took Tom's arm, helping him down the slushy street, her white uniform bright and clean beside his dark, streaked overalls and jacket.

Arriving at the neat frame building where Dr Robinson lived and had his office, Lessie opened the door, passed inside and held it for Tom.

"It's turnen colder, ain' it?" she said, shivering and rubbing her bare arms. Although she had not spoken all the way down the street, now, inside the living-waiting room, she moved freely, reassured by the doctor's nearness.

"We come to see the doctor," she advised his plump, soft-cheeked wife. "This is Mister Reip."

The woman looked at Tom, memory rising slowly and sympathetically in her eyes. "I've heard the doctor speak of you, Mr Reip. You've had a great deal of trouble, haven't you?"

"Thank you, m'am," Tom said, pulling his hat from his head. I come to see about my wife. She's feelen porely."

"Come right in. The doctor's waiting to see you. He received some news for you in the mail this morning."

Lessie edged along beside Tom into the room where Dr Robinson sat at his desk, several books spread before him, partially covering the instruments that were scattered over the glass top.

"Good morning, Tom," he said, extending an arm cordially. "I just got a report this morning—from the examinations. Sit down there. I've got a lot to tell you."

Obediently Tom accepted the chair. Lessie stood at his side, her arm across his shoulder.

"One report came from Ohio State University, at Columbus, and another from Chicago." Searching beneath the outspread books, Dr Robinson found two letters neatly clipped together.

"You know," he said kindly, "we made an examination of Virgil's lungs. The boy wanted it, talked to me many times about it. Well, those reports came back this morning. Your son was right. It is the dust that is killing the men."

Tom edged forward on his chair, passing his hat from one hand to the other.

"Everbody allus said that," Lessie broke in. "Leastways they allus thought it good and hard."

"But we didn't know exactly what it was. Virgil has helped us to find out."

"Ain't it the same as any other kind of dust?" Tom asked. "It just seemed finer, that's all."

"No," the doctor explained, drawing nearer to Tom. "This is silica dust. These reports show without question that the men have been dying from silicosis."

"Silicosis?" Tom queried blankly. "I never heerd of it."

"Then it ain't tunnelitis, like they said?" Lessie broke in anxiously. "That allus did sound funny to me, like they'd made it up."

"Any reputable doctor knows there is no such thing as tunnelitis." He hesitated, flipping the letters with the back of his hand. "These reports on Virgil's lungs," he stated, "prove once and for all that the men in that tunnel are dying from silicosis. The company must have known all along. I don't believe anybody will be able to deny that."

A little dazed, Tom eased back in his chair. "Will they know how to cure it now?" he asked. "Will it do any good?"

The doctor lowered his eyes, staring at the letters. "I've been working since these reports arrived this morning," he said. "I've read everything I can lay my hands on. I'm afraid there is no cure for silicosis."

"None a-tall," Lessie said, her voice loud in the still room. "Lordie, that's awful!"

"Just preventions," the doctor continued. "Most of the trouble could have been prevented if the men had been given proper protection. But there is no known cure."

Tom raised his head, trying to speak, but dropped it again without saying a word.

losing the door of the little shack just below the colored church, Long cut across the dark scar the path made and headed for the street, the bottle of gin beneath his heavy coat, cold and smooth against his hip.

An hour before, he had left the rooming house, plodding his slow way down the hill, three dollars held in one hand inside his pants pocket. He had gone over the unsure footing as rapidly as he dared, his mind filled with the memory of Jim stretched across the bed, his face shoved into a pillow and his shoulders shrugging disconsolately each time Long spoke.

Since the Sunday evening, weeks before, when they had made their wordless way back from the burial field in Summersville, Jim had grown increasingly morose. For days, as the snows began, he remained in the room, sullen and caustic, answering Long in monosyllables and begrudging any intrusion which broke the interminable hours he spent stretched across the rumpled bed.

Of a morning Long would steal quietly about the room, pulling his clothes on in the darkness, his ears cocked toward the bed. Jim never spoke but, tiptoeing down the hall toward the bathroom door, Long was aware that his shadowy movements had been watched, that Jim awaited his departure with silent, bitter resentment.

In the beginning Long had placed a dollar or two beneath the pin dish on the dresser, not wanting to face the awkwardness of urging money on to Jim. But soon after they had visited Owl's grave he came home one evening to find the money untouched. He made no mention of it until he had thrown his work clothes into a corner and stood buttoning his clean shirt before the mirror.

"Christ, Jim, didn't you eat today?" he said, watching through the mirror.

No sound came from the bed.

"Come on. Get up. We'll go downtown and eat. I'm sick of the grub here."

"Go ahead." Jim's words were muted, his arm lying across his face.

"Come on. Maybe we'll see a movie. They've got *Hell's Angels*. I heard it was plenty hot; some new broad."

Jim made no sound, and Long finished dressing, moving briskly and noisily about the room in a cumbersome attempt to dispel the silence.

"Get the hell up out of there, Jim. I'm hungry!" Pulling his heavy coat on, Long got his hat from atop the chair and set it on his head.

"I'm not goin'."

"Jesus Christ, guy, you ain't eaten all day. Come on, get the lead outta your pants!" Reaching down, he yanked Jim's leg, tugging him toward the edge of the bed. "Come on!"

Drawing up his knees, Jim kicked Long's hand away. "Get out and leave me alone!" he demanded sharply.

"Come on, guy," Long said patiently. "Come on."

"Goddamnit, get out of here and leave me alone!" Jim swore, crawling to the far side of the bed. "Go on, get out!"

"What the hell's the matter with you?"

Sullenly Jim turned his face to the wall, not speaking.

"Want me to bring you something?" Long asked, heading for the door. "Anna'll fix it up."

"No."

"Jesus, you got to eat something," Long said, going out. 'You can't live on an empty gut!"

Returning an hour later, he placed the sandwiches and container of coffee on the dresser but, receiving no answer from Jim, he went out again, angry and disturbed.

The following morning the food remained where he had placed it. Coming off the shift that evening, Long saw it was still untouched and the two dollars had not been moved from the corner of the pin dish.

"Hey, look, fellow—you can starve yourself to death if you want to," Long charged, "but you're behaving like a goddamn fool!"

"Get out and leave me alone!"

Long said nothing more until he had dressed and was ready to go. Buttoning his coat, he stood at the foot of the bed.

"Hey, Jim," he said, "let's you and me have a talk."

Sprawled on the bed, Jim made no answer. Irritably he hunched his shoulders, twisting away.

"Why didn't you go out and get something to eat?" Long asked. "How are you goin to get well if you don't eat?" He waited, and when there was no answer he continued, his voice rising with taut anger. "What the hell's the matter with you?" he demanded angrily. "You ain't said two words! You think I'm talkin' to entertain myself? "

"Get out!"

"Get out, my back end! We're goin' to get this thing settled here and now. Are you goin' to get up and eat something or are you goin' to lay there like a damn kid? I'm gettin' fed up with your grouchy——"

Suddenly Jim sprang off the bed, tottering weakly. Grabbing the bedpost to steady himself he whirled about, staring at Long from red-veined eyes. "I'll get out, if that's what you want!" he yelled. "I'll get out right now! I took all the crap from you I'm goin' to. Sure! Sure! You been workin'—you been paying the rent!" Shaking, he crossed to the dresser and snatched up the two dollar bills.

"There, that's yours too! Take it! I'm gettin' out of here!"

Wordlessly Long watched him go to the clothes closet and grab his pants and shirt from the row of nails along the back wall.

"Wait a minute, wait a minute," Long said evenly. "Why didn't you tell me what was on your mind?"

"Go on, get out!" Jim cried fiercely. "You're al'right! You can still work. Just leave me alone!"

"Jim," Long began, his voice lowered and conciliatory, "is that what you've been thinking about, laying there on the bed?"

"What the hell do you suppose I think about—Christmas! You try it sometime."

Long pulled off his heavy coat and tossed it onto the bed. "Look, Jim," he said, seating himself, "we've got to have a talk. I guess I must be pretty goddamn dumb. I thought you was lettin' the cough get you down; I didn't know what was on your mind."

"Well, you know now!" Pulling on his shoes, Jim laced them haphazardly, the sides of his neck throbbing with the exhausting effort.

"Look, Jim, it's been more than a year since I picked you out of that ditch this side of Memphis. We been hittin' it off together———"

"Sure," Jim declared hotly, his mouth white with bitterness, "sure, you were swell! That's another thing I owe you for! Well, goddamnit, I'd a-been better off if I'd busted my damn head wide open! It would have been over quick that way———"

"Cut out that crap!" Long demanded sharply, stiff-arming Jim, knocking him a little sideways. "You sound like you're crazy in the head!"

"Maybe I am," Jim retorted. "I don't give a damn one way or the other."

Long walked back to the dresser, watching Jim haul a sweater over his head.

"Where the hell do you think you're goin'?" he asked presently.

"None of your damn business" Jim said, tossing his shaving brush and razor inside a shirt and tying the sleeves together.

Straightening up Long crossed the room, grabbed him by the shoulders and whirled him about. "I'll tell you where you're goin'," he declared, his voice low and restrained. "You're goin' to stay right here until I get back. I'll get some grub and a bottle of gin. Tomorrow, after I draw my pay, you and me are headin' out of here. That's settled!"

Jim looked at Long across his shoulder, his mouth twisted in derisive silence.

"We'll head for Arizona or New Mexico. Once we get out there we'll throw off that cough in no time. I got thirty-nine bucks saved and fourteen comin'. That'll see us fine."

"I don't want any of your goddamn money," Jim snapped, gathering up the tied shirt. "You'll be throwin' that up to me too."

In great steps Long bounded across the room and grabbed the shirt from Jim's hands. Drawing back, he threw it with all his might into the clothes closet and faced Jim, his upper lip protruding a little at one corner. "Look," he said tensely, "you can give that crap to a lot of people, but you can't give it to me! I said tomorrow you and me were headin' out of here. That don't mean tonight—that means tomorrow! And one more crack out of you about money and I'll knock your damn teeth out! Now set down there until I get back!"

Shrugging morosely, Jim crossed to the large chair and lumped his body into it.

"And get ready to eat," Long said, said, passing through the door. "I'm bringing stuff back."

Hearing Long's footsteps vanish down the hall, Jim got up and made his way to the clothes closet. Bending down, his hand clinging to the doorframe for support, he picked up the bundle and got back to his feet. For several minutes he stood looking at it, cold sweat beading his forehead from the enervating effort. Then, as his body seemed to grow limp with weakness and fatigue, he dropped the bundle and sagged tiredly into bed.

Coming back past the colored church onto the end of the of the sidewalk and through beneath the brightly lighted marquee of the Bijou, Long passed the Ford agency and cut into the Kanawha Cafe, stomping his feet on the step to remove the clinging slush and snow.

Inside he found a seat near the end of the counter and gave Lessie his order for two roast beef and two cheese sandwiches.

"Want mustard on 'em?" Lessie smiled. "It's free."

"Nope," Long replied, easing back so the seat of the stool did not force the bottle of gin from his hip pocket. "But put some ketchup on the roast beef."

Partially opening the swinging door, Lessie called into the kitchen, "Two cheese and two roast beef bleeden, to go!"

"And put a couple bottles of ginger ale in the sack," Lock added. "And lemon, if you've got some."

"Oh-ho," Lessie grinned, cocking her head knowingly.

Anna, who had been talking to a short, neatly dressed man near the end of the counter, left him and walked toward Long.

"How's Jim?" she asked. "I haven't seen him for nearly a week."

"He's okay. Kind of lost his pep, I guess."

"Pete says he stays in his room all the time. Mrs Higgenbottom is worried. She told me this morning he wouldn't even let her in to clean the place."

"He'll be al'right in a couple of days. How's Pete?"

Anna drew in a deep breath, letting it out slowly before she answered. "He's not any better. Worse, if anything. I've been thinking about taking him away somewheres."

"Go to Arizona," Long suggested, "or New Mexico. The air's better out there. He might stand a chance of gettin' well."

"She's talked about them places al'ready," Lessie declared. "Anna's got a map showing where they are. Boy, that'd sure be a far piece to travel."

Mr Hathaway, who had been talking with Anna near the front of the counter, twisted about on his stool. "Did you work in the tunnel too?" he asked Long.

"Sure. Why?"

"Guess you heard then—about it being silicosis."

"Yeah, I heard."

"You think the company will give the men anything for it?"

"What do you think, stranger?"

Before Hathaway could answer Anna interrupted. "That's Mr Hathaway. He sells embalming fluid. He gave Pete and me a lift when we were first coming here."

"Howdy," Long said. "My name's Legg."

Leaving his place, the salesman came down the counter and sat beside Long. "I've been talking to Anna about this silicosis. In my business we run into all sorts of things. When I heard about them sending the boy's lungs away I got in touch with Doctor Robinson. He told me what it was. I did some reading then and talked to several specialists." Hathaway took his hat off, wiped the sweatband with his handkerchief and replaced it. "Yes sir," he repeated, "I've seen all sorts of things in this business. But what that company is doing here is one of the worst disgraces I ever come onto in all my life. I've run into a little of that silicosis before. They've got some in the mines in Pennsylvania, and some in Ohio, where they make pottery and glass. But this is the worst; this is the worst."

"What do you mean?" Long asked. "Ain't it all the same?"

"The way they treated the men up there," Hathaway explained, nodding his head to accent his words. "Driving them into that place when they knew all the time what they were up against."

"He says the company knowed all the time," Lessie added, her voice keen with outrage. "They knowed they was lyen when they called it tunnelitis!"

"You think they did?" Long asked.

"Of course they knew. They sunk test drills, didn't they? They hauled the rock down to Alloy so they could use it in steel processing when they get the plant set up. Do you think they'd do that unless they knew what kind of rock it was?"

Mr Johns slipped quietly in through the swinging door, carrying the sandwiches, and came to a halt at the end of the counter, listening intently.

"And why do you think they broadened that tunnel?" the salesman went on challengingly. "They knew that rock was almost pure silica, that's why. It's the only reason on earth."

"Yep," Long agreed. "We could see that."

"But they didn't give the men masks to wear and fix the ventilators!" Anna's voice, sharp and angry, sounded loud in the long room. "Why didn't they do that, if they knew it was killing the men?"

"They didn't give a hoot," Hathaway went on heatedly. "The Lord knows, the business I'm in a man don't think much about hearing that a few people died. But this—this is different." He eased forward on the stool, drawing nearer Long. "As I say, I've been looking into this silicosis. Now generally when a man gets it he might live ten-twelve years, maybe longer. You see, it depends on how much of that stuff you breathe. In a coal mine the silica content might be only eight or ten per cent. A man could work a whole lifetime in a place like that, and chances are he'd die of something else. But, according to the tests they've been making, that rock up there in the tunnel was almost pure silica, ran about ninety-nine per cent pure. They've got tests showing it."

"Why didn't they tell the men, and they could have gone someplace else to work?" Lessie asked. "Tom wouldn't of worked there, nor Ely or Mark—"

"Me either, you can bet your bottom dollar!" Long declared. "But they never mentioned it."

"I knowed there was something in the dust," Mr Johns offered meekly from the end of the counter. "I seen them fellers losen weight, don't matter how much they et, and I knowed it was somethin they was catchen in the tunnel."

"The company figured they'd finish up the job and get out before anybody knew what was happening to them," Hathaway pointed out. "They thought the men would scatter and nobody would ever know."

"Good God," Long declared, staring down between his legs. "Ain't nobody got a right to do a thing like that, I don't care how big the company is."

"No siree!" Lessie cried vehemently. "And they was all fine people too! Like Pete and Virgil and Mark——"

"And that Owens feller from New York State," Mr Johns added. "I figure he either died or went crazy with worry long before he ever got home. He wasn't no bigger'n a beanpole——"

"That must be why the company is chasing away all the men who can't work," Anna said, stepping nearer Hathaway. "They must want to spread them out as much as they can."

"Sure," Hathaway continued forcefully. "They'll go off somewhere and die, and the doctor will pronounce it pneumonia or consumption or some lung trouble. That's just what the company wants them to do. If they all stay around here together and start dying, it would raise a hell of a stink! People would know about it all over the country."

Long twisted about, looking directly at the fluid salesman. "You say you've been doin some readin' on this silicosis stuff? You know what it is?"

"Sure. Little pieces of dust—so little you have to use a microscope to see them. Well, they get in a man's lungs, in the little places where the air passes from the lungs into the blood stream. See, they don't belong there, so what does the body do? It builds a wall around all of them. Kind of shuts them off so they can't do any harm."

"Shuts 'em off?" Lessie asked incredulously.

Hathaway paused, spreading his hand over the counter. "Say this is the wall of the lung, my hand here. It gets all full of that dust, and the body starts building up a resistance wall, so to speak. That keeps on, and pretty soon the whole lung is covered with this stiff wall. It's almost like a wart. Then, when it gets like that, it gets stiff and the lung can't breathe to do any good. First time a man gets a cold—bang!— and he's gone! Why? Because his lung is too stiff to breathe any more."

"Oh Lord," Lessie exclaimed, her voice filled with wonder and horror. "Is that how it is?"

"That's how it is," Hathaway replied.

"Now I understand," Anna said, nodding her head thoughtfully. "That's why Pete almost drowned. He couldn't get his breath. He was always a good swimmer, but he got out in the river and couldn't get his breath."

Long sat staring at the wrapped sandwiches Lessie had placed before him. "The more of that dust a man breathes, the quicker he would die, eh?" he asked presently.

"Sure; you see, if the silica content had not been so high—nearly a hundred per cent—and if the men had been given proper protection, they wouldn't be dying like they are now. But there was too much of it. That's why they're beginning to die before the company can finish the job and get out, like they planned."

"Jesus," Long gasped. "Jesus, that's awful!"

"Yes, brother. It sure is."

"Tell me, fellow," Long asked, "if a man went where it was warmer, where he couldn't get a cold so easy— would he live longer?"

"He might."

Silently Anna walked away, passing before Mr Johns at the end of the counter and slipping unnoticed into the women's room.

"You think somewhere out West would be all right?"

"Sure. The Southwest would be good. Course if a man had it bad enough he'd die anyhow."

"But it might help some, eh?"

"Sure. As long as he didn't catch a cold or get any lung complication his chances would be better. But he's got to die sooner or later."

"Everyone that's got it?" Long asked somberly.

"I'm afraid so. Just like the ones who're dying today."

"They're dyen fast too!" Lessie exclaimed. "Ever day that ambulance keeps runnen up and down the road with them!"

"And that's another funny thing," Hathaway revealed. "All those men are dying, and that undertaker isn't buying half the embalming fluid he ought to."

"Good Lord," Mr Johns exclaimed. "Good Lord, think of that!"

Long picked up his change and started for the door. "Thank you for telling me them things," he said. "When the company started speedin' up the work and chasin' the sick ones off the place I figured something like that was going on."

"That's what I told Anna," Lessie said, looking about. "Didn't I, Anna? Anna, Anna? Where is she, Mr Johns?"

Mutely he raised his pinkish arm, gesturing toward the women's room.

"Oh, I'll bet she's cryen agin," Lessie declared, staring at the door. For a frozen moment she waited, listening intently, and then, with a gasping sob, ran across between the tables and into the small room.

"The way you look at it," Long asked tensely, "a man would stand a much better chance where it was warm, eh?"

A little embarrassed at the consternation he had caused, Mr Hathaway got up, limping on the thick-soled shoe as he walked toward Long.

"Yes, I think he might. Course if a man left now he wouldn't get anything in case the court makes the company settle with the men."

"No, I guess not," Long said, reaching for the door. "But chances are he'd be dead anyways before the company ever gave him a nickel. I heard the jurors for the trial over at Fayetteville are riding home from the courthouse with men connected with the company. I was thinking a man would be better off if he just headed out for a warmer climate. At least he'd stand a little better chance staying alive, wouldn't he?"

"Sure. Sure. That would be my advice."

Long looked at the man for a still, lengthened moment, nodded curtly and stepped through the door into the snow and slush that covered the street.

34

Three days after Number One had holed through, meeting the dew that had worked its way down from the midway point, Mark Reip was laid off. The facing work, which had been started months before, had followed the drillers, and now, as the hole went through, the steel crews came close behind, affixing the reinforcement bands, and back of them came the leggers, putting in the wooden crosspieces in preparation for the final cement wall which would give the great tube a smooth, curving wall.

A few trackmen were kept on and some of the stronger muckers were converted into a cleanup crew, but in Number One and Two the drillers and chuckers, the dump crews and dinkey crews were paid off and sent home.

Receiving his final pay envelope, Mark went from one foreman to another, trying to secure additional work on one of the crews that cleaned up about the openings. That failed and he went to the foreman of the steel crew and to the legger boss, begging for work, for he knew there was no one else left who might pay the small rent and supply Maw with the few groceries she needed to feed her depleted family.

But the answer was invariably the same. Instead of hiring men the foremen were laying them off, and for each available job the bosses had a hundred applications. Disheartened, Mark came to the end of his search, regretful that Turner Hatch, the foreman who had befriended Tom and Ely and Virgil, had died of silicosis, leaving him with no friend to whom he might make a direct appeal.

Finding the path which led from the end of the bridge through the woods to form the bare, deserted road that bisected the drab shacks that marked Venetta against the riverbank, Mark made his reluctant way home, hating to face Maw and Tom with his last insufficient pay.

Kicking the snow from his shoes against the back wall, he opened the door and stepped into the warm room, smelling the beans and cabbage that simmered on the stove.

"Yore maw's gone to help Daisy," Tom said, propping himself up on one elbow. "She'll be back dreckly."

Mark went into the bedroom, removed his work clothes and, dressing again, stepped out the back door and stood beating his work pants against the wall. For several minutes he pounded them, sending up a thin cloud of gray-white dust that hung in the air long after he had gone inside and closed the door.

At the stove he lifted one potlid after the other, whiffing the air hungrily. Still tense with the news he bore, he flopped down on the bench and began to finger the thin envelope which contained his last pay.

"Pap," he said presently, "I got my walken papers."

Tom made no answer. There was only the thin squeak of the bed as he lowered his body onto the mattress again.

"I'll head out tomorrey and go to the mines," Mark stated, feigning an enthusiasm he could not feel. "Mebby they'll give me some day's work."

"I 'lowed you'd be put off," Tom said. Gaunt and lean, his weathered old face yellow brown against the pillow, his Adam's apple moved like a lump inside his scrawny throat.

"Maw," Mark continued heartlessly, "she's goin to take it hard. We ain't nothin left and we still owe on Virgil's buryen."

"Mebby somethin will turn up, son," Tom consoled. "Mebby the company will pay us a little somethin. We signed up———"

"The company told the men that was fired they'd have to get out of the houses," Mark interrupted. "They're turnen 'em out on the road. Weather like this they'll all get to coughen and die."

"Don't tell yore maw them things, son. It'll only fret her more."

"She feelen any better?" Mark asked, twisting about to face his father. "She talk any today?"

"Not much."

Mark leaned down, elbows on his knees, and began to pick at one thumbnail with the other. "Pap," he said, "there's somethin I been wanten to ask you."

"What is it, Mark?"

"It's bout Maw. Seems like—well, like she's so fergitful anymore. It worries me when I see her sitten round, just looken and looken at nothin a-tall."

Tom made no reply. Lifting the covers slightly, he slipped a thin arm out and laid it across his chest.

"And she's so tetchy anymore, Pap. If she ain't hollerin at somebody she's cryen. Ever time Viney opens her mouth Maw snaps at her. I know Maw, she don't mean nothin by it, but—but I keep wishen there was somethin we could do."

"I guess we done all we can, son. The doctor treated her, but it never seemed to help none. I guess she's eaten her heart out on count of Ely and Virgil."

"Mebby if we was to get back to Slaty it might rest her mind some," Mark said. "It's quiet there and away from where everthin has happened."

"It's a thing I'd like," Tom interposed. "Yore maw's agin leaven the boys here, but if we had the means we would head back. Oncet we got there her mind might get off it——"

"That's what Lessie said," Mark explained. "Maw's goin up there to the graveyard ever day, eaten her heart out. She ain't never goin to get no better lessen we do somethin."

There was no sound in the room until Tom spoke again, the words low and hopeless. "If the company would just give us a little," he said. "It wouldn't take much; just enough to get us back to Slaty."

"I been talken to Lessie," Mark pointed out. "Mebby when we get married we'll stay on here and send you all some ever time we can. If I get took on at the mines I could send five-six dollars a week."

"Was I to work in the fields, stayen out all day, I might stand a chance of throwen off this cough. I'd put in taters, there beneath the ridge——" He stopped, hearing a loud burst of shouting that came from the road before the house. "What's them young'uns yellen so for?" he asked, attempting to rise to his elbows.

"Playen, I reckon," Mark said, getting tiredly to his feet. "I'll go see." Part way to the front door he halted, twisting about. "Don't tell Maw bout me being layed off," he asked. "I'll wait a little. If I get a job tomorrey, then I'll tell her. Most likely she won't worry so much if I don't let her know till I find another job."

"Just whatever you think, son. See what them young'uns is maken so much ruckus for."

Outside, on the roofless porch, Mark looked along the sloppy road. Then, bounding down the steps, he ran toward the place where Viney May, backed up to the dark wall of the Stumps' old house, stood crying and yelling as three half-grown boys pelted snowballs against the wall above her head.

As he reached the road Mark slipped, staggering uncertainly to his feet, and raced over the rutted, snow-splotched road.

"You're crazy in the head!" a wiry thirteen-year-old boy shouted, slinging a snowball at Viney. "Yore whole family is crazy!"

"Leave me be!" Viney shouted, her voice breaking into a loud shriek. "Maw! Maw!"

"Hey, fellers!" a long-necked boy shouted. "Here comes her brother!"

The three hesitated long enough to empty their hands and fled down the deserted street toward the path which led from the upper end of Venetta to the railroad crossing a mile up the river.

Slacking his pace, his breath coming hard, Mark stopped, waiting for Viney May. Crying bitterly, she left the dark torn wall that had been splattered with snowballs and ran toward Mark, her face red and distorted with crying.

"What's the matter?" Mark asked. "What'd they jump on you for?"

"They hit me," she sobbed. "They hit me—here and here!"

"What for?"

"Cause they was teasen me," she said brokenly. "They was teasen me and I hit one with a stick."

"Well, you shouldn't have done it," Mark reprimanded lightly. "You hurt?"

Viney May shook her head, struggling to hold back the tears.

"What were they teasen you for?" Mark asked, leading her back toward the house.

"On count of Maw," the girl admitted, weeping again. "They said she was crazy. They tried to make me say it too."

"They said what?"

"They chased me from school," Viney explained thickly. "They said Maw was a old crazy woman, said she give some blood to the devil. They called her a witch, and I hit 'em with a stick."

Twisting about, Mark looked down the path where the three had fled. Beyond the last house, as the path entered the dark, leafless woods, the boys stood, shouting and flinging snowballs back toward the place where the Tuckers had lived. Mark listened, but their words were carried out over the river by the wind which swept down the hillside.

"Viney, what on earth are you yellen for?"

Maw's voice, coming unexpectedly, caused Mark and Viney May to whirl about. Making her way through between two shacks, Maw had almost reached them before she spoke. Her hair strung loosely from the sides of her head, blown a little by the wind, and her high rugged cheekbones seemed to lift and distort the skin which had come to sag loosely over her face. "What're you yellen like a idiot for?" she repeated. "You know Mister Mullens is down sick! You act like you ain't had no raisen!"

"She hurt herself, Maw," Mark supplied quickly. "She fell and hurt herself."

"Well, come on to the house then." Angrily Maw made her way in great, long strides toward the high-porched shack.

Holding Viney by the shoulder, Mark lagged back, waiting for Maw to get out of hearing distance.

"Don't tell her what happened, Viney," he cautioned firmly. "Don't breathe a word of it."

"I ain't never," the girl answered gravely. "I ain't never."

That night, after they had eaten their beans and cabbage, Mark got his hat and heavy coat from behind the kitchen door and walked down to meet Lessie as she finished work.

As usual the Kanawha Cafe was empty and partially darkened after the supper-hour rush. By the time Mark arrived, coming noise-lessly in at the door and seating himself at the end of the counter, Lessie had cleared all the tables and the room was still but for the clatter of dishes as Mr Johns worked in the kitchen.

"You never had to come tonight, Mark," Lessie said. "It's gitten so cold."

Mark smiled at her and spoke to Anna, who was seated at a table in the far corner. "How's Pete?" he asked. "He feelen any better?"

"Not much. He has to stay in all the time, and he's not used to it."

"Let's go up and set with him awhile," Lessie suggested brightly. "He'll be lonesome. He's all alone since Long and Jim lit out."

"They gone?" Mark asked. "I never knowed."

"Yes, they're gone," Anna replied, spreading a tablet out before her. "Jim was getting worse all the time. They headed for Arizona or someplace out there. Long said he'd get a job in a gas station. They say the air's better out there. It's supposed to heal the lungs."

"Gee," Mark said, taking a step toward her. "Gee, that would be nice. And nice down to Flordey too. When the Stumps headed out they said they'd send us a picture card, but we ain't had a word yet."

"How's your mother, Mark?" Anna asked. "She must be lonesome up there since everybody has moved out."

"The Mullens are still there," Mark reminded quickly. "Mis' Mullens is—is sick, and Maw, she helps her some."

"Mark," Lessie broke in, tugging her hat tightly onto her blonde head. "Mark, I heard a lot of men was let off today. A feller was in and said more was to go next week when they got the openings cleaned up too."

"Yes," Mark answered. "A lot was layed off."

"It's awful to put 'em out of work this time of the year," Lessie declared sympathetically. "Where are they goin to turn to now, that's what I'd like to know."

Before Mark could speak Lessie disappeared into the kitchen. In a few minutes she came back carrying a quart cardboard container which she slipped into a paper sack.

"Anna, I'm taken Pete some soup," she called across the empty room. "Maybe me and Mark can get him to eat it."

"I hope so," Anna replied. "Tell him I'll be up soon's I get through, about nine-fifteen."

Catching Mark's arm, Lessie started toward the door, calling to Mr Johns over her shoulder. Hearing his good night, she spoke to Anna again. "Don't write so many of them letters," she cautioned gently. "You'll make your head hurt agin."

"I'll soon be through," Anna explained, picking up her pencil.

"Anna's writen them letters all the time," Lessie said. "Goodness, some days she gets as many as five or six to answer."

"You'd better knock before you go in," Anna warned as they went out. "Pete won't be expecting you."

As they closed the door Anna bent over the table, carefully rereading the part of the letter she had already written. Finishing, she absently studied the four which still lay spread before her. Two were from Georgia, one from North Carolina and one from Indiana.

Written by men who had formerly worked at the tunnel and who had departed before the reports came back establishing Virgil Reip's death as due to silicosis, they asked if any other men working at the tunnel had developed a persistent lung trouble.

"I got this cough," one explained, "and the doctors don't seem to know what causes it. I'm losing weight all the time. You was always so nice bout writing my letters. I figured you'd let me know if any of the other fellers was complaining. That way I could tell the doctor here and he could treat me for what I got. He thinks now I got consumption, but I don't cough up nothing like he thinks I ought to."

Again Anna glanced over the letter she had started and, unable to continue, she picked up the inquiry written on yellow tablet paper. It was from Reverend Charles Means in Ridgeway, South Carolina.

"Dear Miss," it began in a patiently, elaborately scrawled handwriting, *"My son Lindsey said to me Father if you will let me I will go off and see can I get a good job and I will work and send you some money to support you and by my command he went away in good health and returned with a awful cough. Many times he sent me a little money which you wrote. Another man come back from there and died too. He said the company was going to pay for the men who died for working in that tunnel. Lindsey was a good and obedient boy he always was a good child from his youth he was a member of the Church. He was nineteen years old when he worked in the tunnel. He died of silicosis. I have only one arm and Lindsey was my main dependent and if you will let the company know about me on account of Lindsey's death I will be more than proud for I am a very poor man."*

From,
Chas. Means

Having reread the letter, Anna laid it aside again and picked up her pencil.

"Nobody here knows," she wrote below the paragraph she had finished, "if the company is going to help the men or not. They are having a trial at the county seat, but it does not seem honest the way they are handling it. I will send the company your name and give your son's case to a lawyer if you want me to. Many men are dying here, and a lot of them are walking away to die someplace else. I want to cry every time I think of what has happened here."

 **35**

A week after the lower two openings broke through, the crew that had bored into the earth at the foot of Hawk's Nest set off the final blast, demolishing the thin remaining wall, meeting Number Three beneath the upper spur of Gauley Mountain. As the dust spread and thinned the crews ran forward to meet each other, exhilarated by their accomplishment after long months when they dug blindly ahead, with only the engineers' charts to show that they would eventually meet.

With the final blast the long path of the tunnel was completed. From the foot of Hawk's Nest to Number One opening just above Old Gauley the tunnel ran, surveyor straight, for nearly three miles beneath the ancient old mountain. In time, when the water flowing to the foot of the cragged wall of stone had been diverted into the tunnel, the river would grow shallow and rock bare, meandering its way for seven miles through the old canyons where it had flowed for centuries.

Now, as the last two crews came together, completing the long hole which showed no variation except at the point where the rich vein of silica stone had been struck, the men clasped one another, shouting and calling, like friends who had unexpectedly come together in a strange country. There under the mountain, their voices ringing through the great hole they had made, they laughed and talked and looked with wonder at the thing which they had accomplished.

At no point, from the intake to the outlet, was the drop of one hundred and sixty-eight feet discernible, but the men thought they could see the slow incline and they imagined the water rushing through, like a swift current in a narrow gorge.

"Can't you hear it roaren down through here!" one cried, banging a shovel against the wall. "It'll be enough to drive a man deaf!"

"The boss was tellen me if you'd put a stick in at the upper end it'd come out at the bottom afore you could drive down there in a car!"

A tall, heavily whiskered man stood thoughtfully staring at the high ceiling and wide wall. "All that water goin through here," he said wondrously, "will make enough electricity for the whole damned valley! Light it up like a Christmas tree!"

"Man, O man!"

The first man threw his shovel down, standing with his legs spread far apart. "You s'pose a feller could yell loud enough to be heard all the way through?" Throwing his shoulders back, he tilted his head toward the ceiling while a long, loud shout rose from his throat: "H-e-l-l-o-o!"

Everyone was deathly silent, listening down the long tunnel as the words faded, ringing metallically.

"There ain't no echo," the tall man declared, a little disappointed.

"Must be on count of the dust," another explained. "More'n likely there's too much dust in it yet."

That night, as the men left the tunnel, walking back to Number One, Two and Three camps, they looked at the dark, barren hills, seeing beneath them, as with new eyes, the long hollow line of the tunnel that passed, straight as a die, under the tremendous weight of the mountain. Watching and thinking, they became silent, awed by what they had done, proud in a slow, stubborn way that had no voice but only a deep, confounding astonishment.

The following day, after the muckers had cleaned out, the last drillers, chuckers and dump crews were dismissed. Hundreds of men collected their final pay envelopes, holding them tighter than they ever had before, and returned to the shacks to sit restlessly for a while, to loaf in the commissary and eventually, as the January winds swept down the highways, to wander into Gauley Bridge, listening along the way for some hope of work to be found elsewhere, of some word from the trials in Fayetteville which would compensate those who would never be able to work again.

As January moved on Rhinehart & Dennis began to haul out their machinery. Overnight, it appeared, the work had passed into a new, less dramatic stage. The last drill was silenced and dragged away, and no longer did the trains make their squeaking way toward Alloy with their loads of crushed silica rock.

The dinkey trains and dump cars were lined on a sidetrack, empty and useless, and in a few days the snow covered them as it covered the great blanket of fine gray dust which lay over the ground outside the four openings.

After the rapid, driven activity of the drilling, with the day and night crews forever coming and going, the job seemed almost deserted, for the facing crew had moved far inside, making little noise.

The men, traveling on the road from the tar-paper shacks to Gauley Bridge and back again, looked at the dark holes the openings made and passed on, wordless and bewildered by the sudden way their long familiarity with the work had been ended. Sometimes they would venture near the openings, wanting to revisit the place where they had labored for more than a year. Without work, unable to rest after the prolonged, intense activity, they crept back, aching to see the smooth walls being cemented in place, to walk again through the hole they had helped to bore under the mountain.

"Hey, where you goin' there?"

"I just thought I'd look and see how it was comen. I worked in Number Two."

"The company says stay out. Them's orders!"

"I ain't goin to tetch nothin."

"Get out! You're not allowed on the property!"

"Hell, feller, I worked there. I was on Sam Hoskins' crew. Worked fourteen months."

"Get out, I said! And close that gate behind you!"

In the week which followed notices were posted that the shacks were to be evacuated. Women, going to the commissary for beans and sow's belly, for coffee and meal, saw them and went home, silent, distant-eyed, and they made the beans go farther and ceased buying milk for the coffee. Of a morning the men would rise, leaving the houses early.

"You hear bout work anywheres?" their wives would ask, following them to the door.

"Nope."

"We only got nine dollars left."

"Hell, woman, I know it!"

"We'd best take the young'uns and light out. Mrs Watts heard they was fixen to burn all the shacks down."

"I heerd that two-three places. I can't stop 'em!"

"We could sell our stuff or give it away. We're due to starve if we stay on here."

"Quit naggen me! I'm doin all I can!" He would hurry away, anxious to join the men who clustered the roads, waiting and listening and coughing.

"Well, what's goin to become of us?" she would cry in final desperation. "What on earth is goin to become of us?"

He would tramp down the muddy path toward the highway that led to Gauley. Sometimes as he passed the Jungle he would see families squatted beside the road, their few belongings tied in bundles, the women holding the least of the children in their arms.

"You headen out?"

Curtly they would nod, reproachful and defensive in their helplessness.

"Never heard bout work anywheres, did you?"

"No."

"Well—good luck. Any words from the lawyers yet?"

"That company ain't goin to pay out nothin! They're goin to chase everybody off, like they're chasen us!"

"They run you out?"

"Sure. They're tearen down the shacks so's they can make a golf course for the company bosses. A golf course—Jesus Christ! Putten my missus and kids out in this cold!"

"Well—so long."

"You stayen on?"

"If we can hold out."

"My missus left some cooken pots and a straw ticken in the shack yonder. You're welcome to 'em if you get there afore they tear it down."

"Thank ye. I'll send some of the young'uns."

Lessie and Anna, watching through the large window in front of the cafe, saw the men wander the streets aimlessly, moving from group to group, driven by fear and loneliness and the old hunger for work that made them angry and bitter-tongued.

But for an occasional salesman or transient, the front door was rarely opened during the day, except at mealtime or for one of the dozen or more men who still came to Anna to have their letters written. While they were working they never asked her favor without eating a piece of pie or a sandwich, but now they came, apologetic and hesitant, standing bareheaded near the front door until Anna was free.

"I hate to be any trouble," they would stammer, "but I'm wonderin' if you'd write me a bitty letter to my folks."

"Certainly," Anna always replied. "Come back here."

"If you're busy, I'll step in later."

"I'm not busy. Lessie can take care of everything."

On Thursday, after the last big crew had been laid off, Hance McTeer stood outside the cafe until he saw that it was empty and Anna and Lessie had taken their customary places at a back table where they shared the *Charleston Gazette*.

"Would it be too much bother?" he asked, crumbling his hat in his hand. "I'd like to write my missus."

"Why, Hance," Anna cried, astonished at his thin face. "Hance, I didn't recognize you!"

Aged and yellowed, his face looked like a skull over which the skin had been drawn, and he walked with faltering, unsure steps.

"My Lord!" Lessie exclaimed, springing up. "Whatever happened?" Suddenly she clamped her hand over her mouth, stopping the cry. "Here, set down afore you fall!"

"No, thank ye," Hance said. "I don't want to take yore place."

"Go ahead," Lessie urged. "I stand up so much it don't come natural to set down anyways."

"Where you been, Hance?" Anna asked gently, getting, his tablet from the ledge. "I haven't seen you in two weeks. I thought you had gone back to Joplin."

"No, m'am," he explained. "I been sick. Wes Foster and his wife let me stay with them."

"Has the doctor been seeing you?" Anna asked. "Are you taking treatments?"

"When they layed me off," Hance explained, his breath coming in broken spurts, "they put me out of the company house. After that I couldn't have the company doctor no more. Wes and his woman left for home this mornen. I'm tryen to get to that Coal Valley Hospital, down there at Montgomery."

Half an hour later, when Lessie saw Mark coming up the street, she hastily got her coat and hat and started for the door, trying to conceal the tears that threatened to break from her eyes.

"Good-by, Mister McTeer," she said. "Mark's comen yonder, and I'm goin home with him to see his maw."

"Good-by, young lady." Hance smiled feebly. "You and Mis' Anna has allus been so nice to me."

"I never done nothin," Lessie protested, her voice creaking dangerously. "It was Anna. She's the goodhearted one."

"You been nice too," he insisted. "That feller out there will be lucky to get you."

"Aw," Lessie countered, attempting to smile, "you're just poken fun at me!" Whirling quickly, she ran out the door and into the street.

As she reached the sidewalk Mark caught her arm, speaking her name, and they started toward the bridge. After they had crossed over and found the river path which cut across the low field Mark tugged at Lessie's sleeve, slowing her pace.

"What's the matter, Lessie?" he asked. "You ain't even said howdy."

"Nothin, Mark. Nothin a-tall."

Looking back to see that no one was watching, Mark caught Lessie's other arm and forced her to face him.

"You been cryen, honey," he said. "Tell me what's the matter. It ain't nothin I done, is it?"

"No, Mark," she said, shaking her head.

"Yore eyes is red! Can't you tell me what happened?"

Lessie looked up at him, the tears flooding down her cheeks. With a quick, throbbing cry she threw her arms about his neck, drawing herself tightly against his body. "Oh, Mark!" she sobbed. "I'm scared to death!"

Embarrassed and deeply concerned, Mark's arms encircled Lessie's shoulders as he looked again at the highway to be sure they were unseen.

"What is it, honey?" he urged softly. "What's scaren you?"

"Oh, everythin! The way everbody is gitten sick and dyen, and nobody's doin anythin about it! Why don't somebody do somethin, Mark?"

"Everbody's doin whatever they can," he consoled, brushing his cheek against her hair. "You hadn't ought to cry like that, honey. It ain't goin to help none———"

"I know, I know." Tugging loose, she rubbed both eyes with her hand.

"Let's go on up to the rock," Mark said, sliding one arm down about her waist. "Ain't nobody can see us up there."

Slowly they made their way up the sloppy path, walking close together. As they came to a broad, slushy puddle Mark stepped off the path into the untrampled snow but did not remove his arm from Lessie's waist. Arriving at the large rock, Mark brushed off the loose snow and they sat down.

"They bring any more down from the camps?" he asked rather stiffly, easing Lessie closer to him. "Is that what yore cryen about?"

"No," Lessie said, swallowing the lump that choked at her throat. "That Mister McTeer was in. He's turrible sick, Mark, and he can't get home to his family. He made Anna send them all the money he had, and now he's goin to the hospital in Montgomery, if they'll take him in. Honest, he looks like he was dead already!"

"I guess there's a lot like that," Mark said. "I've talked to 'em afore. They just want to get enough to get home. A man don't like to die away from his people."

Freeing herself, Lessie edged away, twisting about to face Mark. "I wish we could leave now," she said soberly. "If we could take your folks and get back to Slaty, you and me could run the farm. I'm a good worker and, Mark honey, I want us to get out of here in the worst way. Yore paw and maw would feel better, and she could get her mind off the boys."

"I told Pap a'ready," Mark confided. "If we get through till spring we'll head back. We'll get married then and take the folks———"

Lessie slid back, accepting the curve of Mark's arm and leaning her head lightly against the damp shoulder of the heavy jacket which Virgil had received for Christmas more than a year before.

"Mark," she said, "why can't we get married now? Then I could come and live with your folks. I saved near a hundred dollars. It would go a long ways."

"No," he replied. "I'll find some work soon. We'll make out. There ain't no use goin back afore spring. Soon as the winter lets up, and it comes time for plowen, we'll get married and start for Slaty. I figure, if I can get took on at the mines, I can save up enough by then to get started."

"Is it purty, Mark, there on Slaty?"

"Sure. It's awful nice. The house is just a old cabin, but the land lays purty, and a crick cuts acrost the fields. It ain't been worked for near two years. Pap figures the ground will have its strength back by now."

"It sounds real nice, Mark."

"When we was just young'uns," he went on, speaking down across the side of her face, "we thought it was the finest place in the world. Course we never seen anythin else till we come down here."

"We ought to get along good there," Lessie said, pressing her cheek in the cup of his shoulder. "Your pap will get well, and you'll get shet of that cough." With a little jerk she sat up, looking down at Mark's feet.

"Landsakes alive, Mark!" she exclaimed. "Why didn't you say somethin! Yore feet are soaken wet! Come on, we got to get up to the house!"

"They ain't cold," he protested, trying to pull her back down beside him. "Let's set awhile, honey, afore we go up to the house."

"No siree!" she insisted. "We're goin right now. I don't know what I was thinken of! You'll get a fever, sure's anythin! Come on, Mark!"

Begrudgingly he got to his feet, drawing her into his arms as he arose. Recognizing the demands of the movement, Lessie tilted her face, accepting the kiss.

"Gee, honey," he whispered, holding her close. "Gee, I allus liked you from the first time I seen you."

"I like you too, Mark. I allus will."

Again he kissed her, pressing her head back hard against his arm.

"Now that's enough!" she declared peremptorily, pushing him away. "Yore feet must be wringen wet! Come on, let's hurry!"

"Just a minute more, Lessie," he asked, his voice petulant and pleading.

"No sir! You got to get home and get them shoes off!" Freeing herself, she strode up the path, listening for his running feet to overtake her.

He stood watching her hurry up the path, and then, in great long strides, Mark caught up with Lessie, throwing his arms about her waist.

"I guess I know who's going to wear the pants in this family," he chided.

"Well, honest, Mark, you're worser'n a kid!" She stopped abruptly, closely examining his mouth. "We'd better wipe that off," she said, searching for a handkerchief, "or everybody will know!"

"I don't care." Mark smiled, running his tongue in a broad circle about his mouth. "I don't care!"

"Hold still! Stop it, Mark!" Slapping his hand as it sought to pinch her waist, Lessie strained on tiptoes, wiping away the lipstick that reddened his pale mouth.

36

"Lock! Lock!" Daisy cried, attempting to force her arm under his shoulders. "Lock, set up!"

A low smothered sound rose from his throat as he rolled his head from one side to the other, mumbling incoherently.

Outside the wind of a February night pressed and tore at the shack, whistling beneath the thin eaves.

"Lock, get up! Lock!" In the dark room Daisy's voice grew louder, the bed squeaking as she awkwardly moved her heavy body about. Some cold premonition had awakened her from hazardous sleep, causing her to sit bolt upright. As she listened beneath the wind she heard the low gurgling sound that escaped his throat. Frightened, she got to her knees on the bed, straining to lift his shoulders so the congestion which threatened to end his breathing might be relieved. Sluggishly he resisted, moaning audibly.

"For God's sake, Lock!" she cried, tugging at his shoulders, feeling the weight of her own distended belly. "Lock, wake up!"

With his head caught in her arms Daisy tilted back to a squatting position, repeating his name over and over. Finally he began to cough distressedly, his chest knocking against her legs, and a painful groan streamed through his lips.

"Wake up, Lock! Yore choken!" she pleaded desperately. "Cough—cough it out!"

"Huh? Huh?" he whispered, breaking through the heavy phlegmatic stupor which had accompanied the inflammation that filled his disease-hardened lungs. As it gathered, strangling him while he slept, his respiration diminished until Daisy, rising with terrified apprehension, could not hear his breathing but only the faint gurgling that came from deep in his throat.

"You al'right, Lock?" she asked fervently, stacking pillows beneath his shoulders. "Set up now, if you can. I'll light the lamp."

Her feet moved quickly and softly over the bare floor; a match scratched in the darkness, breaking into light, and the room was filled with an unsteady glow.

Grabbing a chair, Daisy hurried back to the bed, her movements cumbersome, for her own body was so large it lifted the flannel gown toward her knees by its distention.

Lock watched her, his eyes wet and red rimmed, his pale lips vaguely shaping the reprimand and caution he could not speak.

"You rest," Daisy whispered, tilting the chair against the headboard so he could lean against it. "I'll dress and go to the Reips. Mark'll fetch the doctor."

"No." Lock halted her, raising a lifeless hand. "You stay here, Daisy. You take care of yoreself."

"Tain't but a step," she protested. "Rest yoreself." Placing his spittle can nearer the bed, she pulled her dress over her nightgown and found her shoes and cotton stockings.

"Daisy, come here and set down," Lock said, reaching out toward her. "It's passed now. I want you to stay here, Daisy."

Obediently she crossed and sat on the bed beside him, tucking the covers about his scrawny shoulders and shoving the loose hair back from his forehead.

"We'd best have the doctor," she insisted softly; "yore wheezen so. If yore catchen a cold, he can stop it, Lock." Her hand continued to caress his forehead, brushing it tenderly.

"Get back in bed, Daisy," he asked. Propped against the back of the chair, his face appeared thin and colorless, the unsteady flicker of the lamp outlining his skull, casting heavy shadows under the ledge of his eyebrows.

"No, Lock. I'll set awhile. You sleep."

"Then get yore heavy coat on, honey, an stir up a fire."

The words were spoken in a low whisper, intimate and close beneath the whining of the wind. Daisy got up from the bed and walked to the stove, her steps soft and bending, as if some unbreakable silence had already crept into the house. With her back turned she stuck several sticks of wood into the gray, cold stove and doused them with kerosene. Not until the flame had leaped up, crackling and moaning as it crowded into the flue, did Daisy lessen her hold on the terrified grief that clogged her throat. Willfully she tried to swallow her weeping so it would not sound above the roar of the fire and of the wind beneath the roof.

Lock's eyes never left her. Seeing the way her shoulders jerked and throbbed, his hand unconsciously began to pat the bed beside him. At last he spoke. Clearing his throat and spitting into the can, he called in a voice that was firm and controlled. "Daisy, you get yore heavy coat on," he said. "It's near yore time, and I don't want you to get down sick."

Day had broken thin and gray to the east above the cemetery hill when Daisy left the kitchen door and ran across the damp, splotchy snow which had fallen during the night. On the Reips's steps, seeing the wind-driven snow which still clung to the rough walls, she knocked twice, waited and then stepped into the shadowy room. In the bleak light she could see Maw crawling from bed.

"It's me, Maw," she called. "It's Daisy."

"Huh? What?"

"Maw," Daisy said, tiptoeing across to the bed. "Maw, I come to ask you——"

"Mark! Mark!" Maw cried, leaping to the floor. "It ain't Mark, is it?"

Daisy grabbed her by the arm. "No, Maw! It's Lock. He's had a choken spell."

"What's the matter?" Tom asked, his voice rising from the bed in a startled cry. "Nettie, what is it?"

In the dim light Maw was still for a moment, then, breaking loose, ran toward the bedroom, crying out her fear. "Mark! Mark! You al'right?" In the murkiness before day her high-pitched voice echoed through the room, desperate and frantic and detached from all else, like a mad, doleful cry heard through darkness.

"What's the matter, Daisy?" Tom demanded, getting up on his elbows in the bed. "Tain't Mark, is it?"

"No," Daisy answered, running into the bedroom. "It's Lock."

"Is he bad?"

Daisy did not answer. Overtaking Maw, she grabbed her by the shoulders, feeling their tense rigidness beneath the coarse nightgown, and whirled her about.

"It ain't Mark!" she repeated several times. "It's Lock. I come to borrey some medicine."

Pushing her aside, Maw bent over Mark, her ear held close to his mouth. Gradually she straightened up, her face blank and uncomprehending.

"That you, Daisy?" she asked.

"Yes, Maw, it's me. Come back in the kitchen."

"Mark's al'right, ain't he, Daisy?"

"Yes, Maw. He's al'right. Come on now, afore you wake him."

"I never heerd you come in."

Back in the kitchen, answering Tom's anxious, fearful questions, Daisy patiently explained that Lock had used the last of his medicine and that she had come to borrow more.

"Nettie," Tom spoke from the bed. "Nettie, it's for Lock. Daisy's come to get some medicine for Lock."

Maw looked down at Tom, her head moving slowly, inquiringly, and, as though startled, she abruptly caught her two thin braids of hair and tied them together at the back of her head.

"You get it, Daisy," Tom whispered. "It's on the shelf there, above the wash box."

As Daisy started across the room Maw fled past her, reached up and got the bottle from the ledge. "It was left from Virgil," she said, the words hollow and detached. "He never lived to use it all."

"Just pour me some out in a glass," Tom intervened, seeing the helpless worried look in Daisy's eyes. "Nettie's forgot."

Finding a glass on the shelf, Daisy emptied half the contents of the bottle in it and placed the glass back of a stack of plates. "Don't let her knock it over," she said, the words coming through pain. "I'll fetch this part back when the doctor comes."

"Ain't no rush," Tom replied. "They's enough there to last me two days."

Nodding, her eyes furtively watching Maw, Daisy went to the door, stepped out and headed over the dark-streaked snow toward the yellow light which came from her kitchen window. She had gone only a short way when Maw's voice, rising shrill and loud from the doorstep, halted her.

"Give him aplenty!" she called. "I never give Virgil enough. That's why he died. Them doctors lied! You got to give him more!"

Biting her lips, Daisy broke into a trot, the heavy weight of her sluggish body causing her to wobble as she went over the clodded ground the cold wind had frozen during the night.

By eight o'clock, when Dr Robinson had parked his car between the highway and the abandoned railway tracks and rode across the river in the stern of Mark's boat, the inflammation had gathered again in Lock's chest.

Frantic, her hysteria rising like the swift upward rush of a storm, Daisy had dragged him from bed, straining to support his slight weight. With one arm about his waist she held him upright, seeing the water gather in his eyes and hearing the low gurgling sound of air breaking through the congestion that continued to fill his incapable lungs.

"Cough it out, Lock," she kept pleading. "Cough it out! The doctor's comen! Lock, spit it out!"

As Robinson rounded the shack and stepped through the kitchen door Daisy's tenseness broke like a wave, and one desperate scream followed another as she sought to hold Lock up and urge the doctor to greater speed at the same time.

"I'm here," Robinson said, trying to stem her grief. "I'm here. We'll do whatever we can!"

"Help him, Doctor!" Daisy begged. "Help Lock. He can't get his breath!"

"Yes, yes." Throwing off his coat, the man grabbed Lock from Daisy's arms, tilting him forward a little in an attempt to get the air into his lungs. In the same motion he pressed his ear to Lock's chest, hearing the fatal telltale whine of breath as it sought to make its way through the accumulated phlegm.

"For God's sake, do somethin!" Daisy screamed, pounding the foot of the bed with her clenched fists. "Do somethin! Do somethin!" Tears, streaming from her eyes, were flung in damp streaks across her cheeks as she shook her head in an effort to evade her growing terror.

Ignoring her, the doctor eased Lock's limp form back against the uptilted chair and grabbed his black satchel, breaking it open. Knowing, as he had known for weeks, that there was no earthly way to avoid the impending death, he snatched up his hypodermic syringe, affixed the needle and quickly applied the narcotic to relieve Lock's pain.

"He ain't goin to die, is he?" Daisy jabbered endlessly, crowding nearer. "He ain't goin to die—he ain't goin to die——"

"I'll do everything I can. You stand back." Daisy moved forward instead, seeking to reach Lock's quiet form. Alertly the doctor grabbed her outstretched hand. "I need hot water," he instructed, trying to distract her. "You put some on!"

Dazed, she backed toward the stove, whirled suddenly and ran to the pail of water sitting in the tin-lined wash box.

As the opiate began to penetrate Lock settled down on the pillow-covered chair, his mouth hanging open and his eyes showing like dim gray blobs through the pale lids.

"He's resting now," Robinson said, thankful that Daisy's busy movements had checked her weeping. "You better go get Mrs Reip."

"Is he al'right?" Daisy asked, her fingers pressing nervously against her swollen lips. "Is it passed, Doctor?"

"We'll do what we can. You go get Mrs Reip."

Daisy crept on slow feet to the door but, once outside, she ran as rapidly as she could across the yards behind the row of deserted shacks and into the Reips's kitchen, not waiting to knock.

Shortly after ten o'clock Lock's head dropped over against his shoulder, and Robinson, listening to his chest and heart, removed the chair and lowered his lean body down onto the bed, saying nothing until he had drawn the covers flatly over Lock's chest.

"Maybe you had better take her out for a while," he whispered to Maw. "I'll call you."

"Huh?" Maw answered numbly. "Huh——"

"Take Mrs Mullens out. I'll call you when it is time."

Breaking free of Maw's arm, which rested over her shoulder, Daisy bounded out of the chair and with both hands grabbed the sides of the doctor's coat collar.

"He ain't dyen, is he?" she demanded, drawing the man's face down near hers. "He ain't—he ain't——" Seeing the doctor's still, compassionate face, she shoved him brusquely aside, stood for a moment staring at the bed and, screaming as though her head cracked with an unendurable pain, lunged to the floor, her arms tearing at the covers and her face struggling to reach the pillow beside Lock's dark head.

The doctor let her cry, standing quietly behind her, his hands reaching down now and again to touch and restrain her shoulders.

Maw moved restlessly, aimlessly about the room, crying from a dry, soundless throat, fingering one object after another and laying it down again. Once she went to the water pail, filled a glass and set it down, as though the errand had held no significance.

After the first heart-torn, convulsive wailing had passed Dr Robinson dragged Daisy up from the side of the bed and helped her into a chair.

"You've got to be quiet," he said tenderly. "You're going to have a baby. It's his child, and you've got to be careful for its sake."

Daisy looked up at him, nodding her grief-torn face, and broke into another spasm of crying.

At two o'clock that afternoon, accompanied by Mark and Lessie, who had taken the afternoon off, Daisy left the shack, her plain black coat buttoned tightly about her neck, and started toward the undertaker's where Lock's body had been hauled soon after the doctor had returned to Gauley Bridge. Over her arm she carried the cheap blue serge suit Lock had bought following the last payment on the stove. Lessie, walking at her side, held a package containing shoes, a shirt and underwear.

No one spoke until they left the road and started down toward the riverbank where Mark's rowboat was tied to the high bare root of a sycamore tree.

Daisy held back, staring at the black water streaked here and there with a thin veil of mush ice, and shook her head.

"She don't want to cross the river," Lessie supplied gently. "She wants to walk."

"It's a lot further round the path," Mark said, his eyes resting on Daisy's heavy body. "It's a long walk."

Spreading the wadded handkerchief she carried over her hand, Daisy held it against her moist face.

"We can go slow," Lessie said, taking Daisy's arm and guiding her toward the path. "We can rest if we get tired."

Alertly Mark caught Daisy's other arm, holding it with firm support, as though he expected her to sag to the ground.

Wordlessly they passed between the rows of empty shacks that had been unreasonably brought to life more than a year before, found the head of the path and made their way toward the bridge. Leaving the iron structure and stepping onto the narrow sidewalk, Mark fell behind, for they could not walk three abreast. Once he attempted to take the package from Lessie but she shook her head, and he relinquished his hold, sensing that the carrying of burial clothes was a duty which women performed alone.

Just beyond the drugstore and before they reached Wayne's temporary office Lessie brought Daisy to a halt.

"You want me to speak to him?" she offered. "Maybe it would be easier if I done the talken."

"I'd be obligeed," Daisy managed, pressing her quivering lips together.

"I'll be glad to, Mis' Mullens. I come with Maw the time Virgil was put away."

They stopped talking until a woman with an armload of groceries and two tagging children had passed.

"Me and Lock's got sixty-two dollars put aside," Daisy said, clearing her throat. "With what the company pays, it might be enough to get a good coffin."

"I'll tell him," Lessie said. "It'll be easier if I do the talken."

"Thank ye."

"What day do you want the buryen?" she asked, drawing close to Daisy's shoulder. "Tomorrey mornen would be nice."

"I'm goin to take Lock home," Daisy said. "I'm taken him back to Cranberry Crick."

"You—you don't want him buried here?" Lessie asked, glancing helplessly at Mark.

"No, I want to take him back home. Paw will bury him up agin the hill. We got a little place there."

"Just whatever you say," Lessie answered, pausing while a truck muttered and choked its way down the street.

"I'd allus feel better in my mind was he nearer home."

"I know," Lessie said softly. "I know you would."

Daisy brushed her eyes with the damp handkerchief, drawing herself erect. "I got to find me a way to get him home," she said. "You reckon they's anybody that would buy my cookstove?"

Lessie and Mark looked up and down the street as though they expected to find some answer along the row of store fronts.

"There's the Dago," Mark said. "Mis' Stump sold some stuff to him."

"He can have the stove for just enough to get us home," Daisy said. "That-a-way we could head out tomorrey. It's the thing I want to do."

"Just you leave it to me and Mark," Lessie said confidently. "We'll see the Dago. He'll pay enough for the stove to haul you back. It's a fine stove."

"Thank ye," Daisy said, starting toward the green velvet-curtained door. "Thank ye kindly."

37

In the weeks after the tunnel had holed through no day passed when a family could not be seen clustered beside the road, holding and dragging their few possessions as they sought to flee the valley. Many abandoned the shacks as the crews moved in to demolish them, leaving behind what they could not carry on their backs, and for miles, east on Route 60 toward White Sulphur Springs and west toward Kentucky and Ohio, pots and pans, brightly painted flower vases and worn work clothes, tied in bundles, could be found along the road where a hopeful load had grown too great.

School children, playing homeward, learned to search for the treasures. The bundles would be ripped open and prodded with sticks as though they were germ infested. But broken dishes and vases made to contain artificial flowers were borne home in proud conquest. Sometimes they would carry the pots and skillets home too, offering them questioningly, but more often they kicked them along the surface of the road or, filling them with rocks, slung them down the mouth of a gulley, listening to hear the faint ring of metal when they struck the floor of the ravine far below.

By the time Lock had died and February was drawing to a close it was not an uncommon sight to see a man, his family and his belongings lumped beside the road, watching passing cars with dull, bewildered eyes, gesturing now and then as a truck approached and sometimes creeping back to the camps at night to sleep in the cold shacks after Slat McCune and the other watchmen had made their rounds. The next morning they would set out again, leaving the shacks before daybreak, afraid of being discovered and jailed for trespassing.

In Boomer and Montgomery, Riverside and Cedar Grove, people living along the highway kept their shades drawn to discourage the endless bedraggled line that trudged along the road, and in Summersville, where the undertaker had been forced by a church committee to separate the colored and the white in the graveyard on the knoll back of his mother's home, a group of women went to the sheriff, demanding that he arrest all vagrants who attempted to spend the night within the town limits.

One, a tall thin-necked woman whose husband was a tax collector, vowed that her home had been violated twice and that a man had tried to inveigle her husband into sleeping with his daughter in return for the use of the tool shed for the night. While her husband was trying to rid the place of them, she declared, one of the man's children had slipped into the kitchen and tried to steal whatever it could lay its hands on.

In other villages complaints were made, and in Gauley Bridge Myrtle Kuhn and the minister's wife attempted to form a committee to force Rhinehart & Dennis to load the people it was dumping onto the community into trucks and haul them back where they came from. A petition was made soon after Number Three and Four had holed through, and Miss Kuhn spent an entire week going from house to house, asking for signers, but her mother was afraid to stay home alone and the venture finally died from a lack of interest.

Often truck drivers stopped, telling a man he could load his family in back, but for the most part they drove past, pretending to be occupied and unaware, for they were disheartened, knowing they could not haul a man far and that they carried him toward nothing at all.

Then, for the two weeks following Lock Mullens' death, a storm hung over the Kanawha Valley. Gathering at night, it bit and howled its way across the hills, tearing at the few remaining shacks and blanketing the bare, drab earth with successive layers of snow. By day it would subside, permitting the sun to glow feebly above Gauley Mountain, and then in the late afternoon, as darkness crept early from the hills, it would rise again, bleak and still and cold before the onslaught of wind and snow.

Driven by the storm, the groups of men no longer clustered about the bridge and before the stores. Mark Reip, leaving the dark-windowed, sway-back shacks at Venetta, saw that the roads were emptied of men but for an occasional straggler who could find no place to live until the storm had passed.

Throughout those weeks there was no day when Mark did not set out after breakfast in search of some kind of work. Going from the coal companies and oil refineries to the electrometallurgical plant being constructed at Alloy, he begged for work, lying when they asked if he had been employed by Rhinehart & Dennis on the tunnel job, for he had long since learned that such an admission flatly canceled his chances for employment.

Late in the afternoons he trudged back into Gauley, stopping to speak to Lessie at the cafe, for no man ever entered the long, odorous room without answering Lessie's insistent demands about work.

"Are the mines at Hugheston goin?" she would implore. "Is there work for a feller at Pratt or Crown Hill or Cedar Grove?"

Some days she would leave the restaurant and walk home with Mark, carrying a crock of macaroni and cheese or a kettle of stew Mr Johns had cooked for her after the noon rush was over. She would place the food on the kitchen table, making no mention of it but always being sure to eat a little before she left, so it would appear that she was not simply bringing it to Maw and Tom and Viney May because they were hungry.

"I allus had a tooth for stew with a lot of taters in it," she would confide. "But Mr Johns, he never has it on the regular bill o' fare. I got to cook it special."

As the second week of the storm passed, breaking the back of winter, the interior of the tunnel was virtually completed and the company renewed its efforts to scatter the last families who still hung on in the shacks. More bills were posted, declaring that all who had not evacuated the houses within ten days would be charged with trespassing and arrested.

Crews were sent to Number Two and Three camps to demolish the houses as they were emptied. Within a few hours of a family's departure the roof and walls would be knocked from the two-by-fours and the framework lowered to the ground. Abandoned pots and skillets, tubs and washboards were dumped into ravines, the broken chairs and bedsteads heaped into a pile and burned.

Negroes, fleeing the camp atop Gauley Mountain where the golf course was to be constructed, crawled into the hollows, trying to build huts with salvaged tin and used lumber stolen by night from the piles that marked the places where their shacks had stood. Five families moved into an old gristmill near the mouth of Turkey Creek, carrying boards into the damp, infested building and laying them across the rotted beams to replace the floor which had long before fallen into decay. During the first week a seven-year-old girl caught pneumonia and died.

The storm finally ceased, and with the first false-promising days Sam Givens, who had left Georgia and the spindly, insufficient cotton rows that spread outward from his tenant door, turned his back on the desolate valley and headed southward to the family he had left eighteen months before.

Thin and weak, he walked over the hill, trying to thumb a ride that would help him toward Virginia and Tennessee and finally into Georgia. Making his way along the state road, facing about with upraised hand each time a motor sounded at his back, Sam recalled the night outside Memphis when Long Legg had returned, carrying Jim over his shoulder, and told of a job he had heard about somewhere in West Virginia.

Long and Jim were gone far to the west and south now, looking for warmer, dryer weather, and the others had vanished with them. Owl Jones was buried, Sam had heard, with a lot of other Negroes in the field somewhere. The rest were gone, searching for work again, looking for something to eat, wanting a place to die.

By the third day Sam had reached Abingdon, wandering strangely, trying to recall the way he had come, trying to remember the colored states, the red and yellow and green ones, his oldest daughter had shown him in her geography book. Once a truck driver had pulled into a gas station, asked for a road map and marked out the way Sam should go, but the following day he got off the route, traveling south but too far to the west.

That night Sam slept in a hut where children waited for the school bus, drawing himself into a tight knot on the hard bench that ran along the back wall. Just before daybreak a cold, penetrating rain pelted the building, splashing in at the open front. Miserably cold, Sam got up, pacing from one end to the other, hoping to ward off the chill that crept along his spine.

For nearly two hours he waited, rubbing his arms and chest, scanning the highway for lights that might emerge from the murky darkness. At six o'clock a truck picked him up, hauling him eight miles. Sam's teeth were chattering, and the chill rose in spasmodic waves to shake his emaciated body.

"Buddy," the driver said, throwing the truck into second, "You'd better get off at the first place and get something to eat. You're shakin' like a dog passin' peach seeds."

"Yeh," Sam replied. "I'll get coffee the first chance."

"You been stuck there all night?"

"Yes. I'm tryin to get to Hawkins. That's down in Georgia."

"You got a long ways. That cough—it sounds like you got consumption."

Pressing his arms to his chest, Sam tilted forward, trying to catch the slight heat that came up through the floor boards.

"Had a brother that had lung trouble once," the driver went on friendlily. "Took him 'bout two years, but he got over it. He never was strong after that, but he didn't die. He was bonier than you are, but soon as he got over the worse of it he began to pick up. Weighs nearly two hundred now; married and got a fine set of kids."

By three o'clock that afternoon Sam Givens had reached Waverly, Tennessee. A succession of short rides had carried him sixty-four miles. The chill had increased, causing the pain to rise across his chest, and for the first time Sam became aware of the heavy premonition which had hung over him since the early hours when he had gotten up from the cold bench in the schoolbus stop. At first it had only been a numbing dread, unnamed and formless, that lay like a heavy weight upon his mind.

Each time he managed a ride something prompted him to ask the same question. "How far is it to Georgia, mister? How far do I have to go to get to Georgia?"

As one short ride after another failed to substantially lessen the distance the dread arose in Sam's mind, gradually taking shape and meaning until, by the time he had climbed down from the rickety truck in Waverly, it had become monstrously clear that he would never reach Hawkins.

Looking up and down the clear rain-washed street, Sam saw the gold letters arched on the window of the post office and, waiting until he had plenty of time to make his way across the street, he went slowly up the few steps and approached the plump bald-headed man at the grille window.

"Somethin' I can do for you?" the man asked pleasantly.

"If you'd be so kind," Sam said, drawing five one-dollar bills and eighty-four cents in change from his pocket. "I want to send this to my missus," he said. "Take out what it costs for the money slip and the postage and send the rest to her."

"Cleaning yourself out, eh?" the man chuckled, reaching for the slender blue-green pad. "What's the name?"

"Missus Sam Givens. We live in Hawkins. Hawkins, Georgia."

Filling in the name and address, the plump man laid down his pen and counted the money.

"That'll leave five seventy-one," he said. "Unless you want to send it special."

"No." Sam thanked him. "Send her the five seventy-one."

The man completed the money order, got a stamped envelope from the drawer and slid the two across the window ledge. "Be sure to keep the stub," he reminded. "That's the little part."

"Mister, would you mind writen on the envelope? My hands are kind of stiff."

"Certainly not. Anything to oblige."

While he addressed the envelope, using the money order as a model, Sam moved nervously about, rubbing his hands against his trouser legs and grasping the window ledge. "If it ain't too much trouble," he stammered finally, "I'd like to put a bitty letter in with it."

"No trouble at all," the man replied cordially. "I've got nothin' to do until the five-forty gets in."

"Just say I'm senden this for her and the young'uns," Sam dictated politely. "Say I'm comen home as soon as I can get there. Say I'm on my way." He waited for the man's fat hand to come to a halt, as he had waited for Anna's many times before, and continued. "Tell her to take good care of the kids, and I'll be home as soon as I can make it."

"You said that before," the postmaster pointed out.

"Oh," Sam apologized, "I guess that's all then."

The man scribbled Sam's name at the bottom, blotted the sheet of paper and handed everything through the window.

"Save the receipt," he repeated, "in case anything goes wrong."

"Yes sir. I'm much obligeed to you."

Folding the letter, Sam enclosed the money order, licked the flap and sealed the envelope by pounding it with the side of his fist. For a brief instant he stood looking at the envelope.

"Just drop it in the slot there." The postmaster leaned forward, indicating the receptacle.

"Yes sir," Sam said, slipping the letter through the slot.

Leaving the post office, he passed along before half-a-dozen stores, looking at their windows with an odd, unreal interest, and headed for the open highway which began at the far end of the village. Beyond the end of the sidewalk he made his slow way for half a mile, looking to either side of the state road for a place to sit down. As he mounted the slight incline the highway followed, leaving Waverly, Sam felt the pain returning to his chest, sharper now and made more intense by the anguish of his labored breathing.

Stumbling off the road, he took several steps toward a large maple set back in a pasture. His throat began to swell, growing red, and below his eyes the flesh seemed to bloat as he fought to overcome the gathered phlegm that blocked his lungs. Before he reached the tree he threw out an arm, pitching forward. His hat rolled to one side, where the wind caught and skittered it across the pasture.

38

On the day following Sam Givens' departure from Gauley Bridge word came from the county seat at Fayetteville that the first trial had resulted in a hung jury. The news spread rapidly, and once again men gathered in tight, anxious groups, trying to understand the difference between an occupational disease and an accidental injury, the grounds upon which the defense had brought the trial to a dead end.

Men who had lost their Class A physical rating and who could no longer pass the examination to secure work elsewhere asked again and again why they had not been warned of the danger, why silicosis was not a compensable disease and, if the company was not responsible for the dead and dying, how could any jury countenance the fact that the contractors had known the lethal qualities of silica rock and yet had taken no precautions to protect them although the silica content was known to be consistently upward of ninety-seven per cent.

"Just like we figured," they would repeat one to the other, "they ain't goin to pay us a cent. They fixed up that trial, and now they're runnen us out of the valley, afraid we'll start trouble."

"Trouble?" an ebony-faced man exclaimed. "I ain't going to have much more trouble on this earth. I'm thinken bout my woman and kids. They the ones that is goin to have trouble."

Almost from the day the trial failed to reach any decision the hopeful anxiety and wishful planning passed from the groups of diseased men who congregated to hear the news. Their talk was slow and sluggish and repetitive, like the mind of a man faced with an unanswerable problem who can neither surmount nor forget it.

"They ain't goin to pay us off," they would commiserate. "They ain't goin to give us a red cent."

"If they was goin to give us anythin, they'd a-give us wet drills and water to lay the dust down with."

"Think of all the water that's goin to come through that tunnel to make power for the company. Millions and millions of gallons, and they wouldn't even give us enough to keep the dust down!"

"Jesus," another responded, "I never thought of it like that! Ain't that a funny thing now?"

"I hate like hell to die," another broke in. "I got a wife and two kids. I always wanted to see the boys grow up."

"Wonder what ever happened to that skinny feller they called Cherry Valley? He was always talken bout his kids."

"Come on, let's go up to the post office. Maybe they're goin to appeal the trial, take it to a higher court."

"Who's goin to appeal it? That Wright feller can't do anything. The company's got him tied up same as the rest of 'em. He was the only one that seen it our way."

"Let's go see anyhow. Won't do no good just standen here."

From one end of the town to the other they walked, repeating their anger and fear, listening hopefully, and as the blob of sun began to come down the sky, darkening the day, they trailed back home, hurt and angry and lost. They ate their potatoes and beans in silence, watching their wives and children irritably, suspicious and maddened when any slight remark could be twisted into a tortured accusation of their helpless inability to work or even to promise to live.

As though the close of the abortive trial concluded their connection with the company and their hope of recompense, the men became silent after the first loud, furious protestations and rarely ventured into Gauley Bridge. Like strangers, suddenly grown alien and aware, they clung to one another, quickly coming to distrust the town, for they were penniless and with no claim to future employment that would validate their presence.

The outward-bound procession grew, a long, tattered parade that dotted the roads leading from the pronged valley. Some left in decrepit cars, their belongings tied on top with spare threadbare tires, and others banded together, crowding into truck beds. With them went the hitchhikers and walkers, straggling along, leaving their furniture behind and tossing away one possession after another when the load became unbearable.

Rumors spread through Gauley Bridge of families living in caves, beneath overhanging ledges and low in the wind-protected ravines that traced their way up the sides of the New River gorge.

Mark Reip, coming back from the oil refinery's employment office at Pratt, told Lessie of seeing a family of four living in a packing case above the road.

"The feller has the cough bad," he explained. "He stays in the box all the time. His woman was beggen along the road."

"Oh, Mark, that's awful," Lessie said, urging a cup of hot coffee onto the counter before him. "Now drink that. You're soppen wet! I told you not to walk so far in the wet."

"The feller over there told me to come back," Mark defended. "I had to see him."

"Why don't you stand in a dry place till you get a lift, like I told you?" she charged, staring down at his wet trouser legs. "Honestly, Mark, yore worser'n a kid!"

"Won't nobody pick you up. There's too many on the roads."

"Well, then, you stay at home till it fairs off. You get soaked to the skin, and you'll start yoreself coughen!"

'I'm warm," he replied. "Feel——" Taking her hand, he placed it against his forehead, being careful that no one saw them from the street.

"Land, it is warm!" Lessie exclaimed. "You sure you don't feel no chill comen on?"

"I'm fine. Just tired."

Lessie settled down on the stool beside him. "Want a piece of pie? You can have it if you want it."

"No. I ain't hungry a-tall."

"How's Maw?"

"'Bout the same when I left this mornen. She just sets in her chair by the winder and rocks all the time. It kind of gets Pap upset, but I reckon she can't help it."

Lessie bent over, leaning her elbows against the counter. "Mark," she said, "it'll be comen April soon now. Why don't we start for Slaty next week?"

"Mebby. If I can get a little day's work."

"You don't need it, Mark. I got enough to get started on. You can pay me back someday. It'd be such a help to your maw."

"Al'right. Mebby, Lessie."

"Gee, I wish we could," Lessie went on, drawing near him. "Let's get married and go right away." She stopped, seeing Mark stare at the kitchen door. "Oh, he can't hear nothin!" she declared bluntly. "Him and Anna have been talken for an hour."

"How's Pete?"

"No better. I think Anna's fixen to leave for Arizoney with him, if she can manage the means. Everbody's leaven, Mark." Again she drew close to him. "Honey, let's get married and head back for Slaty. I'm sick of liven in towns, and I get an awful feelen anymore, stayen on here. Seeing the men stand along the road like crows on a fence rail, and hearen the ambulance going past, makes me all cold inside, Mark. Lookey, if we got back say week after this comen one, you could start plowen, mebby, and yore maw could get her mind off the boys."

Mark unbuttoned his jacket, pushing the sides back beneath his arms. "Gosh, I'm warm," he said fretfully. "I guess I'll go on home."

"Oh, Mark!" Lessie cried, stomping her foot, "yore independent as a hog on ice! Why don't you name it to me?"

"If I don't get work by Saturday a week——" Mark began, then stopped, seeing Anna come through the swinging door.

"What—Mark?" Lessie asked, urging him on. "What?"

He got up, buttoning his jacket. "I'll see you tomorrey," he evaded. "I want to go home and wash. I'm sticky."

"Well," Anna declared, her voice loud and distant. "Well, what do you think!"

"What?" Lessie asked irritably.

"We're leavin! Tomorrow!"

"What?"

"I can't hardly believe it," Anna said, dropping onto a stool. "Look at me shaking!" She held a quivering hand out toward Mark and Lessie.

"Leaven—for where, Anna?" Mark asked.

"New Mexico, I guess. Doctor Robinson thinks that is the best place."

"New Mexico? Land alive, where's that?"

"Five days on the bus," Anna said wondrously. "Mr Johns is lendin me the fare till I get a job. There are lots of road stands out there—"

"Mexico!" Lessie squealed unbelievingly. "Lord, it sounds like yon side of nowhere!"

"Will Pete get better—did the doctor say?" Mark asked.

"Maybe." Still dazed, Anna got up, crossed to the hooks near the women's room and got her coat. "I'm goin to run up and tell Pete. He'll be tickled to death. Nobody on earth has ever been so good to me as Mr Johns. Tomorrow we'll be leavin. Just think of it!" Suddenly she halted, breaking the rapid flow of words, and faced Mark and Lessie. "Do you suppose Pete could ride a bus for five days?" she asked, fright in her voice. "Oh, what if he got sick!"

"Don't you worry about that!" Lessie cried. "You been tryen to find a way to go for weeks. Now you got the chance. Streak out as fast as you can!"

"I know, I know," Anna said confusedly. "I'm goin to. We'll leave tomorrow at noon. But I just wondered." Still mumbling, she slammed the front door and raced across the street to the path that led up the hill.

"Gosh," Lessie exclaimed, watching her through the front window. "Gosh, think of that! Anna and Pete, picken up and leaven just like that!"

"They wanted to go for a long time," Mark reminded her. "Now they got a chance."

"Lordie, I'll miss Anna. And think of Mr Johns," she cried, staring toward the kitchen door. "Honestly, he's the funniest man I ever heard tell of. You never know how to figure him out."

"Lessie," Mark said, his voice low and forlorn, "I'm goin home. I'll see you tomorrow. I'll be down afore the noon bus goes."

"When you get home take your shoes off," Lessie instructed brusquely. "And yore pants too! You must be wet to the skin."

At five minutes after twelve the next day, when the driver had strapped Pete's and Anna's two bags to the top of the bus and covered them with a tarpaulin, he climbed down and accepted their tickets to Charleston.

"When you get there you can buy them on through," he explained. "We'll be leavin' in a couple of minutes."

Anna accepted the stubs and put them in her purse.

Lessie, who had been jiggling from one foot to the other, ran out to the sidewalk and looked through beneath the underpass. "I don't know what come over Mark," she declared. "He named it to me, said he'd be here sure."

"Maybe he got a job," Pete smiled. "Maybe he go to work this mornin'." Pale and shallow-cheeked, he seemed a thin frame upon which his clothes had been draped, and his hands were white and bony as they hung at his sides.

Anna, moving nervously about, was flushed and excited, her blonde hair sparkling with the dampness that hung over the valley. "Well, say good-by to him for us, Lessie. If we don't see him we'll write."

"I'll write too, soon as I get your address," Lessie cried, straining to see across the motor hood of the bus. "Maybe someday Mark and me'll come visit you."

"Sure," Pete grinned. "Sure t'ing."

"Well—well, I guess we'd better get on," Anna decided uncertainly.

Slowly, on unsteady feet, Pete crossed to the cafe door and extended his hand to Mr Johns who stood, his arms wrapped in his apron, excitedly watching the whole procedure.

"So long," Pete said. "We write you too. Maybe you come see us, huh?"

Mr Johns wiped his hands carefully before accepting the farewell. "You watch out for Anna," he said, mouthing the words. Before he released Pete's hand he called over his shoulder to Lessie. "Get the basket," he said. "You almost forgot!"

"Oh Lordie!" With a last backward look toward the underpass Lessie ran into the cafe and brought out a heaping basket, neatly covered with trim white paper. "Here," she said, handing it to Anna. "We worked all mornen on it!"

"What?" Anna stammered. "What is it?"

"Nothin much. Just chicken and a few things. Them buses don't stop very often."

Anna looked at the basket and ran to Mr Johns, throwing her arms about his neck. "Thank you very much," she said, trying to control her voice. "Everybody is so nice!"

Startled, Mr Johns strained his neck forward awkwardly, his cheeks flushing red and his bare arms gesturing aimlessly at his sides.

"He's blushen, Anna!" Lessie cried. "Anna, he's blushen!"

"Come on, lady!" the driver called. "We got to get goin'!"

"Oh, Mark ain't come yet!" Lessie implored, running toward him. "Can't you wait just a few minutes?"

"Nope. We're late now."

"Oh dear," Lessie cried, wringing her hands helplessly. "Good-by! Good-by, Anna!" Realizing that she had not kissed Pete, Lessie released her hold on Anna and ran into the bus after him. As he settled stiffly onto a seat she bent over and kissed him on the mouth, tears breaking free and splashing down her face.

"That's fine!" Pete chortled softly. "That's fine!"

"Good-by, Pete! Good-by!"

Backing away, Lessie bumped into Anna. As they squeezed past one another Lessie grabbed her again, hugging her close, and jumped down onto the sidewalk.

"Hey, don't I get one?" the driver called jovially.

"Oh, hesh!" Lessie cried, wiping the tears across her cheeks.

Backing toward the cafe steps where Mr Johns stood, she continued to wave after the driver had released the brake and rolled out into the street.

Not until the bus had gone down past the drugstore and she had dug into her white uniform pocket for a handkerchief did Lessie notice Viney May waiting on the sidewalk, where she had been concealed by the bus.

"Viney," she cried, "what's the matter? What are you doin down here?"

"The doctor said to come an tell you," the child said backwardly. "Pap said it too."

"Tell me what?" Lessie urged, grabbing her by the hand. "What is it, Viney?"

"Mark," the girl said, her voice loud and frightened. "Mark's got a fever."

"Oh Lord!"

"Pneumoney. He said to tell you pneumoney."

Lessie jerked back to her feet, her fist, holding the crumpled handkerchief, clamping against her lips. For an instant she remained perfectly still, then ran past Mr Johns into the cafe and snatched her coat from the row of hooks at the back.

"What's the matter, Lessie?" Mr Johns asked, backing from her path. "Tain't Mark, is it?"

"He's got pneumoney!" she called back, her face white and ashen. "He's got pneumoney, and it'll kill him sure."

She had run several yards up the street before she halted, fled back and grabbed Viney May by the hand. Trotting as fast as the child's legs would permit, they sped over the bridge and vanished up the low river path.

Mr Johns watched them out of sight, staring helplessly. Once inside, he quickly flipped the catch on the safety lock and shook the door a little to be sure it would not open.

With his face held tensely, as though he were afraid to open his mouth, he went down the long counter and into the kitchen, letting the door swing softly shut behind him.

39

The day was drab, colorless, being neither winter nor spring. A drenching rain had fallen during the night, reducing the last snow to soiled streaks that lay beneath the ridges and in the hollows, gray remnants of the winter which was passing. All morning a mist hung over the valley, low and oppressive, and the rain which had fallen did not recede into the earth but lay in gelatinous puddles; a mucus of slush and blackened water that drained down from the hills.

Warmed by the thawing rain, the acrid stench of the slag heaps rose above the tipples, like steam from a dunghill, and spread over the silt-filled river that broadened with the first of the spring floods. People walking along the roads drew their arms in close their bodies, as if to ward off the smell and inescapable clamminess of the gray mist that strung over the wet earth.

As Maw and Viney May and Lessie, crowded beneath a single black umbrella, trudged their way up the steep road behind Mark's coffin their steps made small squeashy sounds as if their shoes formed a suction in the muddy ground.

Lessie, her arm looped through Maw's and the umbrella held in her hand, walked on one side, her face distorted and drawn beneath the thin veil she had hastily affixed to her narrow-brimmed hat. On the other side Viney May clung to Maw's limp hand, her shoes splattered and thickly soled with an accumulation of mud that broke and fell, then re-formed as she made her way along. Of the three she was the only one who cried aloud, her whimpering breaking from her throat in coagulated lumps.

Between them Maw walked, rigid and incapable of feeling. Her deeply seamed face was set in stoical passiveness, and her eyes, from the pocketed recesses of her head, were dry and dull. The hollows beneath them had turned purple black, like injured flesh, and the rims of her nostrils were raw and red above her colorless mouth. At broken intervals, as they neared the graveyard which spread across the hill above Gauley Bridge, the solemn, dirgeful notes of a hymn sounded from her throat, lilting unreasonably and then subsiding like the thoughtless discord of one who is occupied.

Ahead the young men from the undertaking parlor carried the coffin between them. They walked cautiously, putting their feet down with a hesitant tentativeness, for the clay road, entering the graveyard, was wet and slippery and their load unwieldy. Shoving the white picket gate open, they made their way through, looking back to see that the three who formed the procession were not banged by the broad gate as it swung shut.

Passing over the path which wound between the gravestones, they climbed the knoll toward the far side, where one could look down toward the Gauley River and the clump of dark, rotting shacks that formed Venetta on the opposite bank.

Across Maw's shoulders Lessie's eyes found the Reip shack, high perched and curtained, at the end of the empty row. She saw Tom wrapped in blankets at the window, and her hand clamped the umbrella handle tightly as a wave of loneliness and pity swept through her. Numbed by the task that lay ahead, she sought to shove the fright and apprehension from her mind, remembering old Tom lying on the bed, the bony fingers of his hand forming a fence over his inflamed eyes.

His voice had cracked and broken many times during the hours following Mark's death when he tried to help her with the burial preparations.

Maw had said nothing, sitting in her rocking chair, a vacant dullness forever glazing her dry eyes. She rocked monotonously, her foot kicking the chair into steady motion as she laced and unlaced her fingers in her lap.

"I don't think she knows yet," Tom had whispered against the palm of his hand. "I don't think she knows."

"I'll take care of everythin." Finding a grocery sack, Lessie had wrapped Mark's shoes, his shirt and socks and tie. Back beside the bed, her face frozen with grief, she bent low over Tom so her whispering would not disturb Maw. "Mark, he never had no suit coat, did he?" she asked.

"No, he never," Tom replied. "Ely was the only one that had suit clothes. Mark just had his sweater and that lumberjacket Virgil left." He stopped, swallowing from a dry mouth, and then continued. "You can find my black coat in there agin the wall. You take that to Mark. He's near my size, an it won't look so bad with his pants."

Lessie started to speak but, seeing the deadening hurt in Tom's eyes, she went into the bedroom and got the dark age-greened suit coat, folding it neatly across her arm.

"I allus done everthin I could," Tom said as she recrossed the room. "I worked hard, and we saved. Just seems like everthin was agin us."

"Yes, Tom. I know, Tom," Lessie consoled, swallowing lumpily. "You rest. I'll be back soon's I take these things down."

The path turned, rounding a wire-fenced grave. The low, muffled words of the hymn that Maw had been singing since Lessie had helped her dress for the burial arose again, jerky and tuneless.

As her eyes came back from the blanketed figure in the window Lessie's arm pressed Maw's closer to her, hoping to still the untimely lamentation, but Maw strode along, unaware and unmindful.

Up the path Lessie saw two figures standing beside a piece of outstretched canvas just beyond the graves where Ely and Virgil had been buried. Nearing the plot, a man in overalls stepped forward, dragged the covering from the open grave and went back to the shelter of the broad-branching pine where his mattock and shovel stood propped against the tree trunk.

The bearers lowered the coffin to the canvas cover as the two awaiting figures separated, Mr Johns going to the head of the grave and Reverend Mitchell stepping forward, his head bared, to meet the small procession.

Maw, seeing Ely's and Virgil's graves, stopped in her tracks, freeing her arm from Lessie. No expression stiffed across her face as she stared from one to the other and stepped off the path to brush aside a few small clumps of freshly broken earth that had rolled against the mound where Virgil was interred.

Lessie and the minister exchanged fleet, questioning glances and he walked to Maw's side, touching her arm.

"Won't you stand over here, Mrs Reip?" he asked softly.

Maw looked at him for a long moment and squatted down beside the two graves, as she had many times before, oblivious of the young men who were deftly looping ropes about either end of the bright coffin.

"Come on, Maw," Lessie said. "It's time for the service."

Viney May, left alone, began to sob fitfully, a clenched fist held against one eye.

"I'll stand with you, Maw," Lessie repeated, tugging at her arm. "The reverend is ready to start."

Rising to her feet, Maw squared back her shoulders, her eyes passing with unseeing slowness across the coffin, the open grave and the tarpaulin-covered pile of earth on its farther side.

"If you'll step right over here, Mrs Reip," the minister urged, spreading his Bible over one hand. "If you and the young lady will stand right there——"

Before he finished Maw moved from beneath the shelter of the umbrella Lessie held. Her voice, starting deep in her throat, rose quickly as she began the hymn that wound itself endlessly through her mind.

"'Jesus, Lover of my soul, let me to Thy bosom fly,'" she sang. "'While the nearer waters roll, While the tempest still is high——'"

Nervously the coffin bearers watched her and, with a frightened look at Reverend Mitchell, hastily lowered the coffin into the grave and stepped aside.

Uncertainly the minister gestured toward Lessie. As she broke into tears, crying miserably into her hand, he took up the hymn, joining Maw as he led her a little nearer the grave.

"'Hide me, oh, my Saviour, hide, till the storm of life is past,'" they chanted, Maw's voice strident and without tune. "'Safe into Thy haven guide, Oh, receive my soul at last.'"

At the end of the verse he raised his hand, nodding to Maw, and her voice trailed off, diminishing to a low hum.

Quickly Reverend Mitchell reopened his Bible, reading from the One Hundredth and Second Psalm, his words loud and clear, his eyes turning again and again to Maw's rigid, stoical face.

"'For my days are consumed like smoke,'" he pronounced, "'and my bones are burned as an hearth.'"

The damp mist which had hung over the valley since morning clung about the hilltop, drifting in wisps and causing the black umbrellas to glisten with its moisture. Viney May, her crying reduced to a low whine, gaped at the hole in the ground at her feet.

"'But Thou, O Lord, shalt endure for ever; and Thy remembrance unto all generations,'" the minister intoned.

Lessie, holding Maw's arm in her tight grasp, felt her begin to rock backward and forward as the minister's voice patterned out a chant. Like a whisper, like a voice set free, the low hum began to rise from her throat again.

"'He will regard the prayer of the destitute,'" the minister read, his words coming more rapidly as he heard the strains of the hymn, "'and not despise their prayer.'"

Hurriedly reaching the end of the brief service, as Maw's voice rose and fell, Reverend Mitchell stooped down and picked up a clot of earth. Holding it out over the grave, he crumbled it between his fingers, allowing it to filter down upon the box that rested inside the narrow excavation.

"The Lord giveth," he pronounced, "and He taketh away."

As if by signal, the man who had retired beneath the pine tree came forward, tossed the canvas from over the piled-up dirt and began to shovel it back into the hole, dropping it softly about the bright box.

Viney May, tense and overwrought, began to cry hysterically, her shrill voice tearing through the air like a sharp-edged torture.

Holding her hand to her eyes, Lessie turned about and started down the hill again. Her weeping was hushed, her shoulders shaking with taut desperation. She had taken several steps before she realized that Maw had not moved.

"Come on, Maw," she said, going back and taking her arm. "Come on, we're goin back to the house."

Maw looked at her with remote, lusterless eyes, nodding with a jerky spasmodic movement. Lessie tugged at her arm, trying to get her beneath the umbrella, and they started down the path, followed by Viney May. Back of her came the minister and Mr Johns, walking with short, hesitant steps.

The humming in Maw's throat grew, rising and falling unrhythmically.

"Maw, please. Maw!" Lessie pleaded. "We're goin back to the house now, Tom's waiten."

Maw nodded, no expression crossing her face, and broke into the lugubrious strains of the hymn, her voice, loud and disembodied, ringing out from the hilltop. "'. . . All my trust on Thee is stayed, All my help from Thee I bring . . .'"

Terrified, Lessie twisted about, but the minister's head was lowered and he did not see her. Beyond Mr Johns's umbrella the young men who had carried the coffin stared numb-faced after them.

"Maw," she begged, drawing her arm closer. "Maw, the funeral is over. Don't sing, Maw, please don't!"

"'. . . Cover my defenseless head with the shadow of Thy wing. . . .'"

Down past the gravestones they came, through the broad picket gate and into the slippery clay road. Maw, her body held stiffly erect and her face faded of color and feeling, continued to trace the pattern of the song, her voice lilting unreasonably.

"'. . . . Freely let me take of Thee,'" she sang. "'Spring Thou up within my heart, rise to all eternity. . . .'"

"Oh, Maw," Lessie sobbed, grief and terror gushing from her throat. "Oh, Maw, don't! Don't!"

Ahead of Mr Johns, ahead of the minister, the three skirted figures beneath a single umbrella came down the red clay road toward the valley where two rivers flowed together, forming one.

9 781572 332805